THE FUTURE
OF THE EURO

Edited By

MATTHIAS MATTHIJS
MARK BLYTH

OXFORD
UNIVERSITY PRESS

OXFORD

UNIVERSITY PRESS

Oxford University Press is a department of the University of
Oxford. It furthers the University's objective of excellence in research,
scholarship, and education by publishing worldwide.

Oxford   New York
Auckland   Cape Town   Dar es Salaam   Hong Kong   Karachi
Kuala Lumpur   Madrid   Melbourne   Mexico City   Nairobi
New Delhi   Shanghai   Taipei   Toronto

With offices in
Argentina   Austria   Brazil   Chile   Czech Republic   France   Greece
Guatemala   Hungary   Italy   Japan   Poland   Portugal   Singapore
South Korea   Switzerland   Thailand   Turkey   Ukraine   Vietnam

Oxford is a registered trademark of Oxford University Press
in the UK and certain other countries.

Published in the United States of America by
Oxford University Press
198 Madison Avenue, New York, NY 10016

Library of Congress Cataloging-in-Publication Data
The future of the euro / edited by Matthias Matthijs, Mark Blyth.
pages cm
Includes bibliographical references and index.
ISBN 978-0-19-023323-5   (hardback : alk. paper) — ISBN 978-0-19-023324-2
(pbk. : alk. paper)   1. Euro.   2. Eurozone.   3. Currency crises—European Union
countries.   4. Financial crises—European Union countries.   I. Matthijs, Matthias.
II. Blyth, Mark, 1967-
HG925.F87 2015
332.4'94—dc23
2014032884

3 5 7 9 8 6 4
Printed in the United States of America
on acid-free paper

For Tony Judt

Contents

SECTION III: *The Euro Future*

List of Figures

List of Tables

Foreword

ONE OF THE more minor consequences of the 2007–2008 global financial crisis was some serious soul searching among economists and political scientists for having failed to predict these events. Given its "black swan" nature—low probability and high impact—we might all be forgiven. However, the European sovereign debt crisis that followed two years later invites no such sympathy. There is neither ambiguity about its nature nor its timing, only its final resolution.

The European sovereign debt crisis was in many ways the inevitable consequence of the US financial crisis reaching European shores. But why then, if it was inevitable, were policymakers so blindsided? The euro crisis has called into question the long-term viability of Europe's Economic and Monetary Union. In order to better understand what has gone wrong, how the Eurozone could potentially be fixed, and what the future(s) of the euro might be, including its possible failure, this volume brings together the insights of a dozen scholars on the political economy of Europe, from both Europe and the United States.

This volume is organized according to the various contributors' scholarly expertise and research interests. While a division of labor is a core characteristic of edited volumes, this volume is unique in two respects. First of all, the chapters actually agree to a considerable extent on the main features of the euro and its crisis. Second, they directly engage with and build upon one another. As a result, the whole of the book is much greater than the sum of its parts. We hope that you, the reader, agree with this assessment.

There are many people we would like to thank who have been involved with this project, and we apologize in advance if we omit to mention them here. First of all, this book would not have been possible without the generous funding made available by the Bernard L. Schwartz Globalization Initiative at the School of Advanced International Studies (SAIS) at Johns

Hopkins University. Its academic co-chair, Pravin Krishna, was enthusiastic from the start about the project, and the initial December 2012 workshop in Washington was a success thanks to the research assistance of Ryan Connelly. We are most grateful for all the logistical, administrative, and managerial support from the Initiative's program manager at SAIS, Kelley Kornell. Dean Vali Nasr and Associate Dean for Academic Affairs John Harrington also deserve mention for all their encouragement, and for creating an environment of academic excellence at SAIS.

We also want to thank the Watson Institute for International Studies at Brown University, for sponsoring a conference on the euro crisis in April 2012, where the idea for this edited volume was born. Our conversations with Alfred Gusenbauer, Romano Prodi, and especially Martin Wolf at Brown were particularly enlightening.

It goes without saying that this volume is very much a collective effort, so we owe an immense gratitude to the chapter contributors Kathleen McNamara, Erik Jones, Nicolas Jabko, Vivien Schmidt, Abraham Newman, Mark Vail, Jonathan Hopkin, Wade Jacoby, Craig Parsons, and Eric Helleiner. Furthermore, we want to thank the Council of European Studies for allowing us to build a three-panel symposium around this book project during their annual International Conference of Europeanists in Washington, D.C., in March 2014, as well as Randall Henning, Craig Parsons, and Charles Kupchan for agreeing to serve as discussants on those panels. Others who deserve to be mentioned for their encouragement and sound advice include Jonathan Kirshner, Peter Hall, Dan Drezner, Dan Kelemen, Cornel Ban, Simon Tilford, and Jerry Cohen.

A special mention goes to Björn Bremer, who provided invaluable research assistance during the writing and editing stages of this book. He compiled the bibliography, and proved to be a meticulous editor and proofreader of all the chapters and endnotes. Brian Fox was instrumental in carefully putting together the index for the book. We also thank David McBride and Sarah Rosenthal at Oxford University Press for ably steering the manuscript through the publication process, as well as the very helpful comments from the two anonymous reviewers.

Finally, together with all our contributors, we decided that we wanted to dedicate this book to the late Tony Judt. The debate over the euro crisis was from its inception dominated by financial experts and economic analysts. Judt's unique historian's voice was often very much missed. We think that Judt would have been sympathetic to the main message of this book—that any long-term solution to the crisis experienced by the European Union and its single currency should begin by addressing the political foundations of markets. Tony Judt taught all of us a great deal about Europe and its historical development. We owe him a tremendous intellectual debt. He passed away too soon without leaving us his understanding of what went wrong in this moment of crisis and where we should go from here. With his voice in our ears, we have tried to fill that silence. Whether our collective efforts are worthy of being mentioned in the same breath as Judt's is, however, something that, once again, we will leave to you, the reader, to decide.

Matthias Matthijs and Mark Blyth
Washington, DC, and South Boston, MA
October 2014

Editors

Matthias Matthijs is Assistant Professor of International Political Economy at Johns Hopkins University's School of Advanced International Studies.

Mark Blyth is Professor of International Political Economy and International Studies at the Watson Institute for International Studies at Brown University.

Contributors

Eric Helleiner is Faculty of Arts Chair in International Political Economy and Professor of Political Science at the University of Waterloo.

Jonathan Hopkin is Associate Professor of Comparative Politics in the Department of Government of the London School of Economics and Political Science.

Nicolas Jabko is Associate Professor of Political Science at Johns Hopkins University.

Wade Jacoby is Mary Lou Fulton Professor of Political Science and Director of the Center for the Study of Europe at Brigham Young University.

Erik Jones is Professor of European Studies, Director of European and Eurasian Studies, and Director of the Bologna Institute for Policy Research at Johns Hopkins University's School of Advanced International Studies.

Kathleen R. McNamara is Associate Professor of Government and Foreign Service and Director of the Mortara Center for International Studies at Georgetown University.

Abraham Newman is Associate Professor at the BMW Center for German and European Studies in the Edmund A. Walsh School of Foreign Service at Georgetown University.

Craig Parsons is Professor of Political Science at the University of Oregon.

Vivien A. Schmidt is Professor of International Relations and Political Science, Jean Monnet Professor of European Integration, and Director of the Center for the Study of Europe at Boston University.

Mark I. Vail is Associate Professor of Political Science at Tulane University.

I

Introduction

THE FUTURE OF THE EURO AND THE POLITICS
OF EMBEDDED CURRENCY AREAS

Matthias Matthijs and Mark Blyth

THE PURPOSE OF this book is to move beyond a purely economic under-standing of the euro crisis and its likely aftermath by emphasizing the political foundations of markets. Our goals in doing so are threefold: first, to develop a holistic understanding of what caused the euro crisis, which incorporates political, ideational, institutional, as well as economic and financial factors; second, to determine how the design flaws of the euro can be fixed for the long term; and third, to define which potential futures lie ahead for Europe's single currency and its users.

The book's core proposition is that one should begin by looking at the "minimal" political and institutional conditions required to make a multi-state currency union work. Only then should one ask whether Europe has those conditions in place or is likely to construct them anytime soon. This introductory chapter provides the overall frame for the book and pulls together the main ideas of the chapters. Drawing together the volume's con-tributions, we make three interrelated arguments.

First, we maintain that the *euro problem*—the result of three "forgotten unions" quite distinct from monetary union—developed over a much lon-ger period than a focus on the European sovereign debt crisis of 2010–2012 would suggest. We create an analytical framework for the book, which argues that the currency's lack of "embeddedness" in truly supranational European financial, fiscal, and governance institutions was a significant omission that would eventually come to a head. The great crash of 2008 was merely the catalyst. Those three "forgotten unions" were a financial (and not just bank-ing) union, coherent institutions of supranational economic government (a fiscal union that uses a common debt instrument), and a political union hold-ing comparable democratic legitimacy to the European nation-state.

Second, what we term the *euro experience* shows how the unfinished institu-tional design of the euro led to overall economic divergence across the Eurozone, rather than the convergence that EU leaders had anticipated at Maastricht in the early 1990s. This divergence quietly altered the distribution of economic and political power within Europe prior to the crisis, with real consequences for how the EU has since responded to that crisis. This section highlights how the economies of the Eurozone's big four states—Germany, France, Italy, and Spain—have each changed since and because of the introduction of the euro, and now struggle to live with the commitments that their common cur-rency necessitates. We highlight how the traditional balance of power among Europe's major states shifted dramatically during the crisis, with Germany gaining in clout, the traditional Franco-German engine of European integra-tion sputtering, and the return of the gap between the core "surplus" countries and peripheral "deficit" countries of the Eurozone. We discuss how existing institutions were tested during the euro crisis, noting how the relationship between national and supranational levels of governance underwent a genuine transformation, including a substantial adjustment in the traditional division of labor between legislative, executive, and judiciary branches of government.

Third, and finally, we examine the *euro future* from three different points of view: first, through the politics of its dominant state but reluctant leader, Germany; second, through the capacity of the European Union to transcend this moment of crisis given its past experience; third, through the lens of the broader geopoli-tics of the crisis, asking whether the rest of the world will assist the Eurozone by continuing to accept the euro as a global reserve currency. In the concluding chapter, we focus on the return of national politics in the Eurozone and the European Union, as well as future battles that loom on the horizon. We will also propose a typology on how to think about the future of the euro. Following Nassim Taleb's metaphor, we will distinguish the three different "euro swans"—white, grey, and black—that may grace the euro's future in the years to come.[1]

From Bright to Blight: A Primer on the History of the Present

The euro was created in December 1991 when German Chancellor Helmut Kohl and French President François Mitterrand, together with 10 other

European heads of state, all under the authoritative stewardship of European Commission chief Jacques Delors, negotiated a new "Treaty of European Union" in Maastricht, the Netherlands. At the time, the creation of the single currency was welcomed as a visionary act of international statesmanship and a courageous step toward European political unity.[2] The reasoning seemed straightforward. Through the economic convergence that a common currency was presumed to deliver, EU member states would better align their core national competencies and grow into a more politically integrated region, thereby forever relegating any potential military conflict between them to the dustbin of history.[3] With the international state system still trembling from the triple shock of the fall of the Berlin Wall in 1989, the reunification of Germany in 1990, and the imminent collapse of the Soviet Union at the end of 1991, Economic and Monetary Union (EMU) was Europe's imaginative and bold response to the new geopolitical landscape.[4]

EMU would incorporate a recently reunified Germany into an *ever closer union* and tie Berlin's fate to the rest of Europe through a common currency and a common monetary policy. It would also reassure France and the rest of Germany's neighbors that the long dormant "German problem"—a strong German state at the heart of Europe that was both too dynamic and too big for the rest of the continent to keep up with—would never again resurface. These European elites also shared the view that the forces of globalization, mostly evident in rapidly rising international trade and capital flows, meant a substantial hollowing out of the traditional nation-state, and therefore would require an answer at the supranational level.[5] EMU was therefore also seen as the vehicle that would enable Europe to compete as a unified economic bloc with a rising Japan, a nascent North American free trade area, and other emerging giants in Asia and Latin America.[6] Even though it was acknowledged at the time that the single currency's design was incomplete—a monetary union without a fiscal union—Kohl, Mitterrand, and Delors agreed that this would be addressed at some point in the future.[7] That, at least, was the hope.

During the early 1990s, despite the setbacks of the European Monetary System (EMS) crises of 1992–1993, Europe's focus remained firmly on meeting the "convergence criteria" at the heart of Maastricht's road toward EMU: low interest and inflation rates, fiscal deficits under 3 percent of gross domestic product (GDP), and gross national debt levels below 60 percent of GDP. By 1997, despite the implementation of austerity measures to meet these goals, it was clear that only tiny Luxembourg would meet all four criteria. The EU's leaders therefore made the political decision to focus mainly on the applicants' fiscal deficits, rather than on their overall debt ratios, in order to avoid having a much smaller and predominantly northern euro core to start with. This flexible interpretation and canny massaging of the rules allowed 11 of the then 15 EU members to qualify for EMU membership by 1999. The UK and Denmark opted out, while Sweden decided to wait and then voted against adopting the euro in a referendum in 2003. Greece first needed to make significant progress to improve its fiscal situation, but would join in 2001, just in time for the introduction of euro coins and notes in January 2002.

While the euro initially weakened vis-à-vis the US dollar—the single currency was introduced at $1.17 in January 1999, but steadily depreciated to reach a low of $0.82 during the height of the US "dotcom" boom in October 2000—after January 2002, the euro gradually gained in value, and most Eurozone economies began to grow, in some cases at an unusually fast pace. By the autumn of 2007, the dollar had lost 34 percent of its value vis-à-vis the euro since early 2001. Economists were writing articles and papers about how the dollar's decline would foster the euro's rise.[8] Central banks began to increasingly swap out dollars for euros in their international currency reserves.[9] Supermodels started to insist on contracts denominated in euros rather than dollars.[10] And even the villain in the James Bond movie *Quantum of Solace*, released in 2008, demanded euros as ransom, snidely observing, "the dollar isn't what it once was." France's Gaullist fantasy of a united Europe from the Atlantic to the Urals, finally exercising its own monetary power to counterbalance that of the United States, seemed to be coming to pass. But then, within a very short space of time, the wheels came rather spectacularly off the wagon, and the very existence of the euro was deemed to be at stake.

At the heart of it all was—and at the time of writing still is—a pan-European banking crisis. In short, the funding crisis that had laid waste to Anglo-Saxon "highly leveraged financial institutions" (HLFIs) via the sub-prime mortgage crisis in the United States only fully hit Europe in mid-2009. At first the damage seemed contained, but then European policymakers committed a series of self-inflicted wounds that would turn an Anglo-American problem into a distinctly European one.

First of all, the European Central Bank (ECB) signaled to the markets in May 2009 that they would singularly not engage in quantitative easing in the manner conducted by the Anglo-Americans, which made markets nervous about the liquidity of their bond holdings.[11] The German government then doubled down on this error in March 2010, telling financial markets that neither the ECB nor Germany would act as the lender of last resort for the European banking system, since there was no backstop provision in the EU Treaties, in order to avoid moral hazard. Unsurprisingly, given the huge volume of euro-denominated government debt collectively held by the European banking system, yields on such government bonds became more volatile and began to creep up.

Bond spreads widened over the course of 2010 and 2011 as the market repriced the risk of sovereigns with no printing presses facing possibly insolvent banks with multiples of GDP on their balance sheets and no lender of last resort coming to their rescue.[12] Iceland's and Ireland's fates suddenly seemed much more than mere isolated incidents. The crisis had become systemic. Widening spreads accelerated to critical levels when private liquidity to the European banking system effectively dried up in mid-2011 as US money market funds withdrew from interbank funding markets. As a result, the collateral used for short-term borrowing by European banks, euro-denominated sovereign bonds, fell further in value.[13]

HLFIs going bust have the potential to bring down entire economies, hence the concept of "too big too fail." But what Europe had done, almost without noticing, was to build itself a banking system that was "too big to bail" by any one sovereign, including Germany. Only the massive balance sheet and full commitment of the ECB to provide unlimited liquidity can stabilize such a system. Yet, as noted above, then ECB president Jean-Claude Trichet had expressly disavowed that commitment, passing the buck to the Germans, who duly passed it back to the ECB. Then it was passed around the rest of the Eurozone throughout 2010 and 2011 at one crisis summit after the other, pushing yields up higher and higher.

That basic and indispensable commitment was only given reluctantly by Trichet's successor, Mario Draghi. It had three components. First was Draghi's announcement of the long term refinancing operations (LTROs) for the European banking system in December 2011 and again in February 2012, which pushed 1.5 trillion euro at near zero interest rates into Europe's banks. Second was his emphatic and bold promise to do "whatever it takes" ("within our mandate") to save the euro in July 2012. Third was his concomitant policy initiative of "conditional" outright monetary transactions (OMTs), which promised to buy sovereign bonds *in extremis*, in early September 2012.

Consequently, between the autumn of 2009 and the summer of 2012, Europe experienced a "sovereign debt crisis," which is a rather odd name for a crisis of systemic over-lending by European banks. And European governments responded with austerity policies that exacerbated rather than limited the economic slump that followed. At the time of writing, the euro seems to have survived intact, but only because the private debts of the banking sector were socialized and paid for through draconian cuts in government spending plus, of course, the actions of Mario Draghi at the ECB.[14]

As we enter 2015, financial analysts are bullish again on the euro, pointing out that the global share of central bank reserves held as euros is on the rise again, while sovereign bond yields have fallen to record low levels. The ECB has announced new so-called Targeted LTRO programs aimed at restoring lending to the private sector, made its deposit rates negative in order to push even more money out the door, and launched another bold plan in October 2014 to buy an extra 1 trillion euro in covered bonds and asset-backed securities (ABS) during the last three months of 2014. It seems that the crisis is over. But are we in fact so lucky? Are we back once again to the euro's Bright future after a time of Blight? For even if one believes the banking crisis sketched above has been triaged through the provision of infinite liquidity, if we approach the euro crisis from a focus on the political foundations of markets, we should perhaps not be so sanguine. Perhaps we might conclude that the banking crisis that still lies at the heart of the euro woes was indeed catalytic, but that it was merely one part of a deeper and multifaceted crisis of politics, institutions, and governance that has not at all been resolved.

These interlocking and emergent crises lie in the realm of what the economist Abba Lerner once referred to as "unsolved political problems." He once observed that "economics has gained the title Queen of the Social Sciences by choosing solved political problems as its domain."[15] Economic theories usually start with how the world should be—a model—which presumes that all the relevant political problems have long been solved. All that is left to do, then, is to figure out the most efficient means to get to the end the model prescribes. But such a view of the world assumes away all the politics that in fact make such a world go around. This confusing of the model for the reality it purports to describe lies at the heart of Europe's current condition.

The Political Foundations of Markets: Moving from Optimum to Minimum

There is an old joke about an economist who finds himself trapped on a desert island with only canned food. He quickly assumes the existence of a can opener to solve his predicament. The joke really is not all that funny, but it serves its purpose as a reminder of the limits of economic solutions to what are essentially political problems. As Lerner cautioned, economic theories always start with an idealized version of the world, such as a frictionless market, a rational investor, a representative agent, or in the case of the euro, an optimal currency area. Economists then measure how much the world deviates from this ideal, and the policy solution that logically follows this is to reform the world to become more like the theory.

Vintage 1999 and more recent economic criticisms of the euro as "not fulfilling the requirements of the theory of optimum currency areas (OCA)" are a telling example of this genre, as is Europe's general reform agenda since the outbreak of its crisis.[16] It is undeniable that Europe never met the requirements of the theory, either in whole or in part. There were never any complete markets with cross-border flexibility in all factors of production to absorb asymmetric shocks. Now, after being slammed by banking and debt crises, the current reform agenda of Europe actually seeks to replicate the economists' approach in reality. Through a singular political commitment to structural reform and improving the region's cost-competitiveness without institutional or financial compensation, the euro's reformers in Brussels, Frankfurt, and Berlin seek to make Europe more like the one portrayed in the theory of optimal currency areas—one with symmetric shock absorbers, super-flexible labor markets, and an operative law of one price across financial markets. In the language of the varieties of capitalism literature, European policy elites are trying to take multiple sets of differentiated institutional complementarities, otherwise known as distinct national economies, and turn them into one set of undifferentiated complementary institutions.[17]

Yet such a view of "what is to be done" rather carelessly assumes away the complicated bargains and distributive politics that make integrated markets and a single currency possible in the first place and assure its sustainability over the long term. Such a view begins with the premise that politics is some kind of noise or friction in an otherwise self-equilibrating system that needs to be eliminated. As a consequence, we need rules, pacts, and treaties to constrain politicians whose policy tools should be delegated to technocrats who can safely ignore the demos and get us closer to that optimal world. This is the recent history and the immediate future of the euro—and it has been less than successful of late.

However, if we shift our focus and start with politics as the fundamental underpinning of the system itself—as constitutive of the system's basic institutional design rather than an aberration to be removed by a suitably qualified technocracy—a political account of the euro must start with a theory of minimums rather than optimums. That is, we need to ask, what are the various institutional and political minima required to make a single currency, encompassing a set of integrated markets across distinct national economies,

work? And what are the politics involved in creating those minimum requirements? These questions bring us to the heart of the book and the contributions of its authors.

The Euro Problem: Embedded Currency Areas and Multiple Forgotten Unions

The book begins with Kathleen McNamara's analysis of the politics of
"embedded currency areas" in Chapter 2. McNamara uncovers the minimum
institutional and political prerequisites for a stable currency union from an
examination of past currency unions. She argues that the euro is notably different from every other successful single currency in history in that it has been
fundamentally "disembedded" from the specific social and political institutions that provided a solid and durable foundation for any monetary union in
the past. Markets, she argues, need political authority to create stability. The
lack of governance will hurt the euro going forward more than its objective
shortcomings as an optimum currency area or a set of flexible markets.

The history lessons of previous monetary unions, which McNamara codes
on a continuum from "least embedded" to "most embedded," have a lot to
say about the Eurozone's current predicament. They suggest that European
leaders and their publics will need to channel the historical sociology of Karl
Polanyi, rather than the free markets of Friedrich von Hayek, if they want
to fix the euro's problems. If it is to succeed in the long term, McNamara
believes the Eurozone must be transformed into a truly *embedded* currency
area (ECA). The next three chapters build upon McNamara's opening to give
us greater clarity concerning the three "forgotten unions" that either directly
caused the euro crisis or exacerbated its effects: the "forgotten" financial, economic, and political unions that would constitute a real ECA.

In Chapter 3, Erik Jones views the euro crisis not as a crisis of the euro, but
as a crisis of the single market. Jones argues that when Europe's political leaders pushed for capital market integration and the liberalization of cross-border
banking in the late 1980s and early 1990s, they failed to build common institutions to ensure financial stability. Instead, they held on to *national* institutions for banking regulation, supervision, resolution, and insurance. These
were too small and too fragmented to guard against the risks generated by
the behemoth pan-European banks and insurance firms that emerged in the
single market's integrated financial space. Jones explains why this failure to
construct common institutions to safeguard against the risks generated by
integrated pan-European financial markets was a big mistake. His goal is not

to argue against the view that monetary integration contributed to Europe's problems. Rather, his goal is to show that the absence of any financial union was sufficient, in and of itself, to bring some sort of crisis about. If Europe's policymakers refuse to rectify this situation, Jones fears, they will have to relive the experience.

Nicolas Jabko, in Chapter 4, shows us how the euro crisis is a product not only of Jones's forgotten financial union, but also of a forgotten union of economic governance, parallel to the one lacking in financial markets. Jabko observes that because monetary policy was unified at the EU level, while most other economic policy powers remained in the hands of national governments, an unforeseen conflict between national sovereignty and a new conception of sovereignty that called for its exercise at the European level developed below the radar since the euro's introduction. This conflict became fully evident only after 2009 with the deepening of the Eurozone crisis, but in reality it was, like Jones's forgotten financial union, generated by long-standing "unsolved political problems." For Jabko, the Eurozone crisis is then a crisis of economic governance in a situation of divided sovereignty that compounds the systemic risks generated by the inability to properly regulate financial markets, which Jones highlights. The crisis showed us that while the institutional status quo had become untenable, there was no magic formula to strengthen economic and fiscal governance without further encroaching on national sovereignty, which politicians solely accountable to the national level were simply unwilling to do.

Jabko notes how since the summer of 2011, under the intense pressure of yield spikes and multiple downgrades, member states have de facto moved toward shifting more sovereign powers to the EU level. They have adopted treaty revisions that *could* ultimately reshape the landscape of economic governance, such as the creation of the European Stability Mechanism (ESM) and the "Fiscal Pact" (formally known as the Treaty on Stability, Coordination and Governance). In late 2013, member states endorsed the principles of a single banking supervisory and resolution mechanism, a "pact for growth and jobs," and a "specific and time-bound road map for achieving a genuine economic and monetary union."[18] Yet these steps are, we argue, still too conditional, and in the case of the banking union's single resolution mechanism, still very much contested. Building upon Jones's conclusion, Jabko warns that the crisis will not fully abate as long as the credibility of collective economic governance is in doubt. The solution to that lack of credibility is a further deepening and embedding of political institutions as part of a move toward stronger EU economic governance. But whether that will actually happen is once again likely to remain an "unsolved political problem" in the foreseeable future.

If the forgotten financial and economic governance unions highlighted by Jones and Jabko were the lagged antecedents of the crisis—the accidents waiting to happen—as well as the necessary components of an ECA, then for Vivien Schmidt in Chapter 5, the euro crisis is first and foremost a *political* crisis that is a direct consequence of these hidden fragilities. In particular, she highlights the negative impact on European democracy of the policies proposed and implemented to solve the crisis. These policies—budgetary austerity, wage compression, and a drive for exports—have, Schmidt argues, exacerbated long-standing problems with regard not only to the EU's democratic legitimacy but also to European solidarity.

Democratic legitimacy has suffered not only because Eurozone policies have failed to produce good outcomes, but also because EU citizens have less say than ever over those policies. Indeed, the excessively "intergovernmental" processes of Eurozone crisis governance, in which the ECB acts, the member state leaders in the European Council call the shots, the European Parliament is largely ignored, and the European Commission serves as a secretariat, have unbalanced the EU's long-standing "democratic" settlement in which all three institutions equally pulled their weight. Schmidt further shows us how European democracy suffers a deep crisis of legitimacy that stems from these EU crisis resolution policies. That is, they undercut EU institutions' "output" legitimacy (because of their harmful effects on economic growth and social welfare), they undermine those same institutions' "input" legitimacy (because of their negative effects on citizen participation and representation), and they weaken "throughput" legitimacy (because of rule-making and rule-following that lack efficacy, accountability, transparency, and access).

Taken together, these four chapters demonstrate that the euro crisis is not subject to a simple and singular crisis narrative. It is simultaneously an emergent crisis of finance, governance, legitimacy, and an overarching lack of institutional embeddedness. Overcoming any one crisis is a challenge. The odds against overcoming these obstacles simultaneously and building a real ECA is reason enough to keep some doubts about the euro's future.

The Euro Experience: Mind the Gap

The second section of the book turns from the antecedents and generators of these crises to the actual agents key to resolving them. These are not, in our opinion, the supranational institutions in Brussels. Rather, they are the four main economic and political players of the Eurozone: Germany, France, Italy, and Spain. In this section of the book we examine how these states differentially experienced both the introduction of the euro as well as the decade that followed, which culminated in the euro crisis. Here we investigate whether the euro game has been worth the candle for these countries, how their economies' intermeshing through the euro helped catalyze the crisis in each country, and why they experienced the same shocks so differently.

Collectively the chapters of Section II argue that once economic growth had returned after the 1992–1993 collapse of the EMS and subsequent recession, northern European capital—in search of higher yields—increasingly flowed into southern European markets in anticipation of the formal introduction of the euro in 1999. Financial market participants implicitly assumed that the approaching adoption of the euro in those countries was a de facto guarantee against any inflation or devaluation, which shaved off most of the existing national risk premiums that had prevailed on Mediterranean (and peripheral) country bonds.[19] The initial result of these financial flows was rapid interest rate convergence and a consequent flooding of local bank funding markets, which held as long as economic times were relatively good, between 1998 and 2008, all of which seemed to vindicate the view that the euro had brought about deeper economic integration in the Eurozone. But rather than leading toward convergence, as anyone just focusing on EMU sovereign bond spreads would have discerned, this process had actually resulted in unsustainably large intra-European balance of payments disequilibria between Germany and everyone else, already visible by 2005.

Unintentionally but consequentially, EMU helped to bring about in reality pre-existing popular perceptions of a gap between a seemingly financially more orthodox northern "core" of "surplus countries" that mainly saved, invested, produced, and exported, and a debt-laden southern "periphery" of "deficit countries" that predominantly borrowed, consumed, and imported. This economic divergence, not the expected convergence of the Treaty of Maastricht, made possible by the same institutional design flaws already noted, allowed capital to flow ungoverned across EMU borders. When these capital flows suffered a sudden stop in 2010 as markets grew wary and banking liquidity dried up, the consequence for the periphery was the sudden realization that by joining the euro they had given up their two main national shock absorbers—devaluation and inflation—for a few points less in interest. This left them with "deflation" (or internal devaluation) as the only option on the table, regardless of its effectiveness.[20]

In the absence of any solidarity mechanism at the EU level—where the North would inflate while the South would deflate, or fiscal transfers from North to South to ease the financial blow—the whole burden of adjustment would fall onto the periphery countries via austerity, leaving the core countries Scot-free. As Vivien Schmidt has noted already, the sovereign debt crisis thereby reawakened old political divisions on the European Continent that the euro was actually introduced to put to rest once and for all.

The Reluctant Leader, the Middle Child, and the Troubled South

Abraham Newman, in Chapter 6, demonstrates how the euro crisis has underscored the critical, and unenviable, role that Germany plays in Europe's regional architecture. For Newman, the German government has persistently pushed a policy response that is motivated by a deep concern to avoid moral hazard by other member states, while at the same time doing what needs to be done to stop the situation from becoming critical. This has resulted in a reluctance to fund or favor quick and forceful commitments to regional bailouts or strong interventions by the ECB.

Germany, it should be emphasized, has not been paralyzed in the face of the crisis. As Newman notes, from a pending Greek sovereign default in May 2010 to the Spanish banking crisis in the summer of 2012, Germany has actively engaged on all fronts and has been the most important member of the resolution team. But in these efforts, Germany has played the role of reluctant leader—cautious and circumscribed—which is a caution that has not been without risk, as this halting response has inflated the costs and duration of the crisis by sowing the seeds of market doubt and sparking wider fears of contagion. By always stressing what Newman terms the "moral hazard frame for policy" over other alternative frames that would legitimate a more aggressive response, Germany has managed to both help resolve and help exacerbate the crisis. Given this, it is important to understand why alternative policy frames underscoring either the risks to German exports and growth, or the uncertainties of contagion to Germany (and the rest of Europe), were ultimately rejected by Berlin.

Newman's historical explanation of Germany's crisis behavior focuses on the costs of reunification in the minds of German voters (and as perceived by German politicians) plus the timing of the German economic recovery of the mid-2000s relative to the timing of the euro crisis. These factors, Newman argues, set in motion a set of political dynamics that favored the selection of the moral hazard response over other possible alternatives. In particular, Newman notes how structural reforms enacted in response to the post-reunification economic malaise, as well as the large fiscal transfers from West to East resulting from reunification, seriously undermined any solidarity impulses within the German electorate.

In Chapter 7, Mark Vail builds upon Newman's work by analyzing the politics of France through the frame of its role as Europe's "middle child," with a particular emphasis on the contradictions of its position as a European leader and anchor of EMU despite its relative economic weakness. Vail argues that the competing allures of statism and liberalism in French leaders' views of governance, France's vacillating commitments to Keynesianism and austerity in policy, as well as France's core but increasingly problematic partnership with Germany, have generated a deeply fraught and inconsistent set of trajectories in its financial and economic policy, both domestically and at the European level.

Vail supports his central claim through a careful analysis of the political debates surrounding EMU in the late 1990s, paired with the debates surrounding the European financial and sovereign debt crisis after 2007. In each of these instances, Vail sees French policy guided by commanding but often contradictory political-economic imperatives: French economic autonomy and the desire for political leadership within Europe, the preservation of its historic partnership with Germany as an avenue of influence in the European Union, while protecting and preserving its cherished "statist-liberal" political-economic model. He concludes by suggesting that this balancing strategy has become even less feasible since the euro crisis, while France's growing ineffectiveness at articulating an alternative vision of European economic policy has reduced the chances of a less austere future for the Eurozone as a whole.

Jonathan Hopkin brings this section to a close in Chapter 8 by focusing on the two "troubled" southern European economies whose actions matter most for the future of the euro: Italy and Spain. Hopkin argues that the fate of the euro really hangs on the outcome of the crisis in the southern European democracies, and argues that the social and political dynamics behind the crisis are ill understood. Hopkin's chapter moves beyond the standard narrative of debtor and creditor nations, examining the political and distributional consequences of monetary union within the two largest southern member states.

Rejecting the conventional wisdom of "insiders" (trade unions) benefiting from excessive wages driven up by North-South capital flows, Hopkin shows us empirically that the euro brought big gains to the "sheltered" sectors of these economies—construction, retail, and parts of the public sector—while manufacturing workers actually saw their real wages stagnate. But the policies imposed on the South in response to the debt crisis have come down especially hard on unionized workers and other lower income groups, particularly the young, while protecting politically powerful and protected sectors that gained during the boom years and are able to externalize the costs of adjustment onto others.

According to Hopkin, despite these distributional failings, southern Europeans have shown remarkable resilience in the face of these economic and political challenges and remain largely committed to euro membership. However, he fears that the imposition of multi-year programs of "internal devaluation" constitutes a major natural experiment with very high stakes. It counts on southern European citizens to maintain an unwavering commitment to the euro to justify years of sacrifice with no seeming end in sight. Elections held since the euro crisis began have brought major transformations to what were relatively settled patterns of citizen representation and party competition. Hopkin points to the sharp decline in pro-European sentiment and the tenuous grip on government power of pro-European political forces across all southern countries since the crisis, and cautions that Europe's southern periphery's commitment to the euro will be tested to the limit in the coming years.

The Euro Future: The Return of National Politics, Muddling Through, or Euro Federalism?

What can our evaluation of the "euro problem" and the "euro experience" tell us about the "euro future"? The final section of this book grapples with the critical questions raised earlier: how Europe will deal with its new "German problem" going forward, whether the missing unions can be built into a functional ECA, and which international monetary future awaits the euro—either as a subordinate part of a still dollar-centric global monetary system, or as an integral and central part of a multi-polar international currency universe.

Wade Jacoby's Chapter 9 focuses once again on Germany, but from a different angle than Abraham Newman's analysis in Chapter 6. As Berlin will arguably call the main shots in the euro's evolving institutional design, Jacoby considers both the "timing of politics" and the "politics of timing" behind Germany's policy response to the euro crisis. In regard to the "timing of politics," while German policymakers accept the need to intervene in the sovereign bond markets of other Eurozone members and to secure much deeper integration of governing competencies in general to avoid future crises, they want to pick the optimal time of intervention to maximize the efforts of private actors and to deter public and private behavior that might require more bailouts in the future (here, echoing Newman's moral hazard policy frame). If their central focus is on moral hazard, then their aim is that their intervention should come at the "right" time.

German leaders, however, also face a second and largely separate concern about the "politics of timing." Understandably, German elites feel they cannot launch such very large interventions until they have properly prepared their voters. Given these considerations, they have tended to propose rescue packages both later and smaller than needed to stop the dynamics that were undermining confidence in the euro. Yet each time Germany's elected officials have sold a bailout of a certain envisioned size to their voters, or have argued for even more devolved sovereignty to the EU level, the problem has grown such that the proposed solution is now insufficient to the task. These two problems combine to form a serious dilemma for German politicians going forward. If one focuses primarily on the timing of politics, then patience is a virtue, and elites should wait and minimize future moral hazard concerns. If one focuses primarily on the politics of timing, however, then patience is a vice, as windows of opportunity for stemming the crisis slam shut, one after another. The result is therefore often too little, too late, and too timidly delivered.

In Chapter 10, Craig Parsons and Matthias Matthijs problematize the commonly held view in Brussels that the crisis is a great opportunity for reform and therefore a good thing because "European integration always moves forward through crisis."[21] They aim to expose this view as a persistent and even dangerous popular myth by answering two sets of questions. First, is this view historically correct? Have past major advances in European integration actually tended to follow directly from crises? Second, they examine whether this has been the path actually taken during the Eurozone sovereign debt crisis and to what extent it makes sense to say that the EU has "moved forward" as a consequence of the euro crisis.

Parsons and Matthijs review the historical record of European integration since the early 1950s and answer the first question with a negative. While crisis language has been very common across EU history, no major step in the EU's institutional development responded in any clear way to a widely perceived need for policy changes to solve serious and imminent problems. To the contrary, they argue, the major steps that led to today's EU followed from an ongoing organizational project that advanced despite major contestation among elites (though not publics) about its necessity or even desirability. Their answer to the second question also lies in the negative, noting that while the EU definitely has suffered its first "real" crisis beginning in 2009, they still see Europe's response as reactive, slow, ad hoc, and minimalist.

Nonetheless, they do admit that in some ways the EU has perhaps made itself somewhat better able to respond to similar crises in the future, as per Nicolas Jabko's analysis in Chapter 4, but still has not actually addressed the underlying vulnerabilities noted in the first part of the book in a truly fundamental way. In the view of Parsons and Matthijs, successful projects of reform in huge political organizations rarely, if ever, arise as technically necessary responses to already apparent crises. In such moments, bold ideas are needed since only a positive vision of new European goals will allow the EU to recapture a sense of forward movement. However, in Europe's austere times, such big ideas are mainly conspicuous by their absence.

Finally, Eric Helleiner adds the international political economy dimension to this analysis in Chapter 11. He argues that the future of the euro must be viewed through a lens that focuses not just on intra-European politics but on the international monetary system as a whole. Helleiner argues that for many Europeans, part of the political appeal of the euro has long been that it might serve as a challenge to the dollar-dominated international monetary system. European frustrations over the trajectory of the dollar's value and US policy choices served as a catalyst for strengthening regional monetary cooperation at various moments since the early 1970s. During the 2007–2008 global financial crisis, these European aspirations for the euro's international role came to the surface once again, when many analysts predicted that the US-centered financial upheaval might boost the euro's international role.

Given this context, Helleiner places the euro crisis, and the euro's future, within the ambit of two developments post-2008 that are of great relevance to charting any potential future of the euro. On the one hand, the dollar has shown surprising resilience in the face of the global financial crisis, and effortlessly remains the reserve currency of choice globally. On the other hand, the rise of China's monetary power, primarily linked to its position as the world's creditor, is bound to complicate the dynamics behind the dollar-centric international monetary system.

Helleiner sees these two consequences of the financial crisis as humbling for those Europeans who harbored great aspirations for the euro's future global role. Yet at the same time, they may serve to boost the political prospects for the euro over the longer term. The desire to challenge US monetary power may bolster European backing for reforms that take regional monetary cooperation to the next level. And Chinese policymakers may well help by keeping up their enthusiastic support for the euro, despite the potential for future crises, based on their own geo-strategic goals.

Staying Relevant and Informing Future Policy

Our conclusion to this volume is rather unusual. Rather than simply reiterating all the arguments in short form, we try to tease out the observable implications of each of these sets of arguments for the future of the euro going forward and try to make predictions on this basis.

To retain any claim to relevance this time around, we feel it is incumbent upon scholars who have made their careers talking about Europe to say something about this crisis before it is fully over, no matter what current LTRO-compressed financial markets seem to believe. While there is considerable risk in doing so, we feel that our collective skill set is broad and deep enough to allow us to say something that can anticipate likely outcomes while making a contribution to scholarship that is empirically sound, theoretically informed, and politically relevant. Or that at least is our hope. As usual, time shall be the judge. But we leave that task for the conclusion.

SECTION I

The Euro Problem

2

The Forgotten Problem
of Embeddedness

HISTORY LESSONS FOR THE EURO

Kathleen R. McNamara

Introduction

When euro coins and bills were introduced at midnight on New Year's Eve
in 2002, enthusiastic crowds lined up at cash machines on the Boulevard
Saint-Germain, the Kurfürstendamm, and the Gran Vía to be the first in
their neighborhood to hold the new single European currency in their hands.
The feeling of excitement across the Eurozone was heightened by the sense
that Europe had embarked on a path of historic importance. The naysayers
were few and far between, but they included some vocal American economists who viewed the euro as economically ill advised.[1] Within a decade,
however, "euro euphoria" had turned to "euro phobia" in many quarters, and
the single currency was blamed for exacerbating the hardships of a cataclysmic global financial crisis, a bursting European credit bubble, and sovereign
debt crises spreading across EU member states. The European Parliament
elections of May 2014 demonstrated the deep political cleavages around the
European project and seemed to usher in a new era of political contestation
around the euro, and the European Union more generally. The skeptics'
gloomy predictions seemed to be coming true, and much of the conventional
wisdom explaining the calamitous path of the Eurozone focused on the differing economic fundamentals of the Eurozone member states. Europe, it was

argued, is not an "optimum currency area," making it impossible to sustain a single currency.

This is the wrong diagnosis, however, for Europe's current illness. Instead, the argument in this chapter is that the Eurozone's biggest challenges lie not in its economic suboptimality, but instead in a particular political problem. The design of the Eurozone is notably different from every other successful single currency in history in that it is "disembedded" from the broader social and political institutions needed to provide a solid and durable foundation for monetary union. The euro lacks, quite simply, the political institutions needed for adjustment when the currency is removed from national control. Markets need political authority to stabilize them, and it is this lack of governance that will sink the euro, not its shortcomings as an optimum currency area. In other words, it is the politics—not the economics—that will need to be fixed.

The future of the euro therefore will depend heavily on the reclamation of important lessons from history and a much more political and social reading of the fundamental logics of markets. The history lessons of previous monetary unions have a lot to say about the Eurozone's current predicament. They suggest that rather than trying to mimic the classical markets of Adam Smith, Friedrich von Hayek, and Milton Friedman, European leaders and their publics will need to channel the historical sociology of anthropologist Karl Polanyi if they want to fix the euro's problems. Markets function only when they are embedded within larger formal and informal institutions of political authority. Rather than reach for some optimal set of wished-for attributes, we should understand the minimal conditions that will sustain governance. The future of the euro will depend on a recognition by political leaders, policymakers, and the publics they govern of the importance of designing an embedded currency area to stabilize the euro.

What Underpins the Future of the Euro?

The euro is a historical innovation of startling proportions, as it is the only example in the modern era of a group of states consolidating their currencies into a new, supranational money. Despite its innovations, the euro can be analyzed with two more general theories of what makes a currency area hang together. One, optimum currency area (OCA) theory, dominates how most prominent economic commentators understand the euro today. I argue, however, that this approach is incomplete, as it is missing an account of the various political institutions and conditions that allow for a single currency to be successful. Instead, I propose a theory of what I call embedded currency areas (ECA), which better captures the necessary foundations for managing the slings and arrows of macroeconomic fortune in a single currency zone.

The Market Makes the Currency: Optimum Currency Area Theory

To recognize the problems of the euro, most analysts start with deductive economic theories regarding the conditions under which the move to a single currency is likely to be desirable, that is, the benefits will outweigh the costs, and will be sustainable. The conventional approach centers on the theory of optimum currency areas (OCA), also often referred to as optimal currency area theory.[2] Pioneered by Robert Mundell, the approach begins with the straightforward fact that when you join your currency with others, either as a single currency or as irrevocably fixed exchange rates, your exchange rate can only collectively fluctuate against the rest of the world and can no longer be used for national purposes within that currency zone.[3] In effect, you will lose autonomy in your economic decision-making without exchange rate flexibility. OCA theory then moves to assess the relative costs of adjustment in the new monetary union versus life with an independent currency.

In OCA theory, certain factors have been identified as critical for a monetary union with a single currency to be a net benefit to its members, despite this loss of policy autonomy.[4] In Mundell's original framing of the question, he assumed that the key issue for analysis centered on assessing whether, for any given geographic area, an asymmetric economic shock would better be addressed by individual external exchange rate adjustments, or whether internal adjustments would be adequate to stabilize the economy. For example, what are the policy demands created when Ireland is booming but Germany is anemic, as was the case in 2002? What about the differential effects of the global economic crisis on the Eurozone, as Spain's unemployment soars while Germany's falls? Can a single, common monetary policy address the varied needs of the European states, without the option of using individual exchange rates to adjust? The notion of asymmetry is important here: the monetary union is most challenged when an unexpected shock impacts some parts of the region differently than it does others. If the shock, be it positive or negative, was not asymmetric, then a common external exchange rate adjustment would fix most problems, and individual adjustment through the exchange rate could be forfeited. The ideal monetary union is therefore one where internal adjustments are effective and less costly than an individual region's independent, nominal exchange rate adjustment would be in the face of asymmetric shocks.

Certain factors make it more likely that the internal adjustments will be achievable, from this theoretical perspective. Nominal price and wage flexibility in the currency area is considered to be a key factor in those adjustments.[5] With such flexibility, the assumption is that unemployment or inflation in the face of asymmetric economic shocks might be lessened even without the ability to adjust the economy through the exchange rate. Labor and capital mobility are presumed to be a key way to achieve such adjustment.[6] If both factors of production can move freely throughout the monetary union, then adjustments can more easily happen internally. For example, if one area, say southern Italy, is more severely impacted by an economic shock, and its workers can easily move to another part of the Eurozone that is flourishing, such as the Netherlands, there will be less need for an external exchange rate adjustment, and membership in the euro will be less costly for Italy. Essentially, in this view, the greater the ability of all internal factor markets to adjust through price and wage flexibility to market forces without barriers, the better the single currency will function.

Other economic factors were highlighted in subsequent OCA work as important in determining the success of monetary unions and single currencies. Ronald McKinnon argued that openness to the international economy was a good indicator of whether a single currency made sense for any geographic area.[7] The more open an economy is to world prices, through trade and investment flows, the less "money illusion" there is for the domestic economy (i.e., workers would not be "fooled" for very long by nominal changes in price). This pressure on domestic prices to adjust to competitive levels internationally would mean that the economic merit of exchange rate flexibility would be reduced, as a devaluation in the currency would not likely achieve sustainable growth and employment gains, but would be swamped by the higher costs of tradable goods and increased cost of living. Other elements might also dilute the impact of giving up your currency and make a monetary union more attractive. Peter Kenen posited that the more diverse an economy is in production and consumption, the better it would weather economic shocks.[8] If only certain parts of the economy were struck by downturns at any point in time, the loss of the exchange rate as a tool of adjustment would be less important, according to Kenen, leading him (and others) to argue that groups of countries whose economies were highly diversified are likely to make the most robust partners for a single currency.

Yet this OCA framework, while logical, does not fully capture the entirety of how markets work and risks missing key factors that help determine the likelihood of future success and stability in a currency area. These lacunae produce a striking empirical falsification for OCA theory: no currency union in history, whether successful or not, has actually met all of the requirements of optimum currency area theory. In fact, the key determinant of currency robustness is the existence of political borders, not a currency region drawn because of high factor mobility, openness to the international economy, or sector diversity. State boundaries delineated a vast array of national currencies that hang together despite their imperfect economic structures. The main reason for this can be found in an entirely different view of how markets work, one that looks to political authority, power, and institutions. While this view is anathema to a classical economic view of currency and money, it has both deductive and inductive power in explaining the likely future of the euro, as we will see next.

Politics Makes the Currency: Embedded Currency Area Theory

Currency is always and everywhere a political thing.[9] Contrasting with the rational and abstracted cost-benefit analysis outlined above, my alternative approach seeks to embed market dynamics within a broader set of social and political interactions. It also is an argument against the notion of an optimal rubric for currencies as a guide to the reality of the euro. The idea of the fundamental "embeddedness" of markets comes from the seminal work of Karl Polanyi. In *The Great Transformation*, Polanyi argued that the rise of capitalism upended the traditional relationship between markets, power, and society.[10] Familial or communal ties became subordinate to the market and its seemingly impersonal forces of exchange. But, Polanyi argued, this was not a natural or inevitable process, and it was one that would spawn a powerful backlash of citizens suffering from the social dislocations of liberal market capitalism. This societal counterattack would lead to what Polanyi termed a "double movement," as economic liberalism, on one hand, prompts political demands for social protection by political authorities, on the other. In other words, markets were fundamentally political in nature and would soon become subject to political control.

If we take Polanyi's insight and apply it to the realm of money, currency unions are likely to succeed only as part of a broader series of institutional structures that attempt to stabilize economic interactions within a context of political agreement and a legitimate process for setting economic goals and targets.[11] These institutional setups are inculcated with political and social logics as well as with our more familiar rationalist, economic logics. Economic actors are social beings as well as profit-maximizing creatures, and their perceptions, goals, and desires are shaded by motivations for status, emotional reactions, and larger worldviews and cultural dynamics. These economic actors are likewise "embedded" within larger social institutions that create cultural frames for their actions and onto which those actions reverberate and feed back.[12]

Given this approach, rather than rational, stripped-down market reactions to various economic scenarios in the manner of OCA theory, the determinants of a stable, sustainable monetary union with a single currency should be analyzed in terms of the entire package of elements that are required for monetary unions to succeed. These elements constitute a minimum, rather than an optimal, foundation for monetary union. To analyze the future of the euro, we need to turn from the purely economic understandings of the costs and benefits to an appreciation of the pathways of adjustment in a composite polity. In this embedded currency area (or ECA) approach, key elements bundled together to allow for adjustment include (1) a legitimated generator of market confidence and liquidity, (2) mechanisms for fiscal redistribution and economic adjustment, (3) regulation of financial risk and uncertainty, and (4) political solidarity. Each of these four key elements is further explained below.

First, understanding how money works from an embedded perspective suggests that the market does not itself generate authoritative rules and confidence in compliance with those rules. Instead, there must be some sort of legitimate, centralized political authority that is viewed as both willing and able to provide the public good of stability within the monetary system, allowing for the social construction of market confidence critical to that stability. Central banks developed over the last century as the organizational form in which this sort of authority is vested.[13] The central bank is the tip of the iceberg, the visible expression of the concentration of legitimate political authority in a political system that—ideally—stabilizes expectations about the future of the currency. One key element in the provision of such stabilization of expectations is the acknowledgment, either implicit or explicit, that the central bank will act as a true lender of last resort when needed to stabilize the currency and the broader monetary union. Providing liquidity to markets when money dries up overcomes market failure and demonstrates why markets should be understood as functioning smoothly only when embedded within larger social and political structures.

In addition to the authoritative lender of last resort, a second element important to the stability of monetary unions is a matching fiscal union or economic government.[14] As with the OCA literature, it is instructive to consider what a political entity is giving up when it merges its currency, that is, its exchange rate flexibility. The inability of political authorities to rely on exchange rate depreciation or devaluation to stimulate growth through exports, as for example the Japanese government did in 2013 to revive its moribund economy, can be an unacceptable cost of monetary union. Likewise, if growth is too fast, yet the exchange rate cannot appreciate or be revalued, there is a significant risk of inflation, as in Ireland before the financial crisis of 2008. Rather than look solely to markets for adjustment, the ECA approach suggests the merging together of the fiscal side of economic policy governance. With a broader pool of revenue potential that is spread across the entirety of the currency union, the all but inevitable times when one part of the union is in recession while another part is booming can be smoothed out by transfers from the high-growth regions to the suffering areas through the operation of a system of fiscal federalism. Higher tax revenues from the robust areas will fund automatic social welfare payouts in the faltering regions without the need for highly visible bailout funds transferring from one part of the union to the other. Redistribution in a federal fiscal union can also occur through more explicit targeted ways as well, through programs such as high-speed rail infrastructure investments, tax credits for specific manufacturing plants, or high-tech retraining programs tailored to particular regions.

Another reason that fiscal unions are critical for a monetary union to be successful lies in the need for centralized debt instruments in the single currency. The operation of financial markets in a monetary union with decentralized fiscal policies can create giant pressures on the subordinate political units if there is no monetary union-wide debt instrument to mutualize debt and reduce perceived member state risk. Bond market investors see that monetary union members cannot use the exchange rate to correct the course of the economy, and begin to see their bonds as riskier, putting upward pressure on the national rates needed to borrow. As borrowing becomes more expensive, a vicious circle can be created as higher interest rate charges increase annual deficits and overall public debt levels, further putting stress on the economic performance of the individual currency union member. With a centralized public debt instrument, members can spread the costs of giving up their exchange rates over the entirety of the union and potentially weather temporary downturns more successfully. The flight to safety out of the troubled member state can thereby be mitigated, thus avoiding a liquidity crisis. This would not only help the individual political unit, but also strengthen the unified currency overall.

Fiscal union or economic government is also desirable because of the benefits of balancing monetary and fiscal policy in the macroeconomic "policy mix." Monetary policy (the regulation of the money supply through interest rate changes and open market operations on the part of the central bank) tends to work better if it is done in tandem with fiscal policy (comprising the centralized tax and spending policies of a political unit). A union-wide fiscal policy may be key particularly in a situation where a polity is giving up the ability to tailor monetary policy directly to their political economic circumstances, resulting in what Vivien Schmidt calls a "one size fits none" monetary policy in Chapter 5 of this volume (neither restrictive enough to keep fast-growing economies from overheating, nor lax enough to stimulate growth where it is most needed). Fiscal policy can be targeted much more closely toward specific societal actors and geographic regions, potentially substituting for the shortcomings of a single monetary policy.

The third element needed in the ECA model is authoritative rules regarding banking activities within the union. The combination of monetary and fiscal union needs to be complemented with authoritative rules to reduce the systemic risk in the financial sector. A banking union, composed of a common regulatory framework and a set of security guarantees for bank depositors, as well as resolution funds for financially troubled banks, stabilizes markets by embedding them within larger political structures. If not, the tightly woven monetary and fiscal union means that lax banking regulations and failing banks in one area of the currency union will likely spill over into the broader economy. Risky investment vehicles and undercapitalized banks mean trouble for the entire union because of the working of financial markets and the pressures they will exert on the fiscal, monetary, and currency spheres of activity, as we have seen after the crash of 2008, triggered by the bankruptcy of Lehman Brothers. Markets have been proven to be lacking in the efficient and orderly correction of bad banking activities, making the ability of the broader political and institutional setting to generate regulatory regimes critical for successful monetary union.

These three elements, an authoritative lender of last resort, fiscal union, and banking union, cannot be achieved absent an overarching and robust political union.[15] This fourth part of the bundle that supports currency areas is critical, as all of the above must be situated within a context of broader political solidarity and mechanisms of democratic legitimacy. Political union

Table 2.1 Determinants of Successful Monetary Union

Optimum Currency Area Theory (OCA) (Mundell, McKinnon, Kenen)	Embedded Currency Area Theory (ECA) (McNamara)
Factor Mobility (K & L) (Mundell)	A "True" Lender of Last Resort function (**LOLR**) (*Chapters 3 and 4*, Jones & Jabko)
Wage and Price Flexibility (Mundell)	Fiscal Redistribution, Sovereign Debt Pooling (**Fiscal Union**) (*Chapter 4*, Jabko)
Openness to Global Markets (McKinnon)	Financial Market Regulation, Bailouts, Resolution Mechanisms, Deposit Guarantees (**Banking Union**) (*Chapter 3*, Jones)
A Diversified Economy (Kenen)	Legitimate and Democratic Institutions of Governance (**Political Union**) (*Chapter 5*, Schmidt)

is necessary to create governance rules over the various markets, but also to support the political authority needed to govern beyond mere rules, with the type of discretionary activities of stabilizing and redistributing necessary for successful monetary union. Political union must also be in concert with the prevailing modes of legitimacy of the moment. In the modern era, that means representative democracy. This fourth element pervades the other three and sets the parameters for how the economy develops, including the integrity of the single currency. It speaks to the heart of the model of embedded markets, which assumes that markets will not be able to function without these broader political bargains, social understandings, and democratically accountable public institutions. It can be thought of as the framework necessary to facilitate a sense of social solidarity, facilitating the institutional mechanisms needed to ensure that the losers of economic crisis are compensated in ways adequate to make them feel that they are not being left behind, while not alienating the economic winners. In this regard, a political union is the opposite of the ordo-liberal union that currently structures the institutions of the euro.

In sum, my theoretical perspective sees markets as embedded in larger social, political, and cultural institutions, and therefore generates a very different set of criteria from those found in the optimal currency area literature, as illustrated in Table 2.1. This is no random laundry list of desirable institutions, but rather needs to be understood as deductively generated from an entirely different way of understanding the nature of markets. As outlined in my theoretical discussion above, a model of the economy that sees markets as constructed with power and social logics side by side with economic motivations predicts that isolating money institutionally will not produce the necessary institutional and social stabilizers to sustain a single currency. Moving beyond theory, the historical record on currency unions also strongly bears out the validity of the ECA approach, to which we turn next.

Currency Unions in Practice

Historical cases of monetary integration provide important and instructive lessons for the future of the euro. The simplest historical lesson that we have is that currencies conform to national borders, not to optimum currency areas, and exceptions to this rule have all been relatively short-lived. A sustained monetary union is empirically associated with a high degree of embeddedness in authoritative political institutions, not factor mobility, wage and price flexibility, or diversified and open economies. Modern currencies largely arose as part of state formation processes alongside the rise of the nineteenth-century nation-state, although there have been some examples of currency unions outside the nation-state as well. The currencies that have lasted have all been part of the consolidation of a bundle of activities under a framework of strong political authority. Below, I provide a typology of monetary unions assessed in terms of two variables: the centralization of monetary authority and currency, and the degree of political integration. I use the typology to provide a stylized overview of the historical record on monetary unions, and then parse out some of the details of the variations across different cases of monetary unions in each category. The selected historical record allows for the construction of a comparative qualitative assessment that links the relative sustainability of the currency to the most embedded cases of monetary union (national currencies) to the partially embedded (the euro and the krone of the Austro-Hungarian Empire) and to the least embedded (the Latin Monetary Union and the Scandinavian Monetary Union). This attention to the *degree* of embeddedness and the relative durability of the currency union sets up our analysis about the future of the euro, both here and in the three chapters that follow.

Embedded Currencies: One Money, One Government

Since the nineteenth century, successful modern currencies have had a one-to-one relationship with modern nation-states, with currency unions endogenous to larger projects of state formation and nation building. As previously autonomous geographic units were brought together, usually "through iron and blood," in the words of Prussia's Otto von Bismarck, a range of administrative activities were consolidated by the dominant political authorities.[16] Power was established and institutionalized through policymaking capacity at the center of a bounded geographical territory and population, resulting in a sovereign state. For most theorists, components of modern states generally (but not always) include a unified fiscal system; a common, often imposed, national language; a unified legal system; and, critical for our purposes here, a single currency.[17] Political elites sought to consolidate the levers of control over the economy to the center of a political entity, and currency has been seen as one of those levers. To revise a familiar phrase from Charles Tilly, war makes the state, and the state makes the currency.[18]

National money or currency can be a crucial component of state capacity in times of war, facilitating the collection of revenues, the payment of federal expenditures, and the organization of debt. War can also provide a political opportunity for currency consolidation, as savvy political actors have often taken advantage of crises to consolidate power, using a frame of the "logic of no alternative" to create political conditions to transfer both monetary and fiscal authority to the center.[19] Not just currency, but fiscal policy is a crucial component in this story, as it is the ability to raise revenue and distribute it efficiently that can make the difference between winning a war and being subjugated to a competing power.[20] In addition to the security benefits, a single currency can also aid in the development of a single national market, simplifying transactions and lowering uncertainty across economic actors.[21] Finally, currency is a symbol of political community, and in generating practices around the use of that money in a particular, bounded area, may contribute to nation building if it is positively perceived. However, it can also be a potent symbol for dissolution, as in the case of the Soviet Union and the Austro-Hungarian Empire, discussed further below.[22]

The United States

The development of a single currency in the United States allows us to more closely trace the process of the embedding of currencies, how it happens, and why it matters for the sustainability of a monetary union. The American case represents an example of a fully embedded currency, as it possesses all of the four necessary elements for embedding: a lender of last resort, and overlapping fiscal, banking, and political unions. As the discussion below, highlights, however, these political institutions were gradually built up through historical crises, including both political and military conflicts, and through the pressures of an increasingly complex market system and a series of financial calamities. The demands for governance and the political willingness and coalitional support for the development of a more centralized and powerful political authority over markets as public institutions were pivotal in pushing forward the necessary degree of embeddedness to support the single currency.

The early United States did not have a single currency until the second half of the nineteenth century. The American single currency, the greenback, first replaced a multitude of state currencies and private notes in 1863, during the US Civil War.[23] President Abraham Lincoln's Republican Party muscled through legislation giving the federal government exclusive currency rights once the Southern legislators, opposing more centralization of power, seceded from the union. The currency was viewed as aiding in the war effort by allowing for the rationalization of revenue raising and wartime payments. But it was also a potent symbol of the power of the federal state in the face of the challenges of a disintegrating union, and the various political institutions that came out of the Civil War framed the vigorous development of the American state.[24] The embeddedness of the currency in a putative political union was therefore central to the project of a single currency.

However, the other component parts of embeddedness were not immediately constructed. The authoritative lender of last resort function was only tenuous, as the charter for the US First National Bank was allowed to expire twice, until a permanent US Federal Reserve was finally set up in 1913, after a series of severe financial crises created political will for the centralization of monetary power in a federal reserve board, but only one at the center of a federal system of regional banks.[25] The United States had elements of a fiscal union early on, as Alexander Hamilton, the young country's first Secretary of the Treasury, prioritized the ability to issue and raise debt at the federal level and build a robust financial system. Randall Henning and Martin Kessler argue that the uneasy back and forth over federal bailouts of the states finally resulted in the states passing balanced budget rules in the nineteenth century, but doing so as part of a bargain over a federal state able and willing to provide countercyclical fiscal relief to states in distress.[26] Banking union in the United States likewise was built over time, and took a series of financial crises in the Great Depression to come to fruition. It was not until the Banking Act of 1933 that the Federal Deposit Insurance Corporation (FDIC) guaranteed savings up to $2,500, established the Glass-Steagall banking rules, and, in subsequent legislation, put in force federal oversight of the banking industry.

The US case demonstrates the hard-won but critical relationship between the four elements of embeddedness and the outcome of currency system stability.

Federal Germany

Additional historical cases further illustrate the relationship between the embeddedness of a currency in a broader system of governance and the durability of such a currency. In Europe, the German case highlights the interaction between currency consolidation, war making, and political union, and the ways in which currencies became embedded historically. Germany began the nineteenth century as a highly decentralized, fragmented polity made up of over three hundred independent kingdoms, electorates, duchies, imperial cities, ecclesiastical territories, and estates of imperial kings.[27] Slow and gradual consolidation over the following decades included the Prussians joining with Hesse-Darmstadt in a customs union. This customs union formed the foundation for what would become the German Zollverein in 1834, a loose free trade area with some elements of currency consolidation, including efforts to standardize coins and establish a national central bank.

True monetary union would only occur with the rise of Otto von Bismarck as Minister-President of Prussia in 1862. Bismarck was able to build on the foundations of the Zollverein as he set out to create a modern and united Germany from the various political entities.[28] A gold standard mark was created on July 9, 1873, and the Reichsbank, or German central bank, was established in 1876. The monetary consolidation formed a part of a much larger *Gründungszeit*, or "foundation time" of German state building. The elements of embeddedness identified in our discussion of an optimal embedded currency area were gradually built into the German currency union: political union under Bismarck in 1871, the Reichsbank as a lender of last resort five years later, and a growing fiscal capacity as the German state was gradually built. In keeping with the times, a banking union with tight financial regulations was not created until after the economic collapse preceding World War II, as was true for all of the historical cases. The German mark, however, was clearly nested in a series of political institutions, however imperfect.

Italy and Switzerland

Several other European cases are also instructive. The case of Italy's adoption of a national currency over several years after the *Risorgimento* in the 1860s has been studied by James Foreman-Peck, who found that the unification of the previously sovereign states did not constitute an optimum currency area, with regional disparities beyond the well-known North-South divide.[29]

Instead, it was the larger political framework that stabilized the Italian currency regime, although as we will see further below, Italy soon entered into a larger currency union with its neighbors. Likewise, the Swiss franc came into being—after a brief aborted attempt during the early 1800 Helvetic Republic—with Switzerland's unification through a treaty among 25 sovereign polities in 1848. As the central government took over foreign and military policy, a single Swiss customs union and single market were created, and the exclusive right of coinage was given to the Swiss government. But coin shortages and a desire for standardization in currency matters with a larger group of countries also soon led the Swiss to join the Latin Monetary Union, discussed below.

Partial Embeddedness: One Currency, One Decentralized Polity

There is at least one example of a partially embedded monetary union: Austria-Hungary in the period before and after the turn of the last century. Albeit with important historical caveats, it shares some of the Eurozone's characteristics and represents a midpoint between the embedded national currencies, such as the US dollar, and the disembedded Latin and Scandinavian Monetary Unions discussed below. A currency union between the Austrian Empire and the Kingdom of Hungary ran from 1867 to 1914 as part of the larger Austro-Hungarian Empire or monarchy. Political elites established a single currency system (the krone, or *korona*) with a common central bank, but did not centralize fiscal policy. Instead, they maintained decentralized fiscal capacity to the two states that made up the empire, as well as three autonomous regions, Polish Galicia (under Austria), Croatia (under Hungary), and Bosnia and Herzegovina (administered jointly).

The Austro-Hungarian Empire had an extensive network of political ties and institutions, even as it also had distinct sovereign powers located separately within Austria and Hungary. The Empire had a common monarch in Hapsburg Emperor Franz Joseph I, who served as the ultimate political authority. There was a common army, diplomatic service, and legal system, in addition to its common currency, and a common Austro-Hungarian Bank, located in Vienna. There was a customs union, as well as extensive trade and financial integration across the empire. Yet Austria and Hungary each had their own national political leaders, parliaments, governments, national budgets, and debts.

The Austro-Hungarian currency union was stable for much of the second part of the nineteenth century, with the common central bank controlling the money supply, accumulating reserves, pegging the krone to gold, and maintaining significant independence.[30] However, the decentralized fiscal capacity meant that over time, debts began to rise and markets began to speculate against the solvency of the two states. In addition, ethnic groups within the union began demanding more independence with the advent of World War I and began to loosen their ties with the currency union and rack up large debts.[31] Czechoslovakia and the Kingdom of the Serbs, Croats, and Slovenes left the union, and the monetary union soon fell apart, followed at the end of World War I by the collapse of the larger Austro-Hungarian Empire, whose fate was sealed by the Allied Powers at Versailles in 1919.

Disembedded Money: One Currency, Multiple Polities

Finally, we do have a few cases of disembedded monetary unions, examples of single currencies that were adopted by several separate polities.[32] As predicted by the ECA argument, however, they all struggled and ultimately fell apart as members did not pursue policies that privileged the maintenance of the currency union. The particular reasons for the collapse of the currency unions differed, but they all shared one characteristic: their "disembeddedness" from the panoply of political and social institutions needed to govern money—a central bank, fiscal and banking unions, and political union. The disembedded nature of the currency meant that the legitimate and robust leadership, institutional flexibility, and political cohesion needed to navigate the stresses and strains of monetary union were absent, placing the currencies in peril.

We have two examples of "one currency, multiple polities," and they both demonstrate the difficulties that arise when the instruments of and political support for governance are lacking. They both arose during the pre–World War I era of historical experimentation in political forms, when the modern nation-state was being invented in the second half of the nineteenth century.[33] As national currencies became consolidated in the administrative centralization process occurring across Europe, there were also instances of efforts at creating monetary unions with currencies locked against one another, in effect acting as a single currency. These pre–World War I historical monetary unions were the Scandinavian Monetary Union and the Latin Monetary Union.

Begun in 1866, the Latin Union was composed of France, Italy, Belgium, Switzerland, and eventually Greece. Members agreed to accept each other's coins as legal tender and had a set of standard sizes and fineness for gold and silver coins within the union, among other things. The underlying motivations for the union were, on the economic side, to ease trade and investment through a common monetary standard, and on the political side, France's ambitions to extend its geopolitical power by increasing the centrality of the French franc, on which the Latin currency units were based.[34] As Barry Eichengreen has pointed out, however, the particular issues involved in the Latin Monetary Union involved problems with bimetallism, and the stability sought by forming the union was not easily achieved. As incentives for defection from the agreement rose over time, they ultimately torpedoed the Union altogether.[35] There was no central bank, no common monetary authority, and countries attempted to coordinate their policies without pooling authority or transferring sovereignty to the center, and the union soon devolved into a de facto gold standard–based regime by 1873. Simply put, the stresses and strains of keeping the monetary union together were too much absent the legitimate political authority, institutional and fiscal support, or centralized leadership needed to make the Latin Monetary Union work.

The Scandinavian Monetary Union is the other nineteenth-century example of an attempt at a currency union between multiple political authorities. Beginning in the 1870s, Sweden, Denmark, and subsequently Norway standardized their coinages and allowed for the circulation of national currencies across the Scandinavian borders as their central banks accepted each other's notes at par.[36] Once again, the lack of a common monetary authority or central bank made the management of the Scandinavian Union difficult, as individual states had control over their own monetary policies and there was little sense on the part of market participants that the currencies were truly unified, leading to pressures for movement in the values against each other. Efforts at resisting the market forces were stymied by the disembedded nature of the union, with its lack of centralized or coordinated fiscal capacity or common central bank. The Scandinavian Monetary union was not wholly without political foundations, however, as Sweden and Norway had joined together in a political union from 1814 to 1905. But indicating the importance of political union for building a common currency, the dissolution of that union coincided with the end of agreements to accept each other's financial notes at par. Over the next decade, the Scandinavian Monetary Union crumbled and finally ended completely in 1920. As with the Latin Monetary Union, the Scandinavian experiment in disembedding monetary matters

Table 2.2 Comparing Historical Cases of Monetary Union: The Role of Embeddedness

Most Embedded ←--→ Least Embedded

One Currency, One Political Authority (Sustained)	One Currency, Partial Political Authority (Tenuous)	One Currency, Multiple Political Authorities (Collapsed)
National Currencies (e.g., US dollar/United States 1863–present)	Euro/European Monetary Union (1999–present)	Krone/Scandinavian Monetary Union (1873–1914)
	Krone/Austro-Hungarian Empire (1892–1918)	Interchangeable Currencies/Latin Monetary Union (1865–1927)

from the broader framework of governance institutions and understandings ended in failure.

Our historical survey of all the types of monetary union is captured in Table 2.2.

Understanding the Euro Crisis Through History's Lens

Understood in terms of both theoretical and historical need for economic policy and markets to be embedded in larger frameworks of social and political relationships and institutions, the problems—and thus the potential future paths—of the euro are clear. While the euro initially enjoyed almost a decade of economic good times, the financial crises that developed in late 2008 put severe stress on the Eurozone. What ended up being the worst global macroeconomic shock since the Great Depression also ended up being the perfect storm for testing theories of what really makes a monetary union function smoothly. Troubles had been brewing for a long time, as easy money from various quarters combined with deregulation in financial markets to create massive credit bubbles and asset price rises. European banks were not immune from the litany of financial market "innovations" and the "flip this house" investment culture in holiday villas on the Spanish Costa del Sol and Irish West Coast. The banking crisis that began in the United States in 2008 soon spread to the EU, as European banks' balance sheets took a nosedive and the entire financial machinery in Europe creaked to a halt. Europe was not alone, of course, in its misery, as the United States suffered from similar woes.

But there was a big difference between the ultimate effects of the financial crisis in the US case versus the Eurozone, and the difference really stems from the insufficient embeddedness of the euro in contrast to the dollar. Banking crises in modern times most often result in a state takeover of ailing banks in order to stabilize panicking financial markets and restore overall market confidence. But the result is that a private debt crisis then becomes a sovereign debt crisis.[37] In the case of the United States, the Bush administration, after letting Lehman Brothers fail, stepped in to aggressively stabilize the American banking sector. The 2008 Troubled Assets Relief Program (TARP) was patched together despite conservative congressional complaints and eventually helped stabilize the US financial system. In early 2009, newly elected President Barack Obama enacted a huge stimulus bill, the American Recovery and Reinvestment Act, which distributed money around the country. Additionally, a bailout of the auto industry secured the largest source of manufacturing jobs and put the sector back on track, while every family on the lower end of the income spectrum got a tax refund for several years afterward. The US Federal Reserve has presided over this exercise with the most aggressive injection of money into the US economy, developing and legitimizing new instruments of bond buying in quantitative easing (QE) when interest rates alone no longer provided the punch needed to revive the American economy. While the European Central Bank (ECB), as we will discuss, has also moved beyond its expected mandate, it only started to embrace Fed-style QE well after the acute phase of the crisis was over, in late 2014, in order to fight a persistent deflationary spiral in the Eurozone.

It is not the lack of an optimum currency area that has hamstrung the EU's efforts to match the rebounding of the US economy.[38] Instead, it is the lack of an embedded currency area that has produced divergent outcomes, with devastatingly slow growth and high unemployment in much of southern Europe versus growth and recovery in the US. The problem is that the European Union has only been able to act through one channel, the ECB, to try to ease the broader societal impacts of the Eurozone's financial crisis, the one existing element of an embedded currency on which the EU could build. Yet even the ECB has been working under substantial institutional constraints, with little internal taste on the part of the sober central bankers in Frankfurt for monetizing the debts of its members, overturning the "no bailout" clause in its charter, or moving too far from their historic commitment to price stability above all other goals.[39]

Complicating matters, because it lacks a fiscal union, the EU does not have any power or policy capacity to provide the fiscal stimulus and the special TARP funding found in the US case, which has arguably been a critical reason for the continuing bad performance of many of the European economies relative to the United States. The particular circumstances of the countries with the worst balance sheets—either private debt driven by banking and real estate bubbles, as in Spain or Ireland, or in the case of Greece and Italy, uniquely bad (among the Eurozone countries) political institutions—drove waves of bond market pressures on various countries in turn. As suggested in the literature on currency unions, an asymmetric shock tested the fundamentals of the single currency, and demonstrated the deep shortcomings of the euro. But it is the lack of institutional response at the EU level that sets the euro apart from the other non-optimum currency areas that make up many of the world's dominant national currencies, including, of course, the United States.

On one hand, this should not be surprising, as the EU does not meet the standards of the most successful political form that a currency union can take, that of the modern nation-state. Instead, the EU is a novel hybrid, with some component parts of a federal state, but where key powers, administrative capacities, and political authority firmly remain with the discrete units, the member states. For our purposes, unpacking the component parts vis-à-vis our deductive model helps us evaluate the strengths and weaknesses of the Eurozone. The four component parts identified above as crucial to the overall embeddedness of a currency, that is, a true and authoritative lender of last resort, a financial and banking union, a fiscal and economic union, and a political union, are only weakly represented in the case of the European Union.

The first element, an authoritative lender of last resort, is the area where arguably Europe's monetary union has proven the most sustainable.[40] Founded as a hyper-independent central bank and given a narrow mandate to fight inflation and protect the value of the euro, the European Central Bank has been playing a dramatically more political role than that initially assigned to it by its creators at Maastricht in the early 1990s. Most notably, at the end of 2011, the ECB, under the new leadership of Italian Mario Draghi, issued hundreds of billions of euros in emergency loans to European banks. The policy to some extent mirrored the US Treasury and Federal Reserve's decision in 2008 to bail out American banks in the Troubled Assets Relief Program (TARP). The ECB's new long-term refinancing operations (LTROs) constituted a significant departure from the notion that the ECB would not act to backstop entities in financial distress.

In addition, two new institutional developments also moved the Eurozone closer to having a true lender of last resort capacity. The European Financial Stability Facility (EFSF) was established in May 2010 as a limited liability company, in order to issue state-guaranteed loans for up to 440 billion euro as a first response to the financial distress in Greece. A permanent program, the European Stability Mechanism (ESM), was established in 2012 to provide the funds needed to stabilize financial markets. The ECB's LTRO interventions initially were relatively successful, as the interest rate charged on auctioned bonds in the most pressed member states fell starting in early 2012, allowing for some breathing room. Spain's 10-year bond yields were at 5.5 percent instead of over 7 percent, as they had been in the fall of 2011, and Italy's five-year bonds were selling at yields close to 5 percent, rather than close to 8 percent, as they had earlier. But at various points these interest rates have spiked up again, and the ECB's actions have not been universally applauded.

These new policies and programs have been matched by a much more forceful set of statements from the ECB's executives. In the summer of 2012, muscular remarks by ECB head Mario Draghi pledging his institution's commitment to do "whatever it takes" to save the euro got plenty of attention across Europe and the United States, but it was only one of such statements coming from the ECB as the Eurozone crisis dragged on. Both in terms of its institutional capacity and in terms of its role in the political debate, the ECB has been playing a critical and unexpected role as an unofficial lender of last resort. Yet it is debatable whether it is really fulfilling one of the criteria for stable monetary unions generated by the embedded approach. The ECB's new program of LTROs, begun in 2011, sought to inject money into the faltering European economies, but continuing economic collapse drove the ECB to launch a more aggressive effort, Outright Monetary Transactions (OMT), in September 2012. While OMT allows the ECB to buy up bonds from sovereign member states as well as in secondary markets, a surprising move given the ECB's cautious history, it is both conditional and untested.

The second element, found in all successful cases of currency consolidation, is fiscal and economic union, and this remains the most out of reach in the EU case.[41] Fiscal union comprises the capacity to extract revenue through taxes, to redistribute money through public spending, and to raise additional funds through public debt instruments. The EU currently has none of these explicit functions, although it does redistribute funds through a variety of structural fund programs and other mechanisms. A laundry list of proposals for explicit "Eurobonds" and other ways to mutualize debt in the Eurozone have proved politically inflammatory in some influential circles. Instead of an embedded approach, the EU's leadership and the heads of state and government have aggressively pursued efforts to impose austerity programs of deficit and debt reduction on societies already reeling from the fallout of the financial crisis. The effects look much more like the conditional lending programs and structural adjustment loans of the International Monetary Fund (IMF) than an embedded governance system that could hold together a monetary union. While Ireland has, as of this writing, made it out of its bailout program and met the required conditions of fiscal stringency, Portugal, Spain, Italy, and especially Greece are still mired in recession or stagnation. Nicolas Jabko discusses the missing fiscal union and economic government in greater detail in Chapter 4 of this volume.

The third area of embeddedness needed to sustain a currency, a European banking and financial union, has been slowly working its way through the EU political mill, but effective bargaining on the issue remains elusive. The European Commission, with support from the ECB, has been successful in getting agreement on a single supervisory mechanism (SSM) for the Eurozone's banks, to be spearheaded by the ECB, with a single rulebook for all banks. A European Banking Authority, created in 2011, now spans both the Eurozone and non-euro states as part of the European System of Financial Supervision. However, the regulatory and institutional developments have yet to include elements crucial to the historical cases such as the US, like common deposit insurance, and a single bank resolution program (and common fiscal backstop) in the face of future banking crises. French and especially German political authorities have proven resistant, however, and have stressed at various times a preference for enhanced cooperation rather than ceding power to Brussels and Frankfurt. A prime example is the difficulties surrounding the creation of a single resolution mechanism, which would create a pool of funds to staunch future banking crises. As explained more fully in Erik Jones's Chapter 3 in this volume, the construction of common institutions to safeguard European financial markets is critical for the euro's survival.

Finally, the broader political union that has framed all cases of lasting currency consolidation is likewise missing in the EU case. While the EU has become remarkably institutionalized over the past 50 years, with a constitutional-like legal framework and a series of politics and practices that penetrate deeply into the everyday life of all Europeans, it does not have all of the state-like governance structures of the other examples of currency creation. When, in the midst of the US financial crisis, US Treasury Secretary Henry Paulson stood up with Fed Chairman Ben Bernanke in front of the

US Congress to report on the situation, the world paid attention, and the US polity knew where power lay to make decisions. While the ECB president (first Jean Claude Trichet and then Mario Draghi) has become relatively well known in financial circles, that leader and Jean-Claude Juncker, the head of the Eurogroup at the worst of the crisis, do not have the political profile or confidence of their US counterparts. Indeed, Juncker's successor to head the Eurogroup, Jeroen Dijsselbloem, was an immigration expert with no experience in managing the intricacies of financial crises, which he demonstrated during the Cyprus banking blowup in the spring of 2013. Instead, as Vivien Schmidt argues in Chapter 5 of this volume, the EU "governs by the rules, and rules by the numbers." It has singularly not created the social solidarity and the legitimate political institutions to adequately embed the euro in a larger political framework. With the euro crisis dragging on and on, austerity giving the EU an increasingly bad name, and the political mechanisms for stabilizing the European economy still elusive, creating the political union needed for an embedded currency area will be an uphill battle.

Conclusions

The lessons from history for the future of the euro are clear. Karl Polanyi's insight was that markets, disembedded from broader societal relationships and lacking the political institutions to achieve goals other than market efficiency, would ultimately fail. The same holds true for currencies disembedded from governance structures and the political institutions and social solidarity to underpin that governance. Rather than focusing narrowly, as economists tend to do, on whether the euro is an optimum currency area, we need to understand the importance of creating an embedded currency area, if the euro is to have a future. In this approach, rather than focusing on a wished-for world of economic perfection, we argue for a pragmatic reading of how the political economy works in practice. The construction of the four key elements of currency embeddedness—a central bank to serve as a true lender of last resort, a fiscal and economic union, a financial and banking union, and a political union to govern it all—will be crucial to whether the euro ultimately endures or not. The following three chapters of this volume further flesh out and delineate the dynamics at work in Europe across each of those individual elements. To some degree, they suggest that a halting process is at work to nest the euro in new governance structures. But strong forces continue pushing for austerity and structural reform, emphasizing purely market answers to the euro's ills.

Across the historical cases, there also is a common theme of the wretch-edly difficult political battles fought over proposals to move more authority to a new center of governance within a redrawn political community. From the ultimately successful embedding of the US dollar in the "second foun-dation moment" of nation building during the US Civil War, to the only partial embedding of the Austro-Hungarian krone in a central bank at the heart of a decentralized empire, to the disembedded Scandinavian and Latin Monetary Unions of nineteenth-century Europe, currency has always engen-dered deeply political dynamics. For all its unique features, there is no rea-son to believe that the European Union would be an exception. Despite the strong emphasis on the technical issues around the euro, or the rhetoric about the need for balanced budgets and austerity on the part of all euro member states, the fact is that the political underpinnings of monetary union cannot be shortchanged forever.

The European Union has already demonstrated that deeply embedded governance structures can exist beyond the nation-state. The network of EU regulations that support the Single Market, the multitude of decisions by the European Court of Justice that buffer the impact of markets on EU citizens, and the collaboration across the EU on internal security in a border-less Europe are only a few examples of how the EU has developed capacity and engaged its citizens in its supranational governance structure. The euro, arguably one of the most extreme examples of surrendering sovereign power to the EU level, is in jeopardy because national leaders, rather than embrac-ing the necessity of designing the embedded institutions needed, seem to still be captured by economic orthodoxy and the private interests that support it.

The future of the euro has seemed very dark at many points in time since the outbreak of Europe's sovereign debt crisis in late 2009. At the same time, astonishing and heroic amounts of money and political capital have been spent to bail out insolvent member states and their investors. But not enough has been done to reduce soaring unemployment and the disheartening lack of prospects for young generations of Europeans, particularly in the EU's southern periphery.[42] Markets alone, and prescriptions of austerity to make them run more efficiently, will not fix the euro, nor will they secure Europe's future. The hard-won lessons of history, and the insights of Polanyi's embed-dedness, suggest that it will take more robust EU institutions and the will-ingness to match supranational currency innovations with equal amounts of imaginative political development to save the euro.

3

The Forgotten Financial Union

HOW YOU CAN HAVE A EURO CRISIS
WITHOUT A EURO

Erik Jones

THERE ARE TWO narratives to explain the economic and financial crisis that befell Europe. One focuses on the euro as a multinational currency. European politicians gambled and lost in the late 1990s and early 2000s when they created an Economic and Monetary Union (EMU) out of diverse countries at different stages of development. The euro managed to survive, but only at the cost of relentless austerity and massive unemployment. This is the main gist of Nicolas Jabko's Chapter 4 in this volume.

The other narrative focuses on the single market. When Europe's political leaders pushed for capital market integration and the liberalization of cross-border banking in the late 1980s and early 1990s, they failed to build common institutions to ensure financial stability. Instead, they held on to national institutions for regulation, supervision, resolution, and insurance that were too small to safeguard the banks and insurance firms that emerged in Europe's integrated financial space.

These narratives are not mutually exclusive. Europe's leaders can be faulted on both counts. Nevertheless, criticism of the single currency tends to garner more attention. People find it easier to blame the monetary union that exists than the financial union that was never constructed. There was a short period after the June 2012 European Council summit when Europe's leaders appeared willing to push for common institutions to stabilize European financial markets, but the crisis ebbed once European Central Bank (ECB) President Mario Draghi pledged to do everything necessary to safeguard the euro, and the urgency to build new institutions was quietly forgotten.[1]

The purpose of this chapter is to explain why the failure to construct common institutions to safeguard European financial markets was a mistake. My goal is not to argue with the claim that the monetary integration contributed to Europe's problems. Rather, it is to show how the absence of any financial union was sufficient to bring some sort of crisis about. If Europe's policymakers refuse to rectify the situation, they will have to relive the experience.

Other Priorities: The Initial Oversight

The story begins with the completion of the internal market in the late 1980s and early 1990s. Europe's heads of state and government had three priorities: to strengthen European market competitiveness both internally and in relation to the outside world, to preserve national autonomy and institutional distinctiveness, and to dampen market volatility and so also distributive conflict. The overarching challenge was to reconcile these goals, each of which represented a source of tension. National distinctiveness was an impediment to market competitiveness, both within Europe and at the global level, and any effort to liberalize markets and eliminate national systems of protection would induce volatility and encourage distributive conflict.

The solution was delicately balanced. The single market program rested on a mix of shared norms and the acceptance of national differences. For the trade in manufactures, this was known as "the new approach to technical harmonization and standardization."[2] The underlying principle is that whatever is good enough to trade in one country should be good enough to circulate across Europe as a whole. This principle fit into a broader ethos of market liberalization within which norms, standards, rules, and regulations are all part of market competition. European institutions could provide baselines to prevent the competition from spiraling below minimum thresholds for quality, safety, awareness, or consumer protection. Meanwhile, firms could arbitrage across regulatory jurisdictions within the wider European marketplace.

The need for some sort of financial union, combining common institutions for financial oversight, resolution, and deposit insurance (known collectively as a "banking union") with common risk-free assets, collateral rules, and mechanisms for emergency liquidity provision was not a prominent part of the conversation. The member states did not want a banking union because they preferred to maintain autonomy over their national banking systems and because they did not want to endow the European Commission with this new competence.[3] They did not want to create a common class of risk-free assets or to standardize collateral rules because they sought to preserve the privileged access of sovereign borrowers to credit markets. And they did not make special provision for emergency liquidity provision because either national central banks or an eventual monetary union would ensure that national banking systems remained liquid (even if not solvent).

Gradualism Encourages Blindness—and Leverage

It was easy to live with this oversight. European financial integration was gradual and not instantaneous. The changes were dramatic over longer periods, but they were less noticeable from one year to the next. The adaptation started in the early to mid-1990s as banks and other financial institutions learned to take advantage of the changed market environment. Over time, it spread to asset markets, corporate balance sheets, and government finances as non-financial actors became accustomed to higher rates of return on investments and cheaper and more plentiful credit.

The European Central Bank conducted an early stock-taking of financial sector consolidation soon after it opened for operation in 1999.[4] The benchmarks that it used were the year 1985, when the negotiations of the Single European Act, which led to the completion of the internal market, were in full swing, and 1997, which was the latest year for which it had data available for analysis. What it showed was that the total number of credit institutions in the European Union (EU 15 at the time) fell from 12,526 in 1985 to 9,285 in 1997, with mergers and acquisitions gaining pace over the same period. Much of this activity initially took place within countries as banks prepared for cross-border competition; it gradually spread across countries as well. Meanwhile, the average ratio of banking assets to gross domestic product (GDP) increased from 177 percent in 1985 to 244 percent in 1997.

The integration of European financial markets also sparked a reaction among non-financial actors. Households, firms, and governments adapted to the broader array of financial products and services that were available at lower costs. The most obvious outcome can be seen in housing markets. As traditional mortgage lenders gained access to new sources of liquidity from interbank markets or money market funds, they could translate this liquidity into new mortgage instruments for local borrowers. This did not lead to a convergence in mortgage rates across countries—which were subject to a variety of different regulatory constraints and incentives—but it did encourage the growth of mortgage credit. The result was to increase house prices and, depending upon the regulatory environment, to expand loan-to-value ratios. To give an example, Irish house prices increased sevenfold between the mid-1990s and the start of the crisis; meanwhile, average loan-to-value ratios rose only belatedly, climbing from just under 60 percent in the early 2000s to just under 90 percent by the middle of that decade.[5]

The reaction among other sectors of the economy was less obvious but can still be seen in the data. Firms that benefited from a reduction of the cost of capital could afford to invest in new equipment or retain workers. Hence manufacturing employment in the smaller, peripheral countries of the EU tended to hold up much better than in the core—whether or not firms showed an increase in labor productivity. Although the total population of Germany is only about two-thirds the size of the population living on the periphery of Europe, there were roughly 10.1 million people employed in German manufacturing in 1992 and an equal number of manufacturing workers in Portugal, Italy, Ireland, Greece, and Spain (combined). By 1999, German manufacturing employed 8.3 million; the number of manufacturing workers in the peripheral countries fell to around 10 million. Germany lost another half million manufacturing workers by 2007, bringing the total down to 7.8 million; meanwhile, 9.9 million remained in manufacturing on the periphery.[6] Government finances also benefited. The compression of bond yields put downward pressure on debt servicing requirements. In turn, this made it easier for governments to meet their fiscal consolidation targets while at the same time resisting spending reductions for popular services or entitlements.

The Importance of Being Low

The impact of financial integration over time was to render balance sheets structurally dependent upon low borrowing costs. Any sudden spike in interest rates would make relatively capital-intensive manufacturing workers unaffordable and it would throw government finances into deficit. The scale of this dependence is hard to imagine, not just because it spread across every relative cost structure, but also because it accumulated in the form of either public or private sector indebtedness and net foreign liabilities or assets. This explains how the Italian and Greek governments could sustain public debt levels worth more than 100 percent of GDP, how the Spanish and Irish economies could employ more than 13 percent of their population in construction, and how Dutch households could take on mortgages that averaged over 120 percent of assessed value while carrying debt worth almost 110 percent of GDP.[7]

The adaptation to European financial market integration was different from one country to the next. Ireland and Spain experienced booms in commercial real estate; Hungary and Latvia witnessed an explosion of household borrowing in foreign currency. Meanwhile, the collection of national cases was bound together by the forces of financial interdependence—forces that not only spanned Europe but also linked Europe to the outside world. There is nothing surprising or mysterious about this situation. That was always the intention. What is mysterious is that Europe's political leadership never planned to face a massive common market shock that could cut off their access to credit and so throw the process of financial integration into reverse.[8] That shock came in the late summer of 2007.

Inherent Weaknesses Turn into Fissures

Government regulators became aware of the financial crisis in the United States by July 2007.[9] The crisis moved into public discourse the following August, when the French bank BNP Paribas closed three funds heavily exposed to mortgage-backed securities. The bank's representatives complained about the "complete evaporation of liquidity in certain market segments of the US securitization market."[10] They were not alone. A number of European banks and funds were exposed to losses on investments in the United States. The challenge was to figure out which banks were going to be in trouble as a result. That challenge was not easily met, and so interbank lending suddenly dried up.

Many banks were unwilling to lend to other banks at any price. Credit was not only more expensive, it was also less available. The first institutional victim of this change in financial conditions was the British regional mortgage lender Northern Rock. The problem was not that Northern Rock experienced huge losses in US markets, rather it was that the bank relied heavily on inter-bank lending to service its assets. When that lending dried up, Northern Rock had to turn to the Bank of England for emergency liquidity support. As word leaked out that the mortgage lender would have to rely on emergency liquidity assistance, customers staged a run on the bank's deposits—which many regarded as the first bank run in Britain since 1866.[11]

The Northern Rock debacle illustrates how vulnerable European balance sheets were to changes in the financial environment and specifically to a disintegration of international financial markets. That vulnerability revealed itself again in September 2008, after the collapse of Lehman Brothers. The problem was the same: banks were unwilling to lend to other banks. However, the magnitude was greater this time. By October, the British government was forced to bail out the Bank of Scotland, HBOS, and Lloyds TSB. The explanation given by then newly appointed Financial Services Secretary Paul Myners was: "BS, HBOS and Lloyds were experiencing a professional bank run, where the markets were no longer willing to fund the UK banks. That's why we stepped in. We will never appreciate how close we came to a collapse of the banking system."[12]

Not every country was as able to shore up its finances as the UK. The Irish government faced a similar "professional" (as opposed to "retail") run on its financial institutions. The response was improvised. Ireland's Taoiseach Brian Cowen announced on September 30 that his government would underwrite the liabilities of six Irish-owned financial institutions and one foreign-owned bank. Ultimately, this commitment cost Irish taxpayers more than 64 billion euro. Nevertheless, Cowen saw no alternative: "You see, what was happening at that time was that billions of euros were leaving the country. So we had to stop that and get that money back into the country if possible."[13] The situation in Iceland was more dramatic. The country's three largest banks were not only dependent upon inter-bank markets, but also active in competing for retail deposits in the United Kingdom, Luxembourg, Belgium, and the Netherlands. They were too big for the Icelandic authorities to bail out (or regulate effectively) as well. As the Icelandic banks collapsed due to the global liquidity crunch and due to losses on their asset portfolios, other European governments looked for ways to safeguard deposits that did not leave local taxpayers with paying the bill.[14]

The crisis also extended to countries without large domestic banks, like Latvia and Hungary. In both cases, the main problem was the high level of foreign currency indebtedness. Firms and households need access to foreign currency in order to service these debts. If foreign banks are unwilling to maintain their exposure to domestic markets, foreign currency will become more expensive in terms of domestic currency and may not even be available. Hungary suffered the first problem, with the result that household debt burdens increased as the value of the Hungarian forint declined relative to the euro and Swiss franc. By contrast, Latvia maintained the external value of its currency with the result that domestic liquidity vanished. The International Monetary Fund (IMF) had to support both governments. Hungary received a stand-by agreement on November 6, 2008; Latvia's agreement followed on December 19.

The banks in Hungary and Latvia were heavily exposed to non-euro countries, as well as to debt in euros. The exposure in Hungary was to Swiss francs;

in Latvia, it was to Swedish krona. The explanation in both cases is financial integration and not monetary integration. Domestic firms and households took on significant exchange rate risk when contracting debts in foreign currencies, but they did not seem aware of the potential consequences and they were attracted by the relatively low cost of funding.[15] Moreover, when faced with a choice between more exchange rate risk and more aggressive banking practices, the more aggressive banks won out. Sweden started out as the most important Nordic player in the Baltic States, with just under 43 percent of the region's foreign liabilities in 1999, and it grew its share to more than 70 percent by 2007.[16]

The Greek situation was different. The exposure for Greece was to foreign investors in Greek sovereign debt. Many of these investors held Greek debt because of its status as a "risk-free" asset in the Eurozone. In this sense, they benefited from the high coupons Greece had to offer, the zero risk weighting required for capital adequacy, and the liquidity implicit in the eligibility of Greek sovereign debt as collateral within the Eurozone. The situation was further complicated, however, by the poor state of Greek fiscal accounting. Although most market participants discounted the possibility that Greece would default on its sovereign debt, few knew just how bad the situation might be with Greek government accounts.

Authorities from Eurostat, the European statistical agency, were working with Greek officials to improve their fiscal accounting throughout 2008. They first noticed problems in April with the March estimate that the Greek government had provided for its 2008 fiscal deficit. Eurostat officials visited Greece in June to make an assessment and expressed even larger concerns about Greek accounting. Eurostat officials returned in September to prepare a revision for the government's deficit estimate. The Greek government needed to report that revision to the Council of Economics and Finance Ministers (ECOFIN) in October as part of the procedures for macroeconomic policy coordination. The impact on the figures for 2007 was small but symbolically important; the Greek government had to revise its deficit upward from 2.85 percent to 3.48 percent, which placed it above the 3 percent threshold for special consideration within the excessive deficit procedure.[17] Moreover, the representatives of Eurostat made it clear that the Greek authorities had more work to do in order to clear up their accounts.

In the post–Lehman Brothers context, the market reaction was dramatic. The difference in yields between Greek and German sovereign debt more than doubled in the immediate aftermath of the October debt revision announcement. Capital surged out of Greek financial markets.[18] Investors had become nervous already in April 2008 when the European Commission first complained publicly about the poor state of Greek fiscal accounting; by October that nervousness threatened to become a rout.

Halting Responses and Improvisations

The early European response to the financial crisis was piecemeal and tactical rather than structural or strategic. This is an observation, not a criticism. Strategic action takes time and deliberation. Both elements were in short supply as the crisis unfolded. Hence, the goal was to introduce specific measures to address specific problems, even when the problems were more symptom than cause.

The ECB is a good example of this reactive approach. In 2007, the focus for monetary policy was on liquidity provision to counteract the effects of tightness in inter-bank lending. ECB President Jean-Claude Trichet called an exceptional press conference on August 2 to make it clear that the Governing Council was aware that global financial markets were under stress. Trichet then issued a statement on August 14 to emphasize that the ECB would provide adequate liquidity. Such actions brought only temporary respite. The ECB could help bank treasurers hold their balance sheets together; what the ECB could not do was convince European banks to lend to one another or make it easier for European banks to access global credit.

The challenge with piecemeal action is to manage unintended consequences and negative externalities. The Irish commitment to underwrite bank liabilities, including deposits, offers a good illustration. As Taoiseach Cowen argued, the objective was to stop the hemorrhaging of Irish funds overseas. The unintended consequence was to trigger a flow of funds from non-domiciled banks in Ireland into Irish banks. The Irish bankers were well aware that this would be the effect. Indeed, they joked with one another about the competitive advantage the Irish deposit guarantee scheme would offer.[19] Cowen tried to limit the damage by extending the guarantee to cover foreign branches. Even that was not enough, however, and so Germany quickly followed suit by offering more comprehensive deposit coverage of its own.

European policymakers were capable of taking strategic action, but that required time and deliberation. It also required long-term commitment. British Prime Minister Gordon Brown's leadership of the G20 in responding to the crisis is one illustration; the high-level working group chaired by Jacques de Larosière is another. Brown was an early proponent of the view that governments would have to act decisively to resolve failed or failing financial institutions. He pushed to increase the resources available for balance of payments assistance within the IMF, sought agreement on new rules for banking supervision at the global level, and urged his counterparts to pledge financial resources to stimulate growth in a coordinated fashion. The high point of this activity was the London summit held in April 2009. The "Leaders' Statement" lists actions across a wide front, and even Brown's critics hailed it as a historic turning point. Nevertheless, the momentum Brown generated quickly evaporated, and the G20 failed to emerge as the focal point for global reform. Brown can be credited with galvanizing immediate action, but he did not create a new financial world order.

The high-level working group chaired by de Larosière had more lasting impact. European Commission President José Manuel Barroso commissioned de Larosière to make recommendations to strengthen the European financial system in the immediate aftermath of the Lehman Brothers collapse. De Larosière's group reported back to Barroso in February 2009.[20] The group came up with a clear diagnosis for the origins of the crisis, arguing that the roots can be found in cross-border capital flows and the aggressive "hunt for yield." As a result, the group argued in favor of greater macro-prudential oversight and risk management at the European level. In particular, they made the case for a more effective European crisis management infrastructure.[21] They advocated for the creation of a number of new supervisory agencies, such as a European Systemic Risk Council; they pushed for greater harmonization in deposit insurance and banking resolution; and they called for the elaboration of a more transparent regulatory framework.

The results were mixed. European policymakers established many of the institutions advocated by the de Larosière group (including the rebranded European Systemic Risk Board), and they threw their support behind a renegotiation of the international regulatory framework. Nevertheless, they did not relinquish national controls over banking supervision, and they did little to harmonize banking resolution or deposit insurance. In other words, European policymakers left many of the mechanisms that de Larosière identified at the core of the crisis intact.

European policymakers could act strategically, but they could also fail to respond to problems that appeared far on the horizon. Here the best illustration is Greece, but the point also applies to the subsequent bailout of Ireland and Portugal. Greek sovereign debt markets first got into trouble in March 2008, and then again after the Lehman Brothers collapse in October. Conditions continued to worsen in January 2009 when Standard & Poor's downgraded Greece, raising the prospect that Greek sovereign debt instruments might not qualify as collateral for routine central banking operations. Worse, banks might have to mark Greek sovereign debt to market values and make appropriate provision for losses. Such an event would trigger a major sell-off. Hence German Finance Minister Peer Steinbrück used a February 2009 speech to German business interests to reassure financial markets that the Eurozone countries would not allow Greece to default.[22]

Steinbrück's reassurance helped to bring down the yield differential between Greek and German sovereign debt instruments (see Figure 3.1). For most of 2009, financial market actors worried more about Ireland than about Greece. When the Greek government restated its fiscal account again in October, however, financial market participants asked again whether Germany would bail Greece out. This time they received a different response. The German position changed with the change in coalition from center-left to center-right; instead of reassuring markets that Eurozone countries would prevent Greece from defaulting, the German government insisted that it would only provide assistance once Greece could no longer access private capital. Any doubts about Germany's new position ended with the March 2010 European Council summit, and the Greek government quickly found itself locked out of private capital markets and had to request assistance.[23]

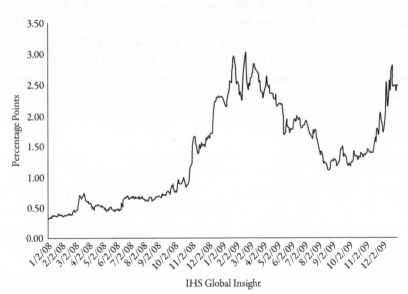

IHS Global Insight

FIGURE 3.1 Greek-German 10-year Sovereign Yield Spread

What followed was a sequence of improvisations. The European Council first sought to provide assistance only for Greece and then had to come back with a more general formula to bail countries out. Europe's leaders then turned to a discussion of private sector involvement, which is a formula for burden sharing that puts some of the costs on participants in financial markets. The threat of private sector involvement triggered a sell-off of Irish debt and a second bailout.[24] Meanwhile, the Greek economy performed below expectations and required further financial assistance. Renewed Greek financial shortfalls raised the prospect of further private sector involvement, which increased incentives for financial market participants to liquidate their positions in the periphery of the Eurozone. Portugal was the next government to request help.

The ECB also improvised. When Greece requested its bailout, the Governing Council of the ECB worried that the subsequent downgrade of Greek sovereign debt instruments would wipe out the available collateral for Greek banks. Hence it suspended the ratings requirements for Greek sovereign debt, making them eligible as collateral so long as Greece did not default. This action made it easier for many banks in northern Europe to shed their exposure to Greece and so offload their debt instruments onto the Greek banks. It also made it attractive for financial institutions with an appetite for risk to profit from the relatively high yields on Greek sovereign debt. The two largest banks in Cyprus increased their exposure to Greece both before and after the May 2010 bailout.[25] In turn, this exposure ensured that there would be a further crisis in Cyprus. The ECB also initiated a securities markets program (SMP) to purchase distressed sovereign debt instruments in secondary markets. This program was limited in size, and any purchases were sterilized in order to avoid creating new liquidity. Nevertheless, the result was to shift more of the exposure to Greece, away from northern Europe and, in this case, onto the balance sheets of the ECB.

The bailouts of Greece, Ireland, and Portugal were connected by European financial markets—both to each other and to the rest of Europe. The contagion was everywhere apparent. That is why Europe's halting responses to the crisis became so important. The failure of policymakers to deal effectively with one country implied new risks for others as well. Market participants based their risk assessments in part at least on how the bailouts were handled. As this process wore on, the European financial crisis evolved into a full-fledged sovereign debt crisis. Moreover, the problem was not Greece, Ireland, or Portugal; it was Italy and Spain.

Fissures Turn into (Big) Breaking Points

The Italian and Spanish cases are revealing for different reasons. Italy highlights the difficulties with reversing the balance sheet adjustments that were triggered by the long process of financial integration. Spain shows how quickly national banking systems and sovereign debt markets can become intertwined. What the two countries have in common is that each is too big to fail. Although European policymakers were able to cobble together sufficient resources to bail out Greece, Ireland, and Portugal, most observers admitted that it would be a stretch to cover Spain as well. Italy, home to the world's third largest bond market after the United States and Japan, was clearly too large.

Italy

The Italian story starts in earnest in July 2011. Before that point, Italian Prime Minister Silvio Berlusconi was able to claim (erroneously but still convincingly) that Italy had escaped much of the crisis; afterward, financial market dynamics would drive him from office.[26] The tipping point was in sovereign debt markets. Although Italy has a large volume of public debt, with roughly 2 trillion euro in obligations in circulation, it also has a good reputation for debt management, and its fiscal position showed a primary surplus—which is an excess of revenues over expenditures net of debt-servicing requirements. In 2007, that surplus was more than 3.5 percent of the country's gross domestic product (GDP). That figure dipped slightly into deficit by 2009, but it was close to zero in 2010 and back in surplus by 2011—in comparative terms, this was exemplary performance. Moreover, Italy did not suffer from excessive net foreign indebtedness. Although Italian banks participated in Europe's integrated financial markets, Italy's cumulative current account deficit for the period from 1999 to 2007 was just 5.5 percent of GDP. This performance compared favorably to 12.6 percent in Ireland, 51.2 percent in Spain, 85.1 percent in Portugal, and 103 percent in Greece.[27] Finally, Italy was a net contributor of liquidity to the euro system, showing a positive balance in its Target2 position for each month from July 2007 to June 2011.

The Italian weakness lay in two areas. One was the addiction of Italian manufacturers to cheap and available credit. The other was the foreign presence in Italian sovereign debt markets. The credit addiction of Italian manufacturers can be seen in the rapid worsening of the country's competitive position as yield spreads opened up with Germany after 2007. The cumulative current account deficit over the four years from 2008 to 2011 was 13.9 percent of GDP—more than double the figure of the eight years before the crisis.[28] Meanwhile, Italian unemployment rose as the spread between Italian and German long-term bond yields increased. Italian manufacturers were profitable while credit was cheap and plentiful; they did not have sufficient productivity to compete when credit was expensive and scarce. By 2011, Italian unemployment was 8.4 percent. It rose more quickly thereafter.

The loss of Italian competitiveness had deep roots that financial integration masked and financial disintegration brought back into focus. The problem associated with foreign holdings of Italian sovereign debt was also deep-rooted, but the manifestation was more sudden. According to data published by the IMF, foreigners accounted for just 6.4 percent of the Italian sovereign debt market in January 1992; by December 1998, they accounted for 27.4 percent. Moreover, the growth of foreign holdings accelerated across the decade.

The turning point came in 2011. Foreign banks became wary of the risk potential in Italian sovereign debt markets and so began to reallocate their portfolios to limit exposure.[29] Given the size of the market, the sales were large and the price swings correspondingly significant. The collective impact of these portfolio reallocation decisions showed up in Italy's net Target2 position. Italy went from a 6 billion euro surplus in June 2011 to a 16 billion euro deficit in July; by September the deficit was 103 billion euro. Moreover, the flood of liquidity pouring out of the Italian economy resulted in a sudden shortage of credit for small and medium-sized enterprises that rely almost exclusively on bank financing. Silvio Berlusconi's government had to prove that it could stabilize government finances while at the same time shoring up macroeconomic performance. It was unable to act decisively on either issue; by November, Berlusconi had to step down from office.

Berlusconi's departure did not solve the Italian problem. Neither did the appointment of two-term European Commissioner Mario Monti to head a technical cabinet with the support of the two largest Italian political parties. The spread between Italian and German bond yields recovered briefly in early December 2011 but then shot up again. It was not until mid-January 2012 that financial markets started to relax the selling pressure on Italian sovereign debt obligations. This marked the start of roughly six weeks of relative stability in Europe. Then the markets turned on Spain.

Spain

Spain's problems were relatively slow to evolve. In the early years of the financial crisis, Spain looked robust. The government had a small debt-to-GDP ratio, and the country's largest banks were among Europe's strongest. Nevertheless, the Spanish economy had three vulnerabilities: weak regional savings banks (or *cajas*), a large share of employment in the construction industry, and a history of excessive growth in both residential and commercial real estate. The government moved first to tackle the savings banks by forcing the smaller institutions to consolidate. Meanwhile, the slow pace of construction activity put upward pressure on unemployment, and the tightening of credit conditions put downward pressure on real estate prices. The result was an explosion of non-performing loans—particularly among the *cajas*. In turn, this led to a self-reinforcing dynamic of more consolidation, tighter credit conditions, lower levels of construction activity, falling real estate prices, and increasing non-performing loans.[30]

The challenge for the Spanish government was not only to address this vicious cycle but also to manage the impact of economic deterioration on government finances. This impact operated through two channels. One was the automatic stabilizers that increase expenditures as revenues decline; the other was the increasing amounts of public money available to sweeten mergers and acquisitions between the *cajas* or to finance banking bailouts. The challenge proved too great for the center-left coalition of José Luis Rodríguez Zapatero—particularly when combined with rising unemployment and persistent European Union calls for increased austerity measures. Zapatero announced in March 2011 that he would not stand for re-election, and he decided in July 2011 that he would dissolve Parliament four months early so that his party could confront the center-right opposition at the polls.

The election of a center-right government led by Mariano Rajoy in November 2011 brought some respite from the markets. Rajoy came to power determined to fix both government finances and bank balance sheets. He was already too late. The consolidated *cajas* were only larger and more vulnerable at this point—Bankia (a union of seven *cajas* and Spain's third largest lender) first and foremost. Moreover, efforts by the Rajoy government to bail out the *cajas* drew unfavorable market attention back to government finances because the more the banks required capital, the deeper the government had to go into debt.[31] The fact that this unfolded against the backdrop of the second Greek bailout made matters worse. Investors who lost money on Greece were unwilling to see Spain (or Italy) as any different. Spanish bond yields bottomed out relative to Germany on March 1, 2012; Italian bond yields bottomed out two weeks later. By early April the yield spreads were back over 350 basis points, or 3.5 percent, which was the

FIGURE 3.2 Yield Spreads with Germany, June 2011–June 2012

threshold figure described by Mario Monti as unsustainable (see Figure 3.2). The Spanish government had to nationalize Bankia in May. The crisis returned in force soon thereafter.

Emergency Measures

The collapse of the Berlusconi government and the nationalization of Bankia were catalysts for successive waves of emergency policy action, both at the ECB and in the Council of the European Union. This action ran alongside changes in the broader pattern for macroeconomic policy coordination that had been evolving throughout the crisis. However, whereas those other changes constituted an evolution in pre-existing institutions and practices, the emergency measures introduced by the ECB and the Council of the European Union represented a fundamental departure.

Long-Term Refinancing Operations to the Rescue?

The program of three-year long-term refinancing operations (LTROs), announced by Mario Draghi soon after he replaced Jean Claude Trichet as ECB president in November 2011, is a good illustration. Draghi argued that banks were struggling to access funding over longer time horizons, and this in turn impaired their ability to provide credit to industry. Hence he created a vehicle through which the ECB would offer unlimited amounts of liquidity for three years at a very low cost and with the possibility of early repayment after the first year. The ECB would make this liquidity available in two tranches—one in December 2011 and the other in February 2012. The only constraint on the banks would be to come up with the collateral necessary to secure what they wanted to borrow.[32]

This point about collateral is important in two senses. First, unsecured lending to banks had dried up both in short-term interbank markets and in the issuance of debt securities. Therefore, banks relied heavily on collateralized borrowing to meet their funding requirements. At the same time, the decline in sovereign bond prices ate away at the volume of collateral that the banks had available. This explains why banks complained about cost of funding and balance sheet constraints as the explanation for why they did not issue more loans.[33]

By looking at the LTROs as a two-stage process, one can see the other sense in which the collateral rules are important. In the first stage, banks could borrow liquidity from the ECB to use in purchasing government bonds and so make a profit from the difference between the low borrowing cost offered by the ECB and the relatively high yields available on distressed sovereign debt. In the second stage, the same banks could use the sovereign debt they purchased to collateralize more ECB loans—which they could use to purchase even more sovereign debt.

The implication here is different from what Draghi announced at the outset. Instead of channeling liquidity to industry, the banks would be propping up sovereign debt markets. Nevertheless, it was clear to most observers that this would be the consequence. Moreover, the effect was welcome— particularly in the Italian context. Italy had an enormous volume of sovereign debt to roll over immediately following the Berlusconi crisis—172 billion euro between December 2011 and April 2012.[34] The threat was that Italy would face an investor strike, particularly in February, when the Italian Treasury needed to roll over more than 50 billion euro in bonds. By providing Italian banks with sufficient liquidity, the ECB insured that the rollover happened smoothly. That is why Italian bond yields fell in February 2012 and the crisis abated. A similar story applies in Spain.

The positive effect of the LTROs was only short-lived. The reason is that the support they offered was asymmetrical. The LTROs could help banks finance governments, but they could not work the other way around. When governments had to finance the banks, the LTROs were not an effective response. Hence while the LTROs tightened the links between national banking systems and sovereign finances, they also made government finances vulnerable to any weakness on the part of the banks. This is where the Spanish crisis becomes important.

More Spanish Flies in the Ointment

The nationalization of Bankia put the Spanish government in a three-way bind. First, Bankia and its holding company, BFA, had held an initial public offering in July 2011, selling almost 60 percent of the newly issued shares to individuals. The decision by the Rajoy government to take control of the bank in May 2012 effectively wiped out the value of their equity stake—disillusioning investors and making it harder for other banks to raise capital.[35] Second, nationalization meant that the government acquired responsibility for the bank's liabilities and performance. Soon after the government took control, Bankia restated its 2011 results to report a 4.3 billion euro loss instead of a 309 million euro profit. Bankia's parent company, BFA, also restated its accounts for 2011, turning a 41 million euro profit into a 3.3 billion euro loss. Loan losses also increased. The government had to pump another 23 billion euro of public money into the bank as a result.[36]

The third part of the bind was the impact of the nationalization on the Spanish government's own cost of capital. Any money that the government borrowed to support Bankia made Spanish sovereign borrowing more expensive in general. Moreover, the loss of creditworthiness by the Spanish government weighed heavily on the price of Spanish bonds in secondary markets—reducing the value of sovereign debt holdings across the Spanish banking system as a whole. This dynamic threatened to push the Spanish economy into a "doom loop" or "death spiral" from which it could not escape. On June 9, 2012, the Spanish government asked the European Union for a 100 billion euro bailout in the form of new resources that could be used to recapitalize Spanish banks. While the initial market response was positive, it took only days to reveal that something more fundamental was required.[37]

The promise of fundamental reform came at the European Council and Euro Area summits held at the end of the month. The initial proposal was to involve the ECB in a single supervisory mechanism (SSM) for European banks with the ability to ensure common standards for soundness across different national jurisdictions. Once that was in place, the European Financial Stability Facility (EFSF) or its successor organization, the European Stability Mechanism (ESM), would be able to channel funds directly into European banks. By implication, national governments would no longer have to borrow money to bail out their own banks. This should sever the link between sovereign finances and national banking systems because bank bailouts would no longer undermine the solvency of national governments.[38]

The single supervisory mechanism and the promise that European funds could recapitalize banks directly were the leading edge of a wider agenda to create a banking union in Europe that would include a common regulatory framework, resolution facilities, and deposit insurance.[39] Some of these elements were already in progress. The common regulatory framework is a good example, as can be seen in de Larosière's report. Others were more aspirational than real. The common resolution mechanism and deposit insurance both fall into this category. Although there was talk of establishing a common hierarchy of creditors and some progress on developing common standards for deposit insurance, there was little movement to mutualize funding to bail out banks or reimburse deposits. Suddenly all parts of this proposal were gaining traction in the wider policy conversation.

There was a new coherence as well. This was not the first time these supports for financial market integration were discussed; it was the first time they were brought together in a consistent manner. More important, the banking union proposals carried the political impetus of the June 2012 European Council summit. Europe's leaders recognized that they faced an imminent crisis. What they needed was a specific plan for implementing this new array of measures and the market confidence to give them time to make it work.

Doing Whatever It Takes?

Both elements were missing—the plan and the confidence. Of the two, the confidence was the more pressing. Bond yields for Spain and Italy continued to increase during the month that followed the June 2012 European Council summit and Euro Area summit statement. Meanwhile, capital flowed from the periphery of the Eurozone back to the core, bank balance sheets in Spain and Italy continued to deteriorate, and the economies of both countries (and much of peripheral Europe) contracted at an alarming rate. Of these factors, the capital flows are easiest to demonstrate. Figure 3.3 provides the Target2 positions for six Eurozone member states—Germany, the Netherlands, Luxembourg, Italy, Spain, and Greece. The first three countries were massive net recipients of capital; the other three net exporters. The spread between the two groups is widest during the summer of 2012.

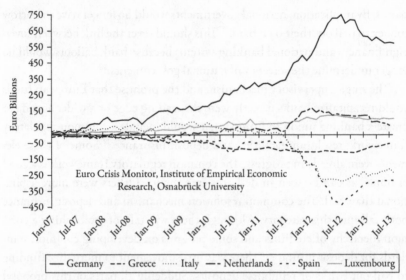

—— Germany --- Greece ⋯⋯ Italy —·— Netherlands - - - Spain —— Luxembourg

FIGURE 3.3 Net TARGET2 Balance within the Eurosystem

By the end of July, Draghi had enough. At a speech to the London finance community, he made a personal commitment "to do whatever it takes to preserve the euro." He also reassured his audience: "believe me, it will be enough."[40] The blunt language Draghi used is confusing. Although he talked about the euro, he was primarily interested in protecting the integrity of the single financial market. Put another way, Draghi's commitment to the euro was qualified. As he made clear from the outset, he is constrained by the mandate of his office. Hence, Draghi's justification for action was to repair the monetary transmission mechanism—the means through which changes in monetary policy are communicated to economic actors across the Eurozone—and to eliminate the premia associated with "convertibility risk" or the possibility that countries will exit from the Eurozone.

This may seem like hair-splitting, but the distinction is important. Both the monetary transmission mechanism and the single market should operate according to the law of one price. Firms need to face the same cost of capital across the single currency (controlling for firm-specific factors) so that any change in the cost of capital will have the same influence on economic activity from one place to the next. Draghi pledged to preserve the euro in order to ensure that there is a single cost of borrowing because well-integrated financial markets are essential to have an effective common monetary policy.

This interpretation of Draghi's motives comes across more clearly in the press conferences he gave in August and September than in the speech he gave in London. In August, Draghi underscored that "risk premia that are related to fears of the reversibility of the euro are unacceptable" and "our greatest concern is financial market fragmentation."[41] The following month, he emphasized that "we need to be in the position to safeguard the monetary policy transmission mechanism in all countries of the euro area. We aim to preserve the singleness of our monetary policy and to ensure the proper transmission of our policy stance to the real economy throughout the area."[42]

Draghi's solution was a departure from previous practice. With the support of the Governing Council, Draghi committed the ECB to purchase "unlimited" amounts of short-term sovereign debt in secondary markets with the aim to safeguard "an appropriate monetary policy transmission and the singleness of the monetary policy."[43] This commitment was not wholly unprecedented. The ECB has always had the option to purchase sovereign debt instruments in secondary markets as part of its open market operations. This option was only exercised once the ECB activated its securities markets program (SMP) in May 2010. The new program of outright monetary transactions (OMT) replaced that early effort.

OMT is different from SMP for several reasons. Governments have to apply for support, they have to accept policy conditionality, and they have no guarantee that the ECB will come to the rescue. Nevertheless, OMT holds out the prospect that the ECB will move into distressed sovereign debt markets with the full weight of its balance sheet. No market participant could hold a short position against such an offensive. That is what Draghi meant when he said "it is pointless to go short on the euro... the euro will stay and it is irreversible."[44]

The new policy was controversial. Bundesbank President Jens Weidmann opposed the new measure both in the Governing Council and in public. Nevertheless, European leaders accepted OMT as necessary. German Chancellor Angela Merkel threw her support behind the new policy; so did German ECB Executive Board member Jörg Asmussen.

Remaining Concerns and New Fissures

The spread between German and Spanish net balances in the Target2 positions peaked in August 2012 and declined thereafter. The spread in German and Spanish sovereign debt yields followed the same pattern. These are the two most obvious indicators of the success of OMT. The Spanish government never had to ask for help officially for the threat of ECB intervention to work. Financial market participants lacked the will to challenge the ECB, even on purely theoretical grounds. In this way, the ECB restored market confidence and bought time for European policymakers to make progress on constructing a banking union and market-structural reform—as ECB Executive Board members emphasized repeatedly in speeches and interviews over the course of the following year and a half.[45]

Nevertheless, the new policy was not wholly successful. OMT did not fully reintegrate European financial markets. Draghi complained repeatedly in monetary press conferences through the first six months of 2013 that the monetary transmission mechanism remained broken, that the cost of borrowing varied widely from North to South, and that what liquidity did arrive in Spanish or Italian banks was not finding its way into new private sector lending. Hence the best that Draghi could claim was that OMT restored sufficient stability to European sovereign debt markets to put fears of a doom loop or death spiral in Spain and Italy to rest. This was a significant achievement, but it left considerable responsibility for action to the member states.

Setting Sights High and Shooting Low

The initial response of the European Council was ambitious. When the Council met in October, it called for a comprehensive approach to create "an integrated financial framework, open to the extent possible to all Member States wishing to participate."[46] The single supervisory mechanism (SSM) was a priority, because its establishment was necessary to unlock the direct recapitalization of distressed banks with funds from the EFSF and ESM. However, the European Council also pushed the establishment of a "single rulebook" for banking supervision that would encompass all banks operating in the internal market (and not just those in the Eurozone). It underscored the importance of legislative efforts to harmonize rules for banking resolution and deposit insurance. And it announced the intention to propose a "single resolution mechanism" (SRM) for those countries that participate in the single supervisory mechanism.[47]

The challenge was to make consistent progress. By the December 2012 European Council summit, it was already clear that the timetable was slipping.[48] Although there was some agreement on the nature of the SSM, there was much concern to strike a balance between the role of the ECB and the responsibilities of national supervisory authorities. The interaction between the ECB's supervisory responsibilities and its primary role in the conduct of monetary policy was also controversial. And there was a need to ensure adequate representation in the SSM for those countries that join and yet do not participate in the single currency. The Council of Economic and Finance Ministers (ECOFIN Council) acknowledged each of these challenges as it deliberated the proposals during the run-up to the December summit. Soon thereafter, the European Council promised to deliver legislative action across a broad front in 2013.[49]

The political momentum was hard to sustain. In part this was due to the complexity of the European legislative process. The European Parliament plays an important role in shaping and approving the necessary institutional reforms. By implication, agreement among the member states is necessary but insufficient. More important, there was no agreement on many of the major issues. Important countries outside the single currency, like Great Britain, objected to the single rulebook and expressed concern about the role of the ECB in shaping financial regulation. Important countries inside the Eurozone, like Germany, refused to share resources for banking resolution and deposit insurance. The German government was willing to accept the European recapitalization of the three largest Spanish banks as a one-off measure, but it was skeptical about any further financial commitment.[50]

Small States Causing Big Trouble: Why Cyprus Matters

The crisis that erupted in Cyprus failed to break this growing inertia. If anything, it had the opposite effect. The government of Cyprus had long known it had a problem. The Cypriot banking system was too large for Cypriot taxpayers to bail out. Worse, it was obviously in need of assistance. The European Banking Authority (EBA) called for the Cypriot banks to rebuild their capital buffers already in December 2011. Soon thereafter, the situation got worse. The country's two largest banks—Bank of Cyprus and Popular Bank or Laiki—had bet heavily on Greek sovereign debt, which they accumulated during the crisis in order to benefit from the relatively high yields that the Greek government had to offer. Moreover, the Cypriot banks relied on Greek debt for routine treasury operations as well as trading profits; they used Greek obligations to post as collateral for central bank borrowing and clearing. When the government of Greece partially defaulted during the second Greek bailout in March 2012, Greek sovereign debt lost its eligibility. This left the Cypriot banks with huge losses on their sovereign debt portfolios and little or no collateral to offer in exchange for routine central bank liquidity. Bank of Cyprus and Laiki had to turn to the Central Bank of Cyprus for emergency support.[51]

From April 2012 onward, the Cypriot banks survived on emergency liquidity assistance (ELA) from the Central Bank of Cyprus, and the ECB's Governing Council made increasingly vocal calls for the Cypriot government to do something to restructure and reform its banks. In March 2013, the ECB Governing Council decided to push the issue by threatening to deny permission to the Central Bank of Cyprus to extend any further liquidity to the banks that were in trouble. Had the ECB followed through with that threat, the result would have been a disorderly default.[52]

What followed was a near disaster, as both the Cypriot government and the ECB mishandled the bailout.[53] The point here is not to rehearse the mistakes that were made; rather it is to focus on the implications. The most important is that the ECB could jeopardize the single currency by acting within its mandate. The Governing Council's threat to deny the Central Bank of Cyprus permission to offer emergency liquidity assistance to the country's two largest banks was within the ECB's mandate—as Mario Draghi pointed out repeatedly.[54] Nevertheless, it forced the government of Cyprus to choose between restructuring the banks, watching them collapse, or exiting the single currency and so releasing the Central Bank of Cyprus from the Governing Council's control. The government of Cyprus chose to restructure the banks; it could also have chosen to exit the euro. The government of Cyprus made this choice because exiting the euro would have made matters worse, not better—not because exiting the euro was impossible.

The lesson for Cyprus was more about the single market than about the single currency. The only way that the Cypriot government could stabilize its banks through the resolution process was to impose controls both on deposits and on the movement of capital across borders. These controls did not take Cyprus out of the euro; they took Cyprus out of Europe's integrated capital markets. Moreover, if the experience of Iceland is any guide, the Cypriot government is unlikely to be able to lift the controls without facing a rapid flight of deposits.

For the countries of northern Europe, Cyprus underscored the importance of private sector involvement and national responsibility. Eurogroup president and Dutch Finance Minister Jeroen Dijsselbloem's comments immediately following the bailout are indicative of this approach.[55] The markets reacted strongly to this position, and Dijsselbloem recanted that Cyprus was not a model for other bailouts. Nevertheless, the desire to protect taxpayers from banking losses and the resistance to pooling either resolution funds or deposit insurance have increased.

The ECB's read on Cyprus was consistent with this preference on the part of the northern member states. In his April 2013 press conference, Mario Draghi made it clear that national banking systems would have to adapt to fit the capacity of national governments to bail them out. Moreover, he stressed that this applied outside as well as inside the single currency:

> Recent experience shows that countries where the banking sector is several times larger than the economy are, on average, more vulnerable. Financial shocks hit these countries harder—simply because of the size of their banking sector—than countries where the banking sector is a smaller component of the economy. We have seen this everywhere, really, beginning with the United Kingdom. So what to do? Well, one thing is to downsize, but other things can be done ... I think people ought to learn from what we are currently experiencing and follow this advice—namely, run your country and your bank much more conservatively.[56]

Beyond that, the positions of politicians like Dijsselbloem and central bankers like Draghi differ. The politicians want to slow down the progress toward banking union because they worry it will lead to transfers across countries and from taxpayers to bond holders. The central bankers want to complete the banking union because they worry that neither politicians nor banks will behave conservatively enough to sustain an integrated financial market. This is true at the top of the financial cycle, where banks compete at the European and global levels. It is also true at the bottom of the cycle, where banks remain dependent for emergency assistance on sovereign finances and national governments. Hence Draghi warned in January 2014 about further financial market disintegration if Europe's leaders did not complete their legislative agenda: "In light of recent experience, we must emphasize that the future Single Supervisory Mechanism and a Single Resolution Mechanism are crucial elements for moving towards re-integrating the banking system and therefore require swift implementation."[57]

Future Prospects

The progress made in completing the banking union since Draghi's January 2014 press conference has been only partial. The ECB has emerged as a single supervisor, and it has worked closely with the European Banking Authority

to undertake a comprehensive assessment of the balance sheets of systemically important financial institutions. These actions fall on the positive side
of the ledger. The elaboration of a common resolution authority with a fund
sufficient to wind up these institutions has been less impressive. Although
the Council managed to find agreement with the European Parliament in
March 2014 on a framework for taking action to resolve failing financial
institutions, critics charge that the decision-making procedures are too cum-
bersome and the funding involved is too limited to address a major crisis.
Meanwhile, no progress is likely in terms of harmonizing deposit insurance
or creating the kind of common backstop that would be required to prevent a
commercial bank run like that experienced by the United Kingdom, Ireland,
Iceland, Greece, or Cyprus. As a consequence, some countries will be able to
weather future storms; others will not.

The fact that the ECB had to launch another round of LTROs in June
2014 and unveiled a new plan to purchase an additional 1 trillion euro of covered bonds and asset-backed securities (ABS) in October 2014, underscores
that more work needs to be done. The cause of the current crisis lies in the
pattern of European financial integration. National governments lowered
barriers to capital flows across borders and then encouraged financial institutions to compete across Europe. These policy actions made sense within the
broader project to complete the internal market. Nevertheless, they sparked
long-term adjustments in the balance sheets of households, firms, and governments that became accustomed to the many advantages that an integrated
European financial market had to offer. Then a shock came along that called
these advantages into question by threatening the viability of major European
financial institutions.

The market response made matters worse, not better. Banks not only
called money back across borders but also worried about lending to other
financial institutions. As the situation deteriorated, they called increasingly on governments for support. However, government finances were also
adversely affected, and in many cases the resources available were too small
to support the institutions most at risk. Central bank efforts to prop up the
financial system were inadequate to the challenge and policy action by governments lagged too far behind market responses. Ultimately, bank bailouts
began to undermine sovereign debt markets even as bond market weakness
further undermined the banks. The real economy also suffered from the lack
of credit, in both the housing and manufacturing sectors. Households lost
incomes and borrowers defaulted on their debts.

This narrative can be told without reference to the euro, even though the creation of the single currency is important for some countries and to some parts of the story. Moreover, the solution to the problem lies in strengthening the internal market and not dismantling the euro. The banking union proposals are part of the agenda. But a comprehensive approach would include other elements like mutualized sovereign debt obligations, strengthened collateral rules, central clearing mechanisms, and other improvements to Europe's financial architecture.[58] The importance of such elements is not immediately obvious. Mutualized debt instruments—called "Eurobonds"—have been a subject of particular confusion. Yet it is hard to see how any financial area can remain integrated when market actors can arbitrage across supposedly "risk-free" assets or when banks and their sovereigns are inextricably intertwined together. Hence, such measures are not only a good idea in the present context, they would also be helpful to Europe in an alternative universe where the single currency did not exist. Indeed, many of these institutional arrangements are being debated in places like Southeast Asia, where EMU remains only a distant prospect.

The crisis in Cyprus was a warning that the situation in Europe is still fragile, even if the immediate threat of turmoil has receded. The threat of a bank run in Bulgaria reveals that countries outside the Eurozone are also vulnerable. Without a financial union, European financial integration remains at risk. Small countries might be manageable with ad hoc responses, but a crisis in Italy would be much more dramatic. The ECB places considerable emphasis on this point.[59] The challenge is to make sure that the necessity to build a financial union for Europe is not forgotten. The architects of the internal market might be forgiven for overlooking the importance of building a financial union both as they nurtured cross-border financial transactions and as they constructed the single currency. The literature they used did not pay much attention to finance, and the objectives they had were very different. Politicians who have experienced the most recent crisis have no such excuse. They can blame the situation on the euro, but they must also recognize the legitimacy of this parallel narrative. Otherwise they risk repeating past mistakes.

4

The Elusive Economic Government and the Forgotten Fiscal Union

Nicolas Jabko

Introduction: The Missing Institutions
of a Supranational Currency

The Eurozone's debt crisis laid bare the shortcomings of its economic governance. Fiscal policies were only imperfectly coordinated, banks that operated largely across borders were regulated primarily at the national level, and large macroeconomic imbalances had been accumulating without attracting much attention. As early as October 2010, a taskforce chaired by EU Council President Herman Van Rompuy advanced a new agenda that received broad support from the member states: "Strengthening economic governance in the EU."[1] In view of the magnitude of the crisis, one might have expected swift progress. By most accounts, however, the buildup of economic capacity and especially fiscal capacity at the EU level has been excruciatingly slow. The new "fiscal compact" and the "compact for jobs and growth" that were agreed upon successively in December 2011 and June 2012 by Eurozone member governments call for "stronger policy coordination and governance" and "a genuine economic and monetary union."[2] Yet the process is still far from completed, as the difficulties in setting up a banking union and coordinating economic and fiscal policies illustrate.

Why has it been so hard to build economic governance that appears to be in the common interest of all? It is tempting to view this as a collective action problem, that is, as a consequence of the fact that member states tend to pursue their national interests at the expense of the common interest. Although there is an element of truth in this characterization—international collective action is always difficult—it is also the case that member states have been able to reach unprecedented agreement on the need for stronger economic governance. France and Germany, the two member states most invested in the Economic and Monetary Union since its creation, have repeatedly stated their commitment to collaborate on building stronger governance for the Eurozone. Of course, words are cheap. But in this case, the survival of the Eurozone was at stake. The member governments were aware of the need to overcome their differences in order to avoid the costs of a collapse, which would have been on a completely different scale than the benefits they could derive from pursuing their self-interests without taking into account the interests of their partners. Faced with emergency situations, they were each repeatedly led to do things that they had sworn they would never do, while never quite doing enough to stop the crisis once and for all. Thus, the slow pace of progress tends to indicate that the problem is much deeper than intergovernmental disagreements based on divergent member states' national interests.

As I argue in this chapter, the puzzling gap between the resilient aspiration for and the still embryonic nature of EU economic governance must be understood against the background of the original motivations for Europe's Economic and Monetary Union (EMU). The aspiration of stronger economic governance remains both alive and in limbo because of a largely unforeseen contradiction between the long-standing concern for national sovereignty and a new conception of sovereignty that called for its exercise at the European level. The fact that Germany, France, and other EU member governments have different views is no longer the main difficulty. More important, the introduction of genuinely strong European economic governance may have a considerable impact on core areas of *national* economic governance. For example, tax policies, labor laws, or pension financing schemes may be affected. Yet all member governments are wary of this prospect, especially so at a time of renewed popular skepticism about the EU. The buildup of an economic union inextricably raises the problem of sovereignty. Not only are national political leaders instinctively reluctant to see their own powers diminished, even for the greater good of the European Union at large, they also cannot easily ignore deeply entrenched conceptions of state sovereignty that resonate with nationally specific ideas about the exercise of power, freedom, and democracy.

The unresolved contradiction between a full integration of monetary policy and a weak integration of other economic policies goes to the heart of the institutional architecture of Europe's Economic and Monetary Union. Fundamentally, EMU is a case in which sovereignty is divided. This results from the design of the EMU by governmental actors at the time of the Maastricht Treaty. Since the main actors could not agree on what a putative "political union" should be about, they agreed to disagree and downplayed their differences. As a consequence, they built an Economic and Monetary Union with major structural problems—exactly the kind of "unsolved political problems" that Matthias Matthijs and Mark Blyth highlight in Chapter 1 of this volume. On the one hand, the transfer of sovereignty goes very far. In the area of monetary policy, sovereignty is fully delegated to the EU level. Powers are clearly unified at the EU level within the European System of Central Banks. Although national central bankers sit on the European Central Bank (ECB) Governing Council and may cast different votes, they ultimately act as a single decision-making body and their decisions cannot be overruled. On the other hand, most other economic policy powers— especially fiscal policy, including the availability of a fiscal backstop for the banking union, which Erik Jones (Chapter 3 of this volume) argues is necessary—remain for the most part national prerogatives.

Today, European leaders aspire to stronger economic governance, but they are still not yet ready to contemplate sharply diminished national prerogatives. In other words, the inconclusive EU economic governance debate should be understood primarily as an expression of "inconsistent preferences."[3] France, Germany, and most other member states—including the ones that bear the heaviest burden in the current crisis—are now engulfed in the same contradiction. No member state is well prepared to relinquish a large swath of its economic policy powers to the EU. In this context, the member states are above all groping for new objectives and trying to fix the problem at the margin.

Three main periods can be distinguished in the debate about and reforms of Eurozone economic government. First, the Maastricht disagreement between France and Germany on how the Eurozone should be governed led to a weak and deeply contradictory economic governance framework. Although the preparation and first decade of the euro were in many ways successful, things started to go wrong, and the shortcomings of pre-crisis governance became increasingly evident. Second, the global financial crisis reignited interest in economic governance and fostered some learning. There was also the beginning of a rapprochement between France and Germany, but at a relatively superficial level. Third, the Eurozone crisis made the matter more pressing and forced the member states to engage in a series of potentially quite significant reforms. These reforms could eventually amount to a considerable reinforcement of economic governance. Stepping back from this periodization and looking forward, it is possible to highlight the lessons that have been learned and the stumbling blocks that remain in the path toward stronger economic governance.

The Shortcomings of Pre-Crisis Economic Governance

The transfer of monetary decision-making power from the national level to the EU level was not a straightforward transfer of sovereignty from the member states to the EU. On the contrary, the shortcomings of Eurozone economic governance can be understood as a result of the refusal to choose clearly between national and EU sovereignty at the time of the Maastricht Treaty. The Maastricht Treaty was a typical diplomatic compromise that reconciled conflicting positions without resolving the underlying conflict. It stated that fiscal policy remained a national prerogative and, at the same time, governments agreed to consider their respective fiscal policies as subject to "budgetary discipline."[4] Nobody seriously wanted to be more precise, as this could have threatened to undermine the fragile consensus reached at Maastricht. From a German perspective, the very idea behind a monetary union managed by an independent central bank was to de-politicize money and to impose fiscal discipline across Europe. Sovereignty concerns were beside the point. The member states should each put their fiscal house in order and let the independent central bank protect the value of the currency—as Germany had done in the past. From a French perspective, however, monetary union was conceived as a way to end a situation in which its *national* sovereignty was battered. In the 1980s, French officials increasingly perceived the European Monetary System as a "Deutsche Mark zone" in which the Bundesbank had become "the bank that ruled Europe."[5] They were seduced by the notion that EMU would reinvigorate, rather than dilute, French sovereignty.[6] The fact that EMU might entail a transfer of sovereignty to the EU level—specifically, to the European Central Bank—was secondary to the desire to escape the strictures of German dominance.

As it emerged in the course of the following two decades, the institutional architecture of EMU reflected, but did not resolve, the deep tension between these two very different conceptions of monetary union. The Stability and Growth Pact, signed in 1997, and the underlying conception of a rule-based EMU was as reviled in France as it was worshipped in Germany. After the surprise socialist victory in the legislative elections of March 1997, Prime Minister Lionel Jospin argued in favor of a *gouvernement économique*—an idea that had first surfaced in the early 1990s—and demanded a rewriting of the stability pact in a direction more conducive to growth. As the notion of *gouvernement économique* seemed to suggest a more active macroeconomic management and a greater role for politics, it soon became an easy sound bite in many French political speeches. Jospin ultimately obtained a relabeling— with the addition of the word "growth"—but not a rewriting of the pact.

Many in the French political elite expressed their desire for a different and "more political" kind of economic and monetary union—and for a more "political" Europe as well. Although nobody was very precise on what *gouvernement économique* actually involved,[7] there was a broad consensus in France on the general notion that the EMU could not be left on automatic pilot by relying only on rule-based governance. EU policies should be authoritative, and they should be pursued boldly. French officials often criticized the excessive legalism of Eurozone governance and its insufficient openness to political debate. Rules were acknowledged as necessary, but they must leave sufficient space for discretionary action, especially in difficult or emergency situations. Policies that are highly reactive to changing economic circumstances should thus not be overly constrained by pre-existing rules.

In contrast to the French insistence on the importance of discretion in economic policymaking, German officials stressed the importance of rules as a necessary framework for any policymaking exercise. They were wary of grand pronouncements that were not followed by concrete effects. Perhaps because of their domestic experience with federalism, they favored a system in which responsibilities are relatively clear and where member states are not forced to follow centrally decided policies with which they often do not agree. More prosaically, they also refused to be placed in a position of bearing the heaviest financial burden of decisions made in Brussels or elsewhere in the EU. As it turned out, Germany's principled support for strong rules also had practical limits, as German officials were not necessarily ready to face the prospect of rules being used against themselves. This became obvious when the German government decided—with help from the French—to block the procedure that the European Commission leveled against Germany's "excessive deficit" in 2003.[8] In the run-up to the 2005 reform of the Stability and Growth Pact, EU bodies and the small member states were the strongest advocates of rule-based rather than discretionary economic governance at the EU level. From the perspective of smaller member states, the independence of the European Commission and of the ECB, as well as the reliance on a rule-based EU economic governance framework, guaranteed against the risk that big countries would throw their weight around in an intergovernmental policymaking exercise.

On the eve of the global financial crisis, the Eurozone therefore emerged from two decades of debate with a weak and deeply contradictory institutional framework. It was not really a strong rule-based regime. Rules had been reinforced on paper, with the European Council's decision to reform the Stability and Growth Pact in 2005.[9] The preventive arm of the Pact was strengthened and made more country-specific, and the reform also mandated consistent trajectories of fiscal consolidation, above and beyond the pre-existing focus on the 3 percent deficit limit. Yet the example of France and Germany demonstrated that there were ways to circumvent the rules without getting caught or suffering the consequences. In effect, the rules were only stringent if the member governments each accepted their logic. And they usually did so only as long as it did not interfere with what they construed as their sovereign prerogatives. The fact that rule-based governance was not a reality was not compensated by a strong discretionary exercise of governance.

To be sure, there was some progress toward more discretionary and cohesive governance within the Eurogroup, that is, the group of Eurozone finance ministers established in 1997. An important milestone was the creation of a permanent chair for two and a half years, which became official in 2007 with the Lisbon Treaty.[10] But this did not necessarily mean that the member states were really governed by anything like a European finance minister. The chairman of the Eurogroup was nothing more than *primus inter pares*, with no real powers or any kind of hierarchical authority over his or her colleagues, as this would have undermined the principle of national economic sovereignty. In effect, therefore, power remained firmly at the national level for all policies other than monetary policy. The question was, would the Eurozone's minimalist economic governance be up to the task in the face of serious challenges?

The Global Financial Crisis as a Spur for Economic Governance

When the global financial crisis started in 2007, it initially seemed that the Eurozone was less vulnerable and was reacting more forcefully than the United States and Great Britain. As the financial crisis suddenly intensified in the fall of 2008, French president Nicolas Sarkozy, acting as rotating chair of the European Council, seized the opportunity to push for a bolder EU agenda. In October, European leaders found themselves under pressure to prevent a meltdown of the European financial sector in the wake of the Lehman Brothers bankruptcy. Sarkozy called for a meeting of Eurozone member states at the level of heads of state and government. EU leaders then issued a "European Action Plan" to shore up the fledgling European banking sector.[11] It spelled out a total commitment of more than 1.3 trillion euro in governmental loans and underwriting of bank capital—well above America's TARP expenditures, even though only a portion of that money was actually disbursed. The French president hailed the plan as the first successful exercise of *gouvernement économique*.[12] By going to the European Parliament to make that point, Sarkozy also wanted to broaden the support for a beefed-up economic governance framework. The European Parliament's favorable response in a resolution passed on November 22, 2008, underscores the fact that its members now saw stronger Eurozone economic governance in a positive light, as a further step toward economic and political integration.[13]

Europe's October 2008 "action plan" was particularly interesting for what it revealed about Nicolas Sarkozy's vision of *gouvernement économique*. From then on, the French president repeatedly expressed his view that the core meaning of economic governance was the coordination and periodic steering of European economic policies by national political leaders. This vision did not necessarily involve formal transfers of powers to the EU level, however. A decision to organize regular Eurozone meetings at the level of heads of state and government is a simple decision to make. Yet such meetings could be an important impulse for EU governance, as shown by the precedent of the European Council—a body that began an informal existence in 1974 and was only formally recognized in December 1991 during the negotiations of the Maastricht Treaty.[14] This vision is also in line with the pre-crisis de facto evolution of economic governance as a primarily informal coordination within the Eurogroup and between the Eurogroup and the ECB, with the Commission bringing mostly technical expertise to the table. Sovereignty thus remains primarily at the level of the member governments, who are collectively in charge of economic governance at the highest political level.

Sarkozy's quintessentially French vision of economic governance had the merit of being more concrete and pragmatic than earlier vague calls for *gouvernement économique*. It could work well when economic interests and policy priorities converged. This is what happened initially, at the outset of the global financial crisis in 2008. National leaders were on the same wavelength in the face of an emergency situation. In the face of a clear threat,

European leaders went full steam ahead in favor of international economic coordination—both among themselves, and vis-à-vis the rest of the world. Internally, the Europeans managed to cooperate among themselves, even in the absence of formal treaty provisions for collective decision-making.

As the Stability and Growth Pact was shelved away for better times, Keynesian ideas were suddenly fashionable again among European policy circles.[15] Likewise, there was a remarkable European willingness to show a united front vis-à-vis the outside world, especially between France and Germany. At the G20 meeting in Washington in October 2008, France and Germany increasingly stood together in opposition to financial deregulation, and in favor of greater international regulatory cooperation.[16] European leaders focused their demands on strengthening international bodies such as the International Monetary Fund (IMF) and the G8, as well as relatively new forums like the Financial Stability Forum (now the Financial Stability Board) or the G20.

Yet Sarkozy's conception of European economic governance did not fundamentally surmount the contradictions of divided sovereignty that the Maastricht Treaty had planted at the heart of Europe's Economic and Monetary Union. Sarkozy's "European action plan" already signaled a problem that would beset subsequent efforts to achieve a coordinated EU response to the financial crisis. A week before the successful announcement of the EU action plan, a meeting of the four EU member governments of the G8 ended in a complete failure. Only when it became clear that all member states shared the same immediate interest in preventing a financial panic did Germany and others come to terms with Sarkozy's idea of a rescue package. The principles of action were adopted in common, but individual governments were careful to make separate announcements for the national details and amounts of funds that they committed to rescuing their national banking systems. The "action plan" that was decided in common is therefore better described as an accumulation of national action plans than as a truly European action plan. The French bank rescue plan, in particular, was quite national in character.[17] Despite the existence of a single market for banking services, there was clearly no banking union even remotely in sight. In this sense, the fact that bank rescue measures were coordinated at the EU level therefore did not at all mean that a durable European economic governance framework was born.

In fact, divisions quickly surfaced on the desirable scale of the stimulus package—especially between Germany and France. The French president initially wanted EU member states to adopt ambitious stimulus plans, so as to kick the European banking system and economy back onto a normal mode. The fact that France held the presidency of the EU in the second half of 2008 also certainly played a role in the French government's high ambition, as Sarkozy wanted the French presidency to be a success. German chancellor Angela Merkel was much more weary of the growing financial burden of public deficits and debts. She initially gave a lukewarm endorsement to the European action plan, and only announced the details of the German plan in January 2009—one month after the end of the French presidency.[18] Although the German stimulus package was ultimately larger than the French one, the German government never recognized it as a rather straightforward Keynesian fiscal spending package, as this did not fit with the dominant national economic policy discourse.[19] Throughout 2009, European leaders thus continued to muddle through the financial crisis. Stimulus plans were implemented, but there was little or no coordination between the different member states.

More generally, the emergence of a durable form of economic governance that would go further than ad hoc coordination in a situation of acute emergency has been extremely difficult. The problem was not that member governments were pursuing different national interests per se. In each case, it would have been perfectly possible to define national interests in a more EU-compatible fashion, without any clear material sacrifice. It is even possible to argue that member states generally lacked vision and hurt their national interests by pursuing go-it-alone tactics.[20] Yet the member states were jealous of their sovereign prerogatives and fundamentally unwilling to put themselves in a position of being told what to do by others. Only when faced with emergency situations and repeated calls for help coming from the European Central Bank or embattled member states did Eurozone member states finally resolve to act in a bold way. Likewise, only when confronted with immediate deadlines or challenges did the Europeans make a serious effort to show a united front to the rest of the world. The Europeans first acted decisively in 2008 to prevent a meltdown of the financial system. But the difficulty of moving together toward a new and sturdier regime of economic governance became considerably more vivid starting in 2010, when the Eurozone was hit by a severe crisis.

The Eurozone Crisis as a Turning Point for Economic Governance

The roots of the European disorder in the face of the crisis are manifold. One bone of contention was the increasingly obvious divergence in competitiveness and external vulnerability among EU member states. Despite a precipitous drop in its export markets in 2008, Germany emerged stronger from the crisis. Its initially strong budgetary position kept the public deficit under control in comparison to others, despite its 2009 stimulus (going from 0.1 percent of GDP in 2008 to a maximum of 4.2 percent in 2010 and back to 0.1 percent already in 2012).[21] Above all, its export competitiveness allowed it to extirpate itself from the depth of the recession much more quickly than its partners. While most of Europe suffered from persistently weak domestic consumer demand, Germany benefited from the quick recovery of emerging economies in Asia and Latin America, toward which it reoriented its exports.[22]

The contrast was especially striking between the German economy and the economies of Greece, Ireland, Portugal, Spain, and later Italy. After accumulating severe public or current account deficits during the boom years of the 1990s and the first decade of the 2000s, these countries were most severely hit by the crisis. They increasingly experienced soaring interest rates in sovereign debt markets—the roots of the Eurozone crisis that broke out in 2010 when Greece and then Ireland had to seek assistance from the IMF and their EU partners. While Germany and (to a lesser extent) other continental European economies weathered the crisis relatively well, the governments of peripheral economies were forced to undertake painful fiscal austerity measures when faced with renewed signs of a banking sector meltdown. It became evident that market actors feared a disorderly movement of sovereign defaults, a Eurozone exit of the weakest member states, and perhaps even a disintegration of the euro itself.

As European leaders slowly came to terms with the vulnerability of their economic governance framework in the face of crisis, they began to take more drastic action in the second half of 2010. In response to intense market pressure, the member states and the ECB adopted a series of emergency measures. The member governments adopted rescue packages for their embattled partners and established a common instrument to help defend countries that faced ever-higher interest rates on their sovereign debts. On May 10, 2010, they announced—in addition to a first 110 billion euro rescue package for Greece—the creation of a European Financial Stability Facility (EFSF).[23] The EFSF was established as a limited liability company, in order to issue state-guaranteed loans for up to 440 billion euro. On May 10, the ECB also decided to start its securities markets program (SMP), a controversial scheme of sovereign debt purchases that effectively came in support of the rescue packages.[24]

When Ireland came under market pressure in the fall of 2010, followed by Portugal in the spring of 2011 and Greece again in the summer of 2011, they all benefited from rescue packages, including EFSF loans—85 billion euro for Ireland in November 2010, 78 billion euro for Portugal in May 2011, and 109 billion euro for Greece in July 2011. When Italy and Spain themselves came under pressure in August 2011, the member states decided to grant the EFSF conditional authority to intervene in secondary debt markets. Before such intervention could become effective, the ECB decided to buy Italian and Spanish debt securities—another very controversial decision within the ECB, leading to the resignation of German ECB Executive Board member Jürgen Stark one month later.[25] Last but not least, the ECB under its new president Mario Draghi decided in December 2011 to offer unlimited three-year loans to Eurozone banks, known as long-term refinancing operations (LTROs).[26] Although Erik Jones rightly points out in Chapter 3 of this volume that the ECB wanted to "channel liquidity to industry," it was also clear when the program was launched that these unlimited ECB loans would be a welcome source of financing to banks that were massively selling peripheral sovereign debt.

The program would thus indirectly help these countries—without violating the Maastricht Treaty, since the ECB was acting in its assigned role as a lender of last resort to private-sector banks rather than directly bailing out member governments.[27] In effect, however, it was clear that the ECB subsidized the banks' holdings of Eurozone member state treasury bonds. To be sure, the LTRO program did not eliminate borrowing cost differentials across the Eurozone. Yet it immediately released interest rate pressures on the debt servicing costs of struggling Eurozone member states, especially Italy and Spain. Although all these decisions were made reluctantly and under extreme market pressure, they amounted to a significant departure from the self-help philosophy of the Economic and Monetary Union as embodied in the Treaty's "no bailout" clause (Article 103).

Just as significantly, the EU has also implemented treaty revisions that could in the long run reshape the landscape of economic governance. At the European Council on October 29, 2010, EU member governments decided that a European Stability Mechanism (ESM) would be created as a collectively underwritten public entity in order to continue the work of the European Financial Stabilization Facility (EFSF) beyond 2013. In exchange for accepting France's idea of a permanent crisis resolution mechanism, German officials obtained support from France for a treaty revision that would authorize economic assistance to other member states only as a tool of "last resort" to preserve stability. On December 17, 2010, the European Council endorsed the French-German proposals, proposing a modification of Article 136 of the

Lisbon Treaty barely a year after it entered into force.[28] On March 25, 2011, the European Council then decided to modify the treaty by introducing a European Stability Mechanism that would be activated if "indispensable to preserve the stability of the euro area." By way of a separate treaty signed on July 11, 2011, the Eurozone member governments then established the ESM, authorized to lend up to 500 billion euro as of June 2013. Like the IMF, the ESM has the status of preferred creditor, thus de facto creating the possibility of haircuts for other (subordinate) debt.

On December 9, 2011, the Eurozone member states agreed on a "fiscal compact," on the early deployment of the ESM in June 2012, and on the establishment of an "emergency procedure" that would enable a qualified majority of member states to trigger financial assistance programs. The "fiscal compact" was subsequently elaborated into a Treaty on Stability, Coordination and Governance, signed by 25 EU member states (all except Britain and the Czech Republic) on March 2, 2012.[29] The treaty calls for national budgets to be "balanced or in surplus" in the medium term (Article 3); the enforcement of this rule is to be guaranteed by stricter EU monitoring and "preferably constitutional" provisions in national legal frameworks; "a correction mechanism shall be triggered automatically" for countries that engage in "significant observed deviations." In addition, the member states agreed that "all major policy reforms that they plan to undertake will be discussed ex ante and, if appropriate, coordinated among themselves" (Article 11).

After a reprieve of a few months, market pressures started to mount against Spain and also Italy, as the news broke that Spain was going to seek financial assistance to recapitalize its troubled banks. This time, investors feared that Spain's regular state debt instruments would become "subordinate" to EFSF/ESM loans. This made repayment of normal treasury bonds potentially less likely, since the senior creditors would be reimbursed first in the event of sovereign debt default. Interest rates on Spain's sovereign debt—and, by contagion, on Italy's debt—therefore shot up to around 7 percent. At the Eurozone summit of June 28–29, 2012, Spanish Prime Minister Mariano Rajoy and Italian Prime Minister Mario Monti therefore united their efforts to obtain short-term measures against the crisis they faced.[30] The member states decided that the EFSF would be authorized to recapitalize banks directly, without going through the troubled banks' home member state and without gaining seniority status. The EFSF/ESM would also be authorized to "respond in a flexible and efficient manner in order to stabilize markets for member states respecting their country specific recommendations and their other commitments"—read Italy. In order to further "break the vicious circle

between banks and sovereigns," the member states also endorsed the principle of a single banking supervisory mechanism, with the ECB at its apex.[31]
Altogether, these measures were an important first step toward a banking
union, with a single bank regulator and implicitly a form of joint and several
liability for European banks. Finally, EU Council President Herman Van
Rompuy was also given the task of developing a "specific and time-bound
road map for achieving a genuine economic and monetary union," possibly
leading to further "[t]reaty change."[32]

Since the summer of 2012, however, the pace of Eurozone governments'
governance reform initiatives has slowed down. One factor is that the unprecedented and quite unconventional activism of the ECB has paradoxically
made the member governments' adoption of reforms seem less urgent. ECB
President Mario Draghi announced in July 2012 that he would do "whatever
it takes" to save the euro.[33] The ECB announced soon thereafter that it was
starting a new program of outright monetary transactions (OMTs), whereby
it could purchase unprecedented quantities of peripheral countries' treasury
bonds in case of an emergency. Erik Jones, in Chapter 3, points out that this
program, like the LTRO program and in line with the ECB's mandate, was
intended to strengthen the monetary transmission mechanism by making
private sector credit more affordable in peripheral countries. Although this
was certainly Mario Draghi's "justification" for the ECB's move, the relief
that it would bring to peripheral member states' borrowing costs was clearly
an expected side effect of the program.[34] Precisely for this reason, the program was adopted very late and long remained controversial among ECB
Governing Council members.

Unlike the Bank of England, the ECB did not clarify early on that it
would stand behind peripheral governments' debts. Paul De Grauwe has
argued that this explains the severity of the confidence crisis that hit these
countries' debt markets.[35] Yet the strident level of internal ECB controversy,
along with many northern European central bankers' long-standing fear of
unleashing more "moral hazard," goes a long way toward explaining why the
ECB made this move at such a late stage in the Eurozone crisis. In the summer of 2012, Bundesbank President Jens Weidmann was the only member of
the ECB's Governing Council who actually voted against the program, but
that was not a foregone conclusion at the outset of the crisis.

In retrospect, the ECB's OMT program appears as a watershed in the
Eurozone crisis. To be sure, it did not pull the Eurozone decisively out of its
economic stagnation.[36] Yet it considerably diminished the market pressure
on the member states that had repeatedly forced Eurozone governments to

come up with emergency responses since 2010. Not very surprisingly, the governments' willingness to adopt common institutional or economic measures declined once the pressure receded. The Eurozone crisis ceased to focus the minds of government leaders on fundamental economic governance reforms or on the need for economic coordination in order to put the Eurozone back on a healthy growth trajectory. The most vulnerable countries no longer felt so vulnerable, while the core member states no longer felt so obliged to make immediate concessions to—let alone help—their partners. Until the last minute, Spanish Prime Minister Mariano Rajoy had refused to admit vulnerability by asking for a bailout package.[37] At the end of 2012, the French president declared that the worst of the crisis was "over."[38]

As for the banking union project, it was distinctively relegated to the back burner as the German government's objections mounted in the run-up to the general elections of September 2013. The crisis over Cyprus's impending bank run provoked another adrenaline rush during the spring of 2013.[39] But as it turned out, the crisis was resolved relatively quickly and does not seem to have really changed the member governments' wait-and-see attitude. As France and Germany celebrated the fiftieth anniversary of the Elysée Treaty signed by Charles de Gaulle and Konrad Audenauer on January 22, 1963, which sealed their reconciliation, François Hollande and Angela Merkel remained remarkably cautious on the strengthening of economic governance.[40] After six months of working together toward common proposals in the run-up to the European Council of June 2013, their most daring institutional proposal was to appoint a "full-time" president of the Eurogroup of finance ministers with "reinforced" prerogatives—not exactly a revolutionary step.

Lessons Learned and Stumbling Blocks

If we take a step back, there are two ways to read the member governments' long-term response to the Eurozone crisis. One reading is that the core European member states are cautiously buttressing EU powers, while addressing the problem of moral hazard at the same time. With the help of the ECB, they are also aiming for a return to long-term fiscal sustainability. In this narrative, European leaders are truly doing their best to build up their economic governance and avert both macroeconomic imbalances and the danger of future sovereign debt crises. They are not only adopting the French idea of stronger discretionary governance, but also making it more compatible with German concerns for fiscal restraint. Thus, they are moving toward a regime that combines stronger discretionary governance with stronger rules, rather than perpetuating the unproductive opposition of the past between a rule-based and a discretion-based conception of economic governance.

This positive narrative can be traced back to 2010, when the French and German governments came to an agreement that they would work together on new economic governance initiatives—and that *gouvernement économique* would henceforth be translated as "economic governance" in joint policy documents.[41] In this sense, the crisis certainly brought France and Germany much closer together than ever before. After more than a decade of stalemate and often-sour French-German controversies on Eurozone governance issues, there has been a considerable rapprochement between French and German views of the euro. In Germany, France's idea of *gouvernement économique* no longer appears so outlandish. The limits of a rule-based regime have become obvious in a situation where, for the time being, member governments retained their sovereignty. As German officials increasingly came to accept the French view that stronger governance was needed, French officials became more acutely aware of the problems posed by diverging economic policies and the potentially devastating effects of public or private indebtedness on the integrity of the euro area. This was an important turnaround for a country whose leaders had often minimized the importance of macroeconomic convergence and eschewed firm commitments on deficit reduction. German officials had always been worried about the risk of macro-imbalances within the euro area—even though they did not always follow the low-deficit principles that they professed—but the novelty was that French officials now shared this long-standing German concern. In other words, the French became more German (so to speak) at the same time that the Germans became more French.

Yet a more skeptical reading of the situation is that European leaders have remained mostly in reactive mode. The considerable rapprochement between Germany and France—especially during the heyday of the "Merkozy" tandem—does not necessarily mean that the implementation of stronger economic governance has become easier. There is still a great deal of confusion as to the concrete forms that stronger economic governance should take. The post-crisis consensus on the necessity to introduce fundamental reform must be understood in this light. It is by no means obvious that member states will be able to agree on fundamental reforms that would truly address the problem of divided sovereignty. For example, the idea of a European sovereign debt market for "E-bonds" was floated early on in the crisis.[42] It built on a rather sophisticated economic policy debate involving established Brussels-based economic policy think tanks.[43] Yet it also met important opposition—not only in Germany but also in France—as it threatened to reopen the Pandora's box of potential limitations on the sovereignty of the member states and transfers of power toward the EU level. It remains to be seen if Jean-Claude Juncker's rise to the presidency of the European Commission in 2014 will give a second wind to his early proposal of a common Eurozone debt instrument. For now, however, Merkel's long-standing and vocal opposition to "Eurobonds" makes even cautious moves in that direction politically tricky.

The same can be said of the banking union project at the current stage of the discussion, with Germany still dragging its feet on the need for a common fiscal backstop to back up the so-called single resolution mechanism (SRM). After a meeting of European leaders on December 19, 2013, European Council President Herman Van Rompuy declared that "everything is falling into place," with a banking union that comprises a single supervisor (housed within the ECB), a common guarantee of deposits, and a debt resolution mechanism in case of bank runs.[44] Yet the banking union as it is currently envisioned has been essentially watered down: debt resolution will remain a national responsibility for a long time, and deposit insurance will be phased in very slowly and will remain limited—with no common fiscal backstop. The danger, then, is that the advent of the banking union will not change the situation and that "banking nationalism" will remain a crippling problem.[45] The prospect of Eurozone banks looking up to the ECB rather than to their national regulators is not a foregone conclusion. It is not clear how much actual clout the single supervisory mechanism (SSM) will be able to muster in the absence of centralized debt resolution and deposit insurance in the foreseeable future. As for the idea of reforming the EU treaty so as to comfort the powers of the EU, French President François Hollande is very reluctant to engage in such an endeavor.[46] His fear is to reopen a painful constitutional debate that sharply divided the country, especially the left, in 2005. And his Socialist Party's dismal performance and the resounding victory of the far-right and Euro-skeptic National Front in France at the European Parliament elections of May 2014 puts Hollande in an even weaker position to support a new EU treaty.

The reality then is that, despite the crisis, all member states remain reluctant to envision the dramatic transfer of significant powers to the EU level. Does the EU need to move squarely toward a form of fiscal federalism? Would such a move be desirable and above all realistic at this point of the crisis and in the present development stage of the euro? These remain for the most part unanswered questions. It is important to realize that they are much more difficult questions to answer than the questions raised by the financial crisis of 2008. At that initial stage of the crisis, member governments could (and did) answer in a primarily domestic fashion, paying only lip service to the idea of EU-wide economic governance. In response to a financial crisis and a recession, they implemented well-known recipes for dealing with recession—a combination of bank bailouts and fiscal stimulus packages at the national level. These recipes were politically controversial and costly, but not completely unprecedented.

The Eurozone crisis was much trickier for two main reasons. First, the Eurozone crisis that started in late 2009 came immediately after the worst of the financial crisis and while Europe was still in recession; this made it more difficult for governments to envision new bailout packages—both from a political and from a financial perspective. Second, the resolution of the Eurozone crisis would have required large-scale institutional innovations for which the various actors involved were absolutely not prepared; it took a long time for everyone to figure out what was required and for unconventional measures and institutional innovations to gather sufficient political momentum. The continuing debate on economic governance only magnifies the member states' dilemma about the consequences of EMU for the locus of economic powers. For now, the EU remains torn between its federal monetary institutions and its still mostly decentralized economic policy institutions.

Meanwhile, economic conditions dramatically deteriorated until the summer of 2012 and remained pretty dismal even after that. Fiscal austerity was implemented in large part to placate financial markets and to protect sovereign debt ratings. Although the escalation of sovereign borrowing costs on financial markets may have been a case of market "mispricing," it seems abundantly clear that fiscal austerity in the Eurozone periphery was not really a freely exercised choice; rather, it was "dictated" by financial markets, in the absence of a clear ECB backstop behind peripheral government bonds.[47] Yet deficit slashing in Greece and elsewhere also came at the expense of other economic priorities, including growth.[48] The controversies that erupted over the tough conditionality of the Greek and Irish rescue plans are enlightening. In the absence of direct levers on Greek budget expenditures or Irish corporate tax rates, core Eurozone member states led by Germany were willing to commit only limited resources. They took a long time to increase the resources and powers of the EFSF. They certainly did not want the EFSF or its successor, the ESM, to become a permanent "transfer" mechanism.

For the same reason, they also refused to endorse proposals to launch "Eurobonds" that would establish a form of joint and several liability among member states. The situation was complicated by the fact that domestic politics entered into the calculations of French and German leaders.[49] Merkel's *Nein* to Eurobonds served to reassure the right of her party and her FDP coalition partner when she asked the Bundestag to vote for a modification of EFSF powers. Meanwhile, Sarkozy's proposal to adopt a "golden rule" of return to a balanced budget enabled him to portray the opposition as fiscally irresponsible in the run-up to the 2012 presidential election. Conversely, France's newly elected president, François Hollande, had to accept the Fiscal Pact in order to establish his fiscal credibility and to legitimize his call for a "growth pact." Hollande obtained a commitment in June 2012 from his European partners on this point, but the agreed-upon budget of 120 billion euro was relatively modest in view of the problems, and moreover it remains largely untapped to this day. If we also consider the slow post-crisis recovery of the French economy and the continuing difficulties of France to abide by its fiscal commitments, it is clear that France is now unable live up to its historical role of partnering with Germany as the "motor of Europe."

Will the somewhat clunky governance framework that emerged from the crisis—including two important treaties that are not regular EU treaties, a "pact for growth and jobs" without yet a clear implementation pathway, and a banking union without any immediate prospect of common debt resolution and deposit insurance—help to steer the Eurozone economy back to a sustainable path for growth and public finances? In order for this to happen, the new framework must not only put the European debt crisis to rest, but also tone down the deep-seated tensions between the aspiration for European sovereignty and the desire to maintain national sovereignty over economic policy. It is useful to keep in mind the fact that economic coordination utterly failed in the 1970s, as member states adopted divergent national responses to the recession. This time, however, the Europeans have been more inclined to work together. There is little doubt that the depth of economic integration today and the fact that Eurozone member states share a single currency are responsible for this relatively new perception of being all in the same boat. The main question remains whether this perception will be sufficient to enable the Europeans to strengthen Eurozone economic governance in such a way as to avoid such crippling crises in the future.

Conclusion

The main reason that fundamental reforms of economic governance have proved so difficult, I have argued, is that the Maastricht Treaty was designed both to centralize the management of a stable currency in the hands of the

ECB and to keep economic policies decentralized at the level of the member states. Since they no longer control monetary policy, member governments have often become extremely protective over their *national* sovereignty in the area of economic and especially fiscal policy. The Eurozone crisis has made clear that the resulting status quo can easily become unsustainable. On the one hand, the fact that governments are caught in the contradiction of divided sovereignty helps to account for the excruciatingly slow pace of economic governance reform. On the other hand, it would be rash to declare Europe's contradictory status quo as *fundamentally* unsustainable. Short of a full-fledged fiscal union, the member states could very well adopt measures that might be considered second-best but that would nonetheless prevent the reoccurrence of a crisis like the one from which they are slowly emerging in 2014.

Clearly, the adoption of a true banking union—complete not just with a centralized bank supervisor, but at least a clear prospect of bank resolution and deposit insurance mechanisms—would be such a step in the direction of radical economic governance reform. Such a banking union would address some of the Eurozone's problems, as it would de facto allow member states to go into default and banks to go bankrupt without provoking a collapse of the entire European financial system. The kind of contagion fears that fueled the recent Eurozone crisis would no longer be as salient, and this could at least put the Eurozone economy on the path of greater stability. In order to completely prevent contagion, a large EU-level backstop that would stand behind the bank resolution authority would also be necessary—even if the backstop remains implicit and does not involve the buildup of a common Eurozone budget in the near future.

A banking union may very well be a more politically realistic objective in the near future than a full-scale Eurozone fiscal policy with a large common budget. It can be pursued as a remedy with low political visibility, although the project runs into trouble when the broader implications, especially the scale of the potential financial commitment, come into focus. Politicians arguably did not fully realize the extensive implications of EMU when they adopted it at Maastricht in December 1991—in particular, the untenable nature of the no-bailout clause if interpreted in an overly strict sense. It may be that, for the same reason, banking union is a more credible option in the short term than fiscal union. The potential financial commitments are no less important and could necessitate the progressive buildup of common budgetary instruments or backstops, but that may come later in successive steps, further down the road.

A banking union would be only a second-best step, however, in the sense that it would not necessarily involve a strong form of economic policy coordination or the buildup of a centralized countercyclical fiscal policy capacity. As such, it would not provide protection against large asymmetric shocks, nor would it ensure an appropriate Eurozone-wide policy mix—something that arguably can only be achieved with a large measure of fiscal policy discretion, if not a common EU budget.[50] In order for such a common Eurozone budget to emerge, the member governments would need to go much further toward surmounting the contradiction between a fully integrated monetary policy and their desire to retain as much economic sovereignty as possible at the national level. For this reason, the buildup of an important fiscal capacity at the EU level remains a relatively distant prospect, even though it would be preferable in terms of macroeconomic policy effectiveness. At this point, there is probably not enough trust in Brussels and among the member states to make the buildup of such fiscal capacity a realistic prospect in the short term, however desirable it may be. A macroeconomically optimal resolution of the deeper contradiction underlying Europe's Economic and Monetary Union is therefore probably still not in the cards in the foreseeable future, as long as the member states are able to keep the specter of a Eurozone collapse at bay.

In a sense, such contradictions are inherent to any federal system. As a political theory, federalism is premised on the existence of multiple levels of sovereignty.[51] The current situation may not be optimal, or even stable in the long run. But federal systems do evolve over time. In fact, the very purpose of federalism is to dynamically accommodate competing claims over sovereignty. In this sense, the newly found consensus in favor of stronger economic governance may only be the beginning of the process. In the long run, there will certainly be a rebalancing of divided sovereignty within the EU. The resulting configuration is essentially impossible to predict. Member states will be tempted to bury their heads in the sand and pretend that the dilemma of divided sovereignty does not exist. Sooner or later, however, the discursive consensus in favor of stronger economic governance will be tested again, and it may not survive under stress. But stress and tensions are also openings for genuine innovations.[52] In the past few years, we have witnessed a modest centralization of economic powers in the form of the ESM, the Fiscal Pact, and the banking union. It remains to be seen whether the collective puzzling over economic governance heralds a new period of integration for the EU, or if it foreshadows the eventual demise of the Eurozone and the renationalization of economic and possibly monetary powers. It may be that we will have to wait until the next crisis of the Eurozone to know the answer to this question.

5

The Forgotten Problem
of Democratic Legitimacy

"GOVERNING BY THE RULES" AND "RULING BY THE NUMBERS"

Vivien A. Schmidt

Introduction

During the euro's sovereign debt crisis, European leaders have become obsessed with rules, numbers, and pacts. This has reinforced an approach that began with the Maastricht Treaty, signed in 1992, which set out numerical targets for inflation, deficits, and debt for member states adopting the single currency; this process was formalized by the Stability and Growth Pact (SGP) of 1997, but accelerated during the Eurozone crisis beginning in 2010. In quick succession, EU leaders signed up for the "Six-Pack," the "Two-Pack," and the "Fiscal Compact," each more stringent on the nature of the rules, more restrictive with regard to the numbers, and more punitive for member states that failed to meet the requirements. In the absence of any deeper political integration that could provide greater democratic representation and control over an ever-expanding supranational governance, the EU has ended up with "governing by the rules" and "ruling by the numbers" in the Eurozone.

What has become clear as a result of the crisis of the Eurozone is that the EU is not just missing an economic union and a fiscal union; it is also missing a political union. During the crisis, the EU abandoned any pretense to respecting the long-standing "democratic settlement" in which Commission,

Council, and European Parliament (EP) all contributed in their different ways to decision-making via the "Community Method." Instead, Eurozone governance combined excessive intergovernmentalism—as EU member state leaders generated the stability-based rules in the European Council while treating the Commission largely as a secretariat—with increased supranationalism. While the ECB pressed the member states to engage in austerity and structural reform in a *quid pro quo* for its own more vigorous monetary interventions, the Commission gained enhanced budgetary oversight powers to apply the restrictive numerical targets. In all of this, moreover, the European Parliament was largely sidelined.

The resulting rules-based, numbers-focused governing of the Eurozone has not only generated problems for the European economy, it has also cast doubts on the European Union's democratic legitimacy and its social solidarity. Prior to the euro crisis, the debate remained open as to whether the EU suffered from a democratic deficit,[1] while many touted the success of the European "social model."[2] This is no longer the case, though diagnoses differ as to the reasons for the deficit and the failure of solidarity. Some fault the deleterious consequences of EU policies of austerity and "structural reform," in particular for the political economies of peripheral member states.[3] Others decry the lack of citizen political engagement in, let alone impact on, EU decision-making, and worry about the concomitant rise in citizen disaffection, accompanied by growing political volatility.[4] Yet others blame the poor quality of EU policy processes, with the increase in supranational and intergovernmental rule to the detriment of the "community method" and any significant involvement of the European Parliament.[5]

These concerns about the impact of the Eurozone crisis on the legitimacy of EU policies, processes, and politics readily translate into concepts used by political analysts who explain the EU's democratic legitimacy in systems terms.[6] Questions about the legitimacy of Eurozone responses include those raised about the *output* performance of EU policies, the EU's *input* responsiveness to citizen politics, and the *throughput* quality of EU governance processes. The first two such legitimizing mechanisms are often seen to involve a trade-off in which more of one can make up for less of the other;[7] there is no such trade-off for the third.

Output legitimacy describes acceptance of the coercive powers of political authorities governing "*for* the people" so long as their exercise is seen to serve the common good of the polity and is constrained by the norms of the community. Input legitimacy represents the exercise of collective self-governing "*by* the people" so as to ensure political authorities' responsiveness to peoples' preferences, as shaped through political debate in a common public space and political competition in political institutions that ensure officials' accountability via general elections.[8] Another way of conceiving of this distinction is as the difference between political authorities engaged in "responsible" as opposed to "responsive" governing.[9] Either way, the interrelationship between the two legitimizing mechanisms can involve a trade-off whereby more *output* performance through effective policy outcomes can make up for less *input* responsiveness, that is, less government attention to citizens' immediate concerns, as expressed in public debates and elections, or vice versa.

Throughput legitimacy sits between the input and the output, in the "black box" of governance.[10] It is dependent upon the quality of the policymaking processes, including the efficacy of the decision-making, the accountability of those engaged in making the decisions, the transparency of the information, and the processes' inclusiveness and openness to consultation with the interest groups of "civil society."[11] The quality of the governance processes, and not just the effectiveness of the outcomes or the responsiveness to citizen demands and expectations, has long been among the central ways in which EU institutional players have sought to counter claims about the poverty of the EU's input legitimacy and to reinforce claims to its output legitimacy. In so doing, they have operated under the assumption that good throughput may operate as a kind of *cordon sanitaire* for the EU, ensuring the legitimacy of EU level output and attention to input. But what they fail to recognize is that throughput quality does not involve the same kind of trade-off as that between output and input. Whereas little citizen input may be offset by effective policy output, and a lot of citizen input can legitimate a policy even if it is ineffective, better quality throughput does not make up for either bad output or minimal input—however efficacious the rules, accountable the actors, or transparent, open, and accessible the process. But bad throughput—consisting of oppressive, incompetent, corrupt, or biased governance practices—is likely to undermine public perceptions of the legitimacy of EU governance, and it can even throw input and output into question by seeming to skew representative politics or taint policy solutions.[12]

Prior to the Eurozone's sovereign debt crisis, the EU seemed to do comparatively well in terms of Eurozone governance legitimacy. Because the EU seemed to have effective output and quality throughput, the minimal political input by citizens did not appear unduly problematic. But with the onset of the sovereign debt crisis in 2009–2010, all of this changed.[13] Output legitimacy plummeted as policies pushing austerity and structural reform led to recession rather than growth. Input legitimacy has been at risk as citizens have become increasingly disaffected from the EU, if not "euro-skeptic," as well as from their national governments as they perceive that policies made at the EU level cannot be changed via national politics. And throughput legitimacy has been compromised by the inefficacy of rescue plans that were too long delayed and only slowly operationalized, as well as by the fact that EU institutional actors seemed more focused on reinforcing the restrictive throughput rules and numbers than on producing better policy output or increasing their responsiveness to citizen input.

Only relatively recently has the EU responded in any significant way to the bad output results and the worsening input politics—by reinterpreting the throughput rules. But although such reinterpretations may indeed ameliorate the situation, they at the same time engender a further problem of legitimacy. In a system in which the obsession with "governing by the rules and ruling by the numbers" has created an increasingly rigid system of packs, pacts, and compacts, any exercise in political or administrative discretion demands rules for stretching or breaking the rules—or at the very least, agreement on who has the authority to make or break those rules.[14] This may help explain why Eurozone institutional actors lately have tended to engage in a discourse that denies that they are actually altering the rules, even though they are.

But why, one might ask, do EU institutional actors then not just change the rules? The obstacles come not only from the continuing divergence in policy preferences, in particular between core and periphery countries, or from differing philosophical ideas about how to govern the economy, which pits neo-Keynesians against neoliberals and ordoliberals. The obstacles also come from the constitutional and legal dimensions of the EU that make changing the (throughput) rules extremely difficult, not to mention building a fuller political union in response to the failures of input-responsive politics and output policy performance. Even where member states' leaders seem to be in greater agreement, the rules by which the EU governs the economy are extremely difficult to change formally, once agreed. Unanimity rules for treaties makes coordinating agreement on what to do, let alone how to do it, very difficult. Changing the rules, once agreed, is even more difficult as a result of the EU's "joint decision trap."[15]

Finally, moving toward any deeper form of economic integration or greater political union has significant implications not only for economic arenas in which the member states have heretofore retained national sovereignty— such as in fiscal policy, as discussed by Nicolas Jabko in Chapter 4 of this volume—but also for political arenas central to the functioning of national democracy. Any further reinforcement of EU level oversight over national macroeconomic policies or budgets, whatever the necessity or appropriateness in light of the Eurozone crisis, reduces even further not only national governmental and parliamentary responsibility for these central policy functions but also their potential responsiveness to the concerns and demands of their national constituencies.

The Output Legitimacy of Euro Crisis Policies

Output legitimacy is a performance criterion focused on policy effectiveness. During the Eurozone crisis, by most economic measures, EU institutional actors failed the test of output legitimacy. Although there have been institutional innovations, these have come very slowly, and have done the minimal, with more focus on instilling discipline than on solving the crisis once and for all. As a result, the economic crisis has gone on and on, while unemployment, poverty, and inequality have been on the rise.

Euro Crisis Policy Content and Rationale

EU institutional actors' main responses to the euro crisis involved setting up loan guarantee mechanisms to shield countries under pressure from the markets, underpinned by intergovernmental agreements (inside or outside the treaties) plus legislative acts that served to reinforce the governance rules first set by the Maastricht Treaty and the SGP. Although many policy solutions to the crisis were proposed—for example, Eurobonds to mutualize debt, a "European Debt Agency" to issue bonds for countries in trouble, a European Monetary Fund to rescue countries in trouble—Eurozone governments did the minimum. They agreed to the Greek loan bailout and a temporary loan guarantee fund, the European Financial Stability Facility (EFSF), for countries in danger of contagion from the crisis in May 2010; a more permanent European Stability Mechanism (ESM), first discussed in 2010, which came into operation in 2013; and a half-baked Banking Union, set up during 2013.

In exchange for the minimal "economic solidarity" embodied by these rescue mechanisms came ever more stringent rules and restrictive numbers for all member states. First came an intergovernmental agreement that established the "European Semester," a framework through which to coordinate member state budgetary and economic policies, which gave the Commission increasing oversight and sanctioning powers. The first major legislative act was the Six-Pack, which provided stronger fiscal and economic surveillance under a new "macroeconomic imbalance procedure" (MIP) for all 28 member states. It more clearly specified how to quantify and operationalize the debt criterion in the "excessive debt procedure" (EDP) at the same time that it instituted a kind of reverse qualified majority voting (RQMV), whereby a Commission decision would be considered adopted unless it was overturned by a qualified majority of the Council. The "Fiscal Compact" that followed was an intergovernmental agreement that mandated even stricter budgetary discipline, with member state signatories expected to enshrine balanced budget rules in national law, preferably constitutional (sometimes called the "Golden Rule"), to be monitored not only by EU institutions but also "at the national level by independent institutions." The subsequent legislative Two-Pack specified further the modalities of surveillance of national governments' budgets by the Commission, along with a timetable that amended that of the European Semester. Moreover, for countries experiencing or threatened with financial difficulties, the Commission would engage in enhanced and ongoing surveillance.

The principles underlying these agreements were largely based on the "Brussels-Frankfurt consensus," which has three basic tenets for Eurozone economic policy: stable money, to be guaranteed by the ECB's role in fighting inflation and ensuring price stability; sound finances, to be assured by the member states, which were to eschew "excessive" deficits and debt; and efficient local labor markets, to be carried out by the member states, with each country responsible for making its own labor market and welfare state "competitive" in whichever way it could.[16] This consensus combines an *ordoliberal* philosophy focused on the need to impose austerity in order to ensure stable money and sound finance via rules-based governance with a *neoliberal* philosophy focused on "structural reform" of labor markets and welfare states as the answer to problems of growth.[17]

EU institutional actors' rationale for instituting the increasingly strict rules-based governance followed from their interpretation of the crisis from the very beginning as a failure to follow the rules of the SGP, which had consecrated the Brussels-Frankfurt consensus on Eurozone economic policy.[18] Seemingly forgotten were the real reasons for the crisis detailed in some of this volume's contributions, including the massive overstretch of the banks and the accumulation of private debt by households; ECB inflation-targeting, which produced increasing divergence rather than convergence; the weakness of euro governance institutions that failed to recognize, let alone warn, member states of the dangers of overheating real estate markets or to exercise sufficient oversight, not just over national finances but also over international banks.

It was as if EU institutional actors had caught a major case of collective amnesia in 2009 and 2010,[19] as they painted the crisis as caused by public profligacy rather than private debt, in what Mark Blyth has called "the greatest 'bait and switch' in history."[20] The narrative that stuck, in particular in Germany, was about the profligacy of the "lazy Greeks" versus "Germans who save," which was then generalized to all the countries in trouble.[21] The framing of the crisis as one of public debt in the periphery fueled resistance to any form of "transfer union," in which northern Europeans would pay for debts accrued in the South, and closed off remedies such as Eurobonds or a European Monetary Fund.[22] The reality was, of course, very different, since although Greece had indeed been profligate in terms of its public spending, the private sector was the main culprit in all the other countries, whether in terms of over-leveraged banks or households. This included some of those hardest hit by the crisis, such as Spain and Ireland, the governments of which had been scrupulous before the crisis in maintaining low public deficits and reducing their sovereign debt.

Euro Crisis Policy Performance

With regard to their output performance, the rules-based austerity policies have appeared at best to be ineffective, at worst to have exacerbated the crisis. Most of the economic indicators of performance dropped significantly across the Eurozone while unemployment reached record highs (12.2 percent in 2013), with many countries much higher (e.g., topping 25 percent in Greece and Spain).[23] Moreover, social solidarity has been in increasingly short supply, in particular because conditionality for program countries has for the most part led to across-the-board cuts in pensions, healthcare, and the social safety net. Close to a quarter of the EU population was at risk of poverty or social exclusion in 2012, while on average 10 percent of the population of the EU was severely materially deprived, with higher numbers in particular in eastern Europe and in Greece.[24]

A Council of Europe report in late 2013 concluded that austerity programs in response to the crisis had undermined human rights in key areas, largely as a result of public social spending cuts, especially in countries under international bailout programs. The report in particular condemned increasing homelessness in southern Europe, Ireland, and the United Kingdom, and failures to provide adequate safeguards to ensure access to the minimum essential levels of food—as governments limited food subsidies—and even of water in the case of Ireland. The troika demanded that public spending in these areas in program countries not exceed 6 percent of GDP.[25]

Critics had warned about the likelihood of such outcomes almost from the very start of the Eurozone response to the crisis. First, economic policies focused on financial stability that assume all countries can tighten their belts at the same time to become more "competitive" ignore the interdependence of surplus and deficit countries and the moving average problem at the heart of such efforts.[26] Second is the very structure of the Eurozone, as a non-optimal currency area in which a monetary policy focused on price stability can only lead to continued divergence rather than convergence,[27] and which would logically push southern European member states into a never-ending downward spiral of wage repression accompanied by the suppression of social and political democracy if they were left without the ability to devalue or to run deficits.[28] Third is what Erik Jones in Chapter 3 calls "the forgotten financial union,"[29] and in particular the incompleteness of the risk pool and insurance mechanism that was put in place more by default than design to respond to the pressures of global financial markets and the challenges of global competition.[30]

Only as the economic output results continued to deteriorate, with unemployment skyrocketing and growth plummeting, did calls for changes in policies come to be voiced. Growth finally became a matter of debate among EU leaders beginning in late 2011, when newly appointed technocratic Italian Prime Minister Mario Monti started talking about the need to focus on growth, and was quickly followed by the campaign discourse of French Socialist presidential candidate François Hollande in early 2012. This had the advantage of revealing that the policies presented as apolitical technocratic solutions that would produce optimum output performance were actually political, and conservative, and that politics therefore also exists at the EU level.[31] But it has been EU politics at the mercy—and the calendar— of national politics. And the discourse did nothing to change the ordo- and neoliberal cast of the policies, which were equally implemented by Monti and Hollande.

Not until the spring of 2013 was there a clear call to action, in particular with the need to address youth unemployment. Moreover, a report by the International Monetary Fund (IMF) in June 2013 most significantly admitted that it had made major mistakes in the bailout of Greece, in particular by assuming that severe austerity would lead in short order to growth, in light of the failure to restructure Greek debt.[32] Although by the summer of 2013 the Commission and EU leaders had all switched to a discourse that focused on growth, it remained mostly empty rhetoric. No measures other than a paltry youth employment scheme had been voted, while EU institutional actors for the most part continued to insist that the way to growth was through structural reform. The only new initiatives, moreover, continued to focus on reinforcing the rules.

Most notable was a proposal introduced in the "Four Presidents' Report" of December 2012,[33] which was reinforced by a joint letter from French and German leaders in May 2013 calling for "contracts" signed between each member state and the Commission.[34] By December 2013, however, the European Council rebuffed Merkel's continued push for such contracts. Moreover, with the arrival of a new Italian Prime Minister—Matteo Renzi— in February 2014, a more focused discussion of growth returned, along with a push for greater flexibility in the application of the rules. Now, in addition to the earlier arguments for increasing EU level capacity to invest so as to jump-start growth, came pressure to enable member states to invest, by easing the rules, both in terms of slowing the pace of deficit reduction and of not counting investment in growth-enhancing areas against the deficit. As of June 2014, however, nothing had been formally changed, nor was it likely to, as Merkel in a speech to the Bundestag insisted that there was no need to change the rules, since the Stability and Growth Pact already contained all the necessary flexibility. But this at least seemed to open the way to greater informal reinterpretation of the rules.

Euro Crisis Politics and Input Legitimacy

Input legitimacy is a criterion focused on citizens' political attitudes and engagement. Much like output legitimacy during the euro crisis, input legitimacy has deteriorated. As the output performance of Eurozone policies has worsened while the hierarchical controls of the EU over national economic governance have tightened, citizens' attitudes toward both their national governments and EU governance have declined dramatically, in lockstep with their economies. This has been most evident in the increasing turnover of incumbent governments, the rise of new parties on the extremes, and a growing loss of trust in the EU as well as in national governments. But while citizens tend to see the EU level as the producer of "responsible" output policies, to the detriment of "responsive" national-level input politics, EU institutional actors nonetheless see themselves as having their own EU-level sources of input legitimacy, along with their trade-offs with output legitimacy. But these, too, have come in for increasing criticism as a result of the Eurozone crisis.

Euro Crisis Challenges to EU Input Legitimacy

Of all the EU-level institutional actors, the European Council has claimed for itself the greatest input legitimacy during the crisis, and has acted accordingly by increasing its intergovernmental decision-making to the detriment of the Community Method, in which the Commission and the Parliament would also have had substantial decision-making input. The argument articulated by Council members was that they, as the elected representatives of the citizens, could best represent their constituencies in the process of intergovernmental decision-making in the Council. German Chancellor Merkel, for example, explicitly commended this new "Union Method" in 2010,[35] as did French President Sarkozy in 2011, who defined a more democratic Europe as "a Europe in which its political leaders decide."[36]

But what EU member state leaders fail to recognize is that leaving the bulk of decision-making to the intergovernmentalism of the European Council and EU Summits—however crucial it may appear in the heat of the crisis—is actually the least input legitimate of processes. First, indirect input can confer legitimacy only on decisions to which leaders agree for their own citizens, not those that they would impose on other member states' citizens. But even if it were legitimate for member states to agree to legally binding austerity measures for everyone, delegating to their agent (i.e., the Commission) the discretionary authority to implement such rules is not similarly legitimate, given the necessarily ad hoc nature of the specific application of those rules to any given country.[37] Second, the Council is not a representative arena as such. Rather, it is more like an international treaty body, in which intergovernmental negotiation gives those leaders with the greatest bargaining power (read Germany) an undemocratic advantage in the closed door negotiating sessions of the Council, as I will elaborate below.

In contrast, the European Parliament, the most legitimate in theory because its members are directly elected by the citizens, suffers in practice from the fact that it remains largely invisible or irrelevant to the majority of EU citizens. This has been borne out in the increasingly high rates of abstention over time from voting in EP elections (with an all-time low participation rate in 2009 of 43 percent), which have long been characterized as "second order" elections in which national political concerns have dominated political debate and voting behavior.[38] This has also been demonstrated in focus group research,[39] as well as in Eurobarometer polls over the years.

The EP elections in 2014 did not do much to reverse this trend, but they did stop the erosion in participation (the turnout rate remained steady at 43.1 percent) and marginally reduced the second-order nature of the election.

Although national political concerns continued to dominate the vote, the debate was more centered on European issues. Moreover, there was a clear politicization of the election campaign—as EP parties ran their separate candidates for Commission president in EU-wide campaigns and held televised debates, even though the results were mixed in terms of citizen interest or awareness. While a majority of voters were aware of the *Spitzenkandidaten* in core European countries like Germany and France, most in the UK were not.

The fact that the Council finally did choose the Commission President from among the winning candidates—against major opposition from British Prime Minister Cameron and initial resistance in other capitals—takes the EU one small step closer to greater input legitimacy, by helping to generate left/right political debates that have a greater chance of spurring citizen interest, and thereby may gradually help to politicize the EU.[40] The one caveat is in the line of "be careful what you wish for." The greatest interest in the EP elections came from the political extremes, whose voters turned out in much greater numbers than those of mainstream parties, helping to make Marine Le Pen's *Front National* the party with the largest number of votes in France and Nigel Farage's UK Independence Party the winner in the UK. The question is, how legitimate is a parliament for which 56.9 percent of the electorate have not voted, and for which, among those voting, close to a third went for extremist parties that have little chance in national elections, where citizens see themselves as having a stake in the outcome? The elections have left the EP with a thinning center, hemmed in by extremists of both right and left. As a result, the majority will necessarily be made up of a "grand coalition" of center right, center left, and liberals, under the leadership of a former Luxembourg prime minister who was also one of the longest standing members of the European Council. Under these circumstances, the politicization of the EU, which was to give citizens a clear choice among parties on the left and right, is lost. And in the end, therefore, such elections could politicize only to delegitimize the Commission and the EP.[41]

But even if input legitimacy is and remains in short supply, so what? A different kind of argument, equally significant in the legitimation of Eurozone governance, is that the trade-off with output performance, as assured by the EU's supranational institutions like the ECB or the Commission, makes up for any deficiencies in input. As another component of ordo- and neo-liberal thought suggests, isolating the institutions carrying out the policies from input politics is as important for output performance as is instituting the right kinds of policies.[42] But this also assumes that a certain modicum of input legitimacy is retained for such non-majoritarian institutions because they operate in the "shadow of politics," as the institutional products of political actors who have the capacity not only to create them and appoint their officials but also to alter them and their decisions if they so choose.[43]

The problem for the EU is that whereas this may apply to non-majoritarian institutions at the national level, it does not as readily to ones at the EU level. Often, such institutions have significant autonomy without any significant or at least sufficient democratic control from the classic "democratic circuit" of parliamentary oversight.[44] Moreover, the decision rules of the EU, and in particular the unanimity rule for treaties, make the policies of EU non-majoritarian institutions almost impossible to alter once established, given the absence of any kind of political government that could force the issue.[45]

The ECB, as the most independent of central banks, is a case in point. Although the absence of even the shadow of input legitimacy can be seen to pose little problem when the ECB remains within its charter-based remit to guide monetary policy, as a trade-off with output legitimacy, it can be problematic when the ECB goes beyond that remit. The ECB is on thin ice with regard to input legitimacy—or output, for that matter—when it pushes more input-legitimate actors like the Council to implement policies focused on austerity and structural reform, or to join with the IMF and the Commission as part of the "Troika" to impose conditionality on program countries.[46] Most problematic in this regard was the secret letter that ECB President Jean-Claude Trichet sent to Spanish Prime Minister Zapatero in August 2011—which Zapatero denied receiving at the time—in which Trichet essentially ordered the prime minister of Spain to decentralize the labor markets, break the monopolies of certain professions, and to institute cutbacks "whatever the circumstances." The revelation of the contents of the letter in the late fall of 2013 unleashed a debate in Spain about how much the president of the ECB had overstepped his bounds, whether by violating his own mandate to focus solely on Eurozone monetary policy, by interfering with the democratic control of elected governments, or in taking over the role of the Commission to make radical recommendations that even the Commission would not have made.[47]

The Commission, much like the ECB, does not have any input legitimacy per se. Commission officials themselves generally see their legitimacy as coming from their accountability to the input legitimate European Parliament, which vets candidates for Commissioner and confirms the Commission as "fit for purpose," but can reject individual candidates and/or impeach the Commission as a whole.[48] Notably, in the course of the Eurozone crisis, neither source of input legitimacy has been central to the Commission's remit, since the Commission has been granted quasi-independent powers and discretionary authority to enforce the various oversight functions of the macroeconomic imbalance and excessive deficit procedures and the European Semester. Such powers have arguably most affected member states' national input legitimacy.

The Commission's power to vet national budgets before governments submit them to national parliaments not only challenges national governments' sovereignty by diminishing their autonomy with regard to budget development. It also undermines one of the main pillars of national parliaments' representative power—control over national budgets—and thereby the principles of representative democracy, in which elected governments are responsible to those who elected them. The fact that the Commission can also sanction governments that do not mend their ways only adds insult to injury. It is therefore not surprising that when Belgium was pressed to further cut its budget for 2013 or face sanctions, Belgian Minister (and EU democracy scholar) Paul Magnette responded with "Who is Olli Rehn?" referring to the Finnish Commissioner for Economic and Monetary Affairs. That the Hungarian PM echoed the thought shows that the spectrum of concern goes from the left all the way through to the (authoritarian) right.

Euro Crisis Challenges to National Input Legitimacy

The ever-increasing sway the Commission has over member state economic and budgetary policies, together with the ever-growing number of Eurozone policies and rules agreed upon by the Council, suggests that the Eurozone crisis has also significantly affected input legitimacy at the national level. Most important, as Peter Mair argues, the EU in the midst of the Eurozone crisis has actually unsettled the balance between the two main functions of national-level political parties in their relations with their constituents. The crisis has forced parties to privilege responsibility over representation, by enhancing their governing role to the detriment of their responsiveness to national electorates.[49] This even includes opposition parties that may have campaigned against the very policies that they will be expected to implement when they gain office, even against "the will of the people."

Citizens have in consequence been left with the sense that they have little recourse in the face of EU-generated policies of which they may disapprove, other than to punish national politicians. The fragmented nature of EU "democracy," in which policies are decided at the EU level but politics—at least in regard to voting for governments—remains at the national level, has meant that citizens tend to hold their national politicians accountable for EU policies.[50] The result has been the increasing cycling of incumbent governments, as voters have punished their national politicians with growing frequency and intensity.[51] Such political volatility has become the rule not only in Greece, Spain, or Italy, but also in the core, with France being a case in point—President Sarkozy was only the second president in the Fifth Republic not to have won a second term. President Hollande has the lowest popularity rating of any president of the Fifth Republic (17 percent in late spring 2014).

Increasing Euro-skepticism or even anti-European—and not just anti-euro—feeling has been seen in all countries. Notably, this has been the case not only in the countries hardest hit by the crisis, in southern and eastern Europe, but also in those largely unaffected by the crisis economically, mainly in northern Europe, as in the case of the True Finns in the 2011 elections in Finland.[52] Moreover, Euro-skepticism has been growing not only on the extremes of the right and the left but also in the center. In a May 2012 Eurobarometer survey, among those saying that membership in the EU was a bad thing, respondents in the center outdistanced those on the left in France, Britain, and the Netherlands, and on both the left and the right in Finland.

Rising citizen disaffection from mainstream parties is also part of this, and can be seen in the growing electoral scores of parties not only on the extremes of the right and the left—as in Greece, where the neo-Nazi Golden Dawn polled 7 percent and the far left Syriza 23 percent in the June 2012 elections—but even in the center—as in Italy with the Beppe Grillo Five Stars phenomenon (with 25 percent of the vote) in the February 2013 election. This in turn makes for greater fragility for governments, with governing majorities on a knife's edge, and greater difficulties for winning mainstream parties to form a government, as in the Italian elections of February 2013— although Italian Prime Minister Matteo Renzi's historical win of 40 percent in the EP elections and Grillo's underperformance relative to his predicted score suggests that Italy, at least for the moment, has managed to reverse the trend. But worse yet in terms of the rise of extremist parties is the possibility that anti-democratic governments will also emerge, as in Hungary. The occasional recourse to technocrats, as with Lucas Papademos's government in Greece and Mario Monti's government in Italy in 2011–2012, however legitimate they may be with regard to the (throughput) constitutionality of such appointments or their potential output results, also raises questions of input legitimacy, given that they are not the people's choice.

Meanwhile, all the unions have been able to do has been to agree to concessions while gaining nothing in return, as in the Spanish pension agreement and the Irish Croke Park deal; at the same time, the most that social movements like the Spanish *indignados* have been able to do is mobilize members for protests and demonstrations that have brought them nothing other than, sometimes, news coverage.[53] Notably, the Council of Europe report in late 2013 condemned governments' side-stepping of regular channels of participation and social dialogue on the pretext of national financial emergency, as well as harsh responses against demonstrators and infringements of freedom of expression and peaceful assembly, as well as reductions in media freedom, in particular in public outlets, such as the closure of the Greek public broadcaster ERT.[54]

The Throughput Legitimacy of Euro Crisis Processes

The challenges arising from the Eurozone crisis not only involve issues related to the input responsiveness of EU institutional actors, or the output performance of EU policies. They also relate to questions of "throughput" legitimacy, which is a procedural criterion focused on the quality of the governance processes by which EU institutional actors formulate and implement the output policies in response to input politics. These processes have become increasingly intergovernmental and supranational (or technocratic) in the course of the Eurozone crisis, leading Jürgen Habermas to warn against the dangers of "executive federalism," in which the tremendous shift of economic and budgetary power to the EU level has occurred without any concomitant increase in citizens' input.[55]

The ECB: From "One Size Fits None" to "Whatever It Takes"

As a non-majoritarian institution, the ECB's deliberate insulation from even the shadow of (input) politics makes it not only more in need to succeed in its (output) performance but also more likely to focus on the (throughput) quality of the rules contained in its mandate. The insistence on sticking to the rules came out most clearly in the first 10 years of the euro, as the first heads of the ECB—first Wim Duisenberg and then Jean-Claude Trichet—incessantly repeated that to maintain the bank's credibility for the markets they needed to follow the ECB's mandate of inflation-fighting while maintaining its total independence from the political pressures of the member states. When Mario Draghi was appointed head of the ECB in 2011, he reiterated this commitment and the Brussels-Frankfurt mantra in his first press conference, insisting that "continuity, credibility and consistency are of the essence in the way we carry out our jobs" and resisting any suggestion that the ECB could act as lender of last resort on the grounds that "the real answer is actually to count on the countries' capacity to reform themselves ... first, put your public finances in order and, second, undertake structural reforms. In doing so, competitiveness is enhanced, thereby fostering growth and job creation."[56]

The problem for ECB governance of the euro is that following the throughput rules, at least as they were originally interpreted, was not necessarily good for output. Even during 2001–2005, it was acknowledged that ECB monetary policy fueled inflation in some countries (Ireland) while producing something close to deflation in others (Germany). But more recently, the ECB monetary policy has come to be acknowledged—even by the ECB itself—as a "one size fits none" system, given that inflation targeting for all member states, rather than leading to the assumed convergence, actually produces increasing divergence in all domains.[57] "The Single Currency did not play by the rules," as Erik Jones has put it,[58] and the ECB as a result decided to move to a more considered view of how to reinterpret the rules in order to produce effective output.[59]

As the Eurozone crisis continued, the ECB incrementally shifted away from strict adherence to the rules in its charter, or at least the original interpretation of them. Notably, however, the ECB remained true to the ideas of the Frankfurt-Brussels consensus, and its underlying ordoliberal principles. Thus, even as it seemingly violated the letter of the Maastricht Treaty's "no bail-out clause" by buying member state debt beginning in May 2010, claiming that this was within the bounds of its remit because it was only buying bonds on the secondary markets, it remained with the spirit of it, by refusing to do what the Fed and the Bank of England did—act as a real lender of last resort (LOLR). This is also when it first began pushing the member states to remedy the problems of the euro's governance, as well as to get their own houses in order through structural reforms. Subsequent unorthodox policy shifts, involving low interest loans to the banks via long-term refinancing operations (LTROs) in late 2011 and early 2012, all were legitimated by suggesting that the output benefits justified "unorthodox" policies (bending the rules).

In July 2012, moreover, as the markets had begun massive attacks against Spanish and Italian sovereign debt, Draghi pledged to go what seemed the last mile, stating that the ECB was ready to do "whatever it takes to preserve the euro," adding, after pausing for effect, "And believe me, it will be enough." To back this up, the bank established the outright monetary transactions program (OMT), which promised the potentially unlimited purchase of Eurozone bonds for countries unjustifiably under market attack.[60] The markets took this as a pledge to act as lender of last resort, which it essentially was, with one significant difference from what central banks ordinarily do— the ECB made clear in September 2012 that it would use the OMT to stop market attacks on Spanish and Italian bonds only if the Italian and Spanish governments asked for it, and after they agreed to a conditionality program in exchange for the ECB's help. By insisting on conditionality through structural reform, the ECB seemed to be trying to legitimize the break with one set of rules in the treaties by reinforcing another. This came largely to the satisfaction of German leaders,[61] with the exception of the more orthodox Bundesbank.

By this time, only the Bundesbank and its head, Jens Weidmann, plus a large number of German economists, were opposed to the ECB's reinterpretation of the rules on the grounds that they violated the charter, and risked long-term inflation. The question of the ECB's right to institute OMT was even taken up by the German Constitutional Court. It pitted Weidmann, who vehemently opposed ECB intervention on the grounds that its remit was to control inflation, and that only the politicians had the legitimacy to deal with the rest, against the ECB's executive board member Jörg Asmussen, who justified the unorthodox monetary policy measures as a response to unusual circumstances, insisting that "[w]e are in a situation of one size fits none, that is why we have extended these non-standard instruments."[62] Significantly, the Constitutional Court's decision, which sided with the Bundesbank's analysis of the illegality of the ECB's never-instituted OMT program, nonetheless referred the case to the ECJ. Subsequently, however—and quite amazingly given its recent stance with regard to the court case—the Bundesbank itself reversed its position, with Weidmann stating in an interview that, in light of a strong currency and the dangers of deflation, the ECB could in fact buy Eurozone member bonds or top-rated private sector assets, thereby opening the door to quantitative easing.[63]

The Council's Governing by "One Size Fits One" Rules

By prioritizing intergovernmental decision-making during the Eurozone crisis, EU member state leaders have shifted the institutional balance increasingly toward the intergovernmental level to the detriment of the joint-decision making process that includes the EP and the Commission. As noted above, to some member state leaders, this posed little input legitimacy problems because they touted the Council as the most legitimate body in the EU. But in so thinking, they fail to acknowledge the fact that rather than being in a representative forum, they are in a bargaining arena in which one country has outsize power. Although academic scholarship on the Council has suggested that even where qualified majority voting occurs, the deliberative mode prevails over hard bargaining because of the focus on consensus,[64] the argument here is that in the Eurozone crisis, where Germany has held all the cards, even where there is deliberation, it occurs in its shadow, such that the Council has ended up with "one size fits one" governing by the rules.

Germany's "power of one" has manifested itself in a range of ways. First of all, the focus on EU economic governance through rules and numbers in successive pacts has largely been due to Germany.[65] Its insistence on governing not just by legislated rules but by their constitutionalization via treaty was evident in such cases as the demand that the EFSF be followed by a constitutionalized mechanism with the ESM, and that legislative agreements such as the Six-Pack (which could be revised through normal EU legislative procedures) be followed by the treaty on the Fiscal Compact (which it could not be).[66]

Second, Germany's power of one has undermined the traditional balance in the "power of two" relationship of the Franco-German couple. Although the relationship between Germany and France went from one of bilateral leadership to a bilateral *directoire* between 2009 and mid-2012, as Sergio Fabbrini has noted, it was a *directoire* dominated by Germany, with Merkel the major partner in the "Merkozy" leadership duo.[67] This can be seen not only in the content of the policies, with the German preference for financial stability having replaced France's focus on solidarity, but also on the processes, as German ideas came to dominate France's concept of *gouvernement économique*—with Commission-administered rules replacing the euro-group discretion that the French had wanted.[68] This was apparent even in Sarkozy's communicative discourse from 2010 to 2012, as he gradually shifted from an emphasis on the importance of "solidarity" for the bailouts to Merkel's consistent talk of "stability."[69]

Third, German leaders, by way of the German Constitutional Court, have largely imposed their country's own rules of input legitimacy on the rest of the EU. Instances include leaders' frequent invocation of the Constitutional Court to delay decisions, most notably with regard to bailing out Greece, the German Constitutional Court's own rulings on democratic oversight of decisions, and the Constitutional Court's hearing on the ECB's various unorthodox programs to save the euro, despite its lack of jurisdiction. The point here is not that member states should do away with the national democratic processes they consider necessary to input legitimacy, but that this can cause serious problems for the efficacy of European decision-making if these kinds of national democratic exigencies were to be multiplied across EU member states.[70]

Finally, Germany has largely imposed its own interests on the rest of the EU.[71] These can be variously understood as the narrow electoral self-interest of the chancellor and her governing coalition, who calculated that a delay in any agreement would enable them to win a major subnational electoral contest (in North Rhine-Westphalia) on May 9, 2010; as financial self-interest with concerns about a "transfer union" and the size of German liability in any bailout; or even, more generously, as the German conviction that "living by the rules" was in Europe's best interest.

To be sure, Germany has also changed its position in response to changing circumstances and pressures from fellow member states and other EU institutional actors as well as from internal German political actors, in particular the Social Democrats.[72] And naturally, Germany was not the only member state promoting this set of ideas, or appealing only to its own electoral constituencies in so doing. Germany's main cheerleaders in Council meetings were the Finns and the Dutch, but there were also the Slovaks and other central Europeans who saw Greece not so much as the profligate cousin as the richer one. Among other EU institutional actors, the ECB, as noted earlier, put very strong pressures on the member states for rules-based solutions, while it is no coincidence that the Commission has been a strong supporter as well (see below). In the development of many of the rules, moreover, the Council president has been equally important in developing a consensus on Eurozone governance by setting up a working group that included the main EU institutional leaders in monetary and economic policy. Germany's power of one, in other words, also lies in the political coalitions constructed with it and around it, to push forward its agenda. And that agenda has changed marginally over time, as the Council's discourse shifted from an exclusive focus on maintaining stability and strict adherence to the rules to one that admitted by 2012 that "growth" was important and, by early summer 2014, that even "flexibility" was acceptable, but only insofar as this stayed within the pre-established stability rules.

The EU Commission's "One Size Fits All"

As befits a bureaucracy, the EU Commission's democratic legitimacy rests less on its Council and EP-derived input legitimacy than on the quality of its throughput processes of governance. In the Eurozone crisis, however, the Commission has seemed to eschew the transparency, openness, and accessibility that characterize its general approach to formulation processes, instead focusing primarily on their efficacy. The euro crisis has largely turned the Commission into a secretariat charged with the technocratic application of rules and numbers. The nature of the rules, moreover—consisting of more and more stringent pacts for "one size fits all" fiscal consolidation—has straitjacketed the Commission, limiting its flexibility with regard to applying the rules in a manner adapted to changing economic circumstances and the often very different needs of the country in question. Ironically, however, it is the Commission itself that designed the straitjacket, since it has been key in drafting the Six-Pack and Two-Pack legislation and in preparing the "Fiscal Compact." Moreover, while these rules essentially tied its own hands, it also tied the hands of the Council through the RQMV, and the hands of the member states through the European Semester. In so doing, at the same time that the Commission has limited its own room for maneuver, it has massively increased its own rules-based oversight and enforcement powers.

In the European Semester, for example, the Commission has the responsibility to monitor developments in each member state using a scorecard, with in-depth country analyses that would enable them to decide whether to place a Eurozone member in a macroeconomic imbalance or excessive deficit procedure, with detailed recommendations, mandatory reporting requirements, and even monetary sanctions. The way in which this is carried out is problematic not only with regard to throughput efficacy, given the rigidity with which the rules are applied, but also with regard to other throughput criteria, such as openness and accountability. For example, the Commission altered its own rules of "collegiality" with regard to the euro crisis, when Commission President Barroso granted autonomy of decision to the Vice President and Commissioner for Economic and Monetary Affairs, Olli Rehn. This has led to a process in which DG ECFIN works out the numbers on its own, largely in secret, makes its decisions, and then informs the Commission, often sending word out to the other members of the Commission on a Monday night for a Wednesday meeting, with little or no explanation of those decisions. There is no possibility to overturn them, and sometimes they are made public even before the other Commissioners have been informed, thereby potentially putting them in an embarrassing position vis-à-vis their own member state governments, which might expect to be forewarned.[73]

Equally important, the rigidity with which the Commission has interpreted the rules and applied the numbers, in particular with the Troika for member states under "conditionality," may stem more from its own ideologically driven choice of strict enforcement, and belief in the ordoliberal output ideas, than Council control or the influence of Germany. We should not forget that already in 2008, with the loan bailout programs for the central European countries, it was the Commission that had pushed for the strictest conditionality, against the wishes of the IMF, making this the "European rescue of the Washington consensus."[74] Thus, even in 2013, when tacit acknowledgement of the failure of fiscal consolidation policies led to agreement to ease the policy on rapid deficit reduction, the Commission stuck to a discourse that claimed that it was prior success, not failure, which allowed for a more flexible policy. Rehn, for example, claimed that things were getting slightly better only because the crisis response offered "a policy mix where building a stability culture and pursuing structural reforms supportive of growth and jobs go hand in hand."[75]

Notably, belief that structural reform produces growth meant not just that the Commission had done little to promote such growth in its own initiatives—including violating the Europe 2020 agenda that sought to create the conditions for growth by promoting employment, improving education, and reducing poverty and social exclusion. It also entailed keeping an inflexible approach to the remaining rules. Thus, Rehn continued to maintain that countries in trouble because of high deficits and debt could not increase their deficits in order to propel growth. Only if they had posted a primary surplus could they do so. In the case of Spain, however, the Commission agreed to change the calculation of the "structural deficit" as proposed by the Spanish government (on the grounds that it underestimated the impact of unemployment) so that it would also have a primary surplus, and thereby could escape applying austerity measures for yet another year. But although the Commission's "Output Gap Working Group" agreed to make an ad hoc methodology change for Spain because the normal calculation appeared so improbable, it did not for others out of "concern in some capitals" about the implications of using better estimates—which might ease up the pressures on program countries.[76]

The most damning criticism of the Commission, however, comes from the IMF, whose recent evaluation of the Greek bailout found that "the Commission, with the focus of its reforms more on compliance with EU norms than on growth impact, was not able to contribute much to identifying growth enhancing structural reforms."[77] The Commission's single-minded focus on the throughput rules may be explained by its assumption that this would serve as a *cordon sanitaire*, ensuring the trustworthiness of the processes and, thereby, their legitimacy. The danger, however, is that the legitimacy of the EU's input and output will be questioned if the Commission's implementation of the rules appears oppressive, as it has to the southern European countries, in particular Greece; biased, because it seems to benefit export-oriented northern European countries; or to be playing favorites, by treating countries differently, as in recalculating the structural deficit for Spain, but not for other countries in similar circumstances.

The European Parliament's "No Size at All?"

If during the euro crisis the ECB started with "one size fits none" rules and the Council continues with "one size fits one" governing, while the Commission remains "one size fits all" ruling by the numbers, then the European Parliament must be seen as having "no size at all." The EP has largely been excluded from most decisions on the euro by EU treaties, as well as in cases where international institutions have been involved—meaning all the loan bailouts and guarantees, with governance by the "Troika" of the IMF, EU Commission, and ECB. The EP's exclusion has thereby also precluded in most instances the parliamentary debates that could serve to amend and/or legitimize policies negotiated behind closed doors by the Council. Moreover, where the EP did have a say, in the Six-Pack and Two-Pack, it largely voted to give the Commission exclusive power to apply the rules, denying itself the ability to oversee the Commission's decision even as it limited Commission discretion by specifying numerical targets for intervention. Here, the heightened sense of crisis, together with the discourse of "no alternative," was such that most MEPs voted in favor of austerity and fiscal tightening—indeed, pushed for more stringent measures than were on the table.[78]

Until the EP gains more say over Eurozone decision-making, it will not have any robust input into current intergovernmental politics, nor can it affect output policies. Notably, the Council has no plans to significantly increase the EP's role in Eurozone crisis governance. Even in the various documents proposing a future "blueprint" for the EU, or in the Four Presidents' Report, the EP is afforded only a "monitoring" role, to debate perhaps, and to provide "accountability," but little more. The only way in which things may change for the EP is as a result of the election of the Commission President via the EP 2014 elections. Ideally, this alternative would help rebalance the EU system not only by ensuring the Parliament greater oversight over the Commission but also by putting the Commission in the shadow of European politics. For the moment, however, the increased input legitimacy of the Commission resulting from the designation of the Commission president via EP elections may not do much to improve the quality of the throughput processes with regard to governance of the Eurozone. Much depends upon the extent to which the EP is able to play upon differences in the Council, say, to push for increased flexibility in Commission oversight of the member states' budgets. But this assumes that the grand coalition of major parties in the EP will be able to reach agreement on a coherent orientation for the Commission, and that this would prevail even over and against Council preferences. Given the EP's limited mandate in Eurozone governance, this is unlikely to happen very soon.

Conclusion

Considering the challenges to democratic legitimacy during the crisis of the euro suggests that the EU needs "output" policies that are more effective, "input" politics that are more responsive to citizens, and "throughput" processes that are more balanced and carried out with greater efficacy and accountability. The question for the EU is therefore not only whether it can get the economics right—by generating economic growth and social solidarity, not endless austerity and destructive structural reform—but also whether it can get the politics right—by enabling citizens greater say over decision-making in ways that serve to rebuild trust while countering the rise of the extremes—and whether it will be able to develop processes that are less intergovernmental and technocratic, with less slavish attention to rigid numerical targets. For any of this to happen, much depends on how EU institutional actors respond to the continuing crisis, and whether they alter the rules and numbers to promote better policy performance as well as to accommodate citizen concerns while opening up decision-making processes to EU and national parliamentary representation. But what is the likelihood that such progressive changes in policies, politics, and processes will come to pass? Is a more balanced political union, in which concerns of all three kinds of legitimacy mechanisms are addressed, at all possible?

For the moment, although EU institutional actors have themselves become increasingly aware of the legitimacy problems, and have taken small steps toward their amelioration, these are by no means enough. As we have seen, the ECB has already moved from its initial "one size fits none" rules of inflation targeting to doing "whatever it takes" for policy results in order to "save" the euro. In exchange, however, the ECB has demanded greater commitment to austerity and structural reform, which may save the euro, but only at the expense of peripheral member state economies. The Council has largely followed the ECB's demands, mainly because the bargaining of EU member state leaders in the European Council has produced a "one size fits one" governing mode, in which the most powerful—read Germany and its northern allies—have largely been able to impose their preferences. And yet, even Germany's position has changed, as it went from a focus on stability above all to one that included a discourse concerned with growth—even though so far little has actually been done to ensure it—and most recently flexibility as well. As for the European Commission, in response to ECB and Council requests, it has devised the "one size fits all" numerical targets by which it has zealously enforced member state compliance to the rules. That said, lately it has begun to soften the rules in response to negative results. Finally, in all of this, the European Parliament has had almost "no size at all," with little role in Eurozone governance. But the appointment of the winning candidate in the EP elections as Commission president may confer greater legitimacy—and therefore potential to exercise discretion—to the Commission. It will also provide some opening to citizens, even if it has initially only increased the presence of Euro-skeptics and resulted in a grand coalition in the EP rather than a more progressive majority.

In the immediate future, therefore, little is likely to change radically, since we cannot expect EU institutional actors to reverse financial stability rules and numerical targets that have become embedded in their practice as well as touted in their discourse—even in the unlikely event that there were to be a shift in the political orientation of the Council following member state elections. But, in a positive take on the future, this does not rule out the incremental reinterpretation of the rules and recalculation of the numbers over the medium term by a Commission with the legitimacy to exercise greater discretion in its economic governance so as to enhance the growth potential of member states' political economies. Such incremental change would also depend upon whether the decision-making system as a whole had reached a new "democratic settlement" in which the Commission president was elected via EP elections, the EP was brought into Eurozone governance alongside the Council, and the ECB was returned to its more limited original responsibility for monetary and banking policy alone. As for the political economic ideas embodied in those evolving rules, one can probably not expect a paradigm shift back to neo-Keynesian expansionism. However, in place of today's "expansionary consolidation" (Schäuble's term - *Financial Times*, June 24, 2010) or, more accurately, "expansionary contraction," given the results of austerity and structural reforms, why could we not see the emergence of a new paradigm of "expansionary stability" or "stable expansionism," in which the stability rules are made compatible with growth-enhancing policies? If this were the outcome, then the euro crisis would have done what past crises have been touted to do: after an initial period of delayed or failed responses, the EU muddles through to a more positive set of results while deepening its own integration. But this is not inevitable, as Craig Parsons and Matthias Matthijs make clear in chapter 10 of this volume. It requires leadership from the EU's institutional actors and heads of government, as well as vision. And currently, at least, these remain in short supply.

SECTION II

The Euro Experience

6

The Reluctant Leader

GERMANY'S EURO EXPERIENCE AND THE LONG
SHADOW OF REUNIFICATION

Abraham Newman

Introduction

One of the great puzzles of the euro crisis is the striking disconnect between the policy position of Germany and much of the rest of Europe and even the world. Countries ranging from France to crisis-ridden states on the periphery have called on Germany to step up and engage in a broad push for solidarity and growth. The international press from the *Financial Times* to the *New York Times* has condemned German policy, casting the German government, and Angela Merkel in particular, as pursuing a failed strategy of austerity.[1] Even the International Monetary Fund (IMF) has criticized the extreme level of structural adjustment being imposed on the crisis-hit countries,[2] and the US Treasury has publicly shamed Germany's persistent current account surplus in the face of regional and global imbalances.[3]

At the same time, the German government has stood by its policy, focusing on the risk of moral hazard by profligate member state governments and its call for austerity and structural reform. Facing attack from all sides, Finance Minister Wolfgang Schäuble described Germany's critics as living in a "parallel universe."[4] In Germany, there is near consensus among the mainstream policy elite supporting the country's approach, marked by the relative absence of the euro crisis from the 2013 German election.[5] In fact, with its euro policies as a reference, the German electorate in September 2013 delivered Chancellor Merkel and her Christian

Democratic Union with the largest electoral success of any party in decades.

German emphasis on individual member state responsibility and reluctance to take on the role of regional stabilizer is all the more surprising in light of its past European and euro experience. First and foremost, the German economy is tightly coupled to the economic future of its neighbors. Roughly 60 percent of German exports have traditionally gone to other European countries, tying future German growth prospects to the success of reform in these markets. Second, Germany has historically played the role of regional guarantor.[6] Many have long argued that German support of the European project results from its desire to undergird a regional order in which Germany prospers.[7]

While some may argue that it is Pollyannaism to think that Germany could have underwritten a swift regional bailout, one only has to look to the US Troubled Asset Relief Program (TARP) as a counterfactual. The US government, along with the Federal Reserve's swap line program, quickly underwrote counterparties in banking systems across the OECD countries.[8] By the spring and summer of 2010, the German government knew the size and risk of delay with the Greek sovereign debt crisis and had received repeated warnings from the US Treasury, the financial press, and market indicators.[9] Why, then, has the German government followed a particularistic solution focused on moral hazard and a narrative of "throwing good money after bad" rather than a solidaristic response centered on "preventing contagion and guaranteeing exports"? More specifically, perhaps, what factors incentivize the moral hazard policy among policy elites and make it electorally successful? More generally, what can be learned about the future of the euro given Germany's response?

In order to make sense of this disconnect, Germany's critics have highlighted a range of factors, including Merkel's personal leadership style to German elite beliefs in ordoliberalism. On the one hand, Merkel is cast as a cautious incrementalist unwilling to risk a grand bargain.[10] On the other hand, German politicians lost in the fog of crisis have turned to deep-seated beliefs about market stability and economic order.[11] While there is no doubt some truth to both of these arguments, they obscure significant facts on the ground. Importantly, there is a domestic electoral dynamic that has rewarded Merkel's leadership and her substantive policy position, which is hard to understand from arguments about leadership style or belief structures on their own. How then can one make sense of the near star-like quality of the unassuming "Schwaebian Hausfrau" as she sweeps up after the crisis-ridden periphery?

The central argument of this chapter is that Germany's euro experience and response to the crisis are deeply tied to its reunification experience. The timing of these two macro-historical events lock German policymakers into a set of political incentives that make alternative policies emphasizing solidarity and burden sharing exceptionally difficult. This relationship works through two primary channels—solidarity exhaustion and structural adjustment misfit. On the one hand, reunification has sapped the willingness of an already skeptical electorate to devote additional resources to bail out its neighbors, undermining the basic logic behind hegemonic stability arguments. After decades of subsidizing and restructuring eastern Germany, the German electorate is wary of committing more money to subsidies they view as largely ineffective.

At the same time, reunification spurred a set of reforms to respond to the competitiveness drag of incorporating a former communist country into the unified German economy. The timing and nature of these reforms relative to the euro crisis have a number of critical consequences. For many Germans, they set up a sinner/saint dynamic in which Germans perceive that they have made painful sacrifices in terms of welfare cuts, wage restraint, and labor market reforms. This, then, helps the electorate justify similar demands of other nations that are now experiencing the euro crisis. Thus the call for austerity and structural adjustment is simply the externalization of their own lived experience. Additionally, these reforms have had real economic effects that have enhanced Germany's export position. As the crisis acts as a drag on the value of the euro in foreign exchange markets, it has had the perverse effect of boosting the export-led German economy. As a result, the German economy has been relatively unscathed by the crisis, experiencing modest growth and record low unemployment rates. In short, the effect of the crisis has been blunted for the German electorate, and thus it is extremely difficult for the German government to engage its citizens in a massive crisis response.

The main point of this chapter, then, is to emphasize the way in which macro political conditions structured the German response to the euro crisis. Rather than focusing on individual leaders or their beliefs, the chapter focuses on the way in which reunification filters Germany's euro experience. Just as the euro crisis is a product of a structural imbalance stimulated in large part by broader regional dynamics,[12] the political decisions of the German leadership have been shaped and constrained by larger regional and structural changes stemming from reunification.

This chapter, then, makes several important contributions to our understanding of the future of the euro. First, and foremost, it makes sense of the radical disconnect between German decision-makers and the rest of the policy community. Given the legacies of reunification, there is little political will within the electorate to support a solidaristic policy path. Rather than being incrementalist or irrational, the German government is responding to the incentives cast by reunification. Second, the approach undermines the fallacy of composition that run rampant in explanations of the euro crisis. Too often, explanatory focus looks at national factors such as leadership or beliefs without considering the larger regional and structural context. Scholars have long cited the relationship between the end of the Cold War and the introduction of the euro.[13] This chapter underscores how the legacies of reunification continue to reverberate through the euro's future.

Germany in the Crisis: Don't Throw Good Money after Bad

The focus of this chapter is to use Germany's response to the euro crisis as a window into its own euro experience more generally. In particular, two things become clear from this latest episode. The first is the public articulation of Germany's role as regional hegemon.[14] For much of the postwar period, Germany stood constrained by the historical legacy of World War II both institutionally and politically. Labeled the "semi-sovereign state," Germany was bound by its constitution to a limited military role globally and faced constant suspicion from its neighbors. These constraints have slowly eroded, however, with reunification and the end of the Cold War.[15]

But the euro crisis has produced a dramatic change in the public acceptance of this new role, both within Germany and regionally. In a remarkable speech in Berlin in 2011, Radoslaw Sikorski, the foreign minister of Poland, declared Germany the "indispensable nation."[16] Similarly, as Mark Vail describes in Chapter 7 of this volume, the twin engines of Europe—France and Germany—have been replaced by Germany as the sole driver. From Sarkozy to Hollande, France has seen its ability to shape the euro crisis response largely neutered by German demands. In part, this is the result of German economic success since 2005, and it is also the reality of its size within Europe. At the same time, policy paralysis within France and its stalled economic recovery have weakened the French position as co-equal. Even Wolfgang Schäuble, finance minister of Germany, reflected in 2010 that only a "leading nation, a benign hegemon or 'stabilizer'" could bring economic stability to the region.[17]

Second, and equally important, the crisis reveals German caution in playing the role of guarantor in this position as regional hegemon. For much of the postwar period, German foreign policy was defined by *Einbindungspolitik*, the notion that Germany's interests were served by regional integration. And repeatedly in the postwar period, Germany made commitments to regional causes, most notably the European Monetary System and the euro, which required considerable solidarity and regional support of its neighbors.[18] The crisis, by contrast, has found Germany asserting the importance of self-responsibility among the member states. Wary of taking on the burden that hegemonic stability provision frequently entails, Germany has been blamed for a failure of leadership.[19]

These two factors—Germany's emergence as the indispensable nation in Europe and its reluctance to guarantee regional collective goods—make its policy position vis-à-vis the crisis central to the future of the euro. In particular, Germany has emphasized its concern for moral hazard in its response to the regional crisis. The German characterization of the euro crisis has been consistent and focused—profligate governments pursued irresponsible policies during the economic boom, and Germany lacked any guarantee that a bailout would alter their behavior. The central narrative coming out of Berlin as early as 2009 focused on the potential moral hazard to German taxpayers of throwing good money after bad in the periphery of Europe.[20] Finance Minister Wolfgang Schäuble summarizes the German position in a 2012 editorial in the *Wall Street Journal*:

Moral hazard is not benign. Setting the wrong incentives would mean stabbing reformist governments in the back. By suggesting that uncompetitive economic structures can endure, we would buoy the populists, scapegoat-seekers and illusion-peddlers who lurk at the fringes of our political landscapes. By discouraging reform, we would not solve Europe's imbalances but make them permanent.

This brings me to another misconception: that the crisis was caused by a lack of solidarity. Solidarity is a noble idea and among the underlying principles of the European Union. It has been very much on display as euro zone member states have stepped in to support those that had lost access to markets.

Solidarity always goes hand and hand with solidity. Because solidarity on its own can also be an empty promise. In their generosity, European welfare systems are unparalleled, both in the world and in history. If we want to maintain such a level of protection in a rapidly changing world, we must ask ourselves where the wealth to sustain it will come from.

Not from a euro-zone budget, the printing press or eurobonds. All of our economies, not just a few, will have to generate this wealth, and they can only do so if they adapt to the rigors of a hyper-competitive world economy. Prosperity is not a God-granted right—it must be earned. [21]

In addition to a diagnosis of the problem, German officials have offered a policy agenda for its solution—austerity.[22] Countries that supposedly lived beyond their means are now required to reign in spending and cut entitlement programs. Adjustment is thus cast as a cost born primarily by citizens in the periphery, who will face declining incomes, real wages, and welfare state benefits. This policy emphasis rests both on the claim that Germany cannot afford to play the lender of last resort for the Eurozone, as well as a claim about fairness in responding to the crisis. Policymakers leverage the strong role of the German Federal Constitutional Court within the German constitution, as it has repeatedly signaled its wariness for delegating budgetary authority to the supranational level, as a further institutional constraint on a solidaristic approach. As Finance Minister Schäuble—again—explains himself in a 2011 editorial in the *Financial Times*:

> . . . it is an undisputable fact that excessive state spending has led to unsustainable levels of debt and deficits that now threaten our economic welfare. Piling on more debt now will stunt rather than stimulate growth in the long run. Governments in and beyond the Eurozone need not just to commit to fiscal consolidation and improved competitiveness—they need to start delivering on these now.[23]

And yet, the moral hazard frame has difficulty explaining the problems facing the Eurozone.[24] For Ireland and Spain, for example, government deficits were routinely below those of Germany and well within the Eurozone Maastricht deficit criteria. Deficits in those countries only ballooned as they were forced, through bank bailouts, to nationalize private debt. A banking crisis, then, turned into a sovereign debt crisis.[25] For still others, such as Italy, the real crisis is one of liquidity. While maintaining a relatively large debt, the government has not had difficulty servicing it so long as there is a market for public debt in Europe.[26] As Germany pushed for self-responsibility, this market quickly evaporated.[27] And while the Greek case is often held up as the

German poster child of the crisis, it seems odd to risk the future of the euro on an economy that is less than 2 percent of the overall EU economy.

To understand the roots of public and private debt in Europe, it is critical to examine structural features of the monetary union.[28] With the introduction of the common currency and pressure by the German Bundesbank to commit the new central bank to fight inflation, interest rates across the Eurozone fell to mirror those in Germany. This was an early signal by the markets (irrationally or not) that there was an implicit bailout commitment within the currency union. In other words, markets assumed that national bonds had the backing of the entire Union (an implicit Eurobond). As interest rates fell in peripheral countries, cheap money rushed into these relatively capital poor countries. Germany profited on two fronts. On the one hand, German banks were among the largest lenders to public and private borrowers in the periphery, with over 300 billion euro in loans to Greece, Portugal, Spain, and Ireland.[29] Once the loans had been made, consumers, firms, and governments in those countries used the money to purchase goods from German exporters. This created current account deficits in the periphery and large current account surpluses in Germany.[30] Moreover, the public assumption of private debt held by governments such as Ireland's, as well as government-orchestrated bailouts in Spain, benefited German banks that had contributed to the unsustainable boom years.[31]

The above discussion of the crisis highlights the selective interpretation by the German government of the problem as well as the solution—moral hazard coupled with austerity. Two alternatives suggest a different set of possible policy prescriptions. The first concerns the risk of contagion and was advocated most vigorously by the IMF as well as the US government. The argument here is that the member state economies are not independent of one another but are linked by market beliefs and fears. Threatening the belief of an implicit bailout commitment would spread the financing troubles beyond small economies such as Greece and Ireland to systemically important countries such as Italy, Spain, and even France.[32] The German government, then, needed to take bold, sweeping action to reassure markets of the ability of the European Union to engage in crisis management. Without such action, the price of the bailout would escalate exponentially. Despite the apparent realization of many of these fears, the German government has resisted the contagion frame since the initial months of the Greek crisis. Citing moral hazard concerns as well as institutional constraints, Berlin has repeatedly rejected proposals for Eurobonds or a shared bailout guarantee.[33]

A second alternative that could have bolstered a more solidaristic hegemonic response focuses on the European market as vital to the German economy. Once again, the German economy becomes inseparable from those of its European member states. Rather than focusing on the potential prices of an escalating bailout, this frame plays on the centrality of the German export industry to the country. If Europe falls into recession, the German export sector will suffer as the majority of German exports go to other European members.[34] In particular, this policy alternative undermines support for deep austerity by Germany's neighbors. As successive French governments have argued, the European Union should focus on promoting growth and use fiscal stimulus if necessary.[35] Given Germany's stable fiscal situation, it is well positioned to spearhead such an initiative. The German government, however, has long resisted this export frame.[36] With German growth stalling in 2013 and 2014, however, the German government is starting to re-examine its long-standing rejection of stimulus and unrelenting commitment to austerity.[37]

While German politicians periodically have made reference to both the risk of contagion or to Germany's reliance on European export markets, these played a relatively insignificant role in German foreign economic policy, particularly in the early phases of the crisis. It is always difficult to determine the exact consequences of counterfactual policy responses. Nevertheless, several independent researchers have concluded that Germany's strict moral hazard approach sparked considerable contagion in the Eurozone crisis.[38] In particular, the German policy response to the Greek sovereign debt problem raised concerns within financial markets that increased interest rates not only for Greece but for Spain and Italy as well. For example, the markets maintained a relatively benign reaction to the repeated recalculation of Greek deficits during 2009. By contrast, interest rate spreads spiked in the wake of official German pronouncements that there was no bailout provision in the Eurozone and that the German government was constrained from acting by the Federal Constitutional Court.[39] As the private market lost faith in the German commitment to member state governments, similar demands were placed on other peripheral economies.

Despite the fact that the moral hazard approach has encouraged contagion across the Continent, it enjoys considerable support within Germany. In a spring 2013 ARD poll, 70 percent surveyed reported that they were satisfied with Merkel's handling of the euro crisis.[40] A spring 2013 PEW Survey found that 67 percent of Germans thought that the solution to the crisis required further cuts to public spending. Similarly, the PEW poll found that

74 percent supported Merkel's management of the crisis. All other leaders in the survey fared considerably worse when evaluated by their national electorates, with David Cameron receiving the second best result at 37 percent.[41] These findings seem remarkably consistent over time, with only 28 percent of Germans responding in a September 2013 Gallup poll that there are better alternatives to the crisis than austerity (by contrast, 80 percent of Spaniards thought there were better alternatives).[42] Michael Schierack, head of the CDU in Brandenburg, bluntly concluded, "The Swabian housewife, who doesn't spend money without getting something in return, is seen by voters as the right leader for Germany in the crisis."[43] Ultimately, Merkel was re-elected chancellor in 2013, winning 42 percent of the vote and gaining nearly 50 percent of the seats in the lower house of parliament, the party's best result in decades. Perhaps equally striking for the future of the euro, the Social Democratic Party in Germany quickly relinquished its call for Eurobonds during the coalition negotiations with the CDU. While mainstream parties across Europe saw their results slashed during the 2014 European Parliamentary elections, Merkel's CDU received the largest vote share on the backs of a campaign based primarily on the chancellor's reputation.

Given that the major concerns of the contagion frame and the export frame have at least in part materialized, both the German government's commitment to the moral hazard argument and its resonance with the German electorate seem puzzling. The next section, then, examines a series of mismatches between events unfolding regionally and within Germany that help to explain Germany's hegemonic reluctance.

From "Sick Man" to "Export Miracle"

The German response to the euro crisis is integrally tied to the ramifications of and its responses to reunification, which have redefined German domestic politics over the last 20 years. This is not simply an argument that reunification has unleashed a "normal" period for German foreign policy, in which Germany may now assert its national self-interests. The end of the Cold War and the Soviet threat has tempered security fears that had motivated deep German commitment to regional integration. Similarly, the peaceful reunification of the country has weakened the long shadow of the past that constrained German foreign policy.[44] While these macro structural and cultural implications of reunification have frequently been employed to explain shifts in German foreign economic policy, this chapter examines parallel changes in the German political economy. In particular, it highlights the economic challenges posed by reunification and how the response to these challenges facilitated the adoption of a moral hazard policy to the euro crisis, as opposed to the more solidaristic contagion or export alternatives. In the end, any of the three alternatives could be conceived as representing the "self-interest" of Germany, so the critical question is to examine why one policy dominated the others and resonated politically.

For the German economy, the real economic crisis started not with the introduction of the euro but in the post-unification period.[45] GDP per capita stagnated in the decade between reunification and the new currency, from $22,692 in 1991 to $23,019 in 2000, with major economic slowdowns happening in 1993, 1995, and 1996.[46] Similarly, unemployment repeatedly broke postwar records and was already persistently above 8 percent by 1994. It was also during this period that Germany's fiscal position deteriorated significantly. With a debt-to-GDP ratio of roughly 40 percent in 1992, the government soon found itself facing a 60 percent debt-to-GDP ratio in 1998.[47] The price tag of big bang reunification, including large regional transfers and monetary union between east and west, put a considerable drag on the German economy. Embarrassingly, Germany violated the euro deficit targets in 2003, which were rules that the German government had insisted upon during the currency's creation in order to reign in profligate spending by other member states.[48] With falling productivity and rising wage costs, the German economy faced stagnant growth well before the introduction of the euro.

While German politicians had pushed for the creation and introduction of the euro, the first years of the currency were particularly rough economically. GDP per capita was stagnant between 1999 and 2004, with official recessions declared in 2001, 2002, and 2004. Unemployment remained consistently over 8 percent, reaching a postwar record of 12 percent, or 5 million unemployed, in March 2005.[49] And even for those with jobs, real net wages were flat, even declining between 2004 and 2008.[50] Additionally, Germany did not experience many of the benefits associated with the currency's introduction, such as lower interest rates or inflation. The German government had long enjoyed lower borrowing privileges, and the strict monetarist policies of the German central bank had kept inflation low. These trends stood in sharp contrast to many other European neighbors who saw wages rise, borrowing costs fall, and growth pick up. Reports of the Celtic tiger in Ireland or the boom years in Spain filled German newspapers and magazines with the implicit contrast to the local economy (see Table 6.1).

Table 6.1 Economic Mismatch in Euro Area Post-Unification

		1992	1999	2005	2011
	Germany	1.9	1.9	.7	3.3
Annual Growth	France	1.5	3.3	1.8	2.0
	Spain	.9	4.7	3.6	.1
Unemployment	Germany	6.6	8.4	11.1	5.9
Rate	France	10.2	12	8.9	9.2
	Spain	18.1	15.6	9.2	21.6

Source: World Development Indicators

Long touted as the postwar economic miracle and considered a rising economic giant in the late 1980s, Germany could not escape the image of the "sick man" of Europe during the 1990s and the first years of the 2000s.[51] Moreover, average Germans repeatedly cited dissatisfaction with the new currency. Despite the fact that inflation remained at a modest level, individuals frequently referred to the *Milchkaffee*-effect—a coffee that used to cost 2 DM now cost 2 euro. This led to the wide perception that the cost of living rose with the introduction of the euro.[52] Given stagnant or falling real wages, the cost of living was in fact rising but not due to the new currency or increasing prices. The overall economic facts were compounded by a slump in consumer confidence and overall faith in the German economy.

In response to the persistent economic slump, the German government, led by Gerhard Schröder, introduced a series of major economic reforms known under the banner of *Agenda 2010*. These reforms, enacted between 2003 and 2004, cut at the heart of the German welfare state, slashing pension and unemployment benefits. Most controversial, the *Hartz IV* reform reduced long-term unemployment benefits to the level of social welfare payments. Credited with introducing flexibility into the labor market and reducing the overall economic burden of social insurance benefits, these reforms continue to represent a major political controversy in German society.[53] The reforms sparked a series of protests across over 100 cities, including some 100,000 people. In many ways, they ended Schröder's career as chancellor, forcing him to resign as party leader in 2004. Seen as a stab in the back to the social democratic agenda, it motivated an internal split within the Social Democratic Party (SPD), giving rise to a new far left party, Die Linke. It is this split and the constant pressure on the left that continue to undermine the

SPD's national ambitions. More generally, the reforms symbolize a retrenchment of the German welfare state and the spread of neoliberal policies on the
Continent.[54]

Whether or not directly connected to these reforms, the German economy entered a new period of growth starting in 2005.[55] Real GDP grew at
over 1 percent a year and unemployment fell. While the German economy suffered in the immediate aftermath of the Great Recession starting in 2007, it
saw a remarkable upswing with the onset of the euro crisis. Economic growth
topped 3 percent in 2010 and unemployment fell to 5.5 percent in 2012.[56] These
figures are all the more striking when contrasted to depression-level GDP figures in many peripheral countries, with Spain alone experiencing over 25 percent unemployment. Germany was once again heralded as the driving force
behind the region's economy, reviving talk of a renewed economic miracle.[57]

The German euro experience is framed by two important macroeconomic
trends. The first is the poor performance of the economy in the wake of the
currency's introduction. This heightened insecurity about the currency limited any political capital or euphoria associated with it.[58] The second macro
trend concerns the mismatch between the German experience with the
currency and that of many of its neighbors. As Germany struggled with
years of stagnation, its neighbors saw their economies blossom. Similarly,
German fortunes improved as other member state economies fell off a cliff.
Unfortunately for Europe, the major economies may finally be falling in
synch, as the German economy contracted in the last quarter of 2012 and
grew at a scant 0.4 percent in 2013.

Reunification Blowback

Reunification, then, resulted in a number of political economy legacies that
have critical consequences for the German response to the euro crisis. On the
one hand, reunification has undermined further German support for solidaristic responses to economic crises. On the other hand, it forced a set of policy
changes that have limited the impact of the crisis, undermining political support for a more aggressive regional response.

Solidarity Exhaustion

There are important parallels between the way Germany has portrayed the
core versus periphery debate in the euro crisis and the consensus narrative
about the economic lessons of reunification. After attempting a massive

intervention to rebuild competitiveness in eastern Germany, elites, media, and the public, which were already pessimistic about such policies, have grown increasingly suspicious of the long-term success of a solidaristic policy. This disappointment in reunification has in many ways transferred both sub-consciously and consciously to the euro crisis assessment and response.

A central tenet of economic reunification focused on the idea of spatial equality—parity in the standard of living across the federal states, which is enshrined in the German Basic Law—under the auspices of a program of reconstruction known as *Aufbau Ost*.[59] In 1991, the government instituted a supplemental income tax, called the *Solidaritätszuschlag* (the solidarity charge), to offset the costs of these efforts. In the 10 years following reunifica-tion, over 1 trillion euro flowed from west to east in financial transfers. These policies have had real on-the-ground consequences, as infrastructure in east-ern Germany is often far superior to that in western Germany, ranging from public facilities such as pools to telecommunications networks and highways.

After an initial public outpouring of support for these policies, however, the discourse around eastern Germany and the policy of regional solidarity has grown increasingly negative.[60] During the mid-1990s and early 2000s (some of the hardest days of the German economic slump), a deep solidarity fatigue emerged in which the results of economic reunification were put in doubt and at the same time a narrative of moral hazard emerged. Economic transfers were increasingly labeled as wasteful, as they produced dependence rather than self-sustainability.[61] The *Die Welt* reporter Uwe Müller summarizes bluntly, "In spite of many billions, which has long since grown to a sum over a trillion, the East is still not able to sustain itself—half of a country is dependent on con-stant infusion of money 'just like a junkie depends on the needle.' "[62]

More than simply a concern of dependence, elites began to directly con-nect the East's experience with the long-standing depiction of economic problems in southern European countries. Helmut Schmidt, former chan-cellor of Germany, warned that if the reconstruction effort was not signifi-cantly reformed, "we'll have a toned-down Mezzogiorno without the mafia in the former GDR. Economically, Germany can perhaps afford that, but politically?"[63] Public debates followed that questioned the continued use of the *Solidaritätszuschlag*. In an interview with former Federal President Horst Köhler, when asked whether people in Mecklenburg-Vorpommern should just accept its lack of competitiveness, he responded:

There were and are currently large differences in living conditions throughout the Republic from north to south and from west to east.

When you want to even them out, you cement in place a state based on subsidies (*Subventionsstaat*) and leave the young generation with an untenable amount of debt. We must move away from the subsidy state. Instead, we need to give people the freedom to realize their ideas and initiatives.[64]

Increasingly, then, a core take-away from reunification for the electorate is the danger of moral hazard that can occur when governments attempt to support uncompetitive regions and the need for these regions to undergo structural adjustment. In a co-authored piece, the influential German economist Hans-Werner Sinn concludes

Along the Elbe, a second Mezzogiorno has emerged, because there, as in Italy, the wage negotiations were handled above the heads of local employees and employers by a third party. And as in Italy, the solution is sought in the form of government transfers as compensation for economic disadvantages, instead of addressing the causes of the problem. Thus a skewed incentive system is created, to which the participants all too easily become accustomed and which is difficult to correct.[65]

It is then almost an identical lens that is reapplied to the crisis-hit countries as is used to describe the policies of reunification—Germany must avoid a cycle of dependence in which subsides replace structural reform. In other words, for many Germans, reunification's solidaristic experiment was deemed a failure, leaving little political appetite for another round.

Structural Adjustment Misfit

At the same time that reunification stoked the fears of moral hazard, it spurred a set of policy reforms that leave Germany strangely out of sync with the rest of Europe. As mentioned earlier, domestic economic concerns stemming largely from reunification pressures pushed the Schröder government to enact a series of reforms to enhance labor market flexibility and reduce welfare state commitments.[66] These reforms have been credited with containing Germany's fiscal commitments and supporting German export growth. At the same time, wage-bargaining contracts negotiated between capital and labor resulted in significant wage restraint.[67] Starting in the middle of the first decade of the 2000s, Germany's current account position steadily improved and it returned to modest growth.

Ironically, as the crisis hit Europe, Germany experienced some of its best macroeconomic performance since reunification. With growth at roughly 1 percent and unemployment steady at 5 percent, the German public faced the surreal experience of being bombarded by bad news about Europe when the domestic economy was relatively strong. In a May 2013 PEW research poll, for example, 75 percent of Germans surveyed reported that they thought economic conditions were good, compared with only 9 percent in France and 4 percent in Spain. Similarly, 77 percent of Germans said their individual finances were good compared to 46 percent in Italy and 15 percent in Greece.[68] Given this disparity in perception, it becomes particularly difficult to motivate the German electorate regarding the severity of the crisis and the need for a comprehensive German response.

Moreover, because reunification forced Germany to impose fiscal and labor market reforms before the euro crisis occurred, the euro crisis, in the short term at least, paradoxically boosted the German economy.[69] As problems started to emerge in 2009 and 2010, a critical consequence of the crisis was a weakening euro. This in turn spurred international exports of German goods, particularly to other growing regions in Asia. A study conducted by Alliance in 2012 estimated that the effect of the euro crisis on the currency's value boosted German exports outside the Eurozone by roughly 5 percent, which would translate into a 1.25 percent boost in German GDP.[70] This largely offset the slowdown in exports from other European countries, insulating Germany from the immediate effects of the crisis.

At the same time, heightened uncertainty over the value of sovereign debt in other European countries lowered borrowing costs in Germany. At one point in the crisis, the German government was able to sell bonds at a negative interest rate. This flight from risk to German bonds further lowered the cost of borrowing for the export sector, consumers, and the government. The perverse effects of the euro crisis, then, can be seen on many dimensions. German business confidence rose unexpectedly with the onset of the crisis, reaching a post-reunification record in November 2010.[71] Carsten Brzeski, an economist at ING Brussels, concluded, "Amidst new financial market turmoil and sovereign debt woes in the euro zone, the German economy seems to be an island of happiness."[72] Even the Finance Ministry noted that the government would save nearly 42 billion euro between 2010 and 2014, owing to falling interest rates.[73] Politically, the timing of economic expansion undermined alternative policy frames, as it was difficult to justify the need for sweeping solidarity in the face of a stable (at times robust) economy. Had reunification not forced structural adjustment in Germany, it is very likely that Germany would have faced the euro crisis in a similar position to other major economies on the Continent, with the French experience serving as a powerful counterfactual.[74]

Statistical versus Real Germany

Finally, the moral hazard frame offers a powerful retelling of the sacrifices made for unification. Despite Germany's return to growth in the second half of the first decade of the 2000s, wages in Germany stagnated.[75] This was due in part to a series of wage bargaining deals struck between business, labor, and the government in the face of stalled growth in the post-unification period, as well as many of the Agenda 2010 reforms.[76] In the wake of these reforms, exports boomed, but on the back of falling living standards. In particular, real wage growth has fallen considerably for lower paid services jobs since 2000.[77] This has helped exports to stay competitive, but with real costs to quality of life. A significant number of Germans thus feel that they have already made large sacrifices due to reunification, and this sociohistorical context shapes their attitude toward the euro crisis. Most notably, the number one concern in Germany in a 2012 PEW survey was not unemployment, the public debt, or inflation, but rising income inequality.[78]

This sentiment found an important expression in the rise of the *Alternative für Deutschland* party during the 2013 election campaign. Founded in 2013, the party is led by a group of conservative academics and intellectuals who oppose the German government's response to the euro crisis. The party actively campaigned for Germany to leave the euro and strictly enforce the no-bailout clause contained in the Maastricht Treaty. And while the party did not cross the 5 percent threshold necessary to enter the Bundestag (it received 4.7 percent of the vote), many blame its entry into the race for the failure of the Free Democratic Party to cross that same 5 percent threshold.

Moreover, the euro crisis allowed the government and German citizens to justify difficult welfare state cuts and real wage stagnation as part of the belt-tightening that all countries need to endure to compete in the global economy.[79] During the boom years, German governments cut social programs and introduced labor market reforms so as to enhance export competitiveness. The moral hazard argument is strengthened by Germany portrayed as the counterfactual, that is, other European governments could have used the period of economic growth to pass hard reforms, rather than engage in reckless spending. Finance Minister Schäuble made the contrast explicit in a series of interviews as he pointed to German structural adjustment in the early 2000s as evidence that similar reforms in the euro area would succeed.[80] He concluded,

> Ten years ago Germany was the "sick man of Europe." We had to tread a long and painful path to become today's engine of growth and anchor of stability in Europe. We too had extremely high levels of unemployment, even long after we started to adopt urgently necessary reforms. But without these reforms there can be no sustainable growth.[81]

At the same time, it allowed German voters to place the responsibility for reform largely on the backs of the governments that had engaged in reckless policies.

Conclusion and Implications for the Future of the Euro

The euro crisis has underscored the critical role that Germany plays in the currency's regional architecture. Importantly, the German government has persistently and often successfully pushed a policy response that is motivated by a concern for moral hazard by other member states. This has resulted in a reluctance to engage in quick and forceful commitments to regional bailouts. This is not to say that Germany has been paralyzed in the face of the crisis, or that it has been absent. From Greek sovereign debt to Spanish banking, Germany has actively engaged the euro crisis and has been an important member—if not *the* most important member—of the resolution team. But in these efforts, Germany has played the role of the reluctant leader—ever cautious and always circumscribed.

This caution has not been without risk. A number of academic and policy analyses suggest that the halting response inflated the cost of the crisis by sowing the seeds of market doubt and sparking wider contagion. It is then important to understand why policy alternatives stressing either German exports or the risk of contagion were rejected.

The central argument of this chapter is that the timing of reunification and the German recovery from it relative to the timing of the euro crisis set in motion a series of political economy dynamics that favored the moral hazard response over the alternatives. In particular, structural reforms enacted in response to the post-reunification economic malaise, as well as economic transfers resulting from reunification, undermined solidaristic impulses within the German electorate and policy elite. German citizens felt that they had already engaged in significant sacrifices to improve their own economy's competitive position. These adjustments would most certainly have been put off if not for the burden of reunification. Moreover, reunification undermined the political support for solidarity that had existed prior to reunification. Finally, the timing of reform put the German economic house in order prior to the crisis. As a result, when the crisis hit, it had the short-term perverse effect of stimulating the German export-based economy.

One of the more general implications of the argument is to refocus attention on the temporal context of regional governance. It is clear that there are considerable interactions between supranational and national policy within Europe. The Europeanization literature, for example, has demonstrated convincingly that considerable variation exists in the implementation of policy across the member states. The argument in this chapter points us in a new direction by considering the timing of decisions made at the level of member states relative to regional policy and how that timing shapes regional opportunity structures.

Moreover, the chapter complicates the notion of self-interest within foreign economic policy. In the context of the euro crisis, it is difficult to discern Germany's objective self-interest. Rather, there is a set of competing claims as to what should be driving national policy. The chapter hopes to help sort out the micro-foundations of support for one "self-interested" agenda over another and thus clarify the fundamental disconnect between German decision-makers and Germany's many international critics.

Finally, the chapter offers a somber assessment of the future of the euro. Given the history of monetary orders that lack the backing of the largest economic player, this erosion of support is particularly troubling. Economic crisis is an inherent part of economic interdependence and integration. In other words, the European project cannot always be a "feel good" story. For much of its history, structural constraints—the end of the Cold War and reunification—worked to bolster German support for an expansive role—hegemonic stabilizer, engine, or leader—regionally. Perhaps more important, market actors believed that Germany had taken on this burden. New structural conditions—the burden of reunification and its policy success—have now created an alternative dynamic, one in which Germany is much more weary of picking up the tab for others.

Ending the bargain, however, comes with real costs. The most immediate implication of this shift for the Eurozone is a widening in economic inequality between the core and the periphery. The cost of lending will continue to diverge as investors price in the risk of default in the periphery and, as a result, competitiveness disparities will grow. As citizens in some regions feel the brunt of these disparities, it risks the political legitimacy of the currency. And given the fiat nature of the currency, such legitimacy is critical for its continued stability. In the near term, German ambivalence will likely undermine the strength of the euro as a global reserve currency. Foreign central banks and investors will face the uncertainty of investing in a currency with a wavering commitment by its largest political power. In the long term, Germany's reticence puts the Eurozone in a precarious position vis-à-vis the next economic crisis, as it has eroded the faith of both market actors and member states in Germany's commitment to crisis management. This, in turn, raises the specter of the interwar monetary order in which no hegemonic authority could stabilize the region.[82]

The central point of this chapter, however, is to underscore that this shift in the German position is not irrational or absurd. Rather, it is the logical result of the incentives created by the interaction between the downstream consequences of reunification and the evolution of the euro—a currency union without a fiscal or political union.[83] Just as reunification played a core role in the currency's birth, it now stands as a significant impediment to its future success.

7

Europe's Middle Child

FRANCE'S STATIST LIBERALISM AND THE CONFLICTED POLITICS OF THE EURO

Mark I. Vail

Introduction: France's Conflicted Euro Politics

This chapter analyzes the legacies of France's "euro experience" and their implications for both France's political economy and the future of the euro. In the midst of the ongoing European debt crisis, the historical ambiguities of France's role in the euro and in the European Union have been thrown into sharp relief. From the immediate postwar period, and in a somewhat different sense after the Socialist "U-turn" of 1983, the related repudiation of reflationary Keynesianism, and the subsequent embrace of the *franc fort* and "competitive disinflation" as central economic strategies,[1] France sought to achieve on the European level the kind of international pre-eminence that it could no longer achieve on its own. In Tony Judt's elegant formulation, "Unhappy and frustrated at being reduced to the least of the great powers, France had embarked upon a novel vocation as the initiator of a new Europe."[2] This goal was bound up in the Franco-German alliance at the heart of the European project, whereby Germany achieved international legitimacy through its commitment to multilateralism, which in turn served as an obstacle to any potentially revanchist agenda (and, more importantly, dampened others' fears of renewed German nationalism).

France, by contrast, connected its economic destiny to the German social market economy, the European Community's largest and most powerful, in the hopes of securing a set of European arrangements that would both enshrine France as the European leader in international affairs and "facilitat[e] the voluntarist economic policies that, it was believed, would speed France's economic modernization."[3] Though the "voluntarist" tendencies of France's model of state-led growth abated somewhat after the 1983 abandonment of the *dirigiste* model, the French state remained a guiding force of French social and economic policy, even after the demise of *dirigisme*.[4] The French conception of the EU continued to rest upon a notion that the country could exert a greater influence in world affairs through its role in the EU while shaping European policy in a more voluntarist (and less "Anglo-Saxon") direction.

Simultaneously, however, France was never either entirely content to live in the shadow of its larger and more economically powerful neighbor or truly reconciled to the doctrinaire monetarism advanced by the Germans and indeed sought to preserve its ostensible status, dating from the earliest days of European integration, as the political leader of the European project. As German economic pre-eminence became clearer in the 1980s and 1990s, France worked to achieve a somewhat awkward synthesis between political leadership within the EU and a Franco-German economic partnership whereby to anchor its strategy of competitive disinflation to the German "external ally."[5] At the same time, it sought to advance an alternative model of economic governance, involving greater integration of national economic policymaking but in the service of a policy agenda both more interventionist and countercyclical than anything that Germany would be likely to tolerate.

The obvious tensions in this arrangement became more acute after German reunification in 1990, which, despite the enormous difficulty and expense involved in integrating nearly 20 million citizens in the former DDR into the West German social market economy, created a potentially even more economically powerful country of 80 million people at Europe's heart, no longer constrained by the geopolitics of the Cold War. Even though, as Abraham Newman argues in Chapter 6, Germany was reluctant to take on a role of regional hegemon, this new political and economic landscape nonetheless presented a stark and unanticipated challenge to France's claims to European political leadership, with President François Mitterrand and others openly fretting about renewed German nationalism and casting about for a new set of understandings of France and Germany's respective roles.[6]

In the run-up to the advent of the euro in the late 1990s, France's effort to reimagine its European role took on added urgency, as the incipient currency union represented both an opportunity and a challenge. It was an opportunity in the sense that France, Europe's second largest economy, stood to benefit from its role at the heart of what euro enthusiasts, both within and beyond France, hoped would become a new international reserve currency with all of the international economic heft that this implied, in the center of a new and powerful economic bloc capable of rivaling the United States. But it was also a challenge that highlighted many of the older ambiguities in France's European role: could France, as Germany's junior economic partner, successfully maintain its putative role as Europe's political leader in the context of a currency union closely (indeed almost slavishly) modeled on the German Deutschmark and the anti-inflationary, monetarist assumptions embedded within it, while also working to use its voice to soften those biases in favor of greater state involvement in the economy?

Equally important, how was France to reconcile its traditional *dirigiste* focus on the state as the engine of national economic development and its long-standing hopes to use its role in the EU to secure such a policy orientation at the European level, on the one hand, with, on the other, a context in which monetary policy was entirely removed from national decision-making processes and fiscal policy was severely constrained (though such constraints would often be recognized in the breach when it suited national interests) by the so-called Stability and Growth Pact designed to protect the euro's value? These ambiguities reflected a deeper conflict among France's reflexive statism, its embrace of the competitive-disinflationary strategy for which the Germans served as an external anchor, and its distrust of the austerity that lay at the substantive heart of the euro project.

As France struggled to define its new role in the early years of the currency union, its older (and increasingly implausible) claims to be Europe's leading voice—its firstborn son, as it were—in the international arena gave way to something more ambiguous, a role that one might view as analogous to that of a family's middle child. This role entailed two features of middle children in particular: the role of mediator in family conflicts and the struggle to be heard above the voices of elder siblings, whose leadership of the European "family" they contest. On the one hand, France was clearly larger and more powerful than the small European states to her north, such as the Benelux countries, and the less economically mighty ones bordering the Mediterranean, with respect to which it had long considered itself to be something of a guide and protector, as well as advocate of a less austere economic model than that favored by its richer, northern European neighbors. On the other, it still had to live in the shadow of the larger and more powerful Germany, struggling to make its voice heard internationally while both remaining loyal to their shared European project and providing a somewhat different vision of what the euro meant and how it should operate. France's effort to walk this line was only partially successful, as the growing discrepancy between French and German economic power both reflected and reinforced a growing imbalance between France's and Germany's respective influence in the venerable Franco-German partnership.

France also became Europe's middle child in another sense, mediating between the increasingly powerful and self-confident Germans and the less affluent, largely Mediterranean states for which Germany's model of export-led growth and massive trade surpluses were neither possible nor particularly desirable. This mediating role reflects a deeper and more substantive ambiguity in France's political-economic outlook. While French elites continue to privilege the state as a key driver and organizing force of the French model of capitalism, they have also embraced a broad project of economic liberalization and, though with greater ambivalence than the Germans, the deflationary and monetarist assumptions at the heart of the euro. Elsewhere, I have characterized these conflicting ideas at the heart of French capitalism as "statist liberalism," embracing both the state's leading role in economic policymaking and a substantively (but constrained) liberal vision of the content of economic policies.[7] Here, I argue that similar ambiguities—between neo-Keynesian statism and monetarist liberalism, between an embrace of the international influence attendant to the euro and deep ambivalence about the monetarist assumptions at its heart—have guided France's inconsistent policy preferences, highlighting its diminishing economic payoffs from the euro and its (often muted but nonetheless real) resistance to the German line in the ongoing European debt crisis. As in its effort to advance a substantive alternative to the German vision of a European economic future modeled on budgetary rigor, export competitiveness, and monetarism, France's efforts to mediate between northern and southern Europe have been undermined by a lackluster economic performance and the resulting tendency of Germany and other northern European countries to view France as an incipient (albeit outsized) member of the Eurozone periphery rather than its core.

Below, I examine France's role as Europe's "middle child" and the tensions at the heart of its "statist liberal" model during the past 15 years. In so doing, I develop this volume's broad focus on the political bargains that underpin the euro by analyzing France's evolving role within the single currency and the tensions between its domestic political-economic model and its long-standing yearning for European influence. I argue that, for whatever political and economic benefits France derived from the euro in the currency union's early days, such benefits have been more recently outweighed by both

political and economic costs, as German insistence on deflationary monetarism in the teeth of the European debt crisis is increasingly at odds with
France's "statist liberal" vision. I argue further that the euro crisis since 2009
has confirmed France's secondary role among Eurozone members, exposing
the implausibility of France's claims to be a co-equal leader of the European
project. In the 1990s and early 2000s, France fared relatively well, though the
euro's anti-growth biases and strictures on fiscal policy precluded an aggressive strategy to deal with the stubbornly high unemployment that persisted
during this period. In the aftermath of the post-2007 global financial crisis, such strictures have become more significant, as French authorities have
struggled to reconcile political and economic leadership in the Eurozone with
the desire to use the power of the French state to foster economic recovery.

As a result, France's long-standing effort to marry its political-economic
fortunes to Germany's ordoliberal system (which marshals but constrains
market forces, privileges high-end exports, and empowers non-state social and
economic actors), while pursuing at home a statist liberal model of top-down,
technocratic economic management coupled with the expansion of market
forces, has proved unfeasible. Even as the ongoing economic downturn has
prompted France to adopt a more statist version of "statist liberalism," the
politics of the European debt crisis have placed the country in the awkward
and increasingly untenable position of mediating between German-led monetarism and austerity and its own pressing domestic economic needs. This
dilemma, exacerbated by a recent record of tepid economic growth that has
weakened France's fiscal balance sheet and therefore undermined its credibility as a counterweight to Germany, has important implications for the
future of the euro, as France's role as the statist voice of countries that reject
the German-led austerity position and its ability to mediate between those
countries and the Eurozone's paymaster have been seriously compromised.
In practice, I suggest that the weakening of this alternative voice will reinforce the Eurozone's tendency toward monetarism and austerity, which may
ultimately have the (presumably unintended) consequence of forcing the exit
from the euro of weaker, peripheral countries such as Greece and Portugal.[8]

Below, I explore briefly the politics of France's position on the euro during
the period of the currency's creation, between the mid-1990s and the early
years of the first decade of the 2000s, when the country made a series of bets
that the euro would both shore up France's influence in European economic
policymaking and guide the substance of that policy in ways that were consistent with France's conception of its economic interests, even as it struggled
to adopt labor-market policies that would promote French competitiveness.

I then turn to the period of the financial and economic crisis since 2008 and focus more particularly on the impact of the Eurozone crisis on the French economy, elaborating on France's responses in fiscal and financial policy and its efforts to guide European responses to the debt crisis and act as a counterweight to Germany. I then return to France's "middle-child" dilemma, offer some observations about the legacies of the "statist liberal" model as they apply to the contemporary European policy context and revisit developments over the past 10 years with a view to sketching out likely scenarios for the fate of the euro and its member states.

France's "Faustian Bargain": European Commitments and National Policy during the Birth of the Euro

On May 10, 1981, François Mitterrand became the first Socialist French president since the advent of the Fifth Republic in 1958, marking the end of the nearly unchallenged Gaullist hegemony that had governed France during the previous two decades. It also embodied hopes for a new economic order in which the working class would be able to share more equitably in the fruits of economic growth. Supported by a large socialist majority in Parliament, Mitterrand and his government embarked upon a program that represented "the highest stage of *dirigisme*," using the powerful executive of the Fifth Republic to develop stepped-up industrial policies designed thoroughly to restructure the French economy while pursuing a "rupture with capitalism."[9] This policy of "redistributive Keynesianism"[10] aimed to enact the left's electoral promises to create jobs, support consumption and incomes, and shelter workers from increasingly widespread economic dislocation. The means by which this new agenda was to be implemented involved reorganizing the supply side of the economy, stimulating demand, "reconquering the domestic market," and relaunching state-funded research and development on a massive scale.[11]

Due to a combination of political as well as domestic and international economic pressures, however, this brave new political-economic order collapsed nearly as quickly as it had begun. In 1982–1983, the government made an abrupt "U-turn," opting for budget cuts and broad-based liberalization in an effort to resolve a series of mounting economic problems and to remain within the European Monetary System (EMS), which it viewed as an essential means of influence over European economic policy and whose limits on currency fluctuation were incompatible with reflationary *dirigisme*. This abrupt shift did not merely end the experiment with *dirigisme*, however; it also initiated a period during which the entire postwar edifice of *dirigiste* policymaking would be dismantled. During the remainder of the 1980s, successive French governments embarked upon an unprecedented project of market making, involving the abandonment of the system of preferential credit and industrial policies that had fueled *les trente glorieuses*, the replacement of bank lending with equity financing for French firms, and the introduction of a competitive financial services sector.[12] This process accelerated under the center-right administration of Jacques Chirac, whose government entered into an uncomfortable "cohabitation" with President Mitterrand in 1986. In five years, France had moved from the epitome of heavy-handed, *marxisant* statism to an acceptance of the market (though still rejecting Anglo-American conceptions of market hegemony) as the guiding principle for its economic development.

The outcome of this period of political ferment was a "statist liberal" model that both preserved the state as the central guide of economic policymaking even as it embraced elements of a more liberal, post-*dirigiste* identity with respect to policy substance. This somewhat schizophrenic political-economic orientation, which led to a series of market-conforming policy changes in the 1990s, would also color France's understanding of the stakes of the nascent single European currency. Even as French elites viewed the euro as desirable from the perspective of both policy substance (creating a Europeanized anchor for its strategy of "competitive disinflation") and process (giving France a prominent seat at the table at which European monetary policy would be made), they (including Jacques Delors himself) were always somewhat uneasy with the monetarist "orthodoxy" enshrined in the euro project, without which German approval was impossible.[13] France was willing to adopt a monetary regime that was more deflationary than it would have preferred for the sake of the political goals of shoring up its influence within European institutions and promoting a single currency that it hoped would enhance its international economic power. In a sense, France was thus making policy from the "outside in," allowing concerns about its role in the EU and the Economic and Monetary Union (EMU) to shape its own domestic policy regime, importing deflation from EMU and Germany for the sake of hoped-for future influence over the substance of European economic and monetary policy.

While this imported monetarism sat awkwardly with the continued prominent role of the French state in domestic policymaking, it did reinforce a pre-existing agenda of marketizing reforms in social and labor-market policy, which, by the late 1980s, had become the central thrust of French economic policy.[14] The "statist liberal" strategy during the mid-1990s and the first years of the 2000s privileged labor-market activation and the reduction of France's stubbornly high unemployment as its central goals. Though driven in part by rising French unemployment, itself a product of a combination of accelerating layoffs in the wake of the abandonment of *dirigisme* and a Bismarckian welfare state whose reliance upon payroll taxes led to high non-wage labor costs, the effort to rationalize and activate the labor market was also a product of mounting French concerns about maintaining competitiveness in an increasingly integrated European marketplace.[15] At the same time, French governments in the late 1990s and the first years of the 2000s displayed an increasing eagerness to rectify a growing fiscal imbalance (the budget deficit had grown steadily, reaching 4.1 percent of GDP by 2003).[16] This was due in large part to the perceived need (often exaggerated as a way of securing political cover for unpopular cuts) to meet the criteria of the Maastricht Treaty and, after 1999, the rules of the Stability and Growth Pact. Although French governments of both left and right were ambivalent about these criteria, which represented obstacles to their statist liberal strategy for economic revival, they also felt that "the painful economic prescription of respecting the Maastricht Treaty was a necessary evil in order for EMU to happen."[17]

In order to reduce unemployment, a goal that had taken on new urgency with the advent of EMU and its associated fiscal strictures, French authorities embarked on a series of labor-market reforms in the late 1990s and early 2000s. The first element of this strategy was to reduce reliance upon early retirement programs, which had become a favored (and politically popular) means of reducing labor supply during the 1980s. These programs offered something for everyone: workers were able to retire early with a minimal loss in income, firms were able to externalize the costs of their restructuring onto the state, and governments could limit the social unrest attendant to economic dislocation.

The second, and more significant, element of France's labor market strategy during this period was a series of reforms of unemployment insurance, which exemplified the country's statist liberal strategy for shoring up competitiveness and reducing fiscal imbalances. In June 2000, French employers and reformist unions (jointly responsible for the administration of France's system of unemployment insurance) struck a bargain that limited access to benefits and imposed significant new obligations upon job seekers. The resulting Plan d'Aide et de Retour à l'Emploi (PARE) ended benefit "regressivity" but made receipt of benefits contingent upon a signed contract between job seekers and the ANPE, or national employment office (the Projet d'Action Personalisé, or PAP), making benefits contingent upon a personalized job-search program.

The best-known and most controversial labor market reforms of this period, however, involved two laws which reduced the standard work week from 39 to 35 hours. The first so-called Aubry Law (named after socialist Labor Minister Martine Aubry), passed in 1998, increased social contribution exemptions to employers but made them conditional upon a firm's or sector's negotiation of a 35-hour weekly work-time limit, accompanied by proportional job creation. The second law, passed in 2000, introduced an exemption on social security contributions that rose with salaries up to 1.8 times the minimum wage (fixed above that level) and established annual limits on work time and overtime for firms or sectors that negotiated new contracts.[18] Aiming to create jobs through a combination of coercion and incentives, the measures were part of the government's efforts to appeal to its constituencies on the left and embodied its self-image as "the counter-current of ultra-liberalism."[19] While such rhetoric reflected the laws' partial political inspiration—an attempt by the new government to shore up support among its leftist constituencies—authorities realized that the law would have to limit costs to employers if the measure were to lead to any significant job creation. Here again, French authorities' statist liberal strategy involved an uneasy synthesis of liberalizing labor market measures designed to shore up French competitiveness and reduce unemployment and a leading role for the state in both guiding the reform process and imposing constraints on micro-economic decision-making.

France's statist liberal strategy thus reflected some of the same ambiguities at the heart of its conception of EMU. A combination of geopolitical aims (e.g., the French desire to constrain German power while preserving a platform for French influence) and economic considerations (the desire to anchor France's "competitive disinflationary" strategy within the EU and securing influence over European monetary policy) led the country to support the structure of a project whose content made many French elites ill at ease.[20] However one might wish to characterize this alloy of factors, it is clear that France's embrace of a highly monetarist, even deflationary set of rules modeled on the Deutschmark was never complete, nor was it entirely consistent with a set of policy commitments involving rationalizing the labor market while preserving some of the Keynesian tenets that had lain at the heart of the *dirigiste* model. During the 1990s and early 2000s, given generally supportive conditions in a recovering international economy and the absence of any serious crises on the European level, France was able to nuance these differences, pursuing a national strategy for labor-market competitiveness never sharply at odds with European constraints on fiscal and monetary policy and indeed reinforced by concerns about sustaining economic growth and redressing the country's fiscal imbalance.

Such a policy regime produced mixed results following the formal introduction of the euro in 1999, with banknotes and coins entering circulation in 2002. Like many of its Continental neighbors, France continued to suffer from chronically high unemployment and sluggish growth, though economic and labor market performance improved somewhat following the downturn of the early 2000s. At the same time, however, unlike Germany and even Italy, France's economic performance declined over the first decade after the euro's adoption, suggesting both constraints on growth and an eroding level of economic competitiveness. In 2004, French economic growth was 2.6 percent of GDP (compared to 1.2 percent in Germany and 1.7 percent in Italy). By 2008 (before the financial crisis and ensuing recession), growth had declined to a relatively stagnant –0.1 percent (collapsing to –3.1 percent in the following year).[21] Though Italian and German growth during this period was similarly slow, unemployment remained higher in France (at 9.3 percent in 2004 and 7.8 percent in 2008) than in Germany or Italy. French budget deficits remained higher than those of either Germany or Italy, and its competitive position collapsed, with the current account declining from 0.5 percent of GDP in 2004 to –1.7 percent in 2008 (see Table 7.1).

France's declining economic performance both reflected and accelerated a growing shift in the Franco-German relationship. In the 1980s, France could plausibly claim to be Germany's economic equal—a powerful (though differently constituted) country at the economic heart of Europe. After a painful period of adjustment following German reunification in 1990, however, and particularly since 2005, Germany's economic success has both legitimized its economic model and constrained France's ability to advance a plausible alternative to it. This economic divergence has reinforced a growing imbalance in the Franco-German relationship, to Germany's benefit and France's detriment. It is no longer plausible for France to claim the status of an equal partner to Germany in either economic or geopolitical terms, with the result that its ability to mediate between Germany and the European periphery has been compromised.

The costs of France's sluggish economic performance have not been limited to its relationship with Germany. With the advent of the post-2007 financial crisis, the deep global recession that followed in its wake, and the

Table 7.1 French Economic Performance in Comparative Perspective, 2004–2008

	France		Germany		Italy	
	2004	2008	2004	2008	2004	2008
Real GDP Growth	2.6%	−0.1%	0.7%	0.8%	1.7%	−1.2%
Unemployment Rate	9.3%	7.8%	10.5%	7.6%	8.0%	6.7%
Current Account (BOP) (% GDP)	0.5%	−1.7%	4.7%	6.2%	−0.3%	−2.9%
Budget Deficit (% GDP)	−3.6%	−3.3%	−3.8%	−0.1%	−3.6%	−2.7%

Source: IMF Statistics at http://www.imf.org/external/data.htm. Various tables.

apparently intractable and increasingly severe European debt crisis, France's slow economic decline forced authorities there to respond aggressively, rendering the previous statist liberal strategy of labor market liberalization and marketization unviable in the short term. As the world economy sputtered to a halt, France was forced to confront the implications of its earlier Faustian bargain and the inconsistencies within its statist liberal model in a new and more straightforward way. In the next section, I argue that, as the proverbial chickens of France's earlier decision to join EMU on German terms came home to roost, different elements of the country's statist liberal model came to the fore, with the authorities embarking on a strategy of modest Keynesian reflation.

As the Eurozone crisis worsened in 2010, furthermore, France once again struggled to square the circle of leadership in the Eurozone with its own distinctive trajectory of state-led domestic economic recovery. If the 1990s and pre-2007 period had been dominated by state-led labor-market reform designed to shore up France's competitiveness and reduce budget deficits in the early days of EMU, the post-2007 period has been characterized by somewhat conflicted resistance to the implications of the terms of EMU to which it had earlier agreed. In the process, France has sought to protect national French economic interests, temper Germany's hard-edged monetarism (though with greater force since the election of socialist François Hollande to the French presidency), and mediate between German economic leadership and doctrinal intransigence vis-à-vis the euro's smaller and poorer members and its insistence on an orthodoxy of austerity that promises to leave such countries to years of economic decline. Doing so has proved increasingly difficult, however, as France's continued efforts to offer a counterweight to Germany, and its related public defense of the broad outlines of Germany's austerity-based strategy for dealing with the crisis, have rendered unavailable the earlier Franco-German strategy of ignoring the Maastricht criteria when it suited them. As a result, France has continued to struggle with the ambiguities of its statist liberal model and the increasingly glaring contradictions between distinctive elements of its European strategy and its own domestic economic priorities.

Statist Liberalism in the Post-2007 Economic Crisis: France as Frustrated Arbiter and Alternative in the Eurozone

From the early 1990s, French authorities had favored a somewhat different understanding of the euro, despite the (somewhat grudging) formal acceptance of monetarist orthodoxy as the apparent price of the project's inauguration. This alternative approach centered on the conception of *gouvernement économique*, meaning a set of democratically elected European institutions responsible for fiscal and other policies historically reserved to member states and designed to act "as a counterpart to the independent European Central Bank."[22] The French hope was that such an arrangement could temper the influence of the austerity-minded Germans and would provide mechanisms whereby to stimulate the Eurozone's economy in the event of economic downturns, while also providing an embryonic core of a future coordinated fiscal union.

As in the early days of the European Community, the French goal was at once procedural and substantive. From a procedural point of view, it would allow the French government to have a continued voice in European level debates over economic policy, a voice viewed as all the more important given the relatively fixed and non-discretionary limits on fiscal policy represented by the so-called Stability and Growth Pact and the monetarist orthodoxy advanced by the highly independent European Central Bank (ECB). Substantively, France hoped to both defend itself against speculative attacks in foreign exchange markets and to preserve its leeway to pursue a selectively interventionist strategy with respect to domestic economic policy. Though such hopes remained frustrated during the 1990s and the early years of the first decade of the 2000s, despite some superficial German overtures in the direction of fiscal coordination, it remained at the core of the French conception of how the euro should eventually work.

The advent of the so-called European "sovereign debt crisis" (more accurately described as a bond-market crisis exacerbated by a deflationary monetary-policy regime)[23] in 2010 brought the differences between the French and German conceptions into sharp relief. This debate was driven by deepening divisions among EU member states about both the merits of the French claim that Europe needed deeper fiscal policy coordination and the intransigence of Germany and her northern European neighbors over the question of loosening some of the fiscal strictures imposed on countries such as Greece, Portugal, and Spain that were under assault by bond markets. In the early days of the crisis, French President Nicolas Sarkozy saw close cooperation with German Chancellor Angela Merkel as the best way of pressing France's case. In substantive terms, Sarkozy hoped to pursue a schizophrenic strategy of what Susan Milner has described as a strategy of "*ri*-lance (a mixture of austerity and Keynesian boosterism to finance innovation and R&D, financed by borrowing), which it sought to coordinate at the European level."[24]

Despite French hopes of tempering Germany's drive to austerity with elements of France's alternative vision, however, Germany's economic might and her necessarily central role in funding a series of (inadequate but numerous) bailouts of Eurozone countries led this "partnership" quickly to devolve into a relatively hierarchical relationship, derided as "Merkozy" by observers, in which Germany effectively led and France followed. Though Sarkozy seemed to view subordination to Merkel as the price of continued relevance (a reprise of France's position during the 1990s), he deeply resented this secondary role and continued to seek ways to constrain or dilute German orthodoxy. After one of a series of tense meetings with Merkel in late 2011 and early 2012, Sarkozy was able only to endorse a vague Franco-German commitment to economic growth, which he claimed "is the priority," without, however, ever convincing Merkel to diverge from Germany's austerity-first strategy, which was inimical to the very growth that both he and Merkel claimed to promote.[25]

Unable to pursue its vision of reflationary *gouvernement économique* on the European level, France retreated inward, centering its response to the crisis on the national level, though operating in the long shadow of the

Maastricht criteria, ECB monetarist orthodoxy, and the fetishization of austerity by Germany and her northern European allies (notably Finland and the Netherlands).[26] The 1990s and the years 2000–2008 were a period in which French policy operated from the "outside in," applying German and ECB-centered orthodoxy in a series of labor market reforms designed to support France's competitiveness and restore fiscal balance. The post-2008 era, however, can be thought of as the converse, with the focus of French policy reverting to the national level in the hopes of saving France's capitalist model and building on the success of the national response to press its case at the European level.

When the scope and severity of the financial crisis became clear in 2008, French authorities acted quickly and in ways that seemed to encapsulate the statist liberal adjustment strategy, even as it was constrained by Sarkozy's rhetorical commitment to austerity and fears that the euro-induced bond market crisis would spread to France. The first element of the government's response was a countercyclical stimulus package, representing one of the first such measures among all advanced economies that were members of the Organisation for Economic Co-operation and Development (OECD). Patrick Devedjian, one of Sarkozy's top economic advisors, expressed a sense of urgency, claiming that "all projects must start in 2009 [. . .] we want rapid results," and criticizing the Americans as having "wasted a lot of time."[27] The package, which amounted to 26 billion euro, or about 1.3 percent of GDP, prioritized public infrastructure projects, including four new high-speed rail lines, a new canal, renovations of public buildings, and investment in public enterprises.[28]

The core of the French response centered squarely on macroeconomic stimulus in classical Keynesian fashion, though it did so mostly through investment and support for business rather than efforts to boost consumption.[29] Sarkozy demanded that public enterprises "accelerate their future investments," since "events command us to move quickly in order to put the brakes on the recession."[30] This sense of urgency was echoed by Budget Director Eric Woerth, for whom the goal was "to spend as quickly as possible." Laurent Wauquiez, Secretary of State for Employment, added, "this is exclusively a policy designed to support job creation."[31] This effort, which was widely viewed by workers as a sop to business, fueled union-led protests demanding support for purchasing power and public employment. The government assumed that the generous network of automatic stabilizers (expanded in the 1980s and 1990s), coupled with renewed economic growth, would accomplish this task.[32] Then-Finance Minister Christine Lagarde observed, "The French model provides shock absorbers that were already in place. We haven't had to reinvent our unemployment, health, or welfare systems."[33]

Faced with mounting protests and following a summit with union leaders, however, the government agreed to an additional 3 billion euro aimed at supporting consumption, in part due to its recognition that the original package would be unlikely to provide a sufficient boost to domestic demand. The package included a 200 euro bonus for recipients of the *Revenu minimum d'activité* (RMA, or France's minimum income benefit), more generous unemployment benefits, and a 150 euro subsidy for low-income households.[34] It thus echoed the initial package's liberal orientation by focusing support on the poor, rather than undertaking a broad attempt to boost incomes across the economy. Taken together, then, the two packages reflected statist liberalism's "statist" (through direct spending and a macroeconomic orientation) and "liberal" (through means-tested income support and support for business) components. Equally important, their modesty relative to the efforts of other G20 countries reflected an understanding of the limits on fiscal expansion represented by European strictures. This constraint was particularly acute for France, whose public finances had never recovered from the collapse of economic growth in the aftermath of the crisis, with its public deficit soaring to 7.5 percent of GDP by the end of 2010.[35] Such limitations undermined Sarkozy's promise to "reconstruct a revitalized capitalism, better regulated, more moral and with greater solidarity,"[36] even if one assumes for a moment that such a promise was sincere.

France's relatively modest stimulus measures were thus focused largely on direct spending designed to revitalize the macro economy. This fact reflected the tension between the statist impulse and the limitations of France's earlier liberalizing turn and the constraints of existing European level strictures on public debt and deficits, as well as Sarkozy's rhetorical commitment to German-led austerity. By 2010, France had spent a total of 38.8 billon euro on stimulus measures (1.75 percent of GDP), less than half the amount spent in the US (3.8 percent). Of that amount, only 6.5 percent was composed of tax cuts (compared to 45.4 percent in Canada and 34.8 percent in the US), with the rest composed of direct spending.[37] About 10 billion euro were spent on public investment, including infrastructure (€1.4 billon), defense (€1.4 billion), publicly funded research (€700 million), monument restoration (€600 million), and subsidies to public enterprises (€4 billion).[38] The package was also quite short-term in focus, with 75 percent of the spending taking place in 2009 and only 25 percent (including the time-delimited income-support measures) in 2010.[39]

This tepid response was particularly surprising given France's relatively dire economic situation: in 2009, French GDP shrank by 3.1 percent and, by the end of the year, unemployment had risen to 9.5 percent, compared to Germany's 7.8 percent.[40] As the Eurozone crisis gathered momentum in early 2010 (developments which I discuss below in more detail), confronting an alarming budget deficit of 7.1 percent of GDP in 2010 and feeling compelled to follow the German austerity lead,[41] Sarkozy therefore proposed a total of 65 billion euro in combined budget cuts and tax increases in 2011, with only 7.5 billion euro scheduled for 2012, and most requiring implementation after the 2012 presidential election. These measures generally favored business and seemed designed to demonstrate commitment to the idea of austerity without enacting serious cuts that might undermine Sarkozy's weakening political position prior to the elections.

After 2010, as bond yields in a number of countries spiked and policymakers struggled to confront revelations about Greece's parlous financial state and the legacies of a decade of serious financial imbalances in the Eurozone, French authorities responded in ways that continued to reflect the tensions within its statist liberal model and the ambiguities and weaknesses of the country's political position in the Eurozone. The deepening crisis confronted France with a dilemma that placed the ambiguities of France's "middle-child" status in stark relief. Prior to the post-2007 global recession, France could maintain the illusion that, despite Germany's greater economic might, the legacies of the Franco-German partnership and French leadership in shaping European institutions (not to mention the fact that Jean-Claude Trichet, the head of the ECB, was a Frenchman) provided it with a co-equal voice in shaping policy within the Eurozone. The sudden realization of the extent of French and German banks' exposure to bad debt in the European periphery,[42] combined with gathering fears that the survival of the euro itself was in jeopardy, however, made France's traditional strategy of generalized public unity with Germany's position and *sub rosa* attempts to soften Germany's austerity line both more difficult and crucial to France's continuing relevance to Eurozone decision-making.

As the crisis gathered steam in 2010 and 2011, Sarkozy met with Merkel several times in an effort to work out a common position, but did so in ways that reflected continued German dominance more than French influence. Sarkozy's preferred strategy differed from the Germans' in several important respects. For Merkel, both the origins of the crisis and the appropriate response to it had to do with rules about fiscal discipline (insufficiently strict and enforceable before the crisis, requiring additional force and applicability thereafter). In addition, she favored maintaining the ECB's independence at all costs and limiting the power of political executives to intervene. Sarkozy, by contrast, emphasized European solidarity (meaning both support for weaker countries' financial systems and the creation of collective debt instruments such as Eurobonds) and a co-equal partnership between political leaders and monetary policymakers at the ECB. The *New York Times* provided an apt formulation of this different vision: "In Berlin, it is a common belief that the euro zone [would] be just fine if it could somehow turn itself into a large version of Germany: respectful of rules, wary of deficits, cautious of over expenditure. As for the French, they never love Europe so much as when they think it is like France: brilliant rhetoric, lots of rules and a capacity to go around them."[43] Given these divergent understandings of both the appropriate response to the crisis and the broader regime of Eurozone governance that it implied, Sarkozy faced a choice of how and to what extent to press these differing priorities, and the extent to which such differences should be aired privately or in the public arena.

The urgency of bailing out teetering peripheral financial systems, Germany's stronger economic position, and Sarkozy's political weaknesses militated in favor of a strategy of substantive concessions to the German line with vague and noisy pronouncements of a "common position" that failed to reflect France's alternative vision in any meaningful way. This unequal relationship was not lost on many observers, and the epithet "Merkozy," ostensibly used to denote a common Franco-German line, really reflected German dominance rather than parity and was generally understood to involve a pejorative reference to French subordination to German whims.[44] As this process played out at a series of summits and other high-level meetings between Merkel and Sarkozy—first at a Franco-German summit at Deauville in October 2010, and then most notably the declaration of a (vaguely defined) "mutual approach" at an October 2011 meeting in Berlin—it became increasingly clear that French relevance to the discussion was preserved only to the extent that France hewed imperatives of austerity. Speaking of France's and Germany's relative influence in governing the crisis, former European Commission President Jacques Delors stated bluntly, "The eurozone crisis has evolved in rhythm with the decisions—and lack of decisions—of Ms. Merkel. It is not nice to say so, but that is how it is."[45]

To be fair, Sarkozy could not shoulder all of the blame for his relative ineffectiveness at pressing the French vision, as he was playing a relatively weak economic hand in a crisis whose urgency and severity lent itself to short-term palliative measures and rule-based quid pro quos. In a context in which such short-term (though ultimately destructive) bargaining dominated, it would be hard for Sarkozy to secure the implementation of a much grander vision of *gouvernement économique* and long-term growth supported by political initiative.[46] On one level, the relative influence of the French and German position came down to the question of which partner was better able to finance the series of bailouts that came to dominate the euro crisis response in 2011. France's economic weakness relative to Germany during this period meant that France had few resources with which to bargain. In 2010, French GDP grew by a modest 1.6 percent, compared to a very healthy 3.6 percent in Germany. At the same time, France had much further to climb out of the depths of the recession in 2009; whereas German unemployment had dropped significantly since the financial crisis's immediate aftermath, declining to 7.1 percent at the end of 2010, French joblessness continued to rise, reaching 9.8 percent in the same year.[47] Even as French authorities confronted a weakening labor market and sluggish growth, their poor budgetary position thus left them with few resources with which to spur growth or job creation or to put any effective pressure on Germany, by necessity the largest paymaster of bailout funds, to alter its stance on austerity or the conditions imposed on recipient nations.

Despite such strictures, after Sarkozy's loss to his socialist rival François Hollande in May 2012, French authorities once again seemed ready to add some substance to the long-standing French claims to represent an alternative to the German policy response to the crisis. Proclaiming that "it's not for Germany to decide for the rest of Europe," Hollande campaigned on promises to reverse Sarkozy's modest spending cuts and adopt new spending initiatives designed to restore growth and create jobs.[48] These included hiring 60,000 additional teachers and subsidizing 150,000 new youth jobs, rolling back Sarkozy's reform that increased the retirement age from 60 to 62, and boosting the annual back-to-school allowance by 25 percent. More controversially, he promised to finance these measures in part through a 75 percent tax on households with annual incomes over one million euro and higher taxes on large firms, while also raising the minimum wage to support consumption. While Sarkozy's variant of statist liberalism tended to favor finance, big business, and investment, Hollande's variant emphasizes universalistic measures to boost consumption and economic equality.

With respect to EU policy, moreover, Hollande's election represented a shift in discourse and the apparent possibility for alterations to some aspects of Europe's new Fiscal Pact, negotiated in December 2011 under Merkel's and Sarkozy's leadership and ratified by most members of the Eurozone in the spring of 2012. Just as France has tried to walk the line between statism and competitive disinflation at home, the country is once again working to move European policymaking in a less deflationary direction, even as Hollande and his government proclaim support for the overall thrust of the fiscal compact. During his campaign, Hollande promised—if elected—to demand the renegotiation of some elements of the pact, particularly in ways that would offer greater support for economic growth as a counterbalance to its single-minded emphasis on austerity. Following his election, Hollande proclaimed that he intended to give "a new direction to Europe" and that "austerity need not be Europe's fate."[49] Such language furnished hope among some leaders in other countries, particularly on the European periphery and on the left, that Hollande's election represented a chance for the revival of a French-style *gouvernement économique*, involving both greater coordination of European fiscal policies and a push to move such policies in a direction more supportive of economic growth. Despite claims by Merkel and German Finance Minister Wolfgang Schäuble that they would not permit any renegotiation of the Fiscal Compact (and that "we cannot work like that in Europe"), German authorities have, largely at French urging, expressed some openness to negotiating additional agreements that might attenuate some of the harsh edges of the austerity regime.[50]

That said, Hollande's promises of a new direction in Europe, away from grinding austerity toward a new emphasis on investment and growth, have come up against some significant economic and political obstacles and will likely prove to be more rhetorical than real. Speaking simultaneously to two audiences—his leftist supporters at home and German and European authorities abroad—Hollande has felt compelled to walk a line between maintaining fundamental commitments to the European Union's policymaking process, on the one hand, and a rejection of much of that regime's substance, on the other. In classic middle-child fashion, France under Hollande is once again trying to reconcile opposing political blocs, a fact that has led to significant inconsistency in both his rhetoric and his policy initiatives. Even as he proclaimed, prior to his first visit to Greece as president, that he "reject[s] a Europe that condemns countries to austerity without end," he sought to establish credibility with his European counterparts and with policymakers in Brussels by honoring a commitment made by Sarkozy to cut the country's budget deficit to 3 percent of GDP, a level at which the ratio of debt to GDP should stabilize, by the end of 2015.[51]

Such promises were unrealistic, given the country's deficit level of 4.8 percent of GDP at the end of 2012 (in excess of the government's target of

4.5 percent), as French authorities were forced to recognize in March, when they revised the 2013 estimate upward to 4.1 percent of GDP.[52] All of these shifting commitments and rhetorical inconsistencies mask a difficult and ironic underlying truth: in order to gain the credibility and influence required to counter the austerity-first regime at the European level, France must first adopt some elements of that austerity regime at home. Such a dilemma poses both political and economic risks for Hollande, whose popularity has been slipping steadily since his election, in part due to frustrations with rising joblessness and sluggish growth, and in part due to perceptions that he has failed to become the promised counterweight to German dominance of European economic policy.[53] It also likely means that France will prove increasingly unable to act as a voice for an alternative, less austere, pro-growth future for the euro, leaving the arrangement predominantly in the hands of northern European advocates of austerity.

Despite the pressures of France's budgetary situation and the challenges of walking the line between credibility and growth, France has come to represent a touchstone for those wishing for the emergence of an anti-austerity coalition to counterbalance the Germans and their northern European allies, consisting perhaps of Spain, Portugal, and, since Renzi's arrival, especially Italy. Leaders in all of these countries (along with Germany's opposition Social Democrats) have increasingly (and with growing sharpness) questioned Merkel and Schäuble's recipe for European recovery, using France as an example of the potential for resistance to the German line. They have also pointed to the economic stagnation of the UK, which has pursued austerity with almost sado-masochistic zeal under David Cameron's coalition government, even though 2013 and 2014 saw the advent of rapid (though distributionally highly inequitable) growth, driven primarily by the development of a new housing bubble.[54] At the same time, however, as many observers predicted at the time of his election, Hollande has felt compelled to adopt some modest austerity measures of his own at home, including 30 billion euro of spending cuts and tax increases adopted in September 2012, which preserved the promised 75 percent marginal rate on top incomes. In part, such a move represents Hollande's wishes to reassure a nervous Germany and bond markets that he is not an old-style Socialist oblivious to economic reality,[55] even though the cuts that he has proposed are actually quite modest by European standards. At the same time, however, they represent a somewhat different vision of the relationship between European and domestic policymaking, reflected in Hollande's concomitant promises to increase spending on consumption and to expand the public sector. Also, and equally important, Hollande prefers to use tax increases rather than spending cuts as a significant ingredient in his recipe for fiscal consolidation, especially during his early years in the Elysée.

Not limited to a pattern of domestic policymaking more comfortable with spending increases and intervention in the economy than his German counterparts, Hollande's policy proposals also differ from Merkel's with respect to his vision for EU policy. He has been among the most vocal advocates of Eurobonds, a greater role for the European Investment Bank, European investments in infrastructure, and other measures designed both to increase policy coordination among member states and to stimulate growth. Hollande is once again trying to reconcile a statist vision of economic development with an austerity-based policy regime in ways that seek some degree of national economic policy autonomy and to soften some of the austerity orientation of European policymaking. Ever the middle child, France is working to establish a clear role among its European siblings in ways that are both true to its statist liberal tradition and consistent with continued relevance and influence in the European conversation about how best to address the most serious crisis of confidence in European institutions since World War II. The euro crisis has shaken voters' faith, not only in the wisdom of particular European policy positions, but rather in the sustainability of the European project as a whole. It remains to be seen how successful Hollande will be in these endeavors, but it is clear that he, unlike his predecessor, has introduced a new and distinctive voice into European policy debates and one with which Germany, despite its status as senior partner, will have to contend in the coming years.[56]

The Middle Child in a Dysfunctional Family: Implications for the Future of the Euro

This chapter has argued that France's statist liberal model of economic development, solidified in the early days of EMU, has created a series of tensions and ambiguities within the country's trajectory of economic policy and its position in the European Union in general and the Eurozone in particular. From the earliest days of postwar European integration, France sought to achieve influence at the European level that it could not achieve on its own, while cementing a close relationship with Germany that would act as the fulcrum of that strategy. Always the junior partner in this relationship in economic terms, France nonetheless saw itself as the spiritual core of European institutions and as the pre-eminent representative of Europe on the world stage.

With the advent of the Maastricht Treaty in the early 1990s and the consolidation of EMU later in that decade, however, this national self-conception proved increasingly difficult to sustain, as France struggled to reconcile its much-vaunted statist model of economic development with the liberal, monetarist economic-policy regime at the core of EMU. In the late 1990s, France managed this contradiction by embarking on an ambitious set of labor market reforms designed to further France's "competitive disinflationary" strategy and adapt it to an increasingly challenging international economic environment. But like Germany, France chose to ignore the strictures of the Stability and Growth Pact when it suited its interests. In contrast to France's initial European strategy, this approach involved an implicit acceptance of the political *and* economic pre-eminence of Germany and, at least in the medium term, the German understanding of the Eurozone as predicated upon fiscal austerity, an anti-inflationary monetary policy, and a de-emphasis of statist strategies for achieving economic growth.

All of the above conformed to and served the interests of Germany's ordoliberal, export-based economy, rather than France's statist liberal model, which relied upon rapid economic growth and significant job creation in order to make liberalization politically viable while preserving the economic sustainability of its social model. This choice effectively meant accepting a relatively stagnant economy and high levels of unemployment, which the euro's fiscal and monetary policy regime prevented it from addressing successfully. In this sense, John Driffill and Marcus Miller are right to claim that the label of the so-called Stability and Growth Pact that served as EMU's foundational bargain is a misnomer, since the Pact "increases unemployment and slows growth."[57] This outcome has both put France in increasingly difficult economic straits and undermined its credibility as an alternative voice to Germany's model of "austerity for all."

These trends were both accelerated and exacerbated after 2009. Though France was able to reconcile EMU with its statist liberal model in the relatively calm 1990s, this task became much more difficult in the aftermath of the post-2007 financial crisis and the "Great Recession" that followed in its wake. As opposed to its approach in the 1990s, when France internalized the deflationary biases of EMU primarily by liberalizing its labor market, in the latter period, the country prioritized domestic policy imperatives and returned to an older, statist pattern of policymaking, enacting a modest Keynesian stimulus package and then shifting to a more pro-growth strategy under Socialist President François Hollande.

The scope of Hollande's tactical shift, however, was constrained by France's earlier embrace of the stringent fiscal criteria for EMU and the strongly felt imperative of preserving its leadership position within a currency union at odds with its preferred economic strategy. Having signed on to a deflationary and anti-growth EMU for largely political reasons, France found itself much more constrained with respect to economic policy than it would have liked in the face of an unprecedented and unexpected financial and economic crisis. If the statist liberal model represented a uniquely French response to the political-economic imperatives of the 1990s, it is clearly less well adapted to the contemporary context of sluggish growth, high unemployment, and an intractable European debt crisis. Even as it struggled to preserve its place at or near the head of the Eurozone policymaking table, then, it did so in ways that undermined the chances of achieving the substantive outcomes that such leadership was meant to foster.

As a result, the imbalances in the Franco-German partnership are unlikely to be resolved. France continues to struggle to define its position in the Eurozone and to offer a coherent alternative model to that advanced by its "elder" German sibling. While François Hollande's election has led to a more explicit embrace of pro-growth strategies at home and rhetorical contestation of Germany's austerity obsession, it seems increasingly unlikely that France can square these rhetorical and political circles. In practice, this means that the future of the euro is likely to be an austere one—a fact which, as other contributors to this volume suggest, might well force the exit of some of its economically more vulnerable members. Even as the orthodoxy of austerity becomes more and more entrenched within the Eurozone, France's ability to mediate between core and periphery will continue to be constrained by the Faustian bargain it made in the early 1990s, when it bought political relevance at the cost of a big part of its statist, pro-growth soul.

In this sense, France's continued calls for some form of *gouvernement économique* would seem to reflect weakness as much as strength; having long ago lost the battle with Germany for lead authorship of Europe's economic future, it is relegated to the second-best strategy of trying to soften the edges of an austere currency union. Though France is unlikely to return to the more liberal market variant of "statist liberalism" that characterized its policy strategy in the 1990s and the first years of the 2000s, it is also unlikely that Hollande will be able to successfully implement at the European level the more pro-growth version that he claims to favor, at least as long as the European debt crisis and prevailing economic stagnation endure. Indeed, the endemic political problems surrounding his administration, along with intensifying recrimination focused on rising unemployment and declining competitiveness, will likely undermine Hollande's capacity to advance an alternative agenda.[58]

If it does, then the chances for the euro to survive, at least in its current form, seem slim indeed. From the beginning, the European project was predicated upon a strong Franco-German partnership, which provided the Germans with legitimacy and the French with the potential to extend the scope of its international influence and economic might in the face of its declining postwar status. It also promised to allow the French to accomplish the kind of economic voluntarism that, at least after 1983, it could no longer accomplish on its own. Its embrace of liberal monetarism and a single currency that inhered those priorities in the 1980s and 1990s, however, effectively traded away its potential to shape the euro in a less austere, more growth-friendly, and more politically and economically sustainable direction. In this sense, Hollande's criticism of Eurozone austerity and French talk of *gouvernement économique* over the past decade is really full of sound and fury, signifying very little. Such objections are much like closing the barn door after the horse has escaped.

French weakness and subordination to the German vision of the euro present European authorities with a stark choice. As many observers have argued, the single currency both depended upon and was designed to drive the development of European political union. All but the most starry-eyed Europhiles recognize that this project has failed.[59] In the absence of some sort of meaningful political union, and the mechanisms of fiscal adjustment and compensation that such would entail, Germany, its rich northern European neighbors, and the ECB must choose between a smaller Eurozone and a different policy regime. If they keep insisting on endless austerity that seems to have become the ECB's orthodoxy, it is hard to envision a Eurozone that retains all of its current members. Such pessimism seems even more warranted in view of the disturbing results of the May 2014 elections to the European Parliament, in which anti-EU parties on the far right, including France's *Front National*, translated anger at the economic effects of austerity and the remoteness of European policymaking processes into electoral success.

If the single currency is to survive in its current form, and to enable it to recover some of its lost legitimacy, European monetary and German economic authorities must be willing to accept greater consumption and inflation in the Eurozone core, some monetization of sovereign debt, and less stringent conditions for fiscal transfers among member states. Given their unwillingness to accept such solutions to date, it seems likely that the euro can survive only with a smaller and more economically homogenous membership. To paraphrase Adolphe Thiers's quip in the 1870s about the relationship between the nascent Third French Republic and conservatism, "the euro will be more accommodating, or it will not exist," at least not in its current form. Whatever officials in the ECB and the European core decide, for reasons both economic and geopolitical, it seems unlikely that France will be able to play a forceful role in bringing about a shift in policy orientation. With respect to Eurozone economic policy, Europe's middle child seems to have become more an obsequious younger sibling than the family mediator or alternative conscience.

8

The Troubled Southern Periphery

THE EURO EXPERIENCE IN ITALY AND SPAIN

Jonathan Hopkin

Introduction

Southern Europe has been in the frontline of the Eurozone debt crisis that developed shortly after the global financial crisis of 2007–2008. Greece and Portugal have both signed up to formal bailouts, while Spain has taken European funds to bail out part of its banking system. Italy, which has so far averted a bailout, poses perhaps the greater existential threat to the euro: it is the largest crisis economy by some distance, and holds the third largest stock of sovereign debt in the world, after the United States and Japan. The "Draghi put"—the ECB's commitment to act as lender of last resort to European governments after rolling out its controversial program of outright monetary transactions (OMT) in September 2012—has shored up the southern European bond markets, but their economies remain mired in deep recession and their political leaderships are shedding credibility at an alarming rate. The fate of the euro hangs on the outcome of the crisis in the southern European democracies, but the social and political dynamics behind the crisis are ill understood. Perceptions of the South are dominated by an awkward combination of fatalistic stereotypes and overly optimistic expectations of deep economic reform.

This chapter argues that current policy toward the South of the Eurozone is predicated on a set of false premises, and is doomed to failure. Some of these premises relate to the design failures of the euro itself, and are well explained elsewhere in this volume.[1] The contribution of this chapter is to explain the impact of euro membership on the southern European political economy, and to assess the political and institutional parameters of the response to the crisis. In particular, the following sections seek to move beyond the standard narrative of debtor and creditor nations, and to examine the political and distributional consequences of monetary union within the southern member states. Understanding the nature of the crisis requires an appreciation of the relationship between winners and losers within each country, and the conflictual and contested politics of how to respond to the austerity and reform programs imposed from outside. The chapter concludes that the current approach to resolving the crisis is doomed to failure precisely because it lacks such an understanding, and as a result risks undermining southern Europe's economic future and even the institutional foundations of its democratic systems. By extension, it threatens the very survival of the euro in its current form.

Joining the Euro: Mistaking the Starting Gun for the Finish Line?

European integration played a key role in the establishment of democracy in southern Europe. The polarized and unstable democracy that emerged out of the collapse of Fascism in Italy was bolstered by its Christian Democratic leaders' close involvement in the creation of the European Economic Community (EEC), which locked the country into the Western bloc and forced the hand of the powerful Italian Communist Party. In Greece, Portugal, and Spain, the prospect of EC membership was crucial in persuading business elites of the virtues of political reform, and the close ties that developed between European socialist parties ensured cross-party support for Europeanization. The economic growth and flows of structural funds enjoyed after entering the Common Market during the 1980s contributed to high levels of popular support for the European project. Joining the euro was therefore seen as a natural step in a historic trajectory of modernization and convergence with the rich and stable democracies of northern Europe.

As a result, the likely consequences of joining the Economic and Monetary Union (EMU) were not the subject of extensive public discussion in southern European countries until after the euro was created. While countries such as France, Germany, and of course the United Kingdom engaged in intense debate on the risks and possible benefits of the single currency, in the southern democracies euro membership was an unquestioned national objective, with only peripheral and mostly extremist political forces offering an alternative view. The overriding sentiment was that participation in monetary union would lock in the gains of EC membership, and would spur further modernization and growth. To the extent that the South's past difficulties with inflation and fiscal policy were considered, the dominant view was that euro membership would provide an anchor and *vincolo esterno* (external constraint) to improve institutions and to facilitate reforms that would otherwise prove impossible.[2]

The run-up to monetary union provided apparent support for this view. The southern countries showed a degree of political commitment to the euro project that discredited critics who had dismissed them as the "Club Med" countries, unprepared for the rigors of monetary union. Spain's Socialist government under Felipe González adopted a tough monetary policy through the 1980s, joining the European Monetary System (EMS), building up currency reserves, and ignoring the protests of González's union allies at soaring unemployment. When the crisis of the EMS Exchange Rate Mechanism hit in 1992, González absorbed the huge political cost in a (failed) attempt to remain inside the EMS even after Italy and the United Kingdom had opted for devaluation. In Italy, after the EMS crisis brought down a long-standing pro-European political elite, a series of technocratic and semi-technocratic governments adopted tough budgetary measures and extensive administrative reforms to stay on track for monetary union.

The social partners played a key role in this process.[3] Trade unions accepted wage restraint and restrictions on public sector spending growth, on the understanding that euro membership would secure investment and employment into the future. The willingness of southern European voters to bear sacrifices for the sake of the euro held out the prospect of continued reform and successful integration into the monetary union. Deficits, inflation, and interest rates converged in timely fashion to meet the Maastricht criteria (the Italian debt-to-GDP ratio of over 100 percent being finessed away). The smooth switch-over to the new currency, with minimal disruption to financial markets and everyday transactions, allayed many of the fears of the skeptics. So why did things go so wrong?

A common response to this question is that European governments, once the key objective of euro membership was in the bag, assumed they could begin to enjoy the benefits of monetary union without facing the political costs of further structural reform.[4] The cross-national econometric evidence for this is mixed,[5] but the European Commission and various European think tanks rebuked southern European governments for their slow progress in meeting reform targets even before the crisis.[6] Strategies of wage moderation agreed between the social partners in the 1990s were relaxed after euro entry,[7] and after the stringent budgetary measures taken to meet the Maastricht criteria on debt and deficit levels, fiscal policy tended to loosen after 1999, although the southern European countries were not the worst offenders (Germany being the first country to breach the 3 percent deficit limit imposed by the Stability and Growth Pact).

The narrative of southern European recklessness has been popular in northern Europe and in the European institutions, as it fits with a diagnosis and a set of remedies to the current crisis that are politically roadworthy in Germany (for reasons that Abraham Newman explains in Chapter 6) and that avoid challenging the essential parameters of monetary union. The focus on fiscal austerity and structural reforms places the onus for resolving the crisis on the debtor nations, instead of focusing on cross-national fiscal transfers or coordinated stimulus measures that would shift the burden onto Germany and would require costly institutional changes at the European level. The introduction of conditionality into the various bailout measures—commitments to specific structural reforms before funds are released—allows European leaders to establish the principle that financial assistance comes at a price, in the hope of reducing moral hazard. The southern countries are served notice that they cannot free ride on the inflationary anchor provided by the euro, and will have to reform in order to secure their future within the currency area.

Beyond its popularity in Brussels, Frankfurt, and Berlin, this narrative is in fact surprisingly widely accepted in the southern European countries themselves.[8] Pew research recently revealed that even after several years of austerity-induced recession, a majority of voters in Italy, Spain, and Portugal wished to remain in the euro, and most favored spending cuts as the best policy to deal with their governments' debt problems.[9] Political and business elites have shown a remarkable degree of commitment not only to the euro project, but also to the measures demanded of them by the European institutions, even though even the IMF has rejected these measures as entirely counterproductive.[10] Moreover, there has been a surprising lack of interest among the debtor governments in coordinating their efforts within the European arena to obtain a more favorable policy mix, in part due to the reluctance of France to play a leadership role, for reasons explained by Mark Vail in Chapter 7 of this volume. The kinds of loose, proto-Keynesian attitudes attributed to the South in various quarters are in fact hard to detect in either public opinion or the political debate.

What is more, the southern European countries have actually made considerable efforts to reform their economic institutions in line with the recommendations made by the European leadership and the policy consensus in organizations such as the Organisation for Economic Co-operation and Development (OECD) and the European Commission. Price controls, restrictions on entry into domestic markets, state ownership of industrial companies, and labor market protections have all been significantly reduced across the southern economies, and on many measures of regulation they have come close to converging with core countries such as France and Germany (see Figure 8.1). Considering the South's history of political control over markets and its legacy of legalistic[11] economic regulation, this constitutes a major transformation of its institutions of economic governance.

Badly regulated product and labor markets and inefficient public spending have certainly been a drag on competitiveness and an impediment to adjustment, making the response to economic shocks difficult. But the southern problem is far from a case of foot-dragging and resistance to reform. If anything, reform has at times been too hasty and has undermined the case for market liberalism, as illustrated in the case of Italian privatizations.[12] Not only did the reforms of the 1990s make less of a difference to the sustainability of the euro project than policymakers believed, in some ways euro entry entrenched some of the most important weaknesses of the southern European political economy.[13] The rest of this chapter will illustrate how the

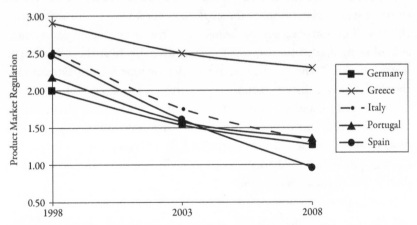

FIGURE 8.1 Product Market Regulatory Reform in Germany and Southern Europe, 1998–2008

Source: OECD, Product Market Regulation (PMR) Indicator (higher values = more regulated product markets) http://www.oecd.org/eco/reform/indicatorsofproductmarketregulationpmr.htm

euro has changed the political economy of southern Europe, and will assess how these changes are shaping the political reaction to the crisis.

Mediterranean Workers: From Restraint to Stagnation

The proximate causes of the crisis in southern Europe are now so well understood that it is difficult to recall how oblivious policymakers were of the risks that were building up in the early years of the euro. In 2005, at the height of Spain's construction boom, the European Commission triumphantly proclaimed that "the story of the Spanish economy in EMU is a dazzling one."[14] Though Italy's economic performance was far less dazzling, there was surprisingly little pressure on the Italian governments early in the first decade of the 2000s to exploit a favorable interest rate environment to significantly reduce its stock of public debt. It has since become clear that the rapid financial integration spurred by monetary union, added to the questionable decision by the European Central Bank to treat all Eurozone government debt as equally valid for collateral, created bubble-like conditions for sovereign debt in the South.[15]

These conditions played out very differently across southern Europe, as they were refracted through varying domestic institutions and economic structures. But what the different cases have in common is that monetary union did not have the desired effects. By smoothing transaction costs, the euro was supposed to complete the single market for finance, "facilitating the efficient allocation of savings to the most profitable investment opportunities and allowing market participants to partly diversify away the risk of asymmetric shocks."[16] The rapid convergence of Eurozone interest rates around those of the low-inflation economies of northern Europe meant a dramatic easing of credit conditions in southern Europe. Policymakers assumed that financial institutions were capable of allocating capital efficiently, and that flows of money to the southern countries reflected real prospects for growth through productivity-enhancing investment. This assumption proved to be a glaring flaw in the euro's design.

Rather than encouraging economic reform and growth, easy credit in fact did little to bring about the kinds of investments needed to make real productivity gains. The large flows of capital from North to South did provide an injection of demand that fueled growth, thus attracting more capital in a classic bubble cycle, particularly in Greece and Spain. But productivity growth remained elusive and much investment was directed into traditional non-traded sectors such as construction (particularly in Spain), or channeled by government and private sector borrowing through to consumption, as in Greece. In Italy falling interest rates facilitated the servicing of its very high public debt levels despite low growth rates. In short, it has become clear that the assumptions of allocative efficiency in Eurozone financial markets were way off the mark. Capital flows instead reflected a "convergence trade," which in the short run made money for banks, but created the conditions for ruinous capital flight when conditions changed.

The boom conditions created in parts of the South by the great wave of money flowing from the North allowed Greece and Spain in particular to build huge imbalances on their current accounts, pushing up real exchange rates.[17] The main beneficiaries of these new circumstances were not, in fact, unionized workers in the industrial sector, whose wage demands remained moderated by market pressures (and the awareness that competitive devaluations were no longer possible), but producers in the non-traded sector of the economy. Although it has become common to blame unions and labor market regulation for the breakdown of wage restraint after euro entry, this ignores the obvious point that employers and governments can also defect on collective agreements, and that workers' wage demands are not the only source of inflation. In fact, the unsustainable conditions of the initial years of the 2000s did not favor unionized core production workers, but instead advantaged economic sectors, which were for the most part inimical to the labor movement.

In Italy, the restraint and reforms of the center-left governments of the 1990s gave way to the election of an uncompromising right-wing government under Silvio Berlusconi in 2001, which dramatically changed the political climate. The Berlusconi government set out to divide the union movement, striking deals with the centrist federations UIL and CSIL and marginalizing the main left-wing union, the CGIL. The employers' federation Confindustria—long dominated by large industrial firms—also had a change in leadership in 2001, with the election of a representative of the small and medium-sized enterprise sector. In consequence, Confindustria collaborated with the Berlusconi government in an attempt to dismantle national-level bargaining in favor of firm-level agreements and to reduce labor protections, leading to a rift with the CGIL.[18] Ironically, this had the effect of relaxing wage moderation, as firms were unable to resist the pressure to set wages in line with productivity gains, after the period of wage stagnation immediately prior to euro entry. Even so, real wages in Italy declined in the 1999–2006 period.[19]

In Spain, too, social pacts had played an important role in meeting the convergence criteria, with public sector workers accepting a pay freeze to meet the Maastricht deficit target and industrial workers signing up to non-inflationary agreements.[20] But boom conditions in the early 2000s, driven by a doubling of foreign direct investment in the first half of the decade and easy credit, relaxed the pressure on unions and employers to curb pay rises, and rapidly falling unemployment increased workers' bargaining power. The lead sector driving growth was construction, as a housing bubble drove reckless overinvestment in new builds, with a consequent boom in demand for low-skilled labor.[21] In these heady circumstances, nominal wage growth outstripped productivity growth, and the ready availability of low-skilled jobs sparked both an acceleration of immigration and a decline in demand for further education.[22] As in Italy, the sheltered services sector was able to exploit buoyant demand conditions to hike prices, limiting real wage growth despite nominal wages rising faster than productivity.[23] Spain's boom in consumption was financed by cheap credit and the "wealth effect" of rising house prices, rather than the growth of real incomes.

In both Spain and Italy, unit labor costs ended up rising rapidly relative to Germany and the Eurozone average, despite workers making relatively limited gains in living standards. The available econometric analysis of wage growth in the Eurozone suggests that our understanding of the reasons for southern Europe's loss of competitiveness needs to be refined.[24] Although unit labor costs did rise faster in the Eurozone periphery than in the core countries, these rising costs did not reflect an unsustainable rise in real wages. Instead, with the exception of Greece, real wage growth in most of the South was only out of line compared to Germany, and remained in keeping with the rest of the Eurozone.[25] The ECB's analysis also reveals that nominal compensation in the industrial sector (the most exposed to competitive pressure) remained stagnant in Spain and barely increased in Italy.[26] So the emerging imbalances cannot be explained in terms of a simple story of union militancy and government profligacy. Instead, the largely neglected role of business elites and other conservative interests needs to enter the equation.

Entrenching a Conservative Coalition: The Unequal Gains of Monetary Union

The experience of economic reform in southern Europe prior to and after Monetary Union reveals a paradox. The prospect of euro entry galvanized southern political leaders and social partners to deploy the standard policy tools to address their historic problems of high inflation and periodic devaluations. Euro entry, ironically, implied the dismantling of the institutional arrangements that had secured low inflation in the run-up to the euro: a national central bank with a credible threat to raise rates if wages did not behave, and a government committed to a tight public deficit target. Joining the euro meant that inflationary price hikes or wage rises would no longer necessarily elicit a policy response from the monetary authority.[27] Given the weak state of the German economy in the late 1990s and the first years of the 2000s, ECB policy would not act to restrain inflation in the southern periphery, and adopted what amounted to an aggressively pro-cyclical policy. Not only did this expose the South to a violent downturn after 2007–2008, it also had major distributional consequences within southern societies.

As we saw in the previous section, core production workers in southern Europe did not make significant gains in living standards during the period of the bubble economy prior to 2008. Neither, contrary to the standard narrative, did the public sector go on an unprecedented spending binge. Instead, the big winners from the resulting boom were to be found in the sheltered sectors of the economy: construction, the services sector (retail, transport, leisure, and personal services), and of course the banks. These sectors had every interest in blocking the kind of reforms that were necessary for the southern European economies to function within the single currency. Ironically, if the requirements laid down in the Maastricht Treaty had positive effects on the institutional development of the southern countries in the run-up to Monetary Union, euro entry itself vitiated or even reversed the progress made by reinforcing a coalition of protected groups whose interests diverged from those of the competitive sector of the economy.

The standard narrative of the euro crisis in the political debate, and even in some academic discussion, has blamed southern European governments for allowing public spending to grow too quickly, leaving them without any room for maneuver when the economy crashed in 2008.[28] The European Commission and other international organizations have identified the inefficiency and corruption of the public sector as a key source of the southern European crisis. The most egregious example of such profligacy was allegedly Greece, whose long-standing tradition of politicians using public money to buy electoral support and even enrich themselves led to a "bloated public sector" and spiraling debt.[29] There is plenty of evidence that the public sector in southern Europe is traditionally subject to partisan political interference, with clientelistic patterns of recruitment, corrupt allocation of public contracts, and weak accountability a characteristic of all the Mediterranean democracies.[30] But there is no evidence that this constitutes a proximate cause of the crisis.

A look at the data (Figure 8.2) shows that the southern European countries do not have particularly high public spending, nor did they exploit falling bond yields to increase public spending before the crisis. Whatever the true extent of clientelism and corruption in the Greek public sector, Greece's government expenditure as a share of GDP is in fact lower than the Eurozone average, and did not show any significant increases until the crisis began in 2007. While Portugal did increase the size of the state after euro entry, the public sector's share of the economy in Greece and Italy remained broadly stable, with a trend over time rather similar to Germany, and Spain's public sector actually shrank relative to GDP. Before the crisis wrecked the southern European economies, increasing the relative size of their public sectors as automatic stabilizers kicked in, government spending was on average considerably lower than in the "virtuous" North.

Neither is there any evidence that southern European governments systematically expanded public employment after monetary union. According to OECD data, Greece did increase the public sector's share of employment between 2000 and 2008 (from 19.3 percent to 20.7 percent), but Italy and Spain both reduced it.[31] The public sector workforce is not, contrary to many

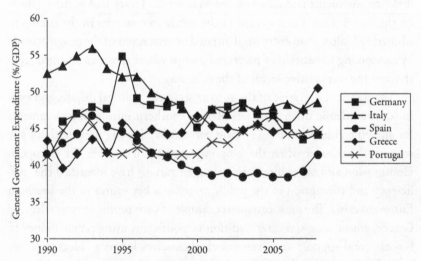

FIGURE 8.2 Government Expenditure in Germany and Southern Europe, 1990–2008 (% GDP)

Source: IMF World Economic Outlook

lazily researched newspaper articles, disproportionately large in these countries. Although the Greek public sector has a higher than average share of the labor force for the OECD, Norway, Denmark, France, Finland, and the Netherlands all have higher shares. In Italy and Spain, the public sector workforce is smaller than in the United States or Britain.[32] The southern tradition of clientelism, corruption, and inefficiency may well make public sector spending less effective in delivering services and redistributing income than in northern Europe, but that is not in itself a cause of the crisis.

In fact, the accusations of "profligacy" are more accurately directed at the private sector of the southern European economies. Government indebtedness in the Eurozone has a much stronger correlation with government revenues than with government spending, and the southern sovereign debt problem is very obviously a result of the collapse of the tax take in the wake of the crisis, rather than any reckless increase in spending. As Figure 8.3 shows, the southern countries had significantly reduced their budget deficits over the 1990s and the early 2000s, and the uptick in government borrowing in Greece and Italy after euro entry was the result of falling tax revenues, not increased spending. If public spending is lower than the Eurozone average in southern Europe, this owes a great deal to systematic

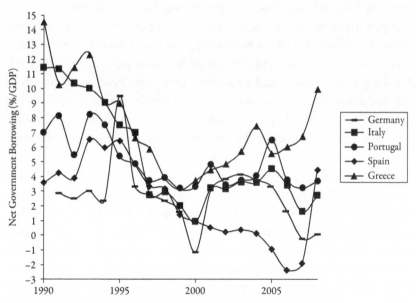

FIGURE 8.3 Government Borrowing in Germany and Southern Europe, 1990–2008 (% GDP)

Source: IMF World Economic Outlook

and long-standing difficulties in levying sufficient tax revenue to pay for a modern state.

Part of the reason that tax revenues swiftly fell off after Monetary Union is that temporary tax hikes had been a key tool for meeting the convergence criteria.[33] For example, in Italy, Romano Prodi's government established a one-off "Europe tax" (*contributo straordinario per l'Europa*) in 1996, which would in principle be reimbursed at a later time.[34] The South's history of running high deficits reflected a common difficulty in reconciling the interests of upper and lower income groups, which tended to be resolved by expanding state spending through borrowing rather than dealing with endemic tax evasion. Although some reforms to the tax regime were made prior to euro entry, developments afterward show that these long-standing problems had not been resolved. The reasons for this are partly structural, but also political, with center-right parties in particular adopting a relaxed attitude toward the widespread under-reporting of income by small businesses and the self-employed.

In Italy, the Berlusconi government exploited the easing of fiscal pressures after euro entry to reward its many supporters in those sectors. With interest rates on Italian public debt dropping sharply, there was some limited scope to cut taxes, as Berlusconi had promised in his high-profile "contract with the Italians," signed on live TV during the 2001 election campaign. The promise to introduce just two tax rates (23 percent and 33 percent) did not come to fruition, but the Berlusconi government did completely abolish inheritance tax in 2001, and tax evasion increased particularly after 2003, breaking a downward trend established under the Prodi governments of the late 1990s.[35] As a result, Italy's primary surplus declined steadily after 2000, although the falling cost of debt servicing allowed the headline deficit figure to remain within the European Commission's 3 percent limit. Strikingly, the brief return to office of Romano Prodi's center-left coalition in 2006–2007 sparked a dramatic increase in tax receipts as business owners and self-employed professionals reported higher incomes in anticipation of a tougher approach by the revenue services. The highly politicized nature of tax collection was revealed in a high-profile spat between Finance Minister Vincenzo Visco and the head of the tax police (*Guardia di Finanza*), Generale Roberto Speciale, who won election to parliament for Berlusconi's center-right after being fired by Visco.[36] On Visco's last day in office in 2008, the Italian revenue service (*Agenzia delle Entrate*) published all that year's tax returns online, an exercise in transparency that lasted less than 24 hours.[37]

The problem of tax evasion is related to industrial structure: southern Europe has the highest proportion of businesses with less than 10 workers in the Eurozone, many of which are family concerns operating in the sheltered sector of the economy (shops, bars, restaurants, transport services, pharmacies, self-employed artisans and tradespeople).[38] Monitoring tax compliance for large numbers of small units is more difficult than in economies with more large companies, and small businesses are concentrated in the sectors more prone to operating outside the formal economy (such as construction and tourism). This diffusion of tax evasion opportunities across broad sectors of the population creates a solid political constituency against a more rigorous and progressive tax collection regime, both through the electoral weight of the numerous small business owners and the self-employed, and through the lobbying of well-organized trade associations.

This anti-tax coalition is oriented toward the center-right and reflects both social and cultural traditions and deliberate political strategies deployed by the conservative, and mostly authoritarian, political elites that governed across southern Europe in the postwar period. In Italy this involved the hegemonic Christian Democrats acting to develop and preserve an urban petty bourgeoisie, which could act as a reliable support base as the numbers of rural smallholders declined.[39] Formal and informal fiscal incentives and a protective system of regulation (for example, restrictions of the size of retail spaces or the number of pharmacies owned by the same company) nurtured a growing social class of self-employed workers and owners of small family businesses. In Spain, the Franco dictatorship's protectionist policies also encouraged the development of small businesses.[40] This industrial culture of small, family-based firms mixed with large, historically state-owned enterprises is common across southern Europe, and is closely linked to the reluctance of center-right parties in southern Europe to embrace market reforms that would expose small firms to greater competition and promote economies of scale.

The transition to the new currency proved lucrative to many small businesses in the southern European service sector, including the retail sector, which in some cases was able to exploit citizens' confusion over the conversion to the euro to trigger dramatic rises in some product markets with limited competition.[41] Southern European inflation rates ran ahead of earnings growth, and the gains for small retail concerns and other small businesses operating in sheltered and heavily regulated markets had significant redistributive consequences, enhancing rents for key supporters of center-right parties while reducing purchasing power for salaried workers, who tended to vote for the center-left. By enhancing price competition in the industrial sector, but maintaining much of the protectionism enjoyed by small-scale service sector actors, euro membership shifted the balance of power within the southern European political economy away from salaried employees and in favor of small business owners and the self-employed.

One area where the euro bubble produced some spectacular gains was in construction and real estate. Spain's housing boom saw prices peak in 2008 at almost twice their 2000 level in real terms, while even in Italy, which did not enjoy significant economic growth in the 2000s, house prices were up 50 percent at their peak.[42] High levels of home ownership in southern Europe meant that the resulting wealth effect was spread across broad sectors of the population, which in Spain had a dramatic effect on consumer confidence and in Italy mitigated the effects of slow economic growth. Politically, the housing boom empowered the real estate and construction industries and deepened their (often corrupt) connections to political representatives, particularly local councilors who had control over planning and zoning decisions, and political nominees in regional banks (the *Cajas* in Spain and the *Fondazioni Bancarie* in Italy).[43]

The political implications of the construction boom demonstrated that rather than eliminating the traditional practices of clientelism and corruption, the restrictions placed on public spending growth by EMU simply displaced the corruption to new areas. Opportunities to hire partisan supporters to public positions were reduced (except to some extent in Greece), but political parties shifted their attention to the corrupt allocation of planning decisions and building permits and the manipulation of public contracts in growing areas such as healthcare and care for the elderly to generate financial resources and political support. In Italy major scandals relating to planning permissions affected the center-left leadership of the Milan province, while corruption in the healthcare sector incriminated the center-left leadership in Abruzzo and the center-right in Lazio. In Spain various scandals relating to construction and planning decisions affected major regions such as Valencia and Madrid in particular. Unlike in the case of traditional clientelism and patronage, these new forms of corruption involved a sharing of rents between party politicians in the public sector and private sector companies.

New forms of corruption and rent seeking also appeared through the privatization process and the increasing resort to private provision of public services. Privatized utilities in southern Europe were sufficiently weakly regulated as to allow energy prices to soar,[44] bringing vast profits to favored investors. The four southern European countries had the highest natural gas prices after Sweden and Denmark, while Italy, Spain, and Portugal were all in the top seven EU countries for electricity prices.[45] Regulatory inadequacies reduced disposable income for consumers while generating outsized profits for private or semi-private energy companies, which in many cases became major players in the financial system. Similarly, privatization opened up opportunities for major private sector investors to take on profitable activities that were often natural monopolies or were protected by state guarantees, for example the Benetton group's acquisition of the Italian Motorway network on terms that some analysts consider excessively generous.[46]

In sum, euro membership proved profitable to a broad set of well-connected and politically mobilized interests that could resist reforms or manipulate the new situation to their benefit. Contrary to the dominant narrative, unionized workers and public sector employees—the classic labor movement "insiders"—were not the big winners of southern Europe's participation in EMU. Instead, groups associated with conservative political forces, such as government-regulated industries in the sheltered sector of the economy and, more broadly, the small business and self-employed sector, were particularly well placed to ride the boom. When boom turned to bust, policy was refracted through this same power structure.

The Crisis: Guess Who Pays?

In much the same way as the EU response to the crisis in the South has been macroeconomically pro-cyclical, the ramifications of austerity have also tended to reinforce the social and political inequalities that emerged in the euro era. Although there has been a mix of center-left and center-right political forces in power across southern Europe in the period since the crisis began, the overriding imperative of deficit reduction through fiscal tightening and the absence of available monetary levers at the national level have meant that policy has been little affected by the electoral process. However, EU interventions, by focusing on short-term deficit reduction and shoring up the financial system, have penalized vulnerable groups, which gained little from the bubble dynamics of the early euro era, and the social stress resulting from austerity is generating serious threats to the medium-term political stability of the region.

The choice for austerity, almost by definition, has regressive distributive consequences. Bailing out investors on the one hand while holding down government spending on the other will, all else equal, favor the wealthy at the expense of middle and lower income groups. In southern Europe, these expectations are borne out by the emerging data on the effects of austerity policies: between 2008 and 2011, the Eurostat poverty rate grew from 18.3 percent to 20.7 percent in Italy, from 18.5 percent to 22.9 percent in Greece, and leapt from 15.9 percent to 21 percent in Spain.[47] Even more dramatic is the increase in unemployment (2008–2013), from 6.7 percent to 12.2 percent in Italy, 8.5 percent to 16.5 percent in Portugal, 7.7 percent to 27.3 percent in Greece, and 11.3 percent to 26.1 percent in Spain.[48] Not surprisingly, this has driven down wages, one of the stated objectives of the fiscal adjustment demanded by the Troika: real wages dropped 20 percent in Greece, 10 percent in Portugal, 6 percent in Spain, and 2.5 percent in Italy between 2010 and 2012.[49] At the same time, EU help has been directed at shoring up the value of government bonds issued by Greece and Portugal, or directly aiding insolvent banks in the case of Spain.

The EU's policy response has therefore piled the burden of Eurozone adjustment not only on the southern European countries themselves, but it has also defined in large part how that burden would be distributed internally. By bailing out states and financial institutions and intervening to shore up bond markets, the European institutions offered massive assistance to the holders of southern European financial assets, and the majority of the benefits went to wealthy interests in the southern European countries themselves, as well as the northern European banks that were exposed to southern debt. At the same time, the policy demands made by the Troika in exchange for financial assistance have mainly penalized wage earners, public employees, and welfare recipients. This approach is in turn driven by the preference for austerity of the German government, the result of Germany's own particular trajectory of stagnation and then recovery since reunification (see Chapter 6 of this volume).

The various memoranda outlining necessary measures as conditions for bailouts paint a picture of the type of economy that EU leaders wish to emerge in southern Europe. Despite the relatively low share of state spending as a share of GDP and the restricted scope of the welfare state in southern Europe, EU conditionality seeks to pare back welfare provision, focusing particularly on the retrenchment of the most developed dimension of social spending in the region: pensions. There are good reasons for adjusting pensions arrangements in southern Europe, in particular given the unfavorable demographics of the southern societies, but the focus on the "sustainability" of the pensions system fails to consider the role that retirees' incomes have in supporting the younger generations, who are less well served by welfare arrangements.[50] Cutting pensions, often presented as a way of securing inter-generational equity, in fact exposes citizens of all ages to increased economic risk,[51] particularly since the European leadership has placed far less emphasis on the expansion of welfare provision for the young, and the deficit reduction requirement makes any increase in spending impossible.

A second major plank of the EU reform drive is to dismantle collective bargaining arrangements.[52] Despite the success of centralized wage deals in curbing labor costs in Germany and other northern European countries, European policymakers insist that decentralization of bargaining to the firm or individual level is the right approach for southern Europe. This dovetails with a long-standing policy priority of the political right in the southern countries, with the abolition of reinstatement rights in Italy (the famous *Articolo 18* of the Labor Code) and the reduction of high dismissal compensation in Spain having been attempted several times before the crisis. Thus the Monti government in Italy made labor market reform a priority, and passed a law that, albeit in a rather ambiguous fashion, sought to increase flexibility in dismissals.[53] In Spain the Rajoy government, freed by its large majority of the need to negotiate with other parties, imposed an apparently more severe reform, which aimed to facilitate a shift toward company-level bargaining at the expense of national and regional agreements.[54] The common pattern across southern Europe has been to undermine collective agreements in favor of a more decentralized, market-driven set of arrangements, under explicit pressure from the European institutions.[55]

The choice for internal devaluation and fiscal austerity as the main response to southern Europe's crisis has marked political and social consequences for the debtor countries. It imposes quite clearly a more liberal set of economic and welfare institutions, and uses the financial vulnerability of the southern countries as a battering ram to force through reforms that have long been urged upon them, but which have met sustained resistance in the past. These reforms favor financial and business interests in the South, at the expense of middle and lower income groups. The so-called "insiders" often blamed for the crisis—stably employed and unionized industrial and public sector workers—have been handed the bill for the crisis, provoked almost entirely by circumstances outside of their control, and from which they did not noticeably benefit. While European structural reform demands have included product market as well as labor market reform, the latter has clearly been the priority, while rent-seeking Small and Medium-sized Enterprises (SMEs) in the sheltered economy have largely been let off the hook. The final section of this chapter assesses the political reactions to these policies in southern European societies.

The Political Response: Populism versus Technocracy

Southern Europe's experience of the crisis amounts to a major social and political experiment. No member state has faced such a sustained economic downturn in the history of the European integration process, and the only comparable case of prolonged economic contraction on the continent is the unpromising case of the 1930s, which put a brutal end to the first democratic experiences of Germany and Spain. Adding to the mix is the relative youth of the democratic regimes established in the 1970s in Greece, Portugal, and Spain, and the turbulent history of democracy in Italy, which experienced a sustained wave of political violence from the late 1960s until the mid-1980s. The choice for austerity constitutes a "crucial case" to test Barry Eichengreen's thesis that internal devaluation is incompatible with democratic rule.[56]

The political consequences of the crisis so far suggest that Eichengreen is right. Since the crisis began, all the parties of government in southern Europe have been defeated and non-traditional political movements have gained new electoral opportunities. If we take the Lehman Brothers bankruptcy as the starting point of the crisis, there have been seven elections in the four southern European countries, of which five have resulted in changes of government (and one was a repeat election held in Greece under a caretaker administration). Table 8.1 shows that incumbents have not only tended to lose power, but have also suffered major (and at times spectacular) declines in electoral support, and that in some cases all the mainstream parties have been collectively penalized by frustrated voters, leading to surges in support for new or previously marginal political parties. The success of populist and other non-mainstream parties across Europe in the May 2014 elections for a new European Parliament shows that this development is not just confined to the South.

The main victims of austerity have been the parties of the center-left that governed in Greece, Portugal, and Spain when the crisis hit. The Portuguese and Spanish socialist parties (PS and PSOE), both of which were in government through the pre-crisis years, suffered serious defeats: the PS in Portugal dropped from 45 percent of the vote in 2005 to 28.1 percent in 2011, while the PSOE in Spain dropped from 43.9 percent in 2008 to just 28.8 percent in 2011, in the space of only one legislature. The Greek socialists (PASOK), who returned to power in 2009 with 43.9 percent of the vote, were reduced to 12.3 percent just three years and two elections later. Even the Italian center-left Democratic Party (PD), in opposition for most of the 2008–2013 parliament,

Table 8.1 Electoral Change and Government Turnover in
Southern Europe, 2008–2013

Election	Government Turnover	Change in Incumbent Vote Share	New Entrants' Vote Share
Portugal 2009	No	−8.4%	0
Greece 2009	Yes	−8.4%	0
Portugal 2011	Yes	−8.5%	0
Spain 2011	Yes	−15.1%	1.8%
Greece May 2012	No	−30.7%	13.1%
Greece June 2012	Yes	−0.9%	0
Italy 2013	Yes	−16%	25.5%

managed to lose 8 percent of the vote, while Berlusconi's People of Freedom party, the incumbent government until a year earlier, lost 16 percent. In short, the mainstream political parties that have articulated governing coalitions for decades have suffered historic defeats, opening up a political vacuum.

Into this vacuum have rushed two entirely contradictory political forces. On the one hand, the near impossibility for professional politicians of winning elections while approving austerity measures brought recourse to governments of technocrats in Greece and Italy. The Papademos government of national unity in Greece in 2011–2012, and the Monti government in Italy in 2011–2013, represented a doomed attempt by the Troika to impose its preferred policies by legislative fiat, bypassing the normal democratic channel of inter-party competition for power. Both men represented the kind of pro-market and pro-business mindset preferred by the Troika institutions: Papademos an MIT-trained academic economist and central banker, Monti a Bocconi-trained academic economist and twice former European Commissioner. The brief and unstable tenure of these governments, subject to the maneuverings of political parties concerned over the electoral fallout from austerity measures, proved technocracy to be little more than an emergency measure to secure short-term objectives.

The failure of both technocratic and partisan governments to end the crisis, and the obvious curtailment of national sovereignty resulting from the various bailout arrangements, opened up a political space for new political forces opposed both to the austerity measures and to the existing political elites. The established parties' shared adherence to the austerity program highlighted the lack of real political competition and exposed the collusive behavior of the main political leaders.[57] In Greece and Italy, the experience of technocracy coincided with an acute crisis of popularity for the mainstream parties, and the rapid rise of new political forces, which expressed resentment toward the "political class" and hostility to the austerity program. The collapse of the PASOK vote corresponded to the remarkable rise of the more populist left party Syriza, which opposed the austerity measures and expressed skepticism toward the European institutions, while on the extreme-right the neo-Nazi party Golden Dawn leapt from almost nothing to 7 percent of the vote. The current pro-austerity coalition in parliament, comprising the conservative New Democracy (ND), what is left of PASOK, and one further minor party, has less than 50 percent of the vote and is only able to sustain a government because of the 50 bonus seats allocated to ND as the largest party under Greece's semi-majoritarian electoral law. The parties of this governing coalition won only 31 percent of the vote in the 2014 European Parliament elections, in which Syriza was the largest party with 27 percent, and the neo-Nazi Golden Dawn came in third—ahead of PASOK—with 9 percent. The Greek party system, relatively stable until 2009, is increasingly polarized and unable to generate cohesive governments.

In Italy the Monti government ended with the scheduled election held in the spring of 2013, which the center-left opposition party, the PD, was widely tipped to win. Monti himself decided to stand for election at the head of a centrist coalition led by a small Christian Democratic party with strong backing from the employers' federation Confindustria. The result of the election confirmed how unimpressed Italian voters were with the austerity measures pushed through by the technocrats. Monti's coalition won a disappointing 10.5 percent, and the PD, which had enthusiastically supported Monti's administration, failed to win its expected overall majority, polling 3.5 million fewer votes than in its defeat to Berlusconi in 2008. The big winners of the 2013 election were the Five Stars Movement (M5S), led by comedian Beppe Grillo, standing for the first time in a national election. The M5S won 8.7 million votes to become the largest single party in the Italian parliament (more than the PD, although the center-left coalition collectively emerged as the largest political force). The PD's disappointing performance led to an internal coup as Matteo Renzi, the rising star of the party's more centrist wing, took over first the leadership and then the prime minister's office, subsequently polling an impressive 40 percent of the vote in the May 2014 European elections.

The M5S and Syriza represent dramatic upheavals in their respective countries' party systems. Though the stability of European electoral politics has declined over the past two decades and new parties have been more and more successful in many countries, the speed with which these parties have grown, conquering more than a quarter of the vote in the space of less than five years, is almost unheard of in recent electoral history. Both parties have latched onto popular resentment over the way in which the crisis is being managed and in diverse ways have challenged the pro-euro mainstream consensus. The M5S has played an ambiguous game on austerity and the euro, but has talked openly about debt restructuring and has promised a referendum on the euro in its 2013 election campaign.[58] Syriza, on the other hand, has remained committed to the euro, but opposed to the austerity measures imposed by the Troika.[59] Both parties express popular frustration at the lack of open political debate and competition between the established party elites. The rise of Matteo Renzi, while helping revive one of the mainstream parties, is also a sign of political change. Not only has he introduced a very new "Americanized" style of leadership to Italy, he has also begun to challenge the "austerian" approach of the European Union to managing the crisis.

In Spain and Portugal, party system change has been less dramatic, but the mainstream parties are still shedding support. In the Spanish case, the most destabilizing development is at the territorial level, with the Catalan nationalist movement's shift toward a pro-independence strategy. Catalonia represents one-fifth of Spanish GDP and is its fourth richest region in per capita terms. Catalan independence is vehemently opposed by the main Spanish political parties, and there is at present no constitutional mechanism for secession to take place. However, surveys suggest that the referendum on independence promised by the Catalan governing parties could possibly deliver a majority for leaving Spain.[60] At the same time, the most successful new party in recent elections, the UPyD, led by former Basque Socialist Rosa Díez, uses a strong anti-regionalist discourse, suggesting a radicalization of the sensitive territorial debate in Spain. The 2014 European elections saw the emergence of an entirely new left party, Podemos, led by a Madrid university professor and talk-show host, which was formed only three months before the poll but managed to win 8 percent of the vote. Alongside the impressive 10 percent won by Spain's historic left party Izquierda Unida, this amounts to a major signal of popular impatience with the performance of the two largest parties, the PP and PSOE, who between them lost the support of almost a third of the Spanish electorate since the 2009 European vote.

These developments pose a very obvious threat to the EU leadership's strategy for dealing with the southern European crisis. The failure of technocracy to provide a sustainable route to imposing internal devaluation leaves the electoral route as the only one available. Yet southern European voters are increasingly reluctant to vote for the reliably pro-European parties that have dominated their party systems ever since the 1980s, and the socialist parties, the key to integrating the working class into a neoliberal economic framework, have suffered the most serious declines in support. By forcing established national political elites to implement painful austerity measures, which have led to further economic collapse, the EU leadership is running the risk of destroying the political forces that have articulated support for European integration and liberalizing reforms in southern Europe.[61] Moreover, the austerity measures have undermined support for the European Union in the South, with only 33 percent of Greeks and 46 percent of Spaniards having a favorable view of the EU in 2013.[62]

The depth of the crisis is placing the democratic institutions at the member-state level, as well as the relations between the member states and the European Union, under unprecedented strain. Although there have been wide and varied grassroots protests against austerity, particularly in Greece and Spain, popular frustration has so far been largely articulated through formal democratic channels. One safety valve is the opportunity of migration, which enables many younger, and particularly better educated, southern Europeans to exercise an "exit" option rather than remain and seek to force change through "voice."[63] This, of course, exacerbates existing demographic imbalances in southern Europe, subtracting the most productive citizens and increasing the relative size of the dependent population. But with unemployment hitting two-thirds of Greeks under 25 years of age, opportunities for migration may prove the best defense against political instability and even democratic collapse.

Conclusion

The debt crisis in southern Europe is first and foremost a particular regional manifestation of the broader global economic crisis that began with the unwinding of an over-leveraged global financial system in 2007, and has been magnified and intensified by the institutional failings of Europe's Economic and Monetary Union. Yet the response to the crisis has focused on the perceived policy errors and historical institutional weaknesses of the southern European states themselves, with a contractionary fiscal policy prescribed as the main remedy. This response has not only decimated the southern European economies by adding a deliberate squeeze in demand to an exogenous demand shock, it also has eaten away at the principal mechanisms for channeling popular participation through democratic institutions: the political parties.

This constitutes a major natural experiment with very high stakes. There is no historical precedent for adjustment on this scale in a democratic context, and the current approach is counting on southern European citizens maintaining an unwavering commitment to the euro to justify years of sacrifice with no end in sight. Even in the best-case scenario, living standards are unlikely to recover in the short term, casting doubt over the sustainability of popular acceptance of the single currency and its institutions. But worse, the current policy mix appears doomed to failure. Italy, carrying a public debt of over 130 percent and with very low average growth since euro entry in 1999, will be unable to sustainably service its debt burden, even with ECB help, unless growth returns. Yet the austerity policies imposed from Brussels and Frankfurt make such growth highly improbable, even in the unlikely scenario of Italy implementing all the recommended structural reforms. In sum, countries such as Italy are being invited to stagnate for the indefinite future, while implementing unpopular policies imposed upon them by largely unelected supranational institutions. Not surprisingly, as soon as a credible politician with popular support has emerged, as in the case of Matteo Renzi in Italy, his first move has been to question the constraints of the Fiscal Compact.

Europe is engaged in a major gamble, and the elections held since the crisis began have brought major transformations to what were relatively settled patterns of citizen representation and party competition in southern Europe. The lack of concern for the electoral process reflects an approach to the political economy in which democratic accountability takes second place to the nebulous notions of investor confidence and credible policy commitments. Bypassing the democratic process is presented as a necessary part of the cure for southern Europe's economic malaise, so that the verdict of the market and the policies of the experts can take center stage in the policy process, overriding citizen demands for social protection.

The success of this strategy rides on whether the European Union's leaders have correctly assessed the southern European electorates' patience and endurance. Needless to say, the collapse of political authority that could result from prolonging the squeeze on the southern European economies threatens the euro project itself. Greece, Italy, Spain, and Portugal constitute a third of Eurozone GDP, and their departure would mean the end of the euro as it has been imagined until now. Such an outcome remains unlikely, and current Eurozone policy assumes that southern Europeans will do "whatever it takes" to stay in the Eurozone, as their remarkable resilience in the face of a catastrophic and abrupt drop in living standards suggests. But the evidence of a sharp decline in pro-European sentiment, as well as the tenuous grip on government power of pro-European political forces across the four countries, cautions that this assumption will be tested to the limit in the coming years. In the absence of a compelling economic rationale for a single currency covering the entire European Union, the euro has always been an essentially political project. Yet, the current crisis is not only undermining the euro, but also the European Union more broadly, encouraging the emergence or strengthening of anti-EU forces and weakening the commitment to the EU not only in the struggling periphery, but also in the bailout-fatigued core. The European project of *ever closer union*, in which each step toward integration begets further reforms, may have run into the buffers. The founders of monetary union may come to regret pinning the future of Europe to a now discredited economic dogma.

The Euro Future

Europe's New German Problem

THE TIMING OF POLITICS AND THE POLITICS OF TIMING

Wade Jacoby

> *It's humiliating that, for the last four years, it has seemed somehow unclear whether the German government's stance on Greece differs significantly from the slogans printed in the tabloid newspaper Bild.*
>
> ULLRICH FICHTNER

Introduction

This chapter is the first of four in this volume specifically addressing the future of the euro.[1] It uses Germany as a prism for the discussion about what might be done next to bolster the euro. Researching the future—always a challenging task—is made harder when multiple state actors contend for prominence on the basis of shifting coalitions at home, all while interacting at an international level. That said, almost everyone accepts that German choices will play the central role in the path ultimately chosen. This chapter thus foregrounds Germany's role in shaping the way ahead, and it does so through an explicitly political framework focused primarily on the electoral implausibility of an alternative German policy course. In so doing, it endorses the broad themes of the volume: that unsolved political issues leave the euro's future "in doubt" and that Germany's leadership has aimed to prevent a full meltdown of the common currency while using the crisis as leverage to oblige structural reforms that it deems essential.

Any discussion about that way ahead presumes some effort to understand how we got where we are. Much analysis of Germany's behavior during the slow motion unraveling and very partial repair of the Eurozone has dwelled on the perplexities of Germany's modest response to a crisis of frightening proportions. Why has the biggest state so often had the smallest imagination? When not being charged with economic illiteracy[2] or a sadistic streak,[3] the general explanation for Germany's conservative, cautious, and incrementalist policies generally have been either ideological—with a heavy emphasis on the importance of ordoliberal thought[4]—or institutional—with the emphasis on ministerial prerogatives, federalist veto points, or active checks from the Constitutional Court.[5]

This chapter adds an electoral dimension to Germany's policy responses. Indeed, while almost nobody abroad is happy with German policy, almost nobody at home has been upset with it. Angela Merkel easily won her 2013 re-election bid over an opponent who offered little substantive alternative when it came to policy toward Europe and who is, in any event, now her coalition partner with an agreement that explicitly rules out debt mutualization. But this chapter goes beyond considering merely "what voters want." For here, as so often, they want many things all at once. German voters overwhelmingly wish to stick with the euro (about 2:1 in summer 2013), but they also support other policies—particularly austerity—that leave the euro highly vulnerable. Rather than merely stressing the obvious point that German voters are conflicted and confused, this chapter injects an element of "time" into what are too often otherwise static considerations of German policy. A focus on time and timing builds on a robust research agenda but one that has tended to emphasize day-to-day policymaking—especially at the EU level—rather than the exceptional and even crisis-driven considerations affected by timing.[6]

Yet timing has mattered greatly in these exceptional circumstances brought on by the euro crisis. Accordingly, this chapter considers both the "timing of politics" and the "politics of timing" under extraordinary decision-making pressure. In the former consideration, while German policymakers accept the need for a massive intervention in sovereign bond markets of other Eurozone members, they want to pick the optimal time of intervention to maximize the efforts of private actors and deter public and private behavior that might require more bailouts in the future. Their central focus is on moral hazard,[7] and their aim is that their political priority—to save the euro—comes at the "right" time and not so early that policy mistakes remain uncorrected. In the latter consideration, a concern about the "politics of timing" means that German elites also feel they cannot intervene until they have properly prepared their voters. However, by the time elites have sold to voters a bailout of a certain envisioned size, the problem has grown larger, such that the envisioned remedy is no longer adequate to the job. Here, the elite focus is centrally on the legitimacy of their policy choices.

Adding to the difficulty, if one focuses primarily on the timing of politics, then patience is a virtue, and elites should wait and minimize future moral hazard concerns. If one focuses primarily on the politics of timing, however, then patience is a vice, as windows of opportunity for stemming the crisis slam shut, one after another. The broad point of the chapter is that the first concern—to avoid cementing an unwise policy status quo in troubled Eurozone states—has consistently won out over the second—to stem the crisis of confidence in the euro.[8]

The argument of this chapter proceeds in three interrelated steps. First, a fundamental and still very much unsolved problem in the European economy consists of imbalances in both trade flows[9] and financial markets.[10] Second, while these imbalances contributed to the crisis in the Eurozone, their resolution—such as it is—has depended primarily on adjustment in the peripheral countries. Meanwhile, Germany, having benefited once as the imbalances accumulated, has benefited again from their subsequent consequences, including the "flight to safety." I call this "Germany's exorbitant privilege."[11] Together, these benefits create conflicting pressures. On the one hand, there is a strong bias toward the status quo that has benefited Germany so handsomely. On the other hand, there is a clear recognition that others in Europe are struggling and that the euro, and its benefits to Germany, are in danger. Germany resolves this dilemma by innovation on the institutions of euro area governance, flanked with a ferocious defense of fiscal austerity and structural reforms. An implication of this is that Germany's exorbitant privilege has helped prevent the rise of an alternative discourse and justified policies that suppress growth in other states. Third, with the taming of the German boom and a 2013 election that strengthened the status quo on Germany's European policy, we have reached an impasse.[12] Yet this impasse cannot be stable: Germany cannot run a persistent trade surplus, avoid meaningful fiscal transfers, and still have a monetary policy with an independent central bank and a "no bailout" policy.[13]

Do Something!

Germany is beset on all sides by those who would have it "do something!" The exhortations began with heads of government in Europe's Mediterranean periphery, and extended to Hungary's socialist prime minister in 2009,[14]

Poland's liberal foreign minister in 2011,[15] the US president,[16] the Italian prime minister, and the European Central Bank (ECB) president in 2012,[17] the European Commissioner for financial matters in 2013,[18] and the US Treasury and European Commissioner (again) in 2014.[19] Some of this criticism is also present in the domestic debate. For example, in April 2010, Joschka Fischer's Düsseldorf speech lamented Germany's waiting on International Monetary Fund (IMF) approval before assisting Greece. Fischer paraphrased Heine: *"Denk ich an [Europa] in der Nacht, bin ich um den Schlaf gebracht."*[20] Vaclav Klaus, a very different politician, expressed in Berlin the next day a similar concern about German dithering. Helmut Schmidt's 2012 *Parteitag* speech blasted the German government for not noticing or not caring that its policies were tearing Europe apart.[21] Thus, there has been concern across the political spectrum, the European continent, and even the Atlantic.

As they have been in the crosshairs of these complaints, one can forgive the Germans for feeling wounded and defensive.[22] Most obviously, Germany *has* done "some things." Many scholars show Germany has done at least an average amount on the fiscal side compared to the rest of the member countries of the Organisation for Economic Co-operation and Development (OECD),[23] especially when compared to a rhetorically activist but fiscally constrained France.[24] Moreover, essentially non-stop summitry between spring 2010 and summer 2012 left an impression in the minds of many German voters of well-nigh frenetic German activity.

It is, however, hard to say *exactly* what Germany has done. Partly, this is down to the proclivity for European leaders to "repackage" what they had already pledged in prior discussions. This criticism can certainly be leveled at the lengthy search for a new set of fiscal rules for the Eurozone states, but it also applies to the emergency bailout packages negotiated to date. For months on end, each summit ground out new pledges that, upon closer inspection, were composed substantially of old pledges.[25]

Voters are confused. Estimates of the size of German commitments vary wildly. As an intermediate starting point, one could look at the 190 billion euro figure cited by the German Constitutional Court in its decision to allow the European Stability Mechanism.[26] On the other hand, by stressing Germany's TARGET2 liabilities of around 600 billion euro, Hans-Werner Sinn once claimed German exposure amounted to 1 trillion euro.[27] Subsequent and regular revisions resulted in a general lowering of these estimates by his institute, such that they were pegged at 541 billion euro in June 2014.[28] Yet since Germany's primary tool has been loans rather than grants and since the loans—apart from bilateral loans to Greece of 53 billion euro in 2010—have all been raised on the markets, it is hard to know what Germany's true exposure has been. In mid-2012, *Business Week* reported that only about 15 billion of Greece's 340 billion euro in loans came from Germany, though other sums did come from international organizations that Germany is party to, including the EU and the IMF.[29] At the extreme, some have argued that none of the "northern" European states has paid a single euro in aid through 2013.[30]

With voters understandably anxious and confused, German policy elites confront European economic problems with several broad and generally reasonable (though not always explicit) assumptions in place: (1) Germany must help because it is the indispensable nation in addressing Europe's economic woes; (2) Germany's own economic and leadership capacities are finite; (3) Germany itself could be damaged by ill-designed rescue efforts; (4) German voters can be made to understand the first point—Germany is indispensable for crisis resolution—only if it is reassured that the government understands the second and third points. In simple terms, the logic—shared across wide swaths of the German elite—can be encapsulated in these four ideas: Germany can do some important things. It cannot do everything. The rescue cannot be allowed to mortally damage the rescuer. Whatever Germany does must bear public scrutiny. The next section shows how these apparently sensible parameters have buttressed a reform argument that cannot work.

The Imbalances Problem

Mark Blyth has shown that in both the United States and Europe, a quintessentially private banking crisis has been rhetorically transformed into a crisis of "public" debt.[31] In an analogous but also complementary fashion, Europe has seen its substantial current account imbalances—again, phenomena that have their primary roots in private consumption and savings choices—recast as crises brought about almost exclusively by faulty political choices, whether of levels of government consumption or improper regulatory coddling of inefficient private producers. No country has done more than Germany to promulgate this understanding of the enduring economic misery in Europe. Debate in the German Bundestag continually invokes the Greek case as exemplary of all the troubled Eurozone states (see below). This understanding justifies a view that German *advice* must be followed before German *money* can do any good. At the same time, German officials have been eager to downplay new and more sober limits on financing current account imbalances as an independent source of stagnation.[32] This section of the chapter explores the implications of Germany's strong and sustained trade surpluses for the politics of crisis resolution—implications that are likely to persist in some fashion going forward. On the "strong and sustained" claim, there can be little doubt. By "sustained," I mean primarily that Germany has run a goods surplus *every single year* since 1951; by "strong," I mean that this surplus was below 2 percent of GDP in only five years since 1950 and has been as high as 8 percent.[33]

The basic idea behind this "imbalances problem" is relatively straightforward and, by now, well understood: as global liquidity increased at the beginning of the first decade of the 2000s, a significant amount flowed to Spain, Ireland, Greece, Portugal, and other states where, despite rapid convergence in interest rates with Germany and others, somewhat higher yields were available.[34] These capital inflows contributed to strong asset bubbles (Spain, Ireland), surging demand (Italy, Greece, Bulgaria), or both (Estonia, Latvia, Portugal).[35] They also created permissive space for steady rises in unit labor costs, even as Germany's stayed flat.[36] As competitiveness eroded in these states, current accounts went heavily into deficit, which required additional capital inflow.[37] Meanwhile, Germany's deep strength in high-quality manufacturing goods whose purchase was enabled by such liquidity provision led to sustained export booms in several manufacturing sectors.[38] As loose monetary policy in the US and Europe boosted liquidity, initial German advantages in intra-European competitiveness were magnified, while the fruits of that competitiveness were recycled back into those countries requiring higher financing to sustain growing levels of consumption.[39]

As noted, German officials resolutely deny that the surpluses of German manufacturing are a cause of the buildup of debt in the European economies.[40] There are two important consequences of the German denial that its permanent surpluses are a problem. The first is that it tends to lead German officials to overestimate the potential of their alternative solutions in *substantive* terms. The second is that it leaves Germans deeply uncertain about the timing of reforms in *procedural* terms. Again, these problems are quite novel and do not fit easily into the theoretical discourse shaped by what we might think of as the "normal" timing challenges associated with the persistent lack of synchronization among the treaty mandates of the European Commission, Council, and Parliament.[41]

In substantive terms, successive German governments have had an interest in maintaining the narrative that the euro crisis is one of public debt since the alternative interpretation—that it is driven in substantial ways by underlying trade imbalances—suggests that Germany may have to bear more of the burden of adjustment.[42] Since trade deficits generally have to be financed by private debt, the alternative narrative opens Germany to the charge that it is private debt, not public debt, that most determines the problems in the Eurozone. This is why debates in the German Bundestag contain constant references to Greece—where the narrative of public profligacy is easier to substantiate—and few references to Spain, which had low debt-to-GDP levels and was running a 4 percent budget surplus at the onset of the crisis.[43] If Greece did not exist, the old CDU-FDP coalition would have had to invent it, as it plays *the* essential rhetorical purpose in their joint crisis narrative. Indeed, in a way, the populist *Bild Zeitung* has already "invented" a Greece that consists almost exclusively of corrupt public officials and a private sector awaiting its early retirement. As German journalist Ullrich Fichtner wryly notes in this chapter's epigraph, it sometimes can be hard to tell in what ways Berlin's official position differs.

In addition to public debt, the German government also stresses a substantial competitiveness gap between Germany and others. This gap is said to result from unrealized structural reforms in the weaker countries, and the German government routinely references prior German reforms as a positive model. Yet Germany's own experience with structural reform in the pre-2008 boom period is likely to be an exceptionally poor guide to such reform during the post-2008 bust.[44] It is far easier to undertake structural reforms at a time when trading partners experience surges of growth since painful dislocations are quickly compensated by new employment. Moreover, the major German reforms prior to 2005 were accompanied not by state austerity but instead were conducted in a period in which Germany was breaking the Stability and Growth Pact rules, with deficit levels well above 3 percent. German voters seem to elide both of these facts—first, that structural reform paid faster dividends when regional growth was strong, and second, that such reforms were not accompanied by austerity but indeed by its opposite. Certainly, Germans have limited appetite for cutting government spending at home. In a 2013 Pew poll, German respondents were second only to Swedish ones in approving current levels of their government's spending.[45] This is good news insofar as Germany is not practicing even more extreme levels of austerity, but it tends to make Germans appear hypocritical in the eyes of other Europeans. Statements like CDU Chief Whip Volker Kauder's comment that "Europe now speaks German"[46] add to this triumphalist tone while ignoring the fact that Germany's sinking debt-to-GDP ratios have come more from strong growth than from austerity, while rising debt-to-GDP ratios in the periphery come *despite* sharp cuts in government spending.

Meanwhile, Germany's policy prescriptions have powerful unproven assumptions. Take the assumption that government austerity does no great harm to general levels of economic activity. There is good evidence, however, that the effects of state austerity on growth are contingent. In a period of normal growth, the effects of austerity might be low, between 0.2 percent and 0.4 percent, as estimated by the IMF. This means that a 1 percent cut in public spending equates to a 0.2–0.4 percent decline in GDP. And yet when monetary policy is not playing an active role, the effects of cuts in public spending may be much higher, from 0.9 percent to 1.7 percent, according to IMF 2012 estimates. The latter figure accords also with historical evidence from the Great Depression—the last time that monetary policy put interest rates at or near the zero lower bound—and suggests a figure of around 1.6 percent.[47]

Would an alternative German government behave differently? In the short term, probably not. It is true that under a "Grand Coalition" that included an SPD Minister of Finance, the German government in 2008–2009 had its own "Keynesian moment."[48] However, the fact that German stimulus spending was right at the OECD average should not obscure the clear reluctance of both parties to talk openly about stimulus. In late 2010, there was a very short-lived effort by the SPD to propose a version of Eurobonds, but this quickly died.[49] Rhetorically, the SPD acknowledges the imbalances issue. For example, party chair Sigmar Gabriel stated in December 2012:[50]

> It is not about having more Europe. It is about a different Europe, a Europe where innovation and competitiveness are actively promoted, and where one doesn't simply believe that markets will do it, a Europe in which Germany does not use low wages and low taxes as a weapon against the competitiveness of its neighbors . . . Of course the imbalance in Europe, especially our current account surpluses, are one cause of the problem.

The problem is that the party understands this is an electorally dangerous message. The 2013 SPD Party Conference virtually ignored the European issue, which played essentially no role in the 2013 campaign and led to no bold shifts in the two parties' coalition agreement of December 2013.

Meanwhile, German officials generally treat the undeniable fact of significant imbalances as an irrelevance, dodging this important debate by posing ludicrous rhetorical questions about whether Germany is expected to "produce inferior goods" as a way of "solving" the imbalance issue. Given the imbalances noted, the intransigence of the German government, and the modest alternative agenda developed by the SPD, the scope for policy reform has been limited. More precisely, whenever Germany has innovated on the monetary policy side, it flanks this with stubbornly conservative policies on fiscal and structural issues.

Why Deutschland *Dithers: Four Scenarios*

Another way to put the "timing of politics" claim is to say that it is too simplistic to charge Germany with pure obstructionism.[51] Instead, the German dilemma in facing the prolonged European financial and economic slump is that they want to intervene neither too early, nor too late, neither too big, nor too small. Their reasons are easily understood from within the ordoliberal paradigm and moral hazard frame.[52] If they are too early, German leaders fear they will exacerbate moral hazard problems. If they are too late, they increase the odds of contagion. If they are too big, they put German taxpayers on the hook for costs that others could and should bear. If they are too small, they run the risk of using up too much of their fiscal room for maneuver—"keeping one's powder dry" is also a metaphor in German—in an ineffective intervention, only to need it later on.[53] Thus, throughout the crisis, German elites have sought to convince German voters that they have a package that is both *timely* and *appropriate*. They have to be "in the right policy place at the right time." If they can do so, they will have public support to put Europe on a better track. To date, however, the government has stayed consistently behind the curve, another metaphor that German policymakers themselves have often employed.[54]

The "timing of politics" dilemma grows from the basic political economy of these four scenarios. The "too early" fear is that rent-seeking machine politics in the Eurozone periphery will not change their ways if rescue comes too quickly. High interest rates are the market's way of delivering the reform message, and bailouts only blunt or muddle this message. German reluctance to jump in too early thus increases pressure for reforms. This scenario imagines the German state pitted against supposedly "austerity-weary" peripheral states in an epic game of fiscal chicken. To blink is to endure another round of a self-reinforcing dynamic in which peripheral governments resist the hard reform choices. These themes—modified only slightly for polite public discourse about one's partners—are a staple of Chancellor Merkel's periodic reports to the German Bundestag. She speaks of the need to export Germany's basic "stability culture" to the rest of Europe and of the urgency of structural reforms that have been too long delayed. Germany, the Chancellor argues, is prepared to take extraordinary steps to flank these domestic reforms, but the central reform agenda lies, in her telling, inside the Eurozone states in trouble.

The "too late" fear is that financial markets will lose confidence in those peripheral Eurozone governments, which will make the rescue more expensive than it would otherwise be. In the worst case, the rescue would be too expensive to contemplate, leading to a Eurozone breakup. This scenario posits that the right policy combination will secure or restore investor confidence. Germany long betrayed little obvious concern with this problem. Indeed, for the first two years of the euro crisis, Germany's obsession with retooling the Stability and Growth Pact into the so-called Six Pack and other fiscal surveillance measures seemed to sidestep the necessary measures on the monetary side.[55] As predictions of a euro breakup multiplied in the summer of 2012 and bond rates for Spain and Italy approached 7 percent, however, the "too late" fear began to take precedence.[56] With Merkel's blessing of the Draghi proposal for outright monetary transactions (OMT) in the summer of 2012, the fear of "too late" gained the upper hand over concerns about moral hazard, at least temporarily.[57]

Germany's "too big" fear is that frightened Eurozone member states might agree on a massive intervention when a smaller, more targeted one would be preferable. Here, the political economy revolves around some of the same rent-seeking fears from the periphery that were present in the "too early" scenario. But there is an additional worry that certain moves might work to the benefit of a few large banks but have relatively little beneficial effect for the rest of the European economy. In the worst case scenario, banks are given "too big" a boost, and they sit on it such that it still makes no appreciable difference to the regional economy, though it may make one or another's balance sheet more healthy.[58] In the German context, the Ministry of Finance experts' report on "strategies for an exit" of the federal government from "crisis-induced participation" in banks crystallizes these concerns.[59]

Finally, the "too small" fear is focused on investor confidence and posits that while large interventions may shock the system back toward a virtuous circle, small and medium interventions only eat up potential rescue resources without actually fixing the core problems. This became known as the "bazooka"[60] debate, in which various EU-level rescue measures were judged inferior and inadequate. A second incarnation of the "too small" fear is that some form of mutualization of new debt—for most Germans, a worrisome possibility raised in the 2012–2013 discussion around banking union—might still be inadequate to relieve states of the crushing burden of older debts. Thus, while very expensive, some mutualization of future debt might be largely irrelevant to solving the ongoing Eurozone problems.

Different combinations of these anxieties have surfaced repeatedly in the German debates. Hans-Werner Sinn has worried that it is possible to go both "too big" and "too early" and, as a result, reward both rent seekers at home (mainly the banks) and abroad (mainly peripheral state governments) at one and the same time.[61] "Too big" and "too late," by contrast, would likely allow some exposed counterparties to benefit from eleventh-hour desperation on the part of the government.[62] Meanwhile, the logic of "too small" is not rent seeking, but rather that it is merely symbolic behavior. This opens the way to different flavors of ineffectiveness, depending on whether the "too small" is "too early" or "too late." For example, the important effect of "too small" and "too early" is to raise the number of market participants that hope for a bailout and, by sending confusing signals, increase the subsequent holdup problems. This has essentially become the mainstream German view of the May 2010 Greece package, which failed to include bail-in mechanisms and is seen to have set the wrong signal going forward that states would bear the full burdens of bank rescues. Germany's main challenge is that it does not have the resources to experiment and to get the rescue wrong in a big way—and still have the capacity to come back and try again. This was already true during the period in which its growth and employment performance diverged wildly from other Eurozone members, and it is even more evident in times when its growth is far more modest. Whatever its strengths, it must choose very carefully the time and modality of its intervention.

Meanwhile, German voters are almost completely ignorant of the imbalance issue in the European economy. German leaders have celebrated export success for so long that they have no effective vocabulary for problematizing export success, even if they were inclined to do so.[63] In any event, they are not so inclined; acknowledging imbalances might threaten to shift some of the burden of adjustment to Germany as a matter of a fundamental course correction. Instead, German leaders have much preferred to contemplate various forms of assistance to manage the effects of imbalances but without taking steps to correct the imbalances themselves. To the extent that Eurozone peripheral countries' current accounts have come back into balance since 2009, this is due far more to import declines than to export gains on their part.[64]

Thinking Slow and Fast: German Patience and Its Exorbitant Privilege

To an extent, the claim that German officials have been resistant to fundamental changes in German policy is contradicted by the many Eurozone policy innovations that have already been tried with German support and sometimes its leadership. It is certainly not correct to say that Germany gets whatever it wants at EU summits. In fact, time and again, Germany has moved from its initial positions—whether that was authorizing and then expanding the European Financial Stability Facility (EFSF), making it permanent under the European Stability Mechanism (ESM), later allowing the ESM to participate in direct bank recapitalization, allowing ECB purchases of government bonds on the primary and secondary markets (Securities Market Program, or SMP), or agreeing to Draghi's line to do "whatever it takes" and the subsequent OMT instrument that it spawned.[65]

As a consequence, the outcome to understand is not German rigidity in any absolute sense. Instead, the pattern has been that the more institutional ground Germany cedes on the monetary side, the more determined it grows to exact changes on the fiscal and structural side. This is an underdeveloped insight in the literature so far, and it helps explain why we have the strange combination of frustration and even rage against ordoliberalism *outside* Germany and the simultaneous despair of many ordoliberals *inside* Germany.[66] Every time there is a new concession to troubled Eurozone states, Merkel doubles down on the calls for fiscal rectitude and structural reform—calls that cannot all be met in electoral democracies. By flanking her institutional concessions in this way, Merkel has, so far, kept both the Constitutional Court and the voters on her side.

The most important caveat to this generalization is the Court's February 2014 ruling that the ECB's outright monetary transactions violate German basic law, which requires Bundestag approval of fiscal and economic policy. Indeed, while most proponents of OMT argue that the ECB could only fulfill its monetary policy mandate with a new instrument that could fix the broken interbank lending market in crisis-hit countries, the Court took a different position, namely that OMT lay outside the ECB mandate because it put the Central Bank in the potential position of incurring losses on bond purchases that could hit national taxpayers without their direct approval.

Thus, there has been policy innovation, but a hallmark of German policy has been slow and deliberate measures, often punctuated by mild backtracking or even outright reversal.[67] This section makes two points about this uneven trajectory. First, it notes coherent reasons for German delaying tactics. Second, it makes the point that Germany began reaping unexpected benefits of the crisis—its "exorbitant privilege"—that actually made it harder to embrace a shift away from the status quo, further cementing this politics of delay.

Citizens of the countries most afflicted by the Eurozone crisis are desperate for relief, but German policy has stressed incremental reforms of the Eurozone framework and, especially, the deeper constitutionalization of fiscal balances already agreed in earlier periods. Why the slow, painstaking reinvention of fiscal wheels when the problems evidently lie so much deeper? The German government has had several aims in buying time, such that the slow pace of reform is overdetermined. To be clear, the German government would love to solve the euro crisis and has, at times, clearly been desperate to do so. But it has judged that no available options were superior to the course it has chosen, and that course, because it required and still requires very extensive adjustment in the peripheral states, is understood to be a long-term project.

First, German delays ensure that fundamental reform impulses must come from the states whose financing models are most under threat. German delays ramp up—or at least fail to relieve—the reform pressure on governments in the Eurozone periphery.[68] Second, moving slowly increases pressure on private counterparties to accept losses or "haircuts." Merkel's insistence that private counterparties accept losses ("adequate participation of private creditors") in the second restructuring of Greek debt suggests that this motive was already operative by the October 2010 Deauville summit, at the latest.[69] Third, Germany sought to use delays to provide a window of time in which its own banks could get healthy after heavy exposure to the bonds of southern European states.[70] Finally, a fourth motive for buying time might have been the significant mismatch between Germany's own very static financial regulatory practices and substantial new experiments in the financial sector over the first decade of the 2000s. Germany has long sought to upload its domestic practices—in function if not always in form—to the European level. While this tendency admittedly had tapered off after the end of the Kohl governments, Germany has no appropriate system of financial regulation to upload.[71] Instead, it has a badly fragmented financial supervisory system that is essentially a permanent tug of war between the Bundesbank (Germany's powerful central bank) and the *Bundesanstalt für Finanzdienstleistungsaufsicht* (or Federal Financial Supervisory Authority).[72]

These are coherent reasons that a Germany eager to solve the euro crisis might still drag its feet on proposed reforms. As a matter of timing, they join with the complexities in the first section in which the German government's obsession with moral hazard complicated efforts to find a solution. Influenced by this inclination toward incrementalism, as the crisis has dragged on in the periphery while Germany enjoyed excellent labor market performance and strong exports, German officials have become more and more wedded to their favored narrative: they both celebrated Germany's excellent record and grew increasingly bold in prescribing "German-style" reforms for troubled Eurozone states.[73]

The final point of this section is that, to all the other reasons for policy conservatism, we have to add that the striking success of the German economy has reinforced Chancellor Merkel's conservatism and that of German voters. Merkel's policies toward the euro crisis have been clearly successful in a political sense, as voters have credited her government with solid management of the German economy and of her European policies. In fact, Pew data (2013) show a massive gap between German attitudes and those in much of the rest of Europe when it comes to the euro crisis.[74] Satisfaction with the economy in Germany was 66 points above the EU average, while smaller gaps separated Germans from the EU average on personal finances (26 percent), European integration (28 percent), and German leadership (48 percent). Only in Germany did a majority (54 percent) still believe that economic integration would strengthen national economies. Perhaps related, German respondents also were, by far, the most likely to support further centralization of power in the EU. Meanwhile, Merkel is Germany's most popular politician. Her approval ratings generally ran a whopping 30 percent above her challenger throughout the 2013 electoral season.

If Merkel has benefited politically, Germany itself has benefited economically to an extent. In fact, as the Eurozone periphery countries began to falter, Germany began to benefit in certain ways from the stress and strain in other parts of the Eurozone. By far the most important of these is the bottoming out of interest rates in Germany. Ten-year rates on German bonds went from above 3 percent to just over 1 percent in the spring of 2013 as the "flight to safety" produced negative real interest rates that dramatically reduced German debt service costs. One estimate, by the Allianz insurance company, calculated German interest savings at around 67 billion euro over several years.[75] Other estimates have been lower, but no one disputes that these benefits have accrued (indeed, the government plays them up in public reports, presumably as a way of countering the fear that German generosity has gone too far). Of course, these low rates have stimulated private investment in Germany as well, an area where rates have been strikingly low for a long time. Another very real benefit has been the influx of skilled labor into Germany from more distressed Eurozone economies. Germany's net labor inflow was 420,000 in 2012.[76] Finally, one could point to the benefits to Germany of the weakness of the euro itself. While the euro has strengthened in the wake of the OMT/"whatever it takes" announcements, there seems little doubt that if Germany had a national currency, its booming economy after 2010 would have led to substantial appreciation. Instead, its export conditions have remained healthy, an advantage Germany shares with only a few other (mostly northern European) states in the Eurozone.

To be sure, this German version of "exorbitant privilege" is clearly not of the same scale or duration as that long enjoyed by the United States.[77] But it has been an unexpected boon that makes the struggles in the Eurozone periphery beneficial to the German economy. Of course, my argument is not that Merkel's government designed these advantages. Instead, the point is that the flight-to-safety dynamics made policies of restraint *that were already wildly popular* in Germany even more popular. With Eurobonds and true fiscal federalism off the table, and with austerity and structural reforms predictably failing to fundamentally alter the crisis dynamics, the search resumed for another tool.

Can Supranational Banking Union Save the Eurozone?

The first major section of the chapter stressed the imbalances of the past, and the second stressed the current predicament. Consistent with the "forgotten unions" theme of the overall volume, this chapter's final section looks to the future and focuses on the plans for a banking union to complement monetary union. This chapter has been animated by the irresolvable tension between a Germany that genuinely seeks a solution to the European financial crisis and a Germany that is determined to minimize the costs of such a solution. The result has been halting and contradictory policy. The previous section showed that in addition to German fears of being called on to rescue other Eurozone states, the crisis in the periphery has actually brought very concrete benefits to Germany, further undermining the political incentives for policy change. The chapter's final section projects this tension forward, looking in particular at the banking union as emblematic of Germany's policy timing and substance dilemmas. Once again, we see a Germany that tends to slow walk the crisis and emphasize fiscal rectitude and structural reform as the solution to the euro crisis.

While the intergovernmental route to economic union is likely to continue the pattern of incremental change, the banking union announced in the summer of 2012 was, at least in principle, due to move much more quickly. A primary trigger for banking union was the awkward combination of supranational banking activity and national regulation, which, in the post-2008 period, had led to widely diverging credit conditions such that similar firms in different states had very different access to capital.[78] Moreover, banking union promised to break the "doom loop" between banks and sovereigns and, as such, promised a way forward without the Eurobonds that Merkel had ruled permanently out of bounds and whose rejection had been codified in her party's coalition agreement with the Social Democrats.

As currently conceived, banking union is to rest on four interrelated pillars: regulation, supervision, deposit insurance, and resolution. These pillars are, however, at very different stages of construction, and some may not happen at all. The outlines of the supervision dimension are fairly clear. Ultimate responsibility for supervision rests with a single entity, the European Central Bank, which has developed a new apparatus to engage in so-called asset quality reviews of systemically important banks, and has taken over supervision of these banks in November 2014. This handover has created what Wolfgang Schäuble has referred to as a "timber-framed" banking union.[79] If he has his way, this will be followed, at a later point, by a substantial change of the European treaties to pave the way for a "steel-framed" banking union. German support for the single supervisory mechanism (SSM) has been contingent upon some accommodation of the politically important savings banks (*Sparkassen*), whose local structure means they have connections in every electoral district in the country.

This will be a major undertaking. Nicolas Véron shows that while the existing treaties can support envisaged legal innovations in both prudential regulation (Article 114 of TFEU) and SSM (Article 127[6] TFEU)—though it is likely that smaller-scale treaty adjustments will be undertaken at a later date—the legal basis for both European-level resolution and deposit insurance mechanisms are lacking and would require a treaty change for a robust basis.[80] My interviews in the German Ministry of Finance and with CDU and SPD officials confirm that while the EU has been able to engage in constitutional innovation through intergovernmental treaties in cases such as the ESM and the Fiscal Compact, the legal basis sought for resolution, in particular, is likely to be more robust and to be sought through the main EU architecture and not as separate agreements. Indeed, in July 2013, the Finance Ministry even obliged formal transposition of an EU provision that had direct effects.

After German objections led to the imposition of a minimum threshold, the ECB now supervises all banks with more than 30 billion euro in assets.[81] This corresponds to more than 130 banks that hold 80 percent of Eurozone banking assets.[82] Starting in late 2013, a process of "publicly-led triage, recapitalization, and restructuring" commenced, leading to the ECB's development of a "manual" by March 2014.[83] The daunting technical challenges have been made somewhat easier by the ECB's better access to clean information than was true of the earlier European bank "stress tests" run by the European Banking Authority headquartered in London. A major impediment, however, lies in the fact that as the ECB uncovers banking problems, the member states will still be responsible for resolving them. This "handover problem" is critical.[84] The ECB has every incentive to ensure that the banks it will take under its supervision have a healthy basis. But the financial resources that will likely be required in any vigorous assessment would need to come from member states. Germany's preference for strictly rules-based regimes for handling such recapitalization and resolution issues is also unlikely to prevail given the likely substantial involvement of politically sensitive creditors—including national pension funds.

German opposition has also prevented the use of the ESM for bank recapitalization, a situation that seems likely to persist until after the handover of authority to the SSM in late 2014.[85] An important consideration will be the extent to which legacy debts can be identified, legally realized, and nationally resolved prior to the handover, if at all. The most credible forward-looking situation would be one in which rigorous European-level reviews and ample national restructuring and resolution funds take place in advance. These are, of course, exactly the circumstances most likely to strike hard at the most fiscally exposed Eurozone states and to open the possibility that, for example, senior unsecured creditors may get far more favorable treatment in fiscally solid states than in those states with more severe funding pressures. That said, ESM ought to be available to backstop these states, if not, as noted, the banks directly. Moreover, Véron argues that markets have, to an extent, priced in large if necessarily uncertain resolution costs for certain Eurozone members, and thus resolution costs ought not to lead to a loss of market access.[86]

On the single resolution mechanism (SRM), we have clear conflict between the Commission and the ECB on one side and the German government on the other. Part of the problem is that there is little clarity

on the size of potential bank losses. Financial journalists have estimated
such losses at 1–1.6 trillion euro, though the higher estimates seem to
assume that bad assets will equate automatically to the need for new capital.[87] Assuming some asset recovery plus available loss provisioning, others
come up with figures closer to 400 billion euro—still daunting but not as
cataclysmic as 1.6 trillion.[88] An additional worry is that any credible asset
quality review and stress test would seem to require frank acknowledgment that holders of bonds of some Eurozone governments face the risk
of at least partial default. This would imply an end to the practice of rating these bonds as zero-risk.[89] And yet any such move would raise future
borrowing costs for governments, possibly sparking financing problems
that would hammer both governments and the banks.[90] As of the summer of 2014, however, European banks had generally made surprising
progress toward raising capital in advance of the fall stress test scenarios.
The *Financial Times* reported that European Tier One capital levels were
nearing 12 percent on average, roughly the same proportion as among US
banks.[91] Furthermore, the ECB's announcement in early October 2014 to
buy an additional trillion euro of covered bonds and asset-backed securities directly from Eurozone banks would help them further strengthen
their balance sheets. Averages can hide a lot of variation, and some important banks may fail the tests. Perhaps a more pressing medium-term challenge will be to shore up profitability levels in Europe's financial sector.[92]

Such difficulties are emblematic of a host of potential problems for a single
resolution authority. When the European Commission announced its plan for
such a European-level resolution authority in July 2013, two problems immediately surfaced. The first was explicit German opposition to the idea of a European
authority in the first place on the grounds that banking problems were a matter
for sovereign states to regulate. Merkel and Hollande released a paper to this end
just prior to the Commission announcement.[93] Second, the Commission failed
to call for the use of the ESM as an initial backstop for such a mechanism.[94]

One major reason for Germany's opposition to several facets of the
banking union is the receding of pressure on the Eurozone and the growing
sense that they can muddle through. Berlin has clearly backed away from
any idea of an early intergovernmental conference that would be required
for any major change to the European treaties. Berlin will still seek the
smaller changes that would allow them to have economic union—essentially, Merkel hopes, in the form of a kind of Lisbon Process with teeth. One
can draw up the intergovernmental contracts noted earlier under existing

treaties, but to either punish or reward (with EU budget funds) contracting states would require treaty change, and there is currently little evidence that Germany could find many member states willing to sign up for such contracts. Germany has also dropped the idea of a "super-commissioner" to enforce budgetary discipline, a Schäuble idea that Merkel never supported. Germany perceives other risks from moving ahead expeditiously. The European Parliament (EP) might oblige a formal convention—they did not do so for the ESM—in part because a larger convention might open the door to greater powers for the EP.[95] Meanwhile, other member states have their own wish list for a treaty change, some uncongenial to Germany, and this seems, for now, to have convinced the German government to trudge forward without a treaty change.

Its overall position puts Germany substantially at odds with the European Central Bank. Jörg Asmussen, who was an economic advisor to Merkel before joining the ECB Executive Board, had made an explicit call for a "European backstop" in a speech in London just prior to the Commission announcement.[96] The Commission proposal, though it does foresee a European agency, would not have resources to help close an ailing bank. Germany's alternative proposal is for a resolution mechanism that coordinates those of the member states. On the one hand, this position perfectly replicates its general orientation against exposing German taxpayers to banking resolution problems in other states. On the other hand, it does nothing to address the issue that many national programs are woefully underfinanced and completely incapable of resolving troubled banks in the states in question. Several academic studies warn that European-level supervision and national-level resolution will lead to misaligned incentives.[97] They mirror the position of the ECB, as articulated by Asmussen, that separate national resolution funds will invite jurisdictional fights that hamper rapid responses to banking crises.[98]

Given the main thrust of this chapter, it is comprehensible why German politics should be fixated on slowing or preventing the establishment of a new authority on deposit insurance and resolution. These activities are traditional areas of national discretion and—more relevant to Germany—pooling liabilities might expose Germany to bank losses in other member states. While this chapter has stressed that German behavior and German rhetoric are often out of sync with one another, banking union appears to be an area where apparent German refusal is indeed built upon a foundation of actual German refusal.

Conclusion: Why Is It So Hard to Get the Right Eurozone Policy at the Right Time?

This chapter has tried to make sense of the future of the Eurozone by looking at Germany's institutional constraints and at the beliefs of ordinary citizens. If Germans sometimes appear dogmatic today, this is a superficial phenomenon. To be sure, there is a veneer of populist *Bild Zeitung*–fueled patter about the need for all of Europe to follow the German model. But this patter is as self-deceptive—because conditions for German structural reforms in the pre-2008 period were far more supportive than today—as it is self-congratulatory, and many Germans do doubt that their government has found the key to the euro crisis in a bracing set of structural reforms of state and market. This uncertainty and tentativeness are sufficient to keep Germany from enacting policies that might have (and perhaps might still) refashion the Eurozone in a more sustainable way. And because the ambivalent and uncertain side of Germany dithers, it gives an additional advantage to those countrymen who defend the untenable status quo, which, in its crudest form, is simply "prosperity for us; austerity for you."

This chapter has made this argument by covering three main issues: the "problem" of trade imbalances, which German leaders and voters do not perceive as a problem at all and around which there has been very little serious debate; the exorbitant privilege that unexpectedly accrued to Germany during the euro crisis and that helps prevent a major course correction by Germany; and the partial banking union now being constructed in a period of relative calm, which has reduced German incentives for a more far-reaching design. The chapter has showed that each of these already complex issues was made more complex by issues of timing. This kind of timing issue goes well beyond the very useful theoretical literature on what one might call the temporal inconsistencies of inter-institutional articulation at the EU level.[99] Instead, this chapter has focused on extended nightmares of timing that have arisen between member states and between constituent parts of the EU in a setting that is anything but routine.

Going forward, there is every reason to think that the imbalance problem—deeply anchored in German fascination with exports and grounded in deep strengths in German manufacturing—will persist in some form. It seems much less likely that the various aspects of Germany's exorbitant privilege will endure. The flight to safety saved Germans tens of billions in financing costs, but can negative real interest rates for one country and punitive ones for another be a stable outcome? This seems doubtful.

And the boom in immigration, while helpful to Germany, may also prove short-lived. An OECD study suggests that most Greek and Spanish immigrants return to their home country within a year of moving to Germany.[100] So what if the imbalance stays, the privilege goes, and the banking union—in any event, a mechanism to deal with future problems but with virtually nothing to say about the resolution of past problems—never really arrives in any full-fledged way?

Until new crises emerge, it seems the current muddling is preordained. German voters have, very recently, heartily approved it and would be unnerved by any decisive steps by the new German government that broke from this course. The current path keeps the pressure for adjustment almost exclusively on other countries, and this is seen as entirely correct in the German debate, owing to the self-evident vice of the deficit countries and the self-evident virtue of the surplus countries. While there has been some recent real wage growth in Germany, public finances remain focused on balance. Indeed, a recent IMF report on Germany felt compelled to caution that the country should not be "over performing on consolidation."[101] Additionally, the December 2013 coalition agreement among the three governing parties foresees only very modest expansionary measures of about 0.1 percent of GDP annually.[102]

Meanwhile, export outlets outside the Eurozone have grown in attraction while established Eurozone customers may have low purchasing power for years to come. Germany's ferocious export boom that started around 2003 eventually led, by 2007, to a more than 100 billion euro external surplus with the Eurozone at a time that Germany's surplus with non-EU states was under 40 billion euro. But times have changed. As the Eurozone stagnated, demand from outside the EU boomed. By 2012, the positions had nearly reversed, with non-EU 27 states running a nearly 100 billion euro deficit with Germany, while the Eurozone deficit had shrunk to about 55 billion euro.[103] Germany has very successfully diversified its export portfolio, and this seems to have eliminated some of their urgency to resolve the Eurozone crisis.[104] The only problem is the specter of trade and currency battles with trading partners around the globe.

But if the muddling is undeniable, it is not clear that the Eurozone will really get through. Whether and how Germany should try to fix the Eurozone also depends on one's view of the medium run. Even presuming the "imbalances" approach stressed here is correct, it is actually not obvious that this euro can be repaired. For the most part, the imbalances argument *tends* to be used by those who question German sanity. The form it takes argues that

Germany profited enormously from this euro, and this is why its austerity mania is *hypocritical* (because Germany gained all along from others' indulgent spending), *unwise* (because it fails to do more to rescue the system that has made it prosperous), and tactically *clumsy* (because it synchronizes deflationary impulses).

But one could also accept the imbalances approach and simply say that while it was good while it lasted, the euro experiment has hit its endpoint and German leaders have concluded that it cannot be reformed for another round. To be sure, this position is one where the glass is acknowledged to be half empty: much of the apparent export success of recent years will have to be compensated by German taxpayers resolving, recapitalizing, or bailing out the German banks that helped finance it.[105] But, according to this view, German efforts to strengthen and retain the Eurozone would just mean throwing good money after bad.

The politics of timing started with the "intrusion" of the German voter into the domain of financial politics, something that has typically been an elite domain in Germany. Banking bailout politics are now so expensive, however, that mass politics has forced its way in. But while German voters are most certainly now paying attention, the dilemma is that by the time politicians convince them of the need to support a certain financial remedy, the Eurozone problems have grown to such a size that this remedy no longer works. A new remedy is required, and the process of explaining the need for it begins again, only this time with increasing voter skepticism that the elites know what they are talking about.

The resulting populist discourse, along with the institutional divisions in German politics, has persistently granted Merkel an important edge in her negotiations. Typically, at the more than 30 EU summits since 2009, Merkel bargains hard but often makes some concessions. A breakthrough of some kind is announced, and a certain collective sigh of relief is registered in Europe. At that moment, other actors in German politics often begin to counter or at least delay what Merkel has agreed. Such actors include the Bundesrat, the Federal Constitutional Court, and, above all, the Bundesbank. These are not entirely quiet rearguard actions, and if they were, they would lose one of their most important effects: to calm German voters.

All of this reverses the usual picture of the "semi-sovereign state" in Germany.[106] According to Peter Katzenstein's formulation, policymaking in Germany moves slowly and deliberately because a plethora of actors are constitutionally empowered to participate in decision-making. Once the system produces a decision, however, the general assumption is that the very corporate partners who gave their assent in the first place will carry it out. What was a hindrance in conception becomes a help in execution. What we are seeing now, however, is a different, in some ways opposite, story. The Chancellor goes to summits and, however grudgingly, agrees to things, which then get walked back in succeeding weeks. Take early summer 2012, when many European leaders thought Merkel had agreed that the ESM could directly fund ailing banks. In subsequent weeks, the Bundesbank strongly disputed this, leaving other European partners wondering. Or take the OMT, which appears to have brought months of relative calm to the financial markets. The German Constitutional Court—as discussed above—has suggested that OMT is not compatible with German basic law. Because the Court asked the European Court of Justice (ECJ) to weigh in, many commentators have assumed that a more euro-friendly court can bless the OMT. But this is not really what Karlsruhe's decision says. Instead, the subtext is far more to call on the ECJ to adapt the OMT to Germany's needs.[107] If the message is "fix it or we will nix it," there may be much more trouble ahead for OMT. Finally, the apparent breakthroughs on banking union in 2012 now appear much less secure once one moves beyond the supervision pillar. Thus, German indecision persists, as does the misery in Europe. There is little reason to expect it to abate any time soon.

10

European Integration Past, Present, and Future

MOVING FORWARD THROUGH CRISIS?

Craig Parsons and Matthias Matthijs

*As on other occasions in European history, this crisis offers a
chance to progress; we must be ready to act on it. Let us not
waste this opportunity to advance European integration.*

PETER PRAET *(Member of ECB Executive Board, 2012)[1]*

Introduction: Moving Forward Through Crisis?

"European integration has progressively moved forward through crisis."
"Europe always emerges stronger after a crisis." "Without previous crises, the
European Union would not have reached the advanced stage it is at today."
Across EU history we have heard such slogans from European heads of state
or government, EU officials, and scholars of European integration as well.
They tend to sing the "Europe moves forward through crisis" refrain almost in
tune whenever the next EU challenge comes along.[2] All echo Jean Monnet's
celebrated words, that "Europe will be forged in crises, and will be the sum of
the solutions adopted in those crises."[3] The chorus swelled to record volumes
with the onset of the euro crisis in the spring of 2010.

The revived prominence of Europe's crisis rhetoric since 2010 is not difficult to explain. It is a reassuring frame that tells Europeans they have sur-
mounted crises before and that the recent storm clouds have a silver lining.
Yet there is a risk in setting today's challenges in such a dominant narrative.
What if the prior construction of the EU did *not* actually arise from comparable crises in the past? What if this time is different? In that case, the

"forward-through-crisis" narrative may encourage complacency at an especially inopportune moment. Europeans who face their first real crisis may conclude that long-term solutions to their current problems will arrive in a functional, even quasi-automatic way. Rather than thinking hard about a political plan or road map that could lead them forward out of the crisis, they may continue to wait for real progress to emerge spontaneously out of mere technocratic tweaks.

This chapter, the second of four in the book's final section addressing the future of the euro, argues that this risk is real. If we define political "crises" in a commonsensical way—as moments characterized by widespread agreement that something fundamental must change in public policy to avoid disastrous near-term consequences—then the euro crisis is without any doubt the first one in the EU's history. None of the past major steps taken toward today's EU featured these elements at all: no especially widespread agreement on major policy problems, and no pressure for immediate decisions under threat of imminent cataclysm. All previous steps did include some crisis rhetoric, certainly, but only in the vague way in which the proponents of almost any substantial step in public policy link it to a "crisis"—by which they just mean anything they see as an important public policy problem. Beyond the rhetoric, all previous major steps to the EU resulted when leaders pursued a positive political plan for European integration amid widespread contestation of whether it was necessary or even desirable at that specific time. The EU was built around a forward-looking organizational project, never as a quick fix to pressing problems.

On the basis of these claims about EU history, we then argue that the European sovereign debt crisis is different from previous episodes in two principal ways. First, this was a crisis: inaction would have brought disaster. Second, this was an acutely political crisis: immediate problems forced EU discussion out of its traditional technocratic sphere, painfully highlighting both distributional conflicts between countries and party-political ideological conflicts over economic policy. For the first time ever, EU leaders felt that they had to pull together quickly and make blatantly political decisions.

As we see it, then, "this time is different" in roughly the opposite way from the phrase evoked by Carmen Reinhart's and Kenneth Rogoff's book on financial crises.[4] Their book, aptly titled *This Time Is Different*, established that the recurring belief among market participants that every new crisis is somehow "different" from the last one has resulted in eight centuries of financial folly. Reinhart and Rogoff tell tales of governments headed into crisis who insist that everything is fine. In European integration, by contrast, leaders have regularly evoked crises where none existed. Now in a real crisis, they face a deep, internalized version of the problem of the boy who cried wolf. In repeating their mantra, they are in danger of persuading the public and themselves that crises naturally generate good long-term solutions for complex institutional reform. Nothing in European history suggests that they do.[5]

What kind of bolder, more proactive political plan might a less compla-cent European leadership provide? That is admittedly hard to say, though we summarize the ways in which EU leaders' responses to the crisis so far are widely seen as falling short of resolving their underlying problems. In any case, the euro crisis suggests that EU leaders' work is not done. Experts agree that the steps taken in recent years mainly help Europe to watch out for crises and react when they hit, doing less to meet the deeper challenges that make Europe vulnerable to such crises in the first place. Europeans can ill afford to adopt the status-quo orientation prevailing in American politics, where any constitutional reform is almost unthinkable. The young EU rests on far more fundamental instabilities than does the old US. Without a positive vision for its future, we fear that the next time will not be so different.

The chapter begins by highlighting the teleologies that have imbued most thinking on European integration by both scholars and politicians, of which the "forward-through-crisis" discourse is one result. Then we survey past steps in the construction of the EU and show that they had little relationship to real crises. Finally, we dissect how the euro crisis is a real political crisis and how the responses to it seem not to represent strong forward movement for the EU overall. Our conclusion is not particularly optimistic, since we perceive many obstacles to the reinvigoration of a more positive and visionary European project, but we very much hope that it spurs some brainstorming in new directions.

The Teleology of Thinking about European Integration

The pervasiveness of teleology—the belief in quasi-inevitable progress toward some end goal or final destination—is striking in most scholarly and active-political thinking about European integration. All scholars of Europe know that the theoretical literature on European integration began with the teleological "neofunctionalist" writings of Ernst Haas.[6] Building on the early integration insights of Europe's "founding fathers" Robert Schuman and Jean Monnet, Haas hypothesized that both the functional interconnectedness of modern economies and powerful positive feedback mechanisms would spread economic integration from one sector to another. Attempts at integration in one sector would soon reveal incentives to integrate other sectors, persuading people that more of their problems were best addressed at the European level. The institutional bodies set up to coordinate early steps—the Commission and other supranational EU institutions—would also circle back to promote further steps by teaming up with interest groups and national officials. Thus the interconnected nature of modern economies and snowballing institutional delegations of power would gradually propel Europe toward a true political union.[7]

Unlike most ivory-tower constructs, Haas's theory both came from and fed back into political beliefs among the actors it studied. As Haas once told one of us as a graduate student, his theory "basically took Jean Monnet's beliefs and made them into social-science hypotheses." Monnet subscribed to a functionalist school of thought in which the destructiveness of nationalist war and the interdependence of modern economies were pressing Europeans to integrate their national political systems. In his view, change would come as the result of these technical processes of necessary adaptation to an evolving world, not out of ideological appeals. As he put it, "[p]eople only accept change when they are faced with necessity, and only recognize necessity when a crisis is upon them."[8] On a practical level, though, he also saw the need to inform people about these "necessities" through a persuasive effort, and he became a tireless advocate for the cause. Haas then came along and made a theoretical prediction that functional interconnectedness and supranational persuasion would indeed drive integration forward.

Though we have no direct evidence of the penetration of "neofunctionalism" beyond scholarly debates, it seems very likely that his work then provided academic legitimacy to Monnet's views in European policy circles and institutions of elite education. Moreover, the political impact of these ideas extended not only to advocates of a United States of Europe, but to many opponents as well. For example, teleological beliefs lay behind the extraordinary steps that French President Charles de Gaulle took to block the further development of the European Economic Community (EEC) institutions during the "empty chair crisis" in the mid-1960s. He and Monnet agreed that the European institutions would tend to accumulate more power, but disagreed on whether the *telos* was desirable or not. The same kind of teleological views run rampant among British Euro-skeptics today, who are convinced that Brussels will inevitably extinguish all hope and light on the Continent.[9] Similarly, the "bicycle theory" of integration—"it must keep going or it will fall over," often evoked by Jacques Delors and others—is related to Haas's teleology and his argument that integration should be conceived as an ongoing process, not an end-state.[10]

Stepping back from Europe for a moment, it is thus fair to say that the dominant narrative on the EU is exactly the opposite of the US myth of the Founding Fathers and their Great Constitution. For Americans, their political system sprang full-formed from the greatest political document ever written. It is stable, and few major improvements are imaginable. For Europeans, the EU is a fundamentally dynamic, partial, and unsteady construct that must and will continue to justify itself by delivering new benefits from "ever closer union." Some look forward to this ongoing development, others do not, but few seem to imagine the EU staying as it is.

Today, most scholars have moved on from neofunctionalism in EU studies or have shorn it of its most teleological elements, but teleology nonetheless remains an active part of the academic scene. Haas himself pronounced neofunctionalism "obsolete" after de Gaulle's attacks on the EEC.[11] This did not evict teleological thinking from EU studies, however, because an equally strong teleological logic also animated the main competitor that came to dominate EU studies in the 1990s. On the surface, Andrew Moravcsik's "liberal intergovernmentalism" is an attack on Haasian logic of runaway institutions, arguing that national governments fully dominate the EU and carefully constrain the growth of supranational power.[12] Yet Moravcsik does not reject that substantial delegations of power have taken place, and the way he explains them replaces the neofunctionalist teleology with another that is even more powerful and widely believed. It is globalization, he suggests, that encourages interest groups to see rising gains in cross-border movements and nudges national governments to seek open and coordinated policies with their neighbors. Moravcsik's EU, which displays "normal politics in an era of globalization," comes across as an even more inevitable product of massive underlying trends than any image from Monnet or Haas.[13] When he explains the euro deal at Maastricht with this logic, as a largely rational-functional response to economic imperatives, he seems to imply that Europeans will do whatever is rationally necessary to fix the euro's problems as well.

Neither in neofunctionalism nor in liberal intergovernmentalism is the notion of crisis a central one, but both nonetheless nourish the discourse of a Europe that moves forward through crisis.[14] The two theories share foundations in rational-functional theorizing in which governments ultimately respond effectively to the demands of interest groups to solve unambiguously real problems. In both approaches, actors are rational enough that they tend to deal with policy problems before they become full-blown crises, leading to accounts that focus mainly on long-term coalition building and bargaining. Still, the bottom-line explanation that both theories give for all past steps in integration is that a large number of interest groups and governments were persuaded—either by functional and political spillover or by the forces of globalization—that something had to be done. For Europe to have come so far, delegating such unprecedented power to supranational institutions, both theories hint that Europeans' past challenges must have been very compelling. Surely these past challenges shaded into actual crises at certain points.

But did they? We argue in the next section that until very recently, the construction of the EU never really displayed a process in which a wide variety of Europeans rallied to new integrative steps as the necessary response to pressing policy challenges.

Past Crises: Overview and Assessment

If history taught the comforting lesson that the EU always advances in crises, what would we see when we looked back at the major steps toward today's Europe? Interpreting any past development as a response to a "crisis"— as opposed to, say, the agenda of a certain political movement, or a bargain between multiple competing agendas, or some other kind of political story— carries strong observable implications. In the approach to a crisis-driven step, we would presumably find a spreading consensus that concrete policy failures called for new solutions at the European level. As policy failures sharpened, persuading many people that immediate steps were necessary, the consensus would extend to broad support for fairly specific solutions. Implementation would follow quickly to prevent the crisis from worsening. Different actors would likely have distinct priorities within the prevailing sense of crisis, leading to bargaining about precise features and distributional aspects of solutions, but few if any responsible actors would dispute the need for broadly similar steps. Throughout this process, the most crucial evidence of genuinely crisis-driven change would be *unusual consensus* that something needs to be done: actors who disagreed about policy priorities in "normal" times would be compelled by crisis to favor a certain collective response.

Unfortunately, EU history does not offer this sort of comfort to crisis-struck Europeans today. Few of these features can be found in any step in the construction of the EU. Of course, the EU as we know it today did arise and evolve to solve some fairly widely perceived problems—a cycle of war, protectionist temptations, monetary instability, stabilization of transitional post-communist polities—but European leaders never confronted a time-pressured sense that failed agreements would be disastrous in the near term. With the exception of broad acceptance of the eastern enlargement, no major element of their substantive deals ever attracted a notable rally of unusual consensus. Widely different diagnoses of policy problems and desirable European-level solutions—including major actors whose first preference at each point was to do nothing—endured through all major deals. Differences were resolved in political maneuvering and bargaining rather than through crisis-compelled convergence.

A book chapter can offer only a brief and impressionistic historical survey to support such broad historical claims. We rapidly touch on the European Coal and Steel Community (ECSC), the failed European Defense Community (EDC), the European Economic Community (EEC), the European Monetary System (EMS), the Single European Act (SEA), Economic and Monetary Union (EMU) in the Maastricht Treaty, and eastern enlargement.[15] We focus disproportionately on French evidence, on which one of us has written extensively, and otherwise note German and British positions as the other most important players in major EU bargains. As thin and selective as our historical glance may be, we think it fully lays to rest the notion that integration has ever advanced through anything like today's euro crisis.

Even advocates of crisis-driven integration tend not to interpret its first step in that light. French Foreign Minister Robert Schuman's proposal that eventually led to the ECSC on May 9, 1950, is conventionally (and rightly) told as the invention of a new organizational model against considerable resistance—a "leap in the dark," as Schuman put it at his press conference—not a reactive response to a consensually understood and pressing problem.[16] Certainly many French and other European elites recognized broad policy challenges to which the ECSC was one solution. For France, the ECSC established a new framework for Franco-German relations that allowed for continued oversight of West Germany (and guaranteed access to its high-quality coal) while meeting American pressures to wind down the Occupation. Neither in France nor anywhere else, however, did most elites rally to it as necessary to prevent imminent disaster. All relevant French interest groups opposed the ECSC treaty through its ratification. Not even a majority of French politicians ever supported it; Schuman bought the last few votes with a side concession on colonial policies.[17] In Germany, Chancellor Adenauer had to overrule hostility from his powerful Economics Minister, Ludwig Erhard, and only shut down the opposition of German industrialists with help from the American occupying authorities.[18] Outside the most Euro-federalist circles, which were generally politically irrelevant, most European elites in the early 1950s would have been perplexed by the suggestion that the ECSC was necessary to avoid an imminent crisis. To both its champions and its opponents, it was a deliberately experimental policy that departed from prevailing wisdom.

The EDC, by contrast, did surge onto the European agenda due to an immediate crisis—but no consensus ever acknowledged it as the right response. This second French proposal came in the early 1950s in response to the outbreak of the Korean War. For Europeans the war itself was not the crisis, however, since few of them shared America's domino fears that it signaled an imminent Soviet invasion of Western Europe.[19] Their crisis took the form of sudden American demands to shore up Western defenses by rearming West Germany. With considerable reluctance, a sizable number of policymakers across Europe agreed to work out a plan that would use the ECSC model to maintain supranational authority over small German units. Again, most interest groups in most countries opposed this model relative to less novel ones—most obviously, simply rearming West Germany within NATO— and military officers everywhere were divided but mostly skeptical.[20] Ratification was achieved in West Germany, Italy, and the Benelux, but in 1952 and 1953 French coalitional politics shifted control of the legislative agenda away from Schuman and his pro-EDC allies. Supported by less than a third of the National Assembly, with new leaders uninterested in making cross-issue payoffs to assemble a majority, the EDC failed. It seemed that the EDC was not necessary after all.

Perhaps, then, a true crisis set Europeans back on the "community" path opened by ECSC? Though venerated historian Alan Milward's economic analysis suggested that the EEC treaty of 1957 was ultimately necessary to "rescue the nation-state," his account largely ignores that few Europeans at the time perceived either a crisis of the nation-state or the EEC as the functional solution to it.[21] After the Messina conference of 1955—now hallowed in EU lore as the launch of the "Spaak Committee" that morphed into the EEC negotiations, which led to the Treaty of Rome—the most common reaction across Europe was disbelief that anyone would consider further talks on the contested "community" model.[22] The British declined to participate, with snide comments that they could not imagine any sort of successful result.[23] Two conditions made a new deal on trade liberalization seem more pie-in-the-sky than unavoidably necessary. First, most French policymakers were convinced that French business could not survive more open competition.

France had effectively reneged on all prior commitments to liberalization in the 16-nation Organization for European Economic Cooperation (OEEC) since 1949.[24] Second, despite a byzantine web of protectionism, intra-European trade was expanding very rapidly in the mid-1950s. Milward notes this "remarkable" growth, musing that a trade pattern often attributed to the EEC was clearly developing before it.[25] If proponents of European free trade had plenty to complain about in the mid-1950s, then, they could point neither to a trade crisis nor to a widespread sense that a new deal was even possible.

In agriculture it may seem more plausible to see a crisis at the time, especially in France. Export subsidies in Europe's largest agricultural producer were reaching budget-breaking levels in the mid-1950s. Successive French governments felt strong pressure to secure international outlets to placate rebellious *paysans*. Yet if the creation of the EEC's Common Agricultural Policy (CAP) has entered legend as the lure that drew France into the Common Market, the fact is that French farmers took a long time even to see a supranational agricultural community as *acceptable*, let alone as critical to solve their problems. An agricultural community was viewed as a Dutch idea that would liberalize farm trade, and almost all French farmers preferred the more familiar vehicle of bilateral export contracts. As Milward notes, French farmers "remained until almost the last moment suspiciously antagonistic of anything more complicated [than bilateral contracts], especially anything that would provide a market for other peoples' surpluses in France."[26] As part of the EEC negotiations, the French government was pleased to secure a transitional period during which the Germans contracted bilaterally to buy French farm exports, while any sort of "common policy" would only begin to be discussed within three years. Not until well into those talks in the 1960s did most French farmers come around to seeing the CAP as likely to be more beneficial than threatening.[27] In sum, no consensus connected a farm crisis to the EEC solution in the late 1950s.

We must regretfully ask readers to look elsewhere for the tale of how the EEC plan overcame these obstacles, since our current object is just to highlight the absence of crisis-driven politics in the EU story.[28] Consider, then, its next substantial step two decades later. The European Monetary System (EMS) was Europe's first enduring response to increased exchange rate volatility in the post–Bretton Woods era. This 1979 commitment to defend fluctuating bilateral bands between currencies responded directly to a concrete policy problem. Broadly varying exchange rates made a mockery of the EEC's goal of a level playing field for intra-European trade. In particular, the Deutschmark (DM) perennially appreciated against other currencies. This asymmetric relationship was vastly worsened by a depreciating US dollar, from which a steady flow of capital went disproportionately into the DM and pushed its value upward. Germany's partners complained that they could not keep up the relative value of their currencies vis-à-vis the DM. German exporters complained of weakening competitiveness.

Nonetheless, the eventual EMS deal did not occur under immediate market pressure, nor did it ever attract especially wide consensus. Instead, it perpetually evoked the political and distributional fights we might expect from a deal intended to hold the DM down and other currencies up. Before, during, and after the EMS agreement, strong-currency advocates applauded outside Germany and grumbled within it, while weak-currency advocates did the reverse. Critics of European authority, such as Margaret Thatcher and the French Gaullists, opposed the deal.[29] Moreover, to the extent that the EMS accomplished its founders' goals—encouraging a convergence of inflation rates and monetary policies by the late 1980s—it did so ironically by nudging Europe toward sharper moments of explicit crisis. That is, the EMS commitments contributed to the concentration of long-term economic evolutions into short-term political crises. The DM's upward drift continued, but what had previously been a gradual process now sparked periodic conflagrations in defense of the EMS thresholds. Currency speculators jumped in to elbow currencies past these targets. Similar crises would have occurred in an EMS-less Europe, certainly, but the EMS rules generated even much more explicit and sharper pressure on policymakers in weak-currency countries to imitate German policies.

The next step in EU history, the Single European Act (SEA) of 1986, probably attracts more crisis-driven rhetoric than any other. All educated Europeans know the tale of "Euro-sclerosis" in the early 1980s—anemic growth, high labor costs, mounting unemployment, and a sense of being surpassed by both the US and Japan—and how it provoked the *relance* of the EEC with the SEA's "Single Market 1992" program and institutional reforms.[30] Also setting the scene for the SEA deal were a series of EEC bargaining impasses over the British budgetary "rebate," CAP spending, and Iberian enlargement that gave its meetings a distinct sense of political crisis at their nadir in 1983. There is no denying that the SEA process featured a masterful orchestration of crisis language to help sell an important political initiative; however, it addressed no immediate policy problems at all. To the contrary, the "1992" program and institutional reforms were long-term shifts whose consequences are still playing out today. And if a superficial historical glance seems to display unusual consensus around the SEA—like the assent of both British conservative Margaret Thatcher and French socialist François Mitterrand, or ratification in the French Assembly by a huge majority of 498 to 35—this impression falls apart under closer scrutiny.

Consider these two examples more closely. Thatcher said explicitly at her press conference after the final deal that she was never persuaded that EEC treaty reform was necessary. She accepted a hard-driven bargain in late-night talks and soon regretted that she had—complaining later (according to some sources) that she was "tricked" by Commission President Jacques Delors on the extent of institutional reforms.[31] Meanwhile, Mitterrand remained skeptical about the liberalization focus of the deal, but reluctantly accepted it in order to obtain the institutional reforms he sought.[32] The SEA's ratifying majority in the French Assembly comprised mainly two parties with internal majorities that disliked the treaty. Mitterrand's Socialists had little enthusiasm for the "1992" liberalizing plan. Most voted the party line because it was difficult to disavow a deal identified personally with their president.[33] Jacques Chirac's Gaullists generally opposed the SEA and took over the government between its signature in March 1986 and its ratification in December. They passed it only grudgingly due to threats to their coalition from their small pro-European allies and pressure from Mitterrand's presidential powers.[34] In our view, these examples are representative of the broader politics of the SEA. Like previous steps in the EU story, it came together thanks to bargains between competing agendas and common dynamics in organizational politics. It featured neither immediate crisis pressures nor unusual consensus around specific European responses.

And what of the single currency deal in the Maastricht Treaty of 1992? Behind the EMU negotiations from 1989 to 1991, it is fair to see two sources of pressure that might qualify as "semi-crisis" conditions. First was the asymmetric burden of EMS commitments in the late 1980s, which were exacerbated by the complete liberalization of capital movements as part of the SEA's "1992" agenda. The ongoing flow of money into the rock-solid DM gave Germany's EMS partners only one way to maintain their EMS pegs: keeping national interest rates slightly above Germany's to keep capital from flowing out of their currencies. The full liberalization of capital movements in 1988 sharpened these pressures, such that any hint that EMS members' rates might stray from Germany's baseline sparked rapid outward financial flows. Though this subordination of other EMS members to German monetary decisions was not necessarily disastrous economically, it was politically difficult to sustain. Second, the fall of the Berlin Wall in November 1989 and the surprisingly rapid reunification of Germany just a year later generated political pressure for a gesture to reassure Europeans— inside Germany and out—that the new Germany would maintain its European commitments.

But as tempting as it is today to think that European leaders felt com- pelled to respond to these conditions, EMS asymmetry and German reuni- fication were more policy problems than immediate crises. Nothing in particular would have happened given inaction on either issue for a few years. Nor did the concrete proposals that led to EMU ever attract broad con- sensus. In France some unusually broad agreement emerged that *something* should be done to escape the asymmetries of the EMS, with major political figures across left and right (including Chirac) arguing in this period that Europe either had to unravel the EMS or move forward to some more bal- anced arrangement.[35] As that "something" became the EMU proposal in the hands of Jacques Delors and advisors to Mitterrand and German Chancellor Helmut Kohl, however, support in France and across Europe fragmented in familiar divisions over economic policies and pro- and anti-Europeanism. Chirac and other sovereignty-conscious figures on the French right opposed the single currency.[36] Most of the French left despised the orthodox monetar- ist conditions in the EMU plan—to the point that Mitterrand relied more on votes from the right to scrape out a *petit oui* in his referendum on the Maastricht Treaty in 1992.[37]

Kohl took steps to ensure that Germany had the kind of non-debate about integrative steps that had been typical in its politics since the 1950s, though everyone suspected what Kohl later admitted: that any popular vote on EMU would have rejected the single currency.[38] The British were certainly not persuaded that any particular new European initiatives were necessary. And obviously the euro's recent travails make it ever more dif- ficult to see EMU as a functional response to compelling policy problems. Many economists warned at the time that the plan suffered from exactly the vulnerability behind today's crisis: enduring differences between national economies would lead to divergent performances over time, especially given large shocks (like, say, the near-collapse of the global financial system in 2008 and 2009).[39]

As the last basic step to the framework of today's EU, consider the admission of post-communist countries, which profoundly reshaped the European club. Here, finally, we encounter a decision to which practically all elites rallied across member states and political divides. Though the prospect of eastern enlargement provoked many debates in the early post–Cold War years, by the mid-1990s it was clear that enlargement would happen. Disagreements were limited to its timing and modalities. Enthusiasm certainly varied widely—from eager British happy to spread out and hopefully water down the EU club, to generally positive Germans concerned about stabilizing their close neighbors, to resigned French or Spaniards worrying about diversion of CAP funds and an EU arena re-centered to the east. By 1994 or 1995 it was difficult, however, to find a non-extremist politician who argued openly against letting in the Easterners. In our view, the most widely shared rationale was stabilization: refusal of the new applicants could lead them to turn away from the West, free markets, and democratization, whereas the prospect of EU membership would create tremendous leverage for reform.[40] Still, even if the end of Europe's division seemed to compel Europeans to a momentous choice about the breadth of integration, a decision that took almost 15 years to implement is hard to describe as a response to a "crisis." Both the motivations and fears surrounding enlargement concerned very long-term trends. At no point did leaders feel major time pressure to act.

In sum, if we assign any real meaning to the word "crisis," the notion that European integration has advanced through crisis is not just questionable. It is entirely wrong. No major advance in European integration has ever occurred under crisis-driven conditions. This short chapter cannot additionally support a view of how European integration *has* occurred, but our selective bits of evidence hint at how we think the main story runs. It is a supply-side story, driven by champions of a positive organizational project, not a demand-side process in which Europeans were broadly compelled by unambiguous problems to agree on endorsing integration in this form. The visionary project of "community-style" Euro-federalism intersected with a variety of other long-term concerns—like keeping Germany in check, subsidizing farmers, taming currency volatility and inflation, or advancing neoliberalism—to construct a certain institutional framework for integration.[41] The end of the Cold War then effectively imposed an extension of that framework to post-communist Europe, creating long-term pressures for enlargement that western Europeans ultimately felt unable to reject.

It is only in recent years that we have had the opportunity to see what it looks like for the EU to address a real crisis, to which we turn next. As we have all seen, it is not pretty.

The Euro Crisis: Qualitatively Different and Insufficient Response

The current crisis facing the euro is the biggest test
Europe has faced for decades, even since the Treaty of
Rome was signed in 1957.

ANGELA MERKEL (Bundestag, May 18, 2010)

Scholars of international political economy see the euro crisis as the most significant aftershock of the global financial crisis and the Great Recession that ensued in 2008–2009.[42] From the point of view of European integration, we argue in this section, it is the first real crisis since the origins of the EU project. We first explain why the euro crisis is different. Then we argue that the EU's responses, while certainly significant by any stretch of the imagination, are widely seen as falling short of long-term solutions to avoid similar crises in the future, as discussed in the first section of this volume. While all previous major steps in European integration did *more* than many relevant actors wanted—vigorously pushing forward-looking organizational plans to the limits of their support—steps taken during the euro crisis have generally been perceived as minimalist and reactive.[43] That should not be surprising: it is what we might reasonably expect more generally from crisis-driven reform in complex institutional settings.

Why This Time Is Different

We believe that the euro crisis is qualitatively different from previous "crises" of European integration. We find that the nature of a supranational sovereign debt crisis, without the legitimate supranational institutions needed to cope with it, laid bare all the structural, institutional, and ideational contradictions that were inherent in the design of Economic and Monetary Union (EMU). The irony, of course, is that the euro was meant to solve these contradictions once and for all by fostering economic convergence. The euro crisis struck at the very heart of the tension between the centrifugal logic of Europe's domestic politics and the centripetal demands of making a common multistate currency function smoothly.[44] We identify two fundamental differences between the euro crisis and the many previous "crises" of European integration. One is the existence of imminent market and political pressure, with the potentially disastrous consequences of inaction. The other is the

ejection of the EU from its technocratic ambit due to the explicit politicization of European decision-making.

The European sovereign debt crisis is in essence the first "real" EU crisis, given that it required a decisive intervention without which the single
currency, and most likely the EU itself, would not have survived.[45] In the
past, whether it was the "empty chair crisis" of the 1960s, or the monetary
crises of the European "snake" in the 1970s, "Euro-sclerosis" in the 1980s,
or the dismemberment of the Soviet Union in the early 1990s, the EEC or
the EU could have stood by and done nothing. There would have been no
financial or economic calamity. The euro crisis was the EU institutions'
first time dealing with real-time financial markets, with national governments realizing that they were helpless in responding to the crisis on their
own, and that swift collective action at the EU level would be needed in
order to stave off pending disaster. More than 20 EU summit meetings
were convened in Brussels to find a lasting and "comprehensive" solution
in just the first 30 months of the crisis. Those meetings underscored the
difficulty of getting 17 national finance ministers to agree on a common
approach. The stakes had never been higher, since inaction would have led
to a breakup of the euro, and maybe even the end of the EU as we knew it.
That existential risk to the project of European integration itself had never
existed before.

The euro crisis has also meant a significant encroachment by the European
Union on national decision-making powers, especially in the realm of fiscal
policy. If Harold Lasswell was right, and "politics" is mainly about "who
gets what, when and how," then the euro crisis was first and foremost a crisis of European politics.[46] During the negotiations over the new Treaty on
European Union (TEU) at Maastricht in December 1991, Helmut Kohl and
François Mitterrand had been careful to avoid transferring significant fiscal
powers to Brussels, fearing a popular backlash against EMU. Instead, they
had opted for broad and numerical "convergence criteria" that all member
states would need to follow. With the new "Fiscal Compact," which was
agreed to in December 2011, Europe took a significant and unpopular step
in directly controlling national member states' budgets. As Vivien Schmidt
illustrates in Chapter 5 of this volume, the failure of the Commission's
"one-size-fits-all" approach to fiscal policy underscores the tension inherent
in Europe's direct interference in what was always believed to be the legitimate preserve of the nation-state. It was one thing to give up sovereignty over
monetary policy in the early 1990s, but quite another step to give up national
autonomy over fiscal policy.[47] For most EU member countries, this really is

one step too far—hence the ambiguity and foot-dragging that characterizes the debate on fiscal union.

Apart from fiscal policy, the euro crisis also saw a "re-politicization" of monetary policy in the European Union.[48] The conduct of monetary policy used to be thought of as a largely tedious, dull, and technical policy domain. It had become widely believed by the late 1980s and early 1990s that one could not trust politicians with one's money.[49] The old, "embedded liberal," belief that monetary policy could be used to achieve domestic economic objectives, like full employment, had been badly battered during the 1970s and 1980s in the wake of the Great Inflation. As price stability replaced full employment as the main objective of economic policymaking, because the short-term trade-off between unemployment and inflation had seemingly collapsed along with the oil shocks and the stagflation of the 1970s, governments eager to convince the markets that they had a credible commitment to long-term price stability started to move toward tying their own hands, following the German example.[50] With a vertical Phillips Curve, the best governments could hope for was to maintain price stability by limiting the growth of the money supply, while using microeconomic "structural" reforms to move back toward full employment.[51] Best practice therefore was to place monetary policy in the supposedly safe hands of unelected technocrats who could run a truly independent central bank with the sole legal and institutional mandate of maintaining price stability.

The neoliberal policy consensus, which had reigned over much of the economics profession since the early 1980s, also helped put to rest the view that monetary policy, especially during economic downturns, could have significant distributive effects. At Maastricht, it was agreed that the European Central Bank (ECB) would not monetize any member country's debt (the "no bailout" clause). The Stability and Growth Pact—with its limits on national deficit and debt ratios—was meant to avoid such a scenario in the first place. During the most acute phases of the euro crisis, it was obvious that the only institution capable of acting was an unelected body based in Frankfurt, which would have to break its politically agreed institutional mandate in order to be successful. While the ECB's decisions were political in nature, they were not subject to democratic control.[52] Faced with turmoil in their sovereign bond markets, national leaders found themselves powerless without the support of a central bank they had no way of influencing.

The euro crisis was the first crisis of EU integration to really uncover the tensions between the democratic incentives in national politics and the institutional logic and non-democratic demands for quick decisions required to successfully run a supranational currency union. With EU leaders primarily accountable to their own national parliaments, they were most likely to do just enough to keep the euro alive, rather than aiming for stronger steps that would forever reassure financial markets that the single currency would function properly.[53] The existing democratic deficit in the European Union, where voters feel far removed from the decisions made in Brussels, would therefore only widen. Of course, the EU has been an elite project from the start, but the euro crisis illustrated that, for better or worse, democratic legitimacy still mainly lies with the nation-state.[54] Compared to past crises, national leaders this time were more reluctant to agree on major steps forward in EU integration, and carefully guarded most of their national decision-making powers. The main difference between the euro crisis and previous crises is that, in the past, the decisions to move forward with further integration were taken on a voluntary basis. This time around, the decisions were thrust upon national leaders by genuine threats of imminent breakdown.

The sovereign debt crisis hence exposed the European Union as a "political" entity, taking it out of its "technocratic" comfort zone. From 1951 to 2009, European integration had been associated with delivering the goods, in terms of fast economic growth and growing prosperity for the West during the first 30 years, and in terms of increased economic freedom during the last 30 years. For the South and the East, European integration meant economic catch-up and convergence, human freedom and dignity, democratic consolidation, and the chance of belonging to or rejoining the West, and reaping all the benefits of becoming modern societies. From 2010 onward, the euro crisis cast the European Commission in the role of "villain" in the Mediterranean—telling them to cut social spending, increase taxes, and push through painful structural reforms, which threatened to tear apart their societies' communitarian social fabric. In Greece and Italy, more directly, the EU was seen as behind the anointing of unpopular technocrats to political office, who were then forced to implement highly political decisions, all without any real say of the people.[55] While the European Union in the past had been associated with greater welfare, it would now be associated with greater pain. Still lacking the democratic legitimacy to be truly effective, throwing the EU into the choppy waters of messy left-and-right politics was always going to be a tough game to play for Brussels' EU officials.[56]

Finally, the euro crisis exposed a growing gap between a northern "core" and a southern "periphery" within the Eurozone. While this gap had been narrowing since the early 1980s—both in economic and democratic-political terms—the sovereign debt crisis laid bare the fragile foundations of the convergence that the euro had brought about between the mid-1990s and 2009.[57] North-South divisions increased after the euro launch in 1999, with labor costs widening and total factor productivity divergences pricing Mediterranean goods and services out of the European market. As the economies of southern Europe and Ireland were booming in the early 2000s, wages tended to grow faster in those countries compared to their trade partners, especially Germany. The persistence of growth and inflation differentials across the EMU have therefore led to diverging movements in international competitiveness and large trade imbalances within the euro area. After Greece announced in late 2009 that its fiscal situation was far worse than previously reported, the analysis in northern Europe quickly became a morality tale of profligate and lazy "Southerners" versus hard-working and frugal "Northerners." This popular image has never really gone away from the debate, and has made calls for EU-wide solidarity, which had buttressed EU integration until then, increasingly ineffective.

The Limits of Crisis-Driven Reform

We are confident that [new measures in the latest euro
rescue operation] will contribute to the swift resolution
of the crisis.

JOSÉ MANUEL BARROSO AND HERMAN VAN ROMPUY
(Joint letter to G20 leaders, October 2011)

In September 2013, Commission President Barroso told the European Parliament that the end of the euro crisis was "within sight."[58] In October 2013, economists at Germany's ZEW think tank declared the crisis "over for now" as a variety of economic indicators turned upward.[59] In an immediate sense they seemed to be right. Bond spreads had declined steadily since mid-2012. The euro had enjoyed a modest but sustained rise. Most parts of the European economy had bottomed out and were showing some signs of growth. At the time of writing, these signs remain weak and erratic, but even Greece re-entered the bond markets in April 2014, and bond spreads are remarkably narrow. By late 2014, the problem was stagnation, not an imminent crisis.

Important things have been done, admittedly, to get to that point. Previous chapters have carefully dissected the steps of European responses (especially Chapter 3 by Erik Jones and Chapter 4 by Nicolas Jabko), so we can simply underscore that collectively they amount to a period of institutional reform in which major new powers have certainly been transferred to the European level. Through the European Financial Stability Facility (EFSF) and its successor, the European Stability Mechanism (ESM), better-off member states accepted a new mechanism to conditionally support those who fall into debt crises. In order for Germany to agree that such funds could ever be disbursed, the Treaty of Stability, Coordination and Governance (the "Fiscal Pact") augmented the Commission's role in overseeing national budgets. Most recently, the member states agreed to launch a single supervisory mechanism (SSM) for banks in the ECB, giving it direct oversight of the largest 150 banks of "systemic importance" and selective surveillance of the rest. Common standards were also set by which national authorities will "bail in" shareholders and bondholders in failing banks before turning to national and European funds for taxpayer-funded "bailouts" (though these will only go into effect in 2018). In a set of developments that were more informal but also more important in directly calming the crisis, the ECB gradually broke out of its original impassive orthodoxy to shore up banks with near-unlimited long-term financing and teetering governments with large purchases of sovereign bonds.

In broader perspective, perhaps the most significant aspect of these new delegations of authority is that they have taken place in the full glare of distributional politics. Richer northern nations have agreed, after endless and agonizing meetings, to front some money for poorer southern ones. True, they attached so many conditions to this support—in the form of pressure for austerity—that to date the negative effects of the conditions are more evident than the positive effects of the support. However misguided the insistence on austerity conditions has been, though, the bailouts and new infrastructure for future bailouts have calmed financial markets. These are major developments in a Europe where the possibility of cross-national transfers was previously limited to haggling over regional development funds and agricultural subsidies that never even approached one percent of the Union's total economic output.

Yet even were we to take a Germanic view of these steps as generous and solidaristic (as opposed to a more French-leaning, or Mediterranean, view of them as an oppressive cure worse than the disease), we would still have to see them as far more reactive than proactive. As Jones and Jabko both emphasize, echoing most other academic and media commentary, the general perception is that these steps have been slow, reluctant, and focused minimally on crisis avoidance. They make Europe somewhat better able to handle crises that have begun to erupt, but not more integrated or stronger in general. This is the most obvious with the ECB's extraordinary actions. Its "outright monetary transactions" (OMTs) have not actually been used. During stable periods these capacities, like the ESM, will presumably sit in the background and have little effect on integration. Stronger oversight of national budgets (the "European Semester") may offer the possibility of evolving in the direction of fiscal coordination, but for the moment it focuses on preventing the worst behaviors rather than developing substantively common behaviors. The banking union deal, while more properly about common policies, has also emphasized common mechanisms to watch for bad behavior far more than bulking up common capacities that could correct it. Member states will now watch banks together in the SSM and treat them more similarly, with shared rules for resolving failures, but the Germans were largely successful in insisting that "there [would] be no European backstops, but rather national backstops" in the single resolution mechanism (SRM).[60] Beyond a shared 55-billion euro fund—roughly one-five-hundredth of the assets of European banks[61]—each country will be on its own.

Wharton School economist Richard Herring calls this "building banking union on a one-legged stool." Without the other legs of a more genuinely "single" SRM and common deposit insurance, he argues, a banking union will not break the multiple constellations of toxic relationships between weak banks and weak sovereigns that have driven the crises in the Mediterranean and Ireland.[62] Overall, then, this round of reform has given Europe new mechanisms for telling banks and governments that they are in trouble and new instruments to save them in extremis. That matters, but it does not do much to alter the core incentives, resources, or rules for economic action that prevailed before 2007. We might expect the increased moral hazard issues of stronger crisis management capacities to roughly balance out with the shaming power of the Commission's fiscal oversight.

What else could Europe do? Besides a "three-legged" banking union, the best-informed economic observers like Jones and Jabko frequently mention some "mutualization" of sovereign debt (the idea, currently moribund, of "Eurobonds"), significant increases in the EU budget in the direction of a proper "fiscal union," improved central clearance mechanisms, plus the never-ending work to "complete the single market" to increase free-flowing economic adjustments on the ground. The basic goal of all such ambitious proposals is to go beyond crisis reaction capabilities to create a Europe in which national economies and their governments are pushed more toward convergence and where flows between them are better able to adapt fluidly to the divergences that remain. In other words, they would be steps to build a better embedded Europe, not just steps to head off imminent disaster.

Our point is not that any such steps will be easy. Nor are we unsympathetic to European leaders' reluctance to look beyond immediate crisis management. To the contrary, we admire anyone who can move the enormous, complex organization of the EU in any direction at all. Today's leaders have fashioned some new tools to calm financial markets and have kept their continent from going over a cliff. (They have simultaneously pushed parts of the continent over a cliff through austerity conditions, but at least in terms of financial markets they have averted a widening meltdown.) To use a slightly different metaphor, perhaps it is not really fair to ask the people at the helm in the storm of the century to develop plans for a better ship while steering clear of the reefs.

It is fair, though, to insist that Europeans not mistake passage of the reefs for construction of a more seaworthy vessel. In particular, they should be careful not to equate their improvisations during the crisis with the kind of political action that built the EU or could rebuild it into something substantially better. This is an especially important message for academics to offer to politicians. Leaders have no reason to know EU history in great detail and thus no reason to question the comforting and politically useful notion that the EU has always moved forward through crisis. Our comparative advantage is that we can step back and see the EU's progress in both breadth and depth.

In sum, then, today's leaders must keep in mind that major transfers of sovereignty that change Europe on the ground—not just bolster it against crises—have never bubbled up mainly out of technical perceptions of policy problems or reactive responses to crises. Substantial policy problems have always existed behind big changes in the EU, certainly.[63] In the ECSC, the EEC, the EMS, the SEA, and the EMU, however, not only did certain leaders tackle substantial policy problems, they advanced very particular (and quite contested) diagnoses of problems and their solutions that connected them to proactive goals of changing Europe in the long term. We can disagree about whether their changes were for the better, of course, but in our view the empirical record is clear that the key leaders in all of these steps followed conscious positive political agendas, rather than being compelled by "crisis" to do anything that was widely perceived as necessary. In each of these cases the main leaders, especially in France and Germany, stepped well beyond their normal domestic support, in a context where many policy options were available, to pursue initiatives that linked policy problems with major new transfers of sovereignty to the European level.

That is what will need to happen if Europe is to move forward after this crisis. Leaders will need to play up some technical problems noted above—including, probably, with some crisis language!—and insist that EU institutional reform is crucial to their resolution. They will need to be popular at home so they can burn political capital to override or pay off the contestation that will arise. And they will also need quite a bit of luck. Unfortunately, the conditions for this sort of polity-building leadership in Europe have become much more challenging since Maastricht in the early 1990s.

Conclusion: Is Forward Movement Imaginable in the EU Today?

We have argued that the common rhetoric that European integration moves forward through crisis, though comforting, is dangerously wrong. Those who care about constructing a viable future for the euro, Europe, and Europeans cannot afford to let historical misrepresentations encourage complacent views that progress in European integration is quasi-inevitable. Whereas the first 50 years of European integration were driven by a coherent and proactive (even aggressive) political project, Europe's leaders in recent years have acted in a very different mode. They have reacted rather desperately to cataclysmic threats with the minimal bargains they could forge between the different populations and organizations they represent.

Once again, we do not mean to suggest that this new mode is surprising. There are good reasons for the absence of a forward-leading vision for the EU today. For one thing, the organization has reached the end of its previous blueprint in monetary union. A single currency was foreseen already in the 1950s, but not even the most ambitious federalists have ever produced a coherent organizational plan about next steps thereafter. Eastern enlargement also set that blueprint in a far wider and more diverse framework. As we have seen, expansion of the club to the East was ultimately the most consensual major reform in the EU's history, but it was also never part of the original vision for the club. All previous thinking about why integration was good for Europeans was premised on bargains among relatively similar West European countries, and inclusion of much poorer post-communist countries left the unfinished blueprint even more uncertain.

Moreover, the "greatest generation" of postwar West European leaders, of which many members perceived integration as an existential issue—either positively or negatively—left active European politics in the first years of the new millennium. Helmut Kohl and Jacques Chirac were the last major figures who entered politics soon after the war but before the EEC became successful. Without a doubt, subsequent political generations have their pro- and anti-Europeans, but they have all grown up in a "community" Europe and tend to be less likely to expend political capital to advance or oppose it (with the notable exception of the British Conservatives, who are a living organizational monument to Margaret Thatcher's hostility to European authority).[64]

Nor do we mean to suggest that the path is wide open for a return to a Europe-building mode. Even if pro-European leaders emerged to champion a new vision that connected policy problems to expanded Euro-authority, we would not be terribly sanguine for their success. The Franco-German couple might use the lingering euro crisis to mobilize new proposals for fiscal union, or might link a new treaty to a common foreign and security policy, but they would face a post-Lisbon EU arena where ambitious treaty reform for the entire EU looks next to impossible. With anti-EU forces far more mobilized than in previous eras, as displayed dramatically in the European Parliament elections of 2014, it is hard to imagine any treaty surviving through all the national opportunities for opponents to sabotage ratification. More likely might be an "enhanced cooperation" framework that could have the additional appeal for core West European members of restoring some separation from British, Danish, and eastern European doubters. Yet this option would face its own challenges, forcing Euro-federalists in Brussels and national capitals to endorse a definitive break with hopes for a coherent United States of Europe.

Europhiles may nonetheless take some heart from another reading of the story we have told. In arguing that integration has never moved forward functionally and automatically out of crisis, we have also emphasized that integration has advanced despite major contestation and uncertainty. This suggests that Europhiles who champion deeper improvements on the flawed euro system may actually have an advantage over their predecessors: where the latter had to frame policy problems in certain ways and invent crises to justify their political agenda, the former can draw on a real recent crisis to make their case.[65] We still hold that the EU will not address its deeper challenges and vulnerabilities until a coherent organizational vision and bold leadership return to champion it, but recent experience of a real crisis may compensate to some degree for the heightened obstacles to treaty reform. If a new generation of Europeanist leaders steps forward to connect the lessons of the euro crisis to "ever closer union," the future of the euro might indeed witness progress toward a more integrated continent. And "crisis" might finally deserve a bit of the credit for it.

II

———————

The Future of the Euro
in a Global Monetary Context

Eric Helleiner

Introduction

The contributors to this volume have focused on a number of intra-European political sources and implications of the euro crisis that will influence the currency's future.[1] This chapter turns to place the euro crisis in more of a global monetary context. For many Europeans, part of the political appeal of the euro has long been that it might serve to challenge the dollar-dominated international monetary system. Indeed, European frustrations with the trajectory of the dollar's value and US policy choices have served as a key catalyst for strengthening regional monetary cooperation at various moments since the early 1970s. During the 2007–2008 global financial crisis, these European aspirations for the euro's international role came to the surface once again when many analysts predicted that the US-centered financial upheaval might boost the euro's international role.

In the end, however, the impact of the global crisis on the euro's international role was very different. Both the global financial meltdown, and the euro crisis that followed, revealed quite starkly the sources of the dollar's global dominance and the associated weakness of the euro's international standing. Moreover, these events drew attention to a new rising international monetary power, China, whose influence on the euro's prospects was felt by Europeans for the first time in a significant way. These two implications of the global and Eurozone financial crises humbled those Europeans who harbored aspirations for the euro's global role.

At the same time, they may serve to boost the political prospects for the euro over the longer term. In particular, they may provide both reinvigorated motivation within Europe and new outside support from China for efforts to address the euro's "missing" unions—financial, governance, and legitimacy—that other chapters in this volume have highlighted. If the efforts were successful and the Eurozone became a more "embedded" currency area, the euro's capacity to grow as an international currency also would be bolstered considerably.

Europe's Global Ambitions

A number of the chapters in this volume have highlighted the limitations of optimum currency area (OCA) theory as a tool for analyzing the euro's prospects. As they have noted, the theory ignores the central importance of the national and regional political and institutional foundations for European monetary cooperation.[2] One further limitation of OCA theory is that it overlooks the significance of the wider global monetary context within which currency unions are created and exist.

That wider context has often played a key role in encouraging currency unions. Its significance has been particularly obvious in colonial contexts, where territories were often merged monetarily as part of broader projects to tie currencies to that of an imperial power.[3] Currency unions in the nineteenth century, such as the Latin Monetary Union, were also seen by some of their advocates as a means to bolster the international monetary power and prestige of member states vis-à-vis outsiders. Key reforms that helped to consolidate domestic territorial currencies within countries were also driven by considerations of the larger global monetary environment. For example, a central motivation for the creation of the Federal Reserve System in the United States in 1913 was that it would help to boost the dollar's international role.[4]

The history of European monetary cooperation has also been deeply influenced by the wider global monetary context. Particularly important has been the desire of European policymakers to reduce their region's dependence on the US dollar and to enhance Europe's monetary power vis-à-vis the United States. This goal arose initially in the context of frustrations with US monetary leadership in the late 1960s, the unilateralism of the 1971 Nixon shock, and the subsequent collapse of the Bretton Woods regime of fixed exchange rates in 1973 after the unraveling of the Smithsonian Agreement. European ambitions to bolster their region's monetary autonomy and power were then reinforced by the dollar's unstable value in the 1970s and 1980s, and perceived efforts by US policymakers to shift the burdens of adjustment to its payments imbalances onto foreigners.[5]

The creation of the euro in 1999 emerged at least partly out of this context. Many of the advocates of the creation of the euro in 1999 saw it as a tool to bolster Europe's power and autonomy within the wider global monetary system. The goal of constraining US influence was often expressed very openly by European policymakers. In its *One Market, One Money* report of 1990, the European Commission praised the way the euro would force the US to become "more conscious of the limits of independent policy-making" and bring greater "symmetry" to the international monetary order. To reinforce the point, it added: "Although the presence of a hegemon may be beneficial as long as it remains the anchor of the system, it is no longer so when it ceases to provide stability."[6]

At that time, the European Commission argued that the euro would be a particularly attractive international currency because it would be backed by an independent central bank that was mandated to pursue price stability. It also noted that the euro would benefit from the fact that unified European money markets would be "the largest in the world."[7] Indeed, Europe's decision a few years earlier to construct a common financial space had also been driven in part by similar international ambitions to challenge US pre-eminence. As Jacques Delors had put it in 1989, financial liberalization was designed to give "our financial centres the opportunity to be among the most important in the world" and "it is this that gives us our say in the world with the Americans and Japanese on debt, on financial flows."[8]

The Euro's Moment to Shine?

These kinds of global ambitions for the euro were reiterated during the 2007–2008 global financial crisis. For example, just before the first G20 summit in November 2008, French President Nicolas Sarkozy made a point of declaring, "I am leaving tomorrow for Washington to explain that the dollar cannot claim to be the only currency in the world."[9] The confidence of Sarkozy and other European policymakers in the euro's international prospects at this time was boosted by the fact that prominent analysts had noted how the currency had become "ever more global" since its creation.[10] For example, the share of the euro in non-industrial countries' reserves had risen from 19 percent to 30 percent since the euro's establishment, while the dollar's share had fallen from 70 percent to 60 percent.[11]

The euro's prospects as a global currency also seemed to be improved by the vulnerability of the US dollar. Even before the outbreak of the 2007–2008 crisis, there had been many predictions of an impending collapse in the dollar's value because of the large current account deficits of the US, combined with its growing external debt. Analysts speculated that foreign creditors of the US might soon withdraw their funding, generating a "financial meltdown in the dollar" that would undermine confidence in the dollar's international role.[12]

This scenario seemed even more possible because many of these foreign creditors were foreign governments. Approximately half of the US current account deficit between 2002 and 2007 had been financed by foreign governments through their purchases of US dollar assets, particularly Treasury bills and the bonds issued by the two US government-sponsored mortgage lending agencies, Fannie Mae and Freddie Mac ("Fannie and Freddie").[13] Some of the large official dollar holders were close US allies, such as Japan and the Gulf states, but others were potential geopolitical rivals such as China, whose foreign exchange reserves had become the world's largest at over 1.5 trillion dollars by the time the crisis began (of which approximately 70–80 percent were in dollar-denominated assets). Analysts speculated that these governments might be tempted to sell dollars as a weapon to achieve political goals, as had sometimes been done in the past.[14] Others noted that selling might be provoked simply by the fact that the costs of holding large dollar reserves were growing in the context of the dollar's depreciation since 2002. At the time of the crisis, Chinese policymakers were in fact facing growing domestic criticism for the poor performance of their US investments.[15]

Even before the outbreak of the 2007–2008 financial crisis, scholars had predicted that a major US recession or financial upheaval could act as a "spark" for a withdrawal from US dollar investments.[16] When the US financial crisis then began, many analysts predicted that foreigners would lose confidence in the US currency and US assets. These fears only intensified when US policymakers responded to the crisis with dramatic interest rate cuts and larger fiscal deficits. Predictions of a dollar collapse were extremely widespread during the early phase of the crisis. As an editorial in *The Economist* put it in December 2007, "a new fear now stalks the markets: that the dollar's slide could spin out of control."[17] Prominent investors such as George Soros also publicly anticipated a flight from the dollar and the end of the dollar's dominant role as an international currency.[18] Even top policymakers, such as US Treasury Secretary Hank Paulson, worried about a collapse in the dollar's value.[19]

In this context, it is not hard to understand why analysts speculated that the euro's time as an international currency might have come. At the very time that investors might lose confidence in the dollar, the euro seemed well positioned to present a credible and attractive international reserve asset for international investors. As one financial journalist put it in March 2008, "Neither the yen nor the D-Mark had a realistic chance of replacing the greenback. But the euro is a real alternative. The Eurozone economy is almost as large as that of the US and may surpass it as it continues to enlarge. Also, the Eurozone bond markets are now almost as deep and liquid as their US counterparts."[20] European policymakers joined in the speculation. For example, in late September 2008, German Finance Minister Peer Steinbrück declared confidently to the German parliament that "the US will lose its status as the superpower of the world financial system. This world will become multipolar." He reiterated the point to journalists later on the same day: "when we look back 10 years from now, we will see 2008 as a fundamental rupture. I am not saying the dollar will lose its reserve currency status, but it will become relative." [21]

The Private Demand for Dollars

In the end, however, this European optimism was short-lived. At the very moment that Steinbrück was predicting the dollar's demise as the world's dominant currency, it was becoming clear that a dollar crisis was unlikely to unfold. Far from collapsing, the dollar's value in fact rose in the second half of 2008 as quickly as at any point since the early 1970s.[22] The dollar's strength revealed clearly some of the sources of its dominance, as well as the weakness of the euro.

To begin with, as during previous international financial crises, private demand for dollars grew because investors plowed into US Treasury bills as a kind of safe haven in the storm.[23] Although the global financial crisis was centered in the United States, US Treasury securities were still perceived as the safest financial assets. Their market was one of the few that remained liquid throughout the crisis, and they were issued by the world's dominant geostrategic and economic power.[24] Euro assets failed to inspire the same confidence. In the absence of a single European fiscal authority, there was no equivalent to the uniquely liquid and deep US Treasury bill market. Italian government securities formed the largest category of outstanding euro-denominated government securities ($1.8 trillion) at the height of the crisis in September 2008, but they did not inspire much market confidence at the time. The second

largest were securities issued by the German government ($1.4 trillion), but
they were much smaller in size than their US counterparts (which totaled
$7.3 trillion) and much less liquid because of its less well developed secondary
market.[25]

Since the early 2000s, international political economy scholars such as
Benjamin Cohen had noted that the euro's international use had also been
held back by concerns about its governance, and thus the broader political
credibility of the whole initiative.[26] Those concerns quickly grew during the
crisis, which highlighted dramatically that the Maastricht Treaty, signed in
1992, had failed to outline clear procedures for the prevention and resolution
of Eurozone financial crises. In the absence of clear rules, Eurozone member
governments responded in unilateral ways to the distress facing individual
financial institutions in their territories. Seeing the lack of coordination,
financial analysts quickly wondered whether European financial integration
could unravel and whether Eurozone unity itself might be threatened.[27] Even
before the outbreak of the European sovereign debt crisis in 2010–2011, questions were being raised about the broader political credibility of the euro in
ways that undermined the euro's ability to compete with the dollar for investor confidence. Those debt crises and their handling then only reinforced
these concerns, and also reduced the liquidity and depth of euro reserve assets
as investors shied away from purchasing the government debt of the afflicted
countries.

The dollar's value was also boosted by several other developments in
private markets that revealed the enduring global importance of the currency. Because of their large dollar borrowing to fund the accumulation of
dollar assets since 2000, many foreign banks required dollars to fund their
positions at the height of the crisis. When interbank and other wholesale
short-term financial markets froze, the intense demand for dollars in this
context of shortage contributed to the currency's appreciation. Also important was the fact that non-US banks and institutional investors had to purchase dollars to square their books and to meet collateral needs as the value
of their dollar assets suddenly deteriorated rapidly with the collapse of the
price of stocks and other financial assets during the crisis. In addition, the
dollar's value was boosted by the unwinding of "carry trades" in which investors had borrowed dollars to invest in higher-yielding instruments in foreign
currencies.[28]

The deep involvement of European banks and investors in dollar-based
markets was particularly striking. Since 2000, many European banks
had been drawn into the US financial bubble and accumulated large

dollar-denominated assets such as mortgage-backed securities in US markets. They had purchased those assets by borrowing dollars cheaply in short-term markets (or by borrowing short-term funds domestically and converting them to dollars via foreign exchange swaps). When sources of short-term dollar funding dried up as the US financial crisis intensified, these European financial institutions were suddenly in trouble, scrambling to secure the necessary dollars to fund their positions.[29] Their demand for dollars not only put upward pressure on the US currency but also left these firms and the European Central Bank dependent on the US authorities as a supplier of emergency dollar liquidity.

They were lucky that US authorities were willing to come to their rescue. Some European institutions received support from the US government's Troubled Asset Relief Program (TARP).[30] The Fed also allowed European financial institutions with branches or subsidiaries in the US to borrow very extensively from its discount window and various emergency facilities.[31] Most important, however, was the fact that the Fed provided dollars to the European Central Bank (ECB) via bilateral swap arrangements, enabling European officials to supply dollar liquidity to local firms and markets.[32] Interestingly, when the Fed first raised the idea of a swap with the ECB in August 2007, the latter rejected the proposal because, in David Wessel's words, "the plan ran up against a strong effort to pin the Great Panic on the United States" at the time.[33] As the crisis worsened, however, the ECB recognized Europe's vulnerability and its need for US help. It accepted a Fed swap in December 2007, and its borrowing from the Fed then grew enormously as the crisis intensified, reaching as high as 310 billion dollars (a figure that was much higher than total borrowing by all countries from the International Monetary Fund [IMF] during 2008–2009).[34]

The dependence of European firms and the ECB on US financial authorities was a striking sign of the euro's subordinate status to the dollar in international financial markets.[35] In the panic, it was dollars—not euros—that were in highest demand. To be sure, the ECB created swap facilities for Poland, Hungary, Sweden, and Denmark that faced potential shortages of euros, but these swaps added up to only 35 billion dollars in total, and actual drawings were small.[36] The Fed also accepted a swap arrangement from the ECB in April 2009, allowing it to access euros, but the swap was never drawn upon.[37] Because of the international role of the dollar, it was US authorities, not European ones, that were called upon to play the role of international lender of last resort.

Foreign Official Support for the Dollar

The dollar's strength during the crisis resulted from the decisions of not just private investors but also foreign governments that refrained from dumping their large dollar holdings. Because of the scale of its reserves, China's role was particularly important. At the height of the crisis in mid-September 2008, US officials received assurances from the top Chinese leadership that they were preventing their own officials and financial institutions from selling US investments.[38] The Chinese government in fact accumulated considerably more dollar reserves during the crisis; its stash of overall reserves grew from 1.5 trillion dollars at the start of the crisis to 2.4 trillion dollars by the end of 2009.[39]

Why did China and other foreign governments continue to support the US dollar during the financial upheaval? Many of them pursued export-oriented economic strategies and had accumulated large dollar reserves before the crisis as a way of stemming upward pressure on their country's exchange rates, thus assisting national exporters. This motivation was strengthened during the crisis, as governments were more concerned than ever to preserve the competitiveness of their export sectors. Chinese authorities, for example, stopped the gradual appreciation of the renminbi (RMB) in July 2008 and kept the currency pegged to the dollar until mid-2010 because of concerns about social unrest stemming from unemployment in their export factories.[40] This Chinese move encouraged other countries whose firms competed directly with Chinese companies to follow suit.

Governments had also accumulated reserves before the crisis for precautionary reasons, as a way of protecting their countries against the kind of crisis that East Asian countries had experienced in 1997–1998.[41] This "self-insurance" rationale for reserve holdings was reinforced by the global financial meltdown in which the war chest of reserves was finally proving its worth as a bulwark against external instability. Rather than dumping reserves, many governments thus sought to preserve and even increase them.[42] The appeal of self-insurance as an economic strategy was also greatly enhanced by the fact that it became clear that developing countries and emerging markets that had accumulated large reserves fared much better than those that had not.

But why were reserves kept in dollars? One reason was that dollars were the dominant currency used in international financial markets and international trade, and thus they were key for intervention purposes. Like private investors, foreign governments were also attracted to hold reserves in dollars because of the unique depth, liquidity, and security of US financial markets, especially the market for US Treasury securities. One Chinese official, Luo Ping, put it as follows in early 2009, when explaining why China continued to buy US Treasury bills during the crisis: "Except for US Treasuries, what can you hold? ... US Treasuries are the safe haven. For everyone, including China, it is the only option ... Once you start issuing $1 trillion—$2 trillion ... we know the dollar is going to depreciate, so we hate you guys but there is nothing much we can do."[43]

The shallowness of European financial markets was a particular problem for foreign authorities with large reserve holdings. As one Chinese official explained, even a small scale shift of Chinese reserves into European markets "would send European government debt yields to the floor and bond prices to the roof, while the consequent appreciation of the euro would seriously damage the European export industry and trigger diplomatic tensions." The central bank governor of the United Arab Emirates made a similar point: "Can the Euro Area absorb large amounts of investment funds from GCC [Gulf Cooperation Council] countries in a short period of time? ... The answer is ... obviously, no."[44] The Eurozone's financial and debt problems also eroded confidence in the euro as a reserve asset among policymakers managing reserve holdings in places such a China, Brazil, and the GCC. Indeed, by the end of 2012, the share of the reserves of developing countries held in euro had fallen from 30 percent at the start of the crisis to 24 percent, its lowest level since 2002 (while that of the dollar remained at around 60 percent).[45]

Before the crisis, governments had also sometimes held reserves in dollars because of broader political and economic relationships with the US. In the case of close US allies such as Japan and the Gulf States, support for the dollar was often linked to these countries' security dependence on the US.[46] Otero-Iglesias and Steinberg even report that US officials directly pressured GCC to curtail their desire to diversify their reserves into euros after the euro's creation.[47] In cases such as these, the prospect of a massive dumping of dollars during the global financial crisis was minimal.

In the all important case of China, scholars have also speculated that the accumulation of dollar reserves was part of an implicit bargain with the US under which the latter accepted underpriced Chinese exports in return for the recycling of Chinese export earnings into dollar assets. Analysts drew a parallel with the pattern of US relations with western European countries and Japan during the 1960s when these US allies built up dollar holdings in the 1960s as part of export-led growth strategies under the Bretton Woods exchange rate system.[48] If the US had undermined this "Bretton Woods II" bargain by closing off its markets to foreign exports, as Nixon did in 1971, Chinese authorities might have reconsidered their support for the dollar during the global financial crisis.[49] But no such move was made by the US.

Indeed, US officials went out of their way to avoid antagonizing their country's major creditor by supporting the burying of an IMF report criticizing Chinese exchange rate policy at the height of the crisis in September 2008.[50] US officials also made efforts throughout the crisis to keep in touch with China and other foreign official creditors, encouraging their investments in US troubled financial institutions and welcoming support for the dollar.[51] Chinese authorities and other foreign governments were also appreciative of the US government's rescue of the various US institutions in which foreigners often had a direct or indirect interest. Particularly important was the support for Fannie and Freddie, whose bonds were held in large numbers by China and other foreign governments.[52]

The risk that China might generate a run on the dollar through unilateral dumping was also minimized by the fact that it had already invested so much in dollar assets. With the size of Chinese claims on the US approximately one-third of Chinese GDP near the start of the crisis, China found itself in a rather dramatic version of what Jonathan Kirshner calls "entrapment" arising from monetary dependence.[53] Chinese authorities now had a very strong interest in the stability of the value of the US currency in which so much of their wealth was held. As Chinese Premier Wen put it in March 2009, "we have lent a huge amount of money to the US. Of course we are concerned about the safety of our assets."[54]

Enduring European International Ambitions

During the global financial crisis of 2007–2008, foreign investors—both official and private—thus chose to support the dollar for a variety of reasons: the unique attractiveness of US financial markets, the centrality of the dollar in private international financial markets, the importance of the US as a destination for foreign exports, its geopolitical dominance, and foreign governments' "entrapment" in the dollar order. Instead of challenging the dollar's international role, the crisis ended up demonstrating what Susan Strange called the wider "structural power" of the US that helped to sustain its currency's dominant global position.[55]

For Europeans, the crisis also starkly highlighted the limitations of the euro's ability to challenge the dollar's international role. For the euro to become a more prominent global currency, it was now clear that European financial markets would need to become more integrated and attractive to foreigners (and even to Europeans, as the European banks' extensive involvement in US securities markets revealed). Particularly important was the need for an equivalent to the uniquely deep and liquid US Treasury bill market. Indeed, investors have been very blunt in declaring that only a federal European bond market will be able to match the attractiveness of the US market.[56]

If the euro were to assume a larger global role, the governance of the Eurozone would also need to be strengthened in broader ways that would inspire greater foreign confidence in the currency's future as a reliable asset. As the ECB pointed out in mid-2013 in discussing barriers to the euro's internationalization, "further efforts are needed both at the euro area and the national level to tackle the fundamental causes of the financial fragmentation in the euro area, and a strengthening of the institutional framework of Economic and Monetary Union will also make a positive contribution to this end."[57] It was also apparent that the euro's international role would be strengthened if European authorities played a more active role in promoting it, including through diplomatic means (as their Chinese counterparts have done vis-à-vis the renminbi since 2009). Since the euro's creation, ECB officials have done very little of this. They studiously declared their neutrality on the issue of the euro's internationalization and stated that the process should be a "market-driven process," rather than something promoted actively by European authorities.[58]

Since the outbreak of the Eurozone crisis, European policymakers have been understandably preoccupied with addressing their internal problems. But in debates about European monetary and financial reform, the issue of the euro's international role has continued to surface. In the past, those advocating stronger European monetary and financial cooperation were able to invoke European frustrations with the dollar's enduring global dominance to support their cause. The same dynamic has emerged in current debates about issues such as the banking union, fiscal union, the creation of a common European public debt instrument, and the broader importance of the euro's future. Top European officials have also discussed the need for the ECB to take a more active role in promoting the internationalization of the euro as part of encouraging a "transition towards a multipolar currency system."[59]

European frustrations with the dollar's enduring dominance have also been expressed in international forums. In August 2010, President Sarkozy called on the G20 to "consider the suitability of an international monetary system dominated by a single currency in a now-multipolar world."[60] When the French government assumed the presidency of the G20 later that year, he was even more direct:

> We must reflect on the appropriateness of a model based on the accumulation of reserves in dollars. I ask you this: doesn't this system render a portion of the world dependent on US monetary policy? Shouldn't we think about the role of SDR [the Special Drawing Rights, the IMF's supra-national reserve asset] and the internationalization of other currencies? Let me be clear. I do not wish in any way to discredit the role of the dollar, which in any event will be prominent. But prominent does not mean exclusive . . . [61]

Of course, Sarkozy's position was in keeping with long-standing French complaints about the dominant role of the dollar in the international monetary system, dating back to the press conferences of Charles de Gaulle during the 1960s. But the experience of the 2007–2008 global financial crisis seemed to intensify the French desire—and that of many other Europeans—to reduce dependency on the dollar and to promote a less unipolar global monetary order. The fact that many scholars assigned part of the blame for the crisis itself to the dollar-dominated international monetary system only seemed to strengthen the European interest in pursuing this goal.[62]

China as a New Player in the Euro's Future

At this time, Europeans found they had a powerful new potential ally in this cause: the Chinese government. In his speech to the first G20 summit in November 2008 in Washington, D.C., Chinese president Hu Jintao had called for "steadily promoting the diversity of the international monetary system."[63] In March 2009 just before the second G20 summit in London, the Chinese central bank governor Zhou Xiaochuan had attracted worldwide attention by calling for an international monetary system centered around a "supra-sovereign" reserve currency, a proposal that was widely perceived as a critique of the dollar and a challenge to US monetary dominance.[64] A few months later, Chinese Secretary of State Dai Bingguo reiterated that China hoped to "promote a diversified and rational international reserve currency system."[65]

Even before the global financial crisis, Chinese officials had already been calling for international monetary reform and expressing frustration with dollar fluctuations and unilateral US monetary policy choices.[66] Like many Europeans, Chinese concerns about their vulnerability to US policy choices and the dollar's instability were reinforced by the experience of the 2007–2008 global financial crisis. From a Chinese standpoint, the financial upheaval demonstrated how the dollar's international role enabled the US to live recklessly beyond its means and then to deflect the costs of adjustment onto others with adverse systemic consequences.[67] The dramatic US monetary easing in response to the crisis strengthened concerns about the risk of China's exposure to dollar depreciation among both Chinese policymakers and the general public. While their country's vulnerability to exchange rate risks left Chinese officials with strong incentives in the short term to defend the dollar, it also encouraged them to explore ways of reducing their dependence on the dollar over the longer term.[68]

Because of these views, Sarkozy reached out to the Chinese leadership in 2010–2011 to support his efforts to reform the international monetary system. Much attention was given to the issue that Zhou had raised: the strengthening of the IMF's supranational reserve asset, the special drawing rights (SDRs).[69] The SDR had been created in 1969 to supplement the dollar's international reserve role, but it made up less than 1 percent of the world's non-gold official reserves by 2008, and its utility was inhibited by limits on its allocation and use. At their second summit meeting, the G20 leaders endorsed a new allocation of SDRs—the first in almost three decades—but the SDR's overall significance in the international monetary system remained very limited. Chinese policymakers initially appeared quite receptive to the French overtures to work together on this issue, but then backed off when French officials joined international calls for Chinese exchange rate policy reform.[70] In the face of wider resistance from the US and others, the initiative to strengthen the SDR quickly ran out of steam.[71]

China's significance to European goals came instead through another more direct channel: support for the euro itself. When the euro had first been created in 1999, Chinese policymakers had welcomed it because of their frustrations with dollar dependence. As China's Foreign Minister Tang Jiaxuan remarked at the time, the euro would "establish a more balanced international financial and monetary system."[72] When the Eurozone crisis broke out in 2010, China's support took a much more active form. Chinese authorities helped boost confidence in the euro through public statements of support and declarations that China was maintaining its reserves in euros in mid-2010 and afterward. More concretely, the Chinese also purchased considerable sums of government bonds of troubled Eurozone countries when the Eurozone's future seemed in jeopardy in early 2011 and at other moments.[73] The scale of the purchases was secret, but it was large enough to provoke financial journalists to note at moments such as early 2011 that "it is no longer just the ECB standing behind the euro. The Chinese are backstopping it, too."[74]

A key Chinese government motivation for supporting the euro was its ongoing interest in a more diversified international monetary order. A strong and stable euro presented Chinese officials with an international asset in which to diversify their reserves. Indeed, they have seen it as the main alternative for diversification, placing as much as 25 percent of their reserves by 2012 in euro assets such as German, French, Spanish, Hungarian, and Greek government debt.[75] Based on interviews in China on this issue, Otero-Iglesias and Steinberg also note the broader value that Chinese officials and analysts place on having a counterweight to the dollar: "Most participants interviewed in China would like to see a move from a unipolar dollar-dominated IMS to a multipolar system, and in this regard they want the euro and Europe to be a strong pole that can function as a counter-weight to the increasingly dysfunctional US dollar-centric system."[76]

China's backing of the euro also reflects some concrete interests. The value of China's existing euro reserves needed to be defended, and the EU was also a major trading partner of China. Chinese initiatives may also have been designed to gain political influence.[77] Jiang notes that countries whose debt has been purchased have supported China on issues within the EU (e.g., the lifting of the arms embargo against China). She also observes that Chinese officials pressed the EU to change some policies toward China (e.g., the arms embargo, recognition of China's market economy status, China's voting share in the IMF) around the time that they purchased bonds of the European Financial Stability Facility (EFSF).[78]

As China's influence has grown, it has become increasingly embroiled in the intra-European politics of the Eurozone. Otero-Iglesias notes that China's active buying of troubled governments' debts in 2011 sometimes frustrated German officials who saw these purchases as undermining the market discipline it was trying to impose on these governments. He reports that the Chinese government increasingly worked more closely with Germany, scaling back its euro buying in order to support German efforts to force poorer members of the Eurozone to accept closer integration.[79] In these ways, it is not just the US monetary power, but also that of China, that has begun to help shape the future of the euro.

Conclusion: What International Future for the Euro?

From its very origins, the project of building a common European currency has been conceptualized as one that would transform the wider global monetary system. If these global ambitions helped to drive the creation of the euro, they deserve some consideration in any analysis of the future of the euro. In other words, the future of European monetary cooperation must be viewed through a lens that focuses not just on intra-European politics but also on the global monetary system as a whole.

In the post-2008 period, two developments in the international monetary system have been particularly significant. The first is the surprisingly enduring global dominance of the US dollar, a dominance whose sources were starkly revealed by the global financial crisis. This development dashed the hopes of Europeans who predicted overconfidently in 2008 that the global financial crisis might boost the euro's international role. The second is the rising international monetary power of China, a power linked primarily—at least so far—to its enormous creditor position. The Eurozone's growing reliance on China's financial support provided yet another reminder of its unanticipated weakness in the post-2008 period.

While these two developments highlighted the limitations of the euro's global ambitions, they may also over the longer term have the effect of strengthening the euro. As in the past, the desire to challenge US monetary power may bolster European backing for reforms that take regional monetary cooperation to the next level. Particularly important would be the creation of a stronger fiscal union that issued common Eurobonds, which could be traded in highly liquid markets whose attractiveness could rival those for US Treasury bills. Also significant would be reforms that address the governance and legitimacy unions highlighted in other chapters in this volume. Even these reforms to strengthen the euro's "embeddedness" as a currency area might not be enough, however, to enable the euro to challenge the dollar's global pre-eminence. As we have seen, the US dollar's international position is also sustained by the broader global role of the US, including its military dominance and its geostrategic and trade relationships with other countries. In other words, the euro's ability to challenge the dollar is closely related to larger issues concerning Europe's strategic and economic position in the world, as well as the willingness and capacity of European policymakers to promote the euro's internationalization more actively and assertively in the future.

Although challenging the dollar's global role is no small task, Europeans with these ambitions may find that they have a new supporter in China. Chinese policymakers share the aspiration of many Europeans to bring greater "symmetry" to the international monetary order and to force the US to become, in the words of the European Commission in 1990, "more conscious of the limits of independent policy-making." Chinese support for the euro was already apparent during Europe's sovereign debt crisis of 2010–2012. If Europe experiences further crises in the context of slow and uneven movement toward closer monetary integration, Chinese support may become important once more in keeping the euro show on the road. Chinese policymakers may even become entangled in intra-Eurozone politics in a more active way as a proponent of reforms that boost the euro's international standing. In these ways, it is clear that the future of the euro depends on politics in the broader global monetary system, as well as those within and among its members.

Conclusion: The Future of the Euro

POSSIBLE FUTURES, RISKS, AND UNCERTAINTIES

Matthias Matthijs and Mark Blyth

European Political Economy and the Importance of Embedded Institutions

In December 2001, on the eve of euro notes and coins going into circulation, Romano Prodi, then president of the European Commission, reflected on Europe's historic leap toward monetary unification in an interview with the *Financial Times*: "I am sure the euro will oblige us to introduce a new set of economic policy instruments. It is politically impossible to propose that now. But some day there will be a crisis and new instruments will be created."[1] The crisis came just under a decade later; a myriad of new economic policy instruments were introduced; and Europe's single currency was pulled back from the brink of collapse in the summer of 2012. The euro survived its first serious crisis. What is more, the Eurozone continued to expand, adding new member states both during and after its debt crisis. Estonia joined in 2011, Latvia in 2014, and Lithuania in 2015. Many observers concluded that Europe's political elites, once again, had gambled and won: the euro was here to stay.[2]

Nevertheless, despite all this exoneration and apparent success, by the summer of 2014 the Eurozone's member states seemed trapped in a rather unhappy marriage. Europeans' trust in their supranational institutions was at an all time low,[3] and Euro-skeptic parties across the Continent recorded their best ever results in the elections for the European Parliament in May 2014.[4] The northern member states found the periphery bailouts hard to swallow, while the southern member states openly resented the uneven imposition of austerity and external demands for structural reform. North and South seemed to be living together despite "irreconcilable differences" as recession made way to stagnation and, in some cases, depression.

Yet the prospect of an amicable divorce, even in the case of depression-battered Greece, was not that appealing. Unlike hard currency pegs, where the original currency remains in circulation, the euro physically replaced all the prior currencies in circulation. Whereas pegs can be broken, unilaterally replacing the euro with a national currency means printing anew. Not only will capital flee as it anticipates this process, import inflation would quickly skyrocket if redenomination occurred. Furthermore, as Greece found out to its despair, when you do not have much of value to sell to the rest of the world, the boost to exports that redenomination should achieve in theory may well fail to materialize in practice. In such a world, once you are in, you stay married.

American Lessons for a European Polity?

There were prior political reasons for such precommitments. One of the main attractions of Economic and Monetary Union (EMU) during the 1990s—especially for Paris-based elites—was not only the importation of Germany's policy credibility and culture of stability, but also the notion that the euro would soon earn Europe the privileges that come with being an international reserve currency. The euro could, in principle, challenge the dollar's monetary hegemony, and Europe's economy would be the main beneficiary.

Ever since the abandonment of the Bretton Woods system of fixed exchange rates, Europe's economies had seen significant currency fluctuations among them during the 1970s and 1980s, more often than not caused by changes in the US Federal Reserve's monetary policy. A common currency, the reasoning went, would remove intra-European exchange rate risk once and for all, and would end the perennial instability of its currency markets. Indeed, as the Prodi quote above suggests, European elites saw EMU as the beginning of a larger process that would eventually lead to a genuine European Constitution—not unlike America's Constitution drafted in 1787 in Philadelphia—that would result in a truly federal European polity. The Europeans, however, could have learned a thing or two from the American experience, if they had paid closer attention to the actual sequence of events in that prior case. Perhaps even more important, and as the analysis of this book makes plain, they should also pay more attention to the concepts of "institutional embeddedness" and "embedded currency areas" developed by Kathleen McNamara in Chapter 2 of this volume.

McNamara drew our attention to the political bargains, cultural norms, and institutional interdependencies that made prior currency unions work, distilling for us the minimum requirements of what she termed an "embedded currency area" (ECA). Those were "(1) a legitimated generator of market confidence and liquidity, (2) mechanisms for fiscal redistribution and economic adjustment, (3) regulation of financial risk and uncertainty, and (4) political solidarity."[5] As McNamara shows us, such embedded institutions tend to evolve over time, preceding and making possible the establishment of later, more obviously economic institutions. The United States serves as a case in point. While the US started out as a political union, the European Union hoped to end as one. In the US, political integration preceded economic union, while in Europe, economic integration was the means to arrive at political union.

As Randall Henning and Martin Kessler noted in an essay for the Brussels-based economics think tank *Bruegel*, rather than ending with one, the US actually started with a limited fiscal union and a common debt instrument.[6] In order to further tie together the nascent federal union politically in 1790, Alexander Hamilton, America's first Treasury Secretary, insisted that the federal government assume 25 million dollars in state debt incurred by the 13 colonies to finance the revolutionary war, and then added it to the existing federal debt owed to France ($11.7 million) and to domestic investors ($42.1 million). Twenty-five million dollars was not a trivial amount at that time, since US nominal GDP was estimated to be around 187 million dollars.[7] Later, the "no-bailout" norm among states in the union was established in the 1840s, once the US was firmly established as a political entity. The US single currency (the "greenback") was introduced another two decades later by President Abraham Lincoln during the US Civil War in 1863 as a means to eventually bind the South closer to the North. A common central bank—the Federal Reserve Board—followed much later, in 1913, while the American banking and financial union, including federal deposit insurance and joint and several liability, was only completed in the 1930s, under the New Deal legislation of President Franklin Delano Roosevelt.[8]

In short, the Americans started with a political union and a federal economic government, complete with a federal debt instrument as well as limited tax levying capacity at the political center. Only much later did they introduce a common currency, a single central bank with the sole right to issue new money, and the equivalent of a banking and financial union. In terms of McNamara's criteria for a successfully embedded currency area, the US got there with the sequence (4), (1), (3), and (2).

The European Union so far has followed a rather different sequence of institution building and political development. The European Economic Community (EEC) started with a customs union of six countries in the late 1950s, agreed on a Common Agricultural Policy in the 1960s, and expanded by adding a few more states in the 1970s and again in the 1980s. The customs union was significantly deepened, becoming a common market with free movement of capital and labor through the Single European Act (SEA) signed in the mid-1980s. With the Maastricht Treaty of 1992, it established a European Central Bank (ECB) in the mid-1990s, followed by the introduction of the single currency, the euro, in 1999 together with a common monetary policy. It was only after two full years of euro crisis, in June 2012, that the idea of a banking union was introduced. A single supervisory mechanism for Europe's systemically important banks was agreed to in late 2013, and went into effect in the autumn of 2014.[9]

Yet, despite these new institutional innovations, Europe today remains without anything resembling a true fiscal union or an economic government, the rules of the "Fiscal Compact" notwithstanding. It lacks a common debt instrument—the so-called Eurobond—and is still far away from a political union that would have the same democratic legitimacy among the citizens of the European Union as the US federal government has with Americans. In other words, the euro as a currency remains fundamentally dis-embedded, in McNamara's terms, from its broader social and political realities, which for the most part in Europe are still based at the level of the individual nation-state.

As no prior currency union composed of multiple large countries seems to have survived without some sort of political union, the importance of McNamara's checklist of what we term "institutional minima" is something European policymakers would do well to keep in mind. Multistate economic projects need to be more fully embedded in existing social and political institutions if they want to be successful in the long term. This is something that America's Founding Fathers seemed to have known instinctively from the very beginning. To date, it does not seem to have penetrated the top echelons of Eurozone policymaking.

Does it then follow that in the absence of such embedded institutions the euro is doomed? Not necessarily, at least not in the short to medium term. Europe and the single currency can continue to muddle through as they have done over the past half decade. The longer-term future of the euro, however, will depend on whether the European Union is able to build the social and political institutions necessary to provide those minima. The chapters in this book suggest both what those minima are and, if built, what possible futures those institutions will face over the next five to ten years.

The Euro's Problem, Experience, and Future: What Have We Learned?

In the first section of the book we explained *the euro problem* as the result of a series of "forgotten unions" that built deep fragilities into the currency's overall architecture. The three forgotten unions of the euro—elaborated on in Jones's Chapter 3, Jabko's Chapter 4, and Schmidt's Chapter 5—are a financial as well as a banking union, institutions of economic governance including supranational fiscal tools, and more effective institutional mechanisms that promote political legitimacy and social solidarity. The main euro problem therefore is, and remains, one of missing "systemic" institutional embeddedness, rather than a lack of "national" competitiveness, labor mobility, wage flexibility, or fiscal restraint.

Erik Jones defines the euro's forgotten financial union as the lack of institutions to manage and regulate cross-border financial flows in a single capital market, which includes a central bank that can act as a true lender of last resort for both Europe's sovereigns and its pan-European banks, as well as a common debt instrument or Eurobond. For Jones, the absence of this financial union was always enough to bring some kind of crisis about, with or without the euro.

Nicolas Jabko added the missing institutions of economic governance to the mix, highlighting the largely unanticipated contradiction between the concern for traditional sovereignty at the national level and a new conception of supranational sovereignty at the European level. He concludes that as long as national elites remain reluctant to see their own powers diminished, the euro's design will remain unfinished and fragile. At the same time, however, those elites cannot easily ignore deeply entrenched notions of sovereignty that resonate with nationally specific ideas about power, liberty, and popular legitimacy.

This latter point is exactly what Vivien Schmidt sees as the final and crucial forgotten union—the political and democratic one that binds all the others together: fiscal, economic, financial, and monetary. For Schmidt, Europe's monetary union lacks legitimate political support mechanisms—at all three levels of democratic input, throughput, and output—as well as long-standing institutions and ideas of intra-European solidarity. The euro's sustainability hence depends on whether it can attract similar democratic support and levels of legitimacy in the future in comparison to what the nation-state enjoys in Europe today.

In Section II of the book, we looked at *the euro experience* from the perspective of its four key member states: Germany, France, Italy, and Spain. Those four economies combined constituted more than 75 percent of the whole Eurozone's GDP in 2013, making them the euro system's principal players.[10] All four experienced both the decade that followed the introduction of the euro and the Eurozone crisis itself very differently. Germany started the 2000s as the "sick man of Europe." France began the decade as the accepted political leader of the Eurozone, while Italy recorded very modest growth rates, but saw its high debt-to-GDP ratio gradually decline. Spain basked in its newfound role as star pupil of the euro growth class. A decade later, after 2010, they all saw their respective roles transformed.

Having benefited from the downward pressure on wages caused by the influx of labor following reunification, and from the export of parts suppliers for their engineering complex to lower cost Eastern European producers, Germany led the euro pack in 2010. (The Hartz reforms had in fact little effect on growth since they primarily produced low wage sheltered service sector employment.) Over the same period France slipped from being top dog to being a middle-ranking euro power, or "middle child," as Mark Vail puts it in Chapter 7, trying to reconcile itself to its new position as a core member state with periphery characteristics. Italy, through euro crisis contagion and the invention of unflattering acronyms linking all crisis-hit Eurozone countries, found itself thrown into the periphery camp, while Spain suddenly went from *wunderkind* to problem child.

Abraham Newman, in Chapter 6, develops an historical explanation for Germany's actions during the euro crisis. Newman argues that Germany's disheartening experience with reunification, plus its ordoliberal tradition and stability culture, combined with the coincidence of its own labor market and welfare reform programs and subsequent economic recovery to determine Berlin's actions. Reluctant to embrace a crisis narrative of contagion risk or a lack of demand in export markets that would have facilitated a more activist or interventionist role, Angela Merkel's various governments played the role of "reluctant leader," adopting a narrative of moral hazard, as well as the need to abide by the rules and implement structural reforms as the only road out of the crisis. This resulted in Germany's preferred policies of austerity and structural reform as the only politically viable solution to the Eurozone's debt crisis, regardless of its dubious macroeconomic merits.

Mark Vail, in Chapter 7, compares France's fall from joint leader of Europe to having to play the role of any family's "middle child"—trying to play the mediator between the northern core and southern periphery member states. But in doing so, France embraces an internal contradiction—binding her economic fate and political prestige to following the preferred policies of Germany and the rest of the North while trying to remain committed, at least rhetorically, to its much-vaunted statist socioeconomic model prevalent in the South. Like most contradictory positions, and standard procedure for being a middle child, no one really cares, and you end up being ignored.

Jonathan Hopkin, in Chapter 8, rejects the standard narrative in both Italy and Spain that explains both countries' woes since 2010 as the inevitable result of greedy unions pricing themselves out of jobs during the boom years. Hopkin, by contrast, shows how the introduction of the euro led to wage stagnation in the Mediterranean countries' manufacturing sectors, which are those most heavily exposed to international competition. The introduction of the euro, however, did bring large gains to the more sheltered sectors such as construction and retail, as well as large parts of the public sector and of course banking. In highlighting this facet of the crisis, Hopkin views the policies of austerity and structural reform in the South as political experiments in how far democracies are willing to go in terms of unemployment to return their economies to fiscal rectitude, since they are targeting the wrong constituencies. Hopkin concludes that the jury is still out, but that the euro's future hangs in the balance. Its future will be determined by how southern Europe will continue to cope with the devastating effects of fiscal consolidation and jobless reform over a decade-long time frame.

In the third and final section of the book, we analyzed *the euro future* from three different points of view. First, how is Europe going to deal with its new German problem? If it is true that Germany's relative power in Europe increased substantially since the first decade of the 2000s, and if its policies have been part of the euro problem rather than the solution, what does that tell us about the single currency's future? Second, is it fair to say, as is often said, that Europe has always moved forward through crisis? And if that is the case, has the euro crisis led to the necessary institutional innovations that will make it possible for the Eurozone to both survive the present and weather future crises? Third, moving beyond Europe's internal dynamics and national political economies, what does the future of the euro look like from an international perspective? What is the euro's place on the world's geopolitical chessboard, which includes, among others, a supposedly declining United States and a fast growing but fragile China?[11]

Wade Jacoby, in Chapter 9, explains how Berlin is torn between what he calls the "timing of politics" and the "politics of timing." On the one hand, Germany accepts its responsibilities as the Eurozone's most powerful member, but it still wants to make sure that bailouts only happen *in extremis*, and that the timing is such that any risk of moral hazard, where the delinquent is encouraged by the bailout to default in the future, is minimized. Time here is a virtue, as the longer one waits, the more the risk of moral hazard is reduced. Yet, at the same time, German politicians feel the pressure of their voters and therefore can only take significant steps in the direction of further integration if they feel that they have sufficiently prepared those voters. Time here is a vice, as any future intervention may be too late. The future of the euro thus depends on how Germany resolves this dilemma. Jacoby argues that this will determine whether we can expect to see any major systemic institution building in the near future, or whether the main governance structures of the euro will remain split between the supranational and national levels.

Craig Parsons and Matthias Matthijs, in Chapter 10, see the euro's future in a rather pessimistic light. They call into question the much-touted view that Europe always moves forward through crisis.[12] While they note that this popular notion of European integration is a reassuring frame for EU policymakers and statesmen, it is actually not borne out by the historical evidence. The European project has in fact almost always moved forward when key players' positive visions of its future institutional development happened to collide, not as a technocratic response to widely perceived problems. Parsons and Matthijs see the euro crisis as Europe's first real crisis, and while the EU has made significant strides toward more integration, especially in the realm of the banking union, they conclude that it falls well short of addressing the single currency's core problem of absent institutional embeddedness.

In contrast, Eric Helleiner, in Chapter 11, paints a more optimistic picture of the euro's future by focusing on the international monetary system. He believes that the euro's future depends upon how long international financial markets will maintain their ostensibly voracious appetite for the US dollar, and what role China will play in the international monetary system as it gradually liberalizes the renminbi (RMB). While for now, the dollar reigns supreme, Helleiner sees a future of relative dollar decline, combined with a gradual rise of the RMB, which could be a positive development for the euro, ending in a perhaps more stable and multipolar currency system.[13]

One thread that all of these chapters have in common is an emphasis on the politics and political economy of the euro and of European integration. The irony of the euro crisis, of course, is that—from Greece and Spain to

Germany and Finland—the crisis brought national politics back into the process of European integration: exactly the outcome the entire post-national project was designed to avoid. Those changing political dynamics, and how national politics will interact with EU level policies, will be crucial in determining which scenario will play out in the euro's future.

The Return of Politics and Possible Futures for the Euro
Four Crisis-Generated Changes That Matter for Europe's Future

Four significant developments in EU politics since 2010 were either the direct result of the euro crisis, or were cultivated and augmented by the policy responses to it, and all four are bound to have consequences for the euro's future. First are the rapidly changing dynamics between Germany and France. Traditionally, the Franco-German couple had functioned as the indispensable motor of European integration. To use former European Commission President Romani Prodi's metaphor, "each one was an equal cylinder in the engine, pushing when the other pulled."[14] That relationship has changed dramatically since the euro crisis. Prior to German reunification, the countries were of relatively equal size, and while Germany could boast a stronger and more dynamic economy, France could lay claim to the EU's political leadership given the catastrophic legacy of World War II for Germany. Yet while they constituted the "twin cylinders," Berlin and Paris always represented two fundamentally different visions of Economic and Monetary Union. While *ordoliberal* and *social market* Germany emphasized the supply side and the need for stability, rules, and fiscal restraint, *dirigiste* and *neo-Keynesian* France stressed the demand side and the importance of full employment, policy flexibility, and solidarity.

The euro crisis saw a noticeable shift in the balance of power away from Paris toward Berlin, which signals a more ordoliberal Europe going forward. While the Social Democratic government of Gerhard Schröder fundamentally reformed the German labor market in the first years of the 2000s, France saw few such reforms under both Gaullist Presidents Jacques Chirac and Nicolas Sarkozy. The latter had pledged a *rupture* for the French economy during his 2007 presidential election campaign, but found it much harder to deliver on that promise once in power. Already by 2006, Germany was beginning to experience faster growth and lower unemployment, and the German government was eager to link this directly to the fruits of its *Hartz* reforms.[15] France, by contrast, saw continuing anemic growth and much higher unemployment, which the Germans then attributed to their lack of reforming zeal.

Once the euro crisis hit, both the media and financial markets scrutinized Angela Merkel's statements much more closely than the comments of either Nicolas Sarkozy or his successor François Hollande. The outcome of the seemingly never-ending series of EU crisis summits of that period largely depended on the stance of Berlin, not Paris. More often than not, the French and German governments would find themselves at odds with one another when it came to crisis responses, but Sarkozy would feel compelled to follow Merkel in her quest for fiscal consolidation and reform to remain relevant. Since 2012, French socialist President Hollande's efforts to shift EU policy away from austerity toward growth and fiscal stimulus proved to be largely irrelevant to actual policy. Again in Romano Prodi's words: "The Germans decide, and the French get to announce it during their joint press conference."[16] There is no doubt that the EU since the euro crisis has moved much more decisively in a "Germanic" direction.

The second big change, one that is particularly disturbing for the goals of the European project, was the return of the North-South gap in the EU. The euro crisis and the implementation of austerity and structural reforms reversed the progress made over the course of the 1990s and the first years of the 2000s in reducing the substantial differences in national income between EU members of the well-off North and the poorer South. Admission to the single currency was supposed to bring the younger (and poorer) democracies of Greece, Spain, and Portugal up to the levels experienced in the rest of Europe. Yet exactly the opposite happened. While the ratio of per capita income (in constant prices) of poor Greece vis-à-vis much more affluent Germany had been steadily improving since the early 1990s to a high of 0.65 in 2007, it worsened again to 0.47 by 2013, a number much lower than the prevailing ratio in the early 1990s. And this was not just a Greek tragedy: the corresponding ratios for Italy's and Spain's per capita income vis-à-vis Germany's were at a high of 0.87 and 0.83 in 2007, and fell to 0.74 and 0.72 in 2013, respectively.[17]

Furthermore, the EU countries of the Mediterranean also experienced a conspicuous erosion of the strength of their democratic institutions and the effectiveness of their governments compared to those in the North since 2010.[18] This adverse evolution has brought new doubts to bear over the old EU mantra of an "ever closer union" and threatened not just the real economic gains that were made prior to the crisis, but also the quality of democracy experienced throughout the union. After all, if Brussels can veto a national parliament's budget, what is the point of electing that parliament in the first place?

Third, the euro crisis has displaced the traditional "community method" of decision-making in the EU in favor of what German Chancellor Merkel referred to as the "union method" in a speech in Bruges in the autumn of 2010.[19] With hundreds of billions of euros in bailout funds needed that were only available directly from the member states' budgets, it should perhaps have been no surprise that neither the European Commission nor the European Parliament on their own could have cobbled together a comprehensive solution. The commitment of those large amounts of taxpayers' money to the European Financial Stability Facility (EFSF) and the European Stability Mechanism (ESM) naturally required oversight by national governments. Nevertheless, this meant that existing "community" institutions were largely sidelined in the decision-making process, with intergovernmental summits putting the European Council firmly in charge of crisis management.

Ironically, however, these supranational institutions may prove to be the long-term winners of the euro crisis. Between 2010 and 2014, the Commission gained sizable future powers in monitoring member states' fiscal policies through the so-called European Semester. The European Central Bank won large discretionary powers not just over monetary policy, but also over banking supervision and resolution. The European Parliament managed to stage a major coup against the European Council by launching a system of *Spitzenkandidaten* during the European elections in May 2014, in which Jean-Claude Juncker as the candidate to lead the Commission of the European People's Party (EPP) was de facto forced on Europe's heads of state and government in June 2014, despite UK Prime Minister David Cameron's desperate efforts to reverse the process and stop Juncker in his tracks. Yet, whether all of this activity adds up to McNamara's minimal conditions of an ECA remains very much in doubt.

Fourth, and finally, the euro crisis reintroduced political and legal tensions between nation-states and the supranational institutions of the European Union, constantly testing the limits of the integration process. As intimated in Section I, the Fiscal Compact, for example, was concluded as an intergovernmental treaty outside the EU Treaties, since Britain and the Czech Republic refused to sign it in December 2011. Once the 25 signatories adopted the treaty in March 2012, they were required to incorporate a balanced budget or "golden" rule into their constitutions, challenging the nature and legitimacy of national constitutions. But the national judicial limits of European integration clashed with the need for system-wide Eurozone solutions most openly in Germany itself. The strongly independent Federal Constitutional Court (FCC or *Bundesverfassungsgericht*) in Karlsruhe had already called into question the democratic legitimacy of the 2009 Lisbon Treaty prior to the euro crisis. In the end, while there were no explicit constitutional objections against the Lisbon Treaty, Karlsruhe did impose limitations to future integration by identifying a number of state functions that were not amenable to integration and which were to be retained at the national level, especially in the realm of fiscal policy.

During the euro crisis, the FCC would rule over the legality of the ESM, the bond buying programs of the ECB, and at the time of writing, is still in the midst of a legal battle with the European Court of Justice (ECJ) in Luxembourg over the legality of the ECB's potential tool of outright monetary transactions (OMT). This legal aspect of the euro crisis added yet another layer of complexity to EU decision-making, periodically fueling uncertainty in financial markets. Given all of this, if Europe wants to build the "missing unions" to make the euro work for the long term, Germany will need to overcome some formidable political obstacles and change its constitution. Everyone else will have to reconcile fiscal centralization and effective national-level democracy, which is not an easy trick to pull off.

Competing Visions of Where Europe Goes from Here

There is no shortage of thinking when it comes to the future of the Eurozone. Both EU institutions and various think tanks around Europe have been looking at how to complete the euro's unfinished institutional framework going forward, detailing the steps necessary to avoid another systemic crisis. All of those competing visions touch upon this book's central concerns, but mostly in an ad hoc and unsystematic manner, often mistaking what is economically and financially desirable for what is politically possible. Indeed, what all such proposals seem to have in common is a rather willful neglect of the role of politics in achieving a more complete EMU.

For example, both the European Council and the European Commission published blueprints for the Eurozone's future in late 2012. Herman Van Rompuy, president of the European Council, in close cooperation with José Manuel Barroso, Jean-Claude Juncker, and Mario Draghi, published a first draft of their blueprint "Towards a Genuine Economic and Monetary Union" in June 2012, in advance of the crucial EU summit that allowed the ESM to directly recapitalize Spain's banking system.[20] What became known as the "Four Presidents' Report" had the advantage of being concise (the June draft was only 7 pages, while the December version was 18 pages), but falls well short of our minimum criteria for an embedded currency area.

While the "Four Presidents' Report" did call for a comprehensive banking union that comprised all European banks, including an effective resolution mechanism, it omitted common deposit insurance from its final draft, and only tentatively called for Eurobonds. The report defined fiscal union mainly as greater centralized budgetary controls and stricter rules—a necessary condition for Eurobonds—and only saw the need for a very limited Eurozone budget in the distant future. It paid lip service to the need for greater democratic legitimacy, mentioning the need for closer cooperation with national parliaments only in passing, omitting the need for any direct democratic choice over policy. The Commission's own "blueprint for a deep and genuine economic and monetary union," released in late November 2012, added very little to the "Four Presidents' Report."[21] They referred to "Stability Bonds" rather than the politically more sensitive term "Eurobonds," but also only after more centralized fiscal controls were in place. It remained vague on the need for a Eurozone budget to absorb asymmetric shocks and mentioned the eventual need for a political union, but without any real specifics on how to get there.[22]

Unburdened by the need to govern, think tank blueprints are more ambitious in scope. *Notre Europe*, the Paris think tank chaired by former Commission President Jacques Delors, commissioned a report on "Completing the Euro" by the Tommaso Padoa-Schioppa Group, coordinated by Henrik Enderlein of the Hertie School in Berlin, which included EMU experts André Sapir, Paul De Grauwe, and Jean Pisany-Ferry.[23] The report, released in June 2012, goes much further than the blueprints of the Council and the Commission. The Padoa-Schioppa Group calls for a US-style Federal Deposit Insurance Corporation and an independent resolution agency to complement the banking union. They made a strong case for Eurobonds and a European Debt Agency to partially finance national budgets, though they also want stricter budgetary controls and stress the right of the Commission to limit the sovereignty of governments that break the rules and accrue too much debt. The report also wants a "cyclical adjustment insurance fund" to serve as the Eurozone budget and protect the currency union against asymmetric shocks, as well as a mechanism for sovereign debt restructuring. This report is obviously much closer to our own analysis. Yet as welcome as such suggestions are, they ignore the institutional, democratic, and electoral problems of getting there, as highlighted in this volume by Jabko, Schmidt, Jacoby, and Hopkin. Unfortunately, you cannot assume away the politics you have in the hope to arrive at the economics you want.

Three more blueprints emerged from German, French, and British initiatives: the Glienicker Group, the Eiffel Group, and the Centre for European Reform (CER).[24] They all also go much further than the Council and Commission blueprints, in that they envision the need for a fiscal union, a Eurozone budget, and a more democratically legitimate political union, but they also stay close to their national traditions.[25] While the Glienicker group—which includes 11 German economists, political scientists, and jurists—makes no mention of common deposit insurance or Eurobonds, they do foresee the need for a limited economic government with a membership fee of 0.5 percent of GDP that could serve to provide unemployment insurance and public goods. They also emphasize the EU's right to limit the sovereignty of governments that borrow too much, but provide no mechanism for sovereign debt restructuring. Glienicker argues that to achieve their political agenda, "the euro area needs a new contractual basis of its own," a "Euro-treaty to replace previous piecemeal reforms."[26]

Hewing to the ideas that Mark Vail indentified in Chapter 7 as being quintessentially French, the Eiffel Group's report—signed by 12 French economists, political scientists, and legal scholars—proposes a Eurozone budget with full tax-raising and borrowing powers, Eurobonds, and a mechanism for sovereign debt restructuring. Eiffel wants "to construct a political Community which is democratic and based around the euro."[27] Their blueprint has an entire section called "method" that discusses the treaty changes and formal democratic procedures that will need to be implemented. But once again, whether those procedures are politically feasible is a question left unanswered.[28]

Finally, Philippe Legrain's report for the London-based Centre for European Reform, "How to Finish the Euro House," is probably the most ambitious and well thought out proposal, in terms of what needs to be done, that we have encountered.[29] It is also the most realistic when it comes to outlining what will actually happen, as opposed to outlining the future one would like to see. To work well, Legrain argues, the Eurozone needs to do four things: (1) try to prevent problems from emerging; (2) limit problems when they arise; (3) resolve problems "promptly, fairly, and safely"; and (4) be democratically legitimate. That is, the Eurozone needs to be properly accountable insofar as it embodies real democratic choices.[30]

This assessment comes closest to what we have defined as the outcomes of an embedded currency area in this volume. The CER report, however, is realistic enough politically to see that this will not happen overnight, if at all. Legrain suggests four possible futures for the Eurozone: a Germanic one, a technocratic one, a fiscally federal one, and a flexible (or de-centralized) one. Ideally, the Eurozone would move toward a fiscally federal Eurozone, but that is also politically the least likely option. Legrain fears that the current political trajectory of Europe has the Eurozone on a path toward a combination of a Germanic and a technocratic union, which falls far short of his ideal blueprint, and ours too, since it still treats politics as an error to be eliminated rather than a foundation from which to build. Legrain concludes that the current path Europe is on may ultimately lead the euro to disintegrate. However, though he is not hopeful, Legrain does allow for the possibility that a new crisis may "provide the political momentum to create a fiscally federal eurozone."[31]

From Blueprints to Black Swans: Europe's Possible Futures

Blueprints for the future of Europe are not like the blueprints for a building. The latter tend to correspond quite closely to what is actually built. The former usually end up quite far away from the future they purport to produce. The more complex the blueprint, and the further into the future it projects, the greater the risks and uncertainties that multiply within the structure. In order to make further sense of the future of the Eurozone given the many concerns raised in this book, we elaborate here on the future of the euro using the "black swan" metaphor originally developed by Nassim Nicholas Taleb.[32] Rather than chart still further paths, in part because we largely agree with Legrain's analysis, we use an extension of Taleb's metaphor in this final part of our concluding chapter to chart the likely economic, financial, and political threats facing the euro going forward. We envision three kinds of "euro swans"—white swans, grey swans, and black swans.[33]

First, *white swans* are events that present us with a potentially knowable economic or financial risk. There is a definable probability of them occurring, along with a reasonable estimate of their impact. Economic policymakers and individual market participants can hedge themselves against the impact of such white swans because insurance, to some degree, is possible. White swans are what former US Defense Secretary Donald Rumsfeld referred to as "known knowns."

Second, *grey swans* shade from risk toward uncertainty, but constantly wander between the two states. The future gets more complicated—and much more unpredictable—with grey swans. Grey swans happen when (mainly) political events—like a referendum, a national election, or an important parliamentary vote—about which we may know the actual timing but not the magnitude of their impact, upset other more knowable variables. Grey swans may be less likely to happen than white swans, or at least the probability that they could be estimated accurately is lower, but they could potentially bring a much bigger shock to the system. They are both Rumsfeld's "known unknowns" and his "unknown knowns."

Third, *black swans* are those extraordinary events that have a completely unknown probability. These are Rumsfeld's "unknown unknowns," and are uncertain in the deepest sense of the word. We cannot know what they are in advance, but we do know that their impact will be devastating.[34] Black swans are particularly pernicious because they have no determinately related historical precedents, no set date, and elaboration from past data usually makes one more blind as to what is actually coming.

In sum, white swans are what we expect to see. They lie in the middle of the distribution of possible risks. Grey swans take us outside these parameters, out beyond our one or two sigma comfort zone. Black swans lie hidden deep in the tails of the distribution of possible futures.

Europe's White Swans

White swan events are a dime a dozen: a fall in Purchasing Managers Indices (PMIs), an upturn in consumer confidence, or a rise in the euro-dollar exchange rate despite ECB actions. They are trivial, in the sense that they are everyday occurrences, but that does not mean that they are unimportant. One example comes from Helleiner's focus in Chapter 11 on the international role of the euro. The fact that central banks outside Europe loaded up on euros prior to the crisis acted as a positive white swan for Europe insofar as it meant that during the crisis the euro-dollar exchange rate held up much better than a lot of currency traders expected. This adding of euros to everyone's reserves created a prisoner's dilemma situation among central banks. If any of them tried to move out of euros, it would have triggered a run on the euro, which would have hurt them all. As such, it became in everyone's interest not to sell euros despite the currency's systemic crisis, and stability was unexpectedly assured.

Another example of a possibly positive white swan is the ECB's ongoing (at the time of writing) Asset Quality Review (AQR) of Europe's troubled banking system. Europe faces what might be called a "Goldilocks dilemma" in its attempt to reform its banking system.[35] As noted in this book by several of the authors, the European sovereign debt crisis was only triaged when ECB President Mario Draghi poured nearly one trillion euro of public money (LTROs) into the European banking system in December 2011 and March 2012. The result of all this cash hitting the banking system was to incentivize periphery banks to buy local sovereign bonds. Because of the yield compression this causes, if austerity policies are loosened and growth accelerates, then interest rates will have to rise. As that happens, the periphery banks holding all these bonds will see their asset base shrink in value as yields go up, bond prices go down, and their balance sheets become impaired. So growth cannot get "too hot." Given this, the ECB needs low rates, more LTROs, and a host of monetary tricks such as the introduction of negative deposit rates in June 2014 and the direct purchasing of covered bonds and asset-backed securities (ABS) as announced in October 2014 to allow the banks to clean up their balance sheets, one non-performing loan at a time, in an environment of relatively slow growth.

However, not only is such a process painfully slow, if growth is "too cold" these policies cannot work since only higher rates of growth will allow the banks to repair their balance sheets as new "performing" loans replace their "non-performing" loans. Given this constraint, where growth can be neither too hot nor too cold, the AQR provides the ECB with a way to triage the worst offenses of the banking system without setting off a general panic. Bad bank solutions, such as Ireland's National Asset Management Agency (NAMA), may become more palatable to other states in the wake of the AQR. This could have a positive effect on the needed downsizing and recapitalization of the European financial sector, despite the Goldilocks constraint. Such white swans, should they occur, will be good for the euro's long-term future.

Europe's Grey Swans

Grey swans are more serious, in terms of magnitude, and tend to be more negative. We know something is coming, we just do not know when or what its magnitude will be. At a most general level, the politics of building embedded institutions is a grey swan. This is seen in Erik Jones's admonishment that without a full financial union, given the realities of cross-border banking by multinational banks that all effectively borrow their currency (since none of them prints the euro), some kind of accident waiting to happen is still there, despite recent reforms. We just do not know what it is yet, or how it will play out.

Jonathan Hopkin's Chapter 8 on Italy and Spain hints at another grey swan. Turning around Italy's debt position and cleaning up Spain's banks are arduous projects that could take a decade to complete. If the policy menu to achieve these ends is unending fiscal austerity, then quite apart from deflationary risks or GDP shrinkage, the sheer political sustainability of such policies comes into question. Asking people to vote once for austerity—even twice—is plausible if there is light at the end of the tunnel. If, however, all that seems possible is the lengthening of the tunnel, then either democracy refuses the policy menu or the enforcers of the policy menu ignore democracy. The replacement of the democratically elected Greek and Italian leadership by veteran EU technocrats at the height of the crisis in November 2011 was no aberration. It was an inevitable product of this tension. If it breaks out again, which is likely, and democracy wins, which is also likely, all that remains in doubt is the magnitude of the shock it sends to the euro itself.

Wade Jacoby's insights on the timing of politics and the politics of timing in Germany also have great bearing here. While it is easy to blame Germany's austerity-fetishism for making the crisis a lot worse—and indeed there is merit in such a claim—the "democracy versus markets" problem highlighted by Hopkin in the South bites hard in Germany, too. Germany may be the Eurozone's biggest economy, but at a shade under 3.5 trillion dollars in GDP, it is only 29 percent of Eurozone GDP and a mere 8.75 percent of the value of the total asset footprint of the European banking sector.[36] As such, Germany can only be expected to swallow so much of everyone else's problems.[37] It is in this context that the timing of politics—the desire to minimize one's own risk of exposure to someone else's moral hazard—combines with the politics of timing—the "right" moment to sell a policy to the public—to create leadership that is likely always going to be insufficient to fully resolve the crisis and safeguard the euro's future.

Other grey swan–type events include popular referendums. Scotland voted on its independence on September 18, 2014 with 55 percent of Scots deciding to stay in the union. If it had decided to break away from the rest of the United Kingdom, the knock-on effects to European markets could have potentially been very large. It could have created a shadow bond market for Scottish debt (amusingly called "kilt-edged securities") separate from British debt that would have weakened the British fiscal position. What was left of the UK could then have voted to leave the EU, just as Scotland would have been petitioning to get back in, all while using the Bank of England's money. The union seems safe for now, but Catalonia in Spain and Flanders in Belgium may well follow Scotland's example by announcing referendums of their own, bringing greater instability and enormous uncertainty over the status of their respective countries' large sovereign debt stocks.

Europe's Black Swans

By definition, black swans cannot be predicted, and past data, such as the analysis of this book, can make one less prepared for their arrival, rather than more. But having said that, there are a few imaginable "unknown unknowns" out there worth mentioning that are extremely underpriced and could yet generate huge risks.

The first is the "Treaty on Stability, Coordination and Governance," also known as the "Fiscal Compact."[38] This treaty came into effect in March 2012, mandating that national budgets be "balanced or in surplus"[39] with enforcement guaranteed by "preferably constitutional"[40] provisions embedded in national legal frameworks. In other words, parliaments are to vote away their last set of fiscal powers. Countries that produce "significant observed deviations"[41] from the numbers enshrined in the treaty will be fined. Furthermore, the so-called Six-Pack, consisting of five regulations and one directive, which entered into force in December 2011, includes a "Macroeconomic Imbalance Procedure."[42] This procedure allows member countries to have a maximum current account deficit of 4 percent or a surplus of 6 percent of their respective GDPs. Given that imports and exports sum to zero, that surplus of +2 percent must be offset somehow. Either surplus countries reduce their surpluses, which they are not going to do voluntarily, or deficit countries have to run permanently tight policies to offset the surpluses, given the common currency. If this is the case, the Fiscal Compact and the Six-Pack themselves are risk generators of unknown value for the euro since they will more than likely produce macroeconomic outcomes in non-surplus countries that will add to the political instability that Hopkin highlights in Chapter 8.

A second black swan that lies hidden in the tail would be the unexpected return of a 1930s-style authoritarian regime to one of the Eurozone member states. A future and sudden rise of extremist parties—Golden Dawn in Greece and Marine Le Pen's Front National in France come to mind—could force those countries to withdraw from the Eurozone or the EU altogether. A significant anti-democratic turn by a non-euro member state, like Hungary, is also not unthinkable, and would have a profound impact on the future of the EU. Meanwhile, even further out in the tail, the Middle East may blow up and start a nuclear arms race if Iran gets an atomic bomb. Putin's Russia may invade the Baltics (which are all three euro members) under the ruse of "protecting Russian minorities," and the American economic recovery may falter, triggered by a new financial meltdown, impacting the economies of China, India, and Brazil, and ultimately the northern European export machine. However, if the deflationary trends in the eurozone itself continue beyond 2014, we may not need such exotic birds to do the damage at all. Existing policy continuing on autopilot may be all that is required.

What Does All This Mean for the Future of the Euro?

Such events could have huge consequences, or they may never come to pass. A seemingly minor white swan may cause serious damage to the currency's long-term future. Black swans may never take flight or, at the risk of stretching the metaphor, a whole flock may settle over Europe. We simply do not know. But what we can say on the basis of this book is the following:

- Without developing a political process to legitimately embed its economic and financial institutions, the future of the euro will be fragile at best.
- We know which institutions need to be built in finance, governance, and politics to make it work. They are detailed in the first section of the book. What Europe has built to date falls far short of these minima.
- There are no sustainable technocratic solutions to the euro problem, which is an inherently political one, and will need political solutions. Democracy is not a mere error term in the non-linear regression of governance.
- The major current risks to the euro stem from the attempt to make national-level austerity and structural reform superior objectives to restoring Eurozone growth and championing EU political reform.
- The future of the euro will be decided in Germany, Spain, and Italy. France has lost its leadership position in Europe, and has yet to find a role.
- The timing of politics outside Germany will eventually dominate the timing of German politics and the future of the euro.
- The Eurozone will gradually take over the EU in institutional importance, which will have significant consequences for the "euro-outs" like the UK, Sweden, and Denmark. The outs may at some point face a painful choice between joining the euro and leaving the European Union altogether.
- The euro's international position may help it at the margin, but it is European domestic politics that will determine its future in the end.

What we know for sure is that the Eurozone, assuming we still have a euro a decade from now, which is far from certain, will look very different from how it looks today. More countries will likely have joined by 2025, including Denmark, Poland, and possibly Hungary, while some other countries, like Greece, Cyprus, and Portugal, may well have opted to leave. Some of the missing unions—maybe common deposit insurance or some version of a Eurobond—may have been introduced, with others still lagging far behind or remaining politically unthinkable. The global economy will continue to develop, and the individual national varieties of capitalism that constitute the European economy will continue to evolve in divergent as well as convergent ways.[43] Germany may well be struggling by 2025, while France could see an economic revival—it has happened before—and its demographics are much better. Britain may have left the European Union altogether. Belgium may no longer exist.

In closing, we are reminded of the observation made by the Greek philosopher Heraclitus (535–475 BC) that "no man ever steps into the same river twice, for it is not the same river and he is not the same man." Like Heraclitus's river, the Eurozone is a dynamic system that continues to advance and flow. The men and women in Europe's corridors of power also change, as does the nature of Europe's democracies and peoples' expectations of their national governments and of the European Union. As the next generation of leaders takes office, they will likely have very different ideas from those of Kohl, Mitterrand, and Delors, or Merkel, Hollande, and Barroso.

Heraclitus tells us that the man was different the second time around, precisely because he had already waded into the river once before. The experience of the euro crisis should therefore have taught current and future leaders to put the euro on a more solid footing. In order to do so, all we can hope is that Europe's future leaders will approach the question of the single currency by beginning with the political foundations of markets. We dare even dream that they may have internalized the main lesson of this book, that a common currency is not a technocratic endeavor but a political choice: it needs to be fully embedded in democratic institutions to keep earning its legitimacy every day. The economist Abba Lerner, who we cited at the beginning of Chapter 1, once observed that economic transactions constitute "solved political problems." The euro is not there yet: Europe still has a long way to travel in order to solve its single currency's intrinsically *political* flaws. Only then will the Eurozone be able to fundamentally resolve its *economic* ones.

Notes

CHAPTER 1

1. Taleb 2010; Blyth 2009; and Matthijs 2012b.
2. See Gilbert 2012, chapter 7, pp. 143–171; Calleo 2011; and Parsons 2003, chapter 7.
3. For earlier "functionalist" thinking on European integration, see Haas 1968.
4. Calleo 2003.
5. Milward 2000.
6. Calleo 2003, chapter 12.
7. Marsh 2011, pp. 153–155.
8. See, for example, Eichengreen, 2005.
9. As Eric Helleiner points out in Chapter 11 of this volume, the share of the euro in non-industrial countries' reserves had risen from 19 percent since the euro's establishment to 30 percent in 2008, while the dollar's share had fallen from 70 percent to 60 percent.
10. Bloomberg News 2007.
11. Trichet 2009.
12. Blyth 2014a.
13. Shin 2012.
14. Blyth 2013a, chapter 3.
15. Lerner 1972, p. 259.
16. See, for example, Bayoumi and Eichengreen 1993; Feldstein 1997; Frankel and Rose 1997, 1998.
17. See Hall and Soskice 2001; and Hall 2014.
18. Van Rompuy et al. 2012.
19. A European Commission directive in 2001 that mandated all euro denominated debt be treated equally as (de facto AAA) collateral in repo transactions simply turbocharged this process further.

20. Matthijs 2014b.
21. This view is dominant in both EU scholarly as well as policy elite circles. Recent scholarly examples: Gross 2011; and Schmitter 2012. Examples of policymakers: Merkel 2010a; and Van Rompuy 2011. See Chapter 10 in this volume.

CHAPTER 2

1. Most prominently, Feldstein 1997.
2. Reviews of OCA theory include Mongelli 2002.
3. Mundell 1961.
4. I am using monetary union, currency union, and single currency somewhat interchangeably to mean a geographic area with one monetary policy and one currency or irrevocably locked exchange rates.
5. Friedman 1953.
6. Mundell 1961.
7. McKinnon 1963.
8. Kenen 1969.
9. Kirshner, ed. 2003; Helleiner 2008.
10. Polanyi 1957. See also Berman 2006; Blyth 2002.
11. A subtle analysis of the relationship between Polanyi's ideas, monetary law, and EU law is found in Everson and Joerges 2012.
12. Abdelal, Blyth, and Parsons 2010.
13. Erik Jones's Chapter 3 in this volume further elaborates on the role of central banks in monetary unions.
14. See Nicolas Jabko's Chapter 4 in this volume for a full explanation of the importance of fiscal union.
15. The importance of political union and democratic legitimacy is explored in Vivien Schmidt's Chapter 5 in this volume.
16. On the European experience, see Tilly, ed. 1975; Evans, Rueschemeyer, and Skocpol, eds. 1985. For the US experience, Burnham 1970; Stephen Skowronek 1982; and Bensel 1991.
17. Poggi 1978, p. 93.
18. Tilly 1985.
19. McNamara 2002.
20. McNamara 2002; McNamara 2003; and McNamara 2011.
21. McNamara 2011.
22. On the Soviet case, see Woodruff 1999.
23. This section draws on McNamara 2002, as well as on McNamara 2011.
24. See Bensel 1991.
25. Binder and Spindel 2013.
26. Henning and Kessler 2012.
27. Mattli 1999.

28. Holtfrerich 1993.

29. Foreman-Peck 2006.

30. Flandreau 2003.

31. Flandreau 2003.

32. The classical gold standard of the nineteenth century has some similarities to the Eurozone in that the fixed rate commitment meant that adjustments had to be made through other policy instruments than the exchange rate. However, as an intergovernmental agreement, it did not have aspirations toward any sort of collective decision-making such as that implied by a currency union. For a more complete treatment of the gold standard in terms of its lessons for EMU, see Matthijs 2014b.

33. Spruyt 1996; Anderson 1983; Weber 1976.

34. Flandreau 2000; Eric Helleiner 2003; Einaudi 2001.

35. Eichengreen 2008.

36. Eichengreen 2008.

37. Reinhart and Rogoff 2009.

38. The Eurozone does not match all the criteria of the OCA models according to Eichengreen and others; see Eichengreen 1991. However, recent analysis shows more mobility in the factors of production among the core countries of Europe, as the single market has deepened, advances in social welfare portability across the EU has allowed for more labor mobility, and financial integration has taken off. See Rose 2008.

39. On how the ideational underpinnings of the ECB created these constraints, see McNamara 1998.

40. See Erik Jones's contribution to this volume (Chapter 3) for a full accounting of the role of the ECB in the euro crisis.

41. Fiscal union and "economic government" in the EU are further explored in Nicolas Jabko's Chapter 4 in this volume.

42. See Matthijs 2014b as well as Chapter 8 by Jonathan Hopkin in this volume.

CHAPTER 3

1. Jones 2014.

2. Pelkmans 1987; Schreiber 1991.

3. Vipond 1991.

4. European Central Bank 1999, pp. 15–16.

5. Duffy 2012.

6. Annual Macroeconomic (AMECO) database, European Commission.

7. International Monetary Fund 2011, p. 15; Vandevyvere and Zenthoefer, pp. 12, 17.

8. Obstfeld 2013.

9. White 2012, p. 19.

10. Gangahar and Jones 2007.

11. White 2012, p. 19. A few commentators from Birkbeck College lament that there was actually a bank run in the UK as recently as 1910. See Daripa, Kapur, and Wright 2013, p. 72.
12. Kingsley 2012.
13. Brennan 2013.
14. Thorhallsson 2013.
15. Kulish 2008.
16. International Monetary Fund 2007, p. 26.
17. Eurostat 2008, p. 7.
18. Merler and Pisani-Ferry 2012, p. 6.
19. Osborne 2013.
20. De Larosière 2009.
21. De Larosière 2009, p. 12.
22. Benoit and Barber 2009.
23. Jones 2010.
24. Bank for International Settlements 2010, pp. 11–12.
25. Kambas 2013.
26. Hopkin 2012a.
27. AMECO database.
28. AMECO database.
29. Arslanalp and Tsuda 2012, p. 30.
30. Royo 2013, pp. 203–205.
31. Royo 2013, pp. 196–201.
32. Draghi 2011b.
33. European Central Bank 2012a.
34. Italian Treasury 2011, p. 3.
35. Martinuzzi, Wu, and Plenty 2012.
36. Royo 2013, p. 199.
37. Jenkins 2012.
38. Euro Area 2012.
39. Howarth and Quaglia 2013, pp. 103–104, 107–110.
40. Draghi 2012a.
41. Draghi 2012b.
42. Draghi 2012c.
43. European Central Bank, 2012c.
44. Draghi 2012b.
45. Mersch 2014; Cœuré 2013; Asmussen 2013b.
46. European Council 2012d, p. 7.
47. European Council 2012d, pp. 7–8.
48. Howarth and Quaglia 2013, pp. 111–113.
49. European Council 2012e, pp. 3–4.
50. Howarth and Quaglia, 2013, p. 113.

51. Jones 2013b, pp. 85–86.
52. Steinhauser, Stevis, and Walker 2013.
53. Jones 2013b, pp. 81–94.
54. Draghi 2013.
55. Der Spiegel 2013.
56. Draghi 2013.
57. Draghi 2014.
58. O'Rourke and Taylor 2013, pp.186–188.
59. Draghi 2014.

CHAPTER 4

1. European Council 2010.
2. European Council 2011b, 2012b.
3. Elster 1986; March 1994.
4. European Union 1992, Maastricht Treaty, Article 104c (now Article 126).
5. Marsh 1992.
6. Jabko 2006, pp. 147–178; Dyson and Featherstone 1999, pp. 124–245.
7. Pisani-Ferry 2006.
8. Heipertz and Verdun 2010.
9. European Council 2005, Annex II.
10. European Union, 2007, Lisbon Treaty, Protocol on the euro group, Article 2.
11. Agence France Presse online 2008b.
12. Sarkozy 2008.
13. European Parliament 2008.
14. Interview with French government official, Paris, November 6, 2008.
15. Skidelsky 2009.
16. Bloomberg News 2008.
17. Jabko and Massoc 2012.
18. Bloomberg News 2009.
19. Vail 2011.
20. Bastasin 2012. On Germany in particular, *Financial Times* columnist Wolfgang Münchau has repeatedly made the argument that many of the key decisions adopted during the Eurozone crisis were self-defeating. See, for example, Münchau 2010.
21. OECD 2013.
22. See both Chapter 6 by Abraham Newman and Chapter 9 by Wade Jacoby in this volume.
23. Council of the European Union 2010.
24. On the controversy within the ECB, see Irwin 2013, pp. 229–232.
25. European Central Bank 2011a. On the controversy, see Irwin 2013, pp. 320–321.
26. European Central Bank 2011b.

27. Author interview, Elysée Palace, January 2012.
28. The treaty modification was possible under the "simplified revision procedure" (Article 48.6), which authorizes limited treaty modifications after a unanimous vote of the member governments at the European Council.
29. European Council 2012a.
30. Spiegel and Chaffin 2012.
31. European Council 2012c.
32. European Council 2012b.
33. European Central Bank 2012b.
34. Irwin 2013, pp. 351–352, 380–382.
35. De Grauwe 2011.
36. Darvas, Pisani-Ferry, and Wolff 2013.
37. Mallet and Spiegel 2012.
38. Hollande 2012.
39. Hall 2013.
40. Hollande and Merkel 2013.
41. Interview, French President's office, Paris, November 2, 2010. Thus, in July 2010, the French and German finance ministers presented to the Van Rompuy taskforce a joint position paper titled "European Economic Governance: A French-German Paper" (in French, "Gouvernement économique européen: papier franco-allemand").
42. Juncker and Tremonti 2010.
43. Delpla and von Weizäcker 2010; Gros and Mayer 2004.
44. Van Rompuy 2013.
45. Véron 2013b.
46. Hollande 2013b.
47. De Grauwe and Ji 2012; De Grauwe 2012.
48. Blyth 2013a.
49. On the national dimension of the Eurozone crisis, see especially Bastasin 2012.
50. Wolff 2012; McNamara, Chapter 2 in this volume.
51. Hamilton, Madison, and Jay 1987; especially #31, 39, and 62.
52. However, see Chapter 10 by Craig Parsons and Matthias Matthijs on whether the EU really moves forward through crisis.

CHAPTER 5

1. E.g., Caporaso and Tarrow 2008; Majone 1998; Moravcsik 2002 vs. Follesdal 2006; Mair 2006; Hix 2008; and even Majone 2009.
2. See, e.g., Barbier 2008.
3. Scharpf 2012b, 2013, 2014; Blyth 2013a; Höpner and Schäfer 2007; Baccaro and Armingeon 2013.
4. See, e.g., Kriesi et al. 2008; Mair 2006; Franklin and van der Eijk 2007; Hooghe and Marks 2009.

5. Scharpf 2012b; Fabbrini 2013; Schmidt 2013.

6. The systems approach largely built on that of David Easton (1965).

7. E.g., Scharpf 1999; Majone 1998.

8. Scharpf 1999, 2014.

9. Mair 2013; Mair and Thomassen 2010.

10. Schmidt 2013a; see also Zürn 2000; Benz and Papadopoulos 2006. Note that Easton (1965) uses the term "throughput," but limits it to administrative processes.

11. See, e.g., Heritier and Lehmkuhl 2011; Dehousse 2011; Smismans 2003; and see discussion in Schmidt 2013a.

12. Schmidt 2013a.

13. Schmidt 2013c.

14. Thanks to André Sapir for this comment, made in the wrap-up session of the Conference on "Europe in a Post Crisis World," Center for European Studies, Harvard University (Oct. 31–Nov. 1, 2013).

15. Scharpf 1999, 2012, 2014.

16. Jones 2013a.

17. On ordoliberalism, see Ptak 2009; Dullien and Guérot 2012; Blyth 2013a; Schmidt and Thatcher 2013.

18. See discussion in Nicolas Jabko, Chapter 4 in this volume.

19. See Barbier 2012.

20. Blyth 2013a.

21. See Newman, Chapter 6 of this volume.

22. Schmidt 2013b.

23. See Hopkin, Chapter 8 of this volume.

24. Eurostat 2013.

25. Council of Europe 2013.

26. See, e.g., Skidelsky 2013; Matthijs and Blyth 2011; Wolf 2013.

27. Enderlein et al. 2012.

28. Scharpf 2013, 2014.

29. See also Chapter 2 by Kathleen McNamara in this volume.

30. Schelkle 2014.

31. Matthijs 2014b.

32. International Monetary Fund 2013.

33. Van Rompuy et al., 2012.

34. Those contracts pledged even more binding adherence to the rules, as well as structural reform where deemed necessary.

35. Speech at the College of Europe in Bruges (November 2, 2010).

36. Speech in Toulon on the Eurozone crisis (December 1, 2011).

37. Scharpf 2013b, pp. 138–139.

38. Franklin and van der Eijk 2007; Mair 2006; Hix 2008.

39. Duchesne et al. 2012.

40. See Hix 2008.
41. Schmidt 2013a.
42. See, e.g., Majone 1998; see also discussion in Schmidt and Thatcher 2013.
43. Scharpf 2012b; Schmidt 2013a.
44. Héritier and Lehmkuhl 2011, pp. 138–139.
45. Scharpf 2012b; see also Schmidt 2013a.
46. Eichengreen 2013.
47. Peréz 2013.
48. View expressed by a senior Commission official, September 26, 2013.
49. Mair 2013; see also discussion in Laffan 2014.
50. This is what I have elsewhere described as "policy without politics" at the EU level, "politics without policy" at the national. See Schmidt 2006.
51. Bosco et al. 2012.
52. Taggart and Szczerbiak 2013; Usherwood and Startin 2013.
53. Armingeon and Baccaro 2013.
54. Council of Europe 2013.
55. Habermas 2011.
56. Draghi 2011a.
57. Enderlein et al. 2012.
58. Jones 2013a.
59. See Jones, Chapter 3 of this volume.
60. See discussion in Jones, Chapter 3 of this volume.
61. Braun 2013, p. 6. See also Newman, Chapter 6 of this volume.
62. Asmussen testimony, FT, June 12, 2013.
63. Euractiv 2014b.
64. Novak 2010; Puetter 2012.
65. See Newman, Chapter 6, and Jacoby, Chapter 9, in this volume.
66. Laffan 2014.
67. Fabbrini 2013.
68. For more detail, see Boyer and Dehove 2011; and Vail, Chapter 7, and Jabko, Chapter 4, in this volume.
69. Crespy and Schmidt 2013.
70. Dehousse 2011.
71. See Newman, Chapter 6 of this volume.
72. See Jacoby, Chapter 9 of this volume.
73. View expressed by a senior Commission official, September 5, 2013.
74. Lutz and Kranke 2011.
75. Rehn 2013.
76. Dalton 2013.
77. International Monetary Fund 2013b, p. 31.
78. Barbier 2012.

CHAPTER 6

1. Wolf 2013; Krugman 2012a; Hawley 2011.
2. International Monetary Fund 2013b.
3. US Treasury Department 2013.
4. Wolfgang Schäuble 2013c.
5. Andrei Markovits 2013.
6. Abdelal 1998; Banchoff 1999; Grieco 1996.
7. Katzenstein 1997.
8. Congressional Oversight Panel 2010.
9. Jones 2010.
10. Beck 2013.
11. Newman 2010; Berghahn and Young 2013.
12. Matthijs and Blyth, Chapter 1 in this volume.
13. Banchoff 1999; Grieco 1996.
14. It is important to note that the term "hegemon" is used in reference to the international political economy literature on financial crises, which dates back to the work of Charles Kindleberger (2013). The central insight is that the global economy often requires a guarantor that can resolve potential collective action and cooperation problems. Leading powers, "hegemons," have an interest in playing this role and covering the costs of smaller states "free riding," as they benefit disproportionately from the smooth working of international trade. Many German interlocutors resist the term "hegemon" as it raises normative concerns stemming from Germany's role in World War II. The idea invoked here is not that of a revanchist power but rather an actor capable of motivating and supporting cooperation. In many ways, it is similar to the "engine of Europe" concept, which refers to the central role of Germany in promoting regional integration. German audiences much more readily accept this idea.
15. Katzenstein 1997; Bulmer and Paterson 1996.
16. Sikorski 2011.
17. Schäuble 2010.
18. Abdelal 1998; Banchoff 1999.
19. Matthijs and Blyth 2011.
20. Jones 2010.
21. Schäuble 2012b.
22. Blyth 2013a.
23. Schäuble 2011.
24. Hopkin, Chapter 8 in this volume.
25. Matthijs and Blyth 2011.
26. Blyth 2013a.
27. Jones 2010.
28. Moravcsik 2012.

29. Ewing 2010.
30. Rosenthal 2012.
31. Gore and Roy 2012.
32. BBC 2010.
33. Jones 2010; Czuczka and Parkin 2011.
34. Economist 2013.
35. See Vail, Chapter 7 in this volume.
36. MNI 2011; Donahue and Czucka 2012; Gomez 2013.
37. Boell and Reiermann 2013.
38. Jones 2010; Creuset 2014.
39. Creuset 2014.
40. Euronews 2013.
41. PEW Research 2013.
42. Gallup 2013.
43. Bloomberg News 2012a.
44. Katzenstein 1997; Bulmer and Paterson 1996.
45. Harding and Paterson 2000; Kitschelt and Streeck 2003.
46. GDP per capita is reported in current prices. See World Development Indicators.
47. World Development Indicators.
48. Heipertz and Verdun 2010.
49. World Development Indicators.
50. German Institute for Economic Research 2009.
51. Dornbusch 1933; Hardin and Paterson 2000.
52. Traut-Mattausch et al. 2004.
53. Vail 2010; Streeck and Hassel 2003.
54. Kitschelt and Streeck 2003; Streeck and Hassel 2003; Streeck and Tampusch 2005.
55. Dustmann et al. 2014.
56. World Development Indicators.
57. Reisenbichler and Morgan 2012.
58. Risse 2003.
59. Berentsen 2006.
60. Johnson 2011.
61. Johnson 2011.
62. Müller 2006.
63. Schmidt as quoted in Müller 2006, p. 29.
64. Focus Magazin 2004.
65. Giersch and Sinn 2000, p. 15.
66. Vail 2010.
67. Dustmann et al. 2014.
68. PEW Research 2013.
69. See also Jacoby, Chapter 9 in this volume.

70. Broyer, Petersen, and Schneider 2012.
71. Black and Vits 2010.
72. Black and Vits 2010.
73. *Der Spiegel* 2013.
74. Vail, Chapter 7 in this volume.
75. Vail 2009.
76. Vail 2009; Reisenbichler and Morgan 2012.
77. Dustmann et al. 2014.
78. PEW Research 2013.
79. Mallaby 2012. See, for example, Vitzthum 2011.
80. Schäuble 2013c.
81. Schäuble 2013b.
82. See McNamara, Chapter 2 in this volume.
83. Kindleberger 2013.

CHAPTER 7

1. Jabko 2006, p. 157.
2. Judt 2006 [2005], p. 153.
3. Loriaux 1991, p. 242.
4. In the words of Jonah Levy, Mari Miura, and Gene Park 2006, p. 95: "[T]he road to *dirigiste* rollback is paved with new state interventions. . . . [D]e-*dirigisation* was purchased at the expense of expanded state activity in the social arena."
5. Loriaux 1991, p. 253.
6. In a statement that reflected both his apprehensions and a misreading of the geopolitical context, Mitterrand said, "I don't have to do anything to stop it, the Soviets will do it for me. They will never allow this greater Germany just opposite them." Quoted in Judt 2006 [2005], p. 640.
7. Vail 2014, pp. 63–85.
8. As Jonathan Hopkin argues in Chapter 8 of this volume, voters across Southern Europe may well lose patience with the German-led austerity agenda, which seemingly condemns them to years of economic suffering.
9. Levy 1999, p. 19.
10. The term is Peter Hall's, in Hall 1986, p. 193 ff.
11. Cohen 1989, p. 309.
12. Levy 1999, p. 260.
13. Jabko 2006, pp. 166–169.
14. For a full discussion, see Vail, 2010, chaps. 5 and 6.
15. Unemployment, which had been a mere 2.7 percent in 1973, rose to an unprecedented 12.3 percent by 1994. Join-Lambert et al. 1997, p. 198.
16. OECD 2012.
17. Jabko 2006, p. 171.

18. Direction de l'Animation de la Recherche, des Etudes, et des Statistiques (DARES) 2002, p. 10.

19. Agence France Presse Wire Service 1997.

20. For a full discussion, see Parsons 2003, especially chap. 7.

21. All data in this section were drawn from OECD and IMF databases at http://www.oecd-ilibrary.org and http://www.imf.org/external/data.htm

22. Jabko 2006, p. 168.

23. For a full discussion of this rhetorical feint, see Blyth 2013a, especially chaps. 1 and 3.

24. Milner 2011, p. 190.

25. Huffington Post 2012.

26. On the lack of economic government, see Nicolas Jabko's Chapter 4 in this volume.

27. Schwartz 2009, p. B1.

28. Cornudet 2008, p. 2.

29. The other significant element of Sarkozy's "statist liberal" strategy was an aggressive bailout and forced merger of several major French banks. See Jabko and Massoc 2012.

30. Delacroix 2008, p. 4.

31. Agence France Presse Online 2008a.

32. In 2005, France spent 1.2 percent of GDP on non-contributory income support, compared to 0.6 percent in Germany. ILO 2010, p. 264.

33. The Economist 2009, p. 28.

34. Cornudet 2009, p. 3.

35. Economist Intelligence Unit 2011, p. 6.

36. Quoted in Boutté 2010, p. 187.

37. Prasad and Sorkin 2009; and Horton 2011, p. 115. Estimates of overall fiscal stimulus during this period vary slightly, as a result of differing treatment of such factors as automatic stabilizers and differences between outlays and expenditures. But these figures represent the middle range of available data.

38. Delacroix 2008.

39. OECD 2009.

40. Surprisingly, France's stimulus measures were much more modest than those of Germany, a country normally associated with fiscal rectitude and a dislike of state intervention in the economy. For a detailed discussion, see Vail 2014.

41. OECD 2012.

42. At the end of September 2011, the four largest French banks shouldered a combined €63.3 billion in sovereign debt in Ireland, Spain, Portugal, Greece, and Italy (with €7.7 billion in Greece alone), among the highest levels in the Eurozone. Cour des Comptes 2012, pp. 96–97.

43. Ockrent 2011.

44. One senior European official had famously observed that the partnership "serve[d] to hide the strength of Germany and the weakness of France." Quoted in *The Economist* 2011b.

45. Peel and Carnegy 2013.

46. It is also worth pointing out that Sarkozy faced re-election in 2012 amidst deteriorating poll numbers as a result of France's economic woes and his own foibles. He thus had little political capital left to spend on a public fight with Germany over Eurozone policy.

47. OECD 2011, pp. 11, 43.

48. Wittrock 2012.

49. Cowell and Kulish 2012.

50. Wittrock 2012.

51. Carnegy 2013a.

52. Carnegy 2013b.

53. Bruno Le Maire, Sarkozy's former European affairs minister, put it this way: "France has got to regain credibility with Germany and that only comes through the economy, fixing growth, unemployment, and the debt. Nothing works without this." Peel and Carnegy 2013. See http://www.ft.com/intl/cms/s/0/37c2ae62-6182-11e2-9545-00144feab49a.html#axzz3FBZ5N9mN

54. Such skepticism among political elites has paralleled a growing, if limited, disenchantment with the austerity-only recipe. Spiegel and Ehrlich 2013.

55. The Economist 2012.

56. Much will also depend on Hollande's ability to keep his fractious Socialist government in line, something that the beleaguered and often ham-fisted president, whose approval ratings have plummeted in the wake of a series of scandals and other missteps, has often struggled to accomplish. One of the clearest examples of such political mismanagement came with the leaking of an internal Socialist Party memo condemning Merkel's "selfish intransigence" over austerity. Carnegy 2013c.

57. Driffill and Miller 2003, p. 42.

58. In the words of Dominique Moïsi, "[B]y navigating with excessive prudence between the logic of the bond markets (no Keynesian policy) and that of his Socialist party inside (no courageous measures to free up the labour market), he has reached the exact opposite result. He has encouraged a climate of negative expectations and suspicion vis-à-vis the efficiency of the state." Moïsi 2013. See http://www.ft.com/intl/cms/s/0/c452f694-a038-11e2-a6e1-00144feabdc0.html#axzz3FBZ5N9mN

59. For a range of perspectives surrounding this core contention, see "Forum: How Germany Reconquered Europe: The Euro and Its Discontents," *Harpers* (February 2014): 33–43.

CHAPTER 8

1. See all four chapters in Section I of this volume.

2. Ferrera and Gualmini 2004.

3. Rhodes 2001.
4. Fernández-Villaverde, Garicano, and Santos 2013.
5. Alesina, Ardagna, and Galasso 2008.
6. See, for example, Tilford and Whyte 2012.
7. Tilford and Whyte 2012.
8. See, for instance, Royo 2013.
9. Pew Research 2013.
10. Blanchard and Leigh 2013.
11. Hopkin and Blyth 2012.
12. De Cecco 1998.
13. Simoni 2012.
14. European Commission 2005.
15. Blyth 2013a, chap. 2.
16. Trichet 2005.
17. Krugman 2012b.
18. Baccaro and Pulignano 2011.
19. See Andersson et al. 2008, Table 5, p. 22.
20. Royo 2001, p.14.
21. At one point, a quarter of all Spanish male workers were employed in construction: Fernández-Villaverde 2013, p. 13.
22. Fernández-Villaverde 2013, p. 12.
23. Royo 2001, p. 49.
24. Andersson et al. 2008.
25. Andersson et al. 2008, Tables 3, 4, p. 19.
26. Andersson et al. 2008, Table 8, p. 29.
27. Hancké 2012, p. 21.
28. See the assessment of this debate in The Economist 2011a.
29. Sfakianasis 2012.
30. Hopkin 2012, pp. 198–215.
31. Data from OECD, Employment in General Government and Public Corporations as a Percentage of the Labor Force, 2000 and 2008. Available at: http://www.oecd-ilibrary.org/sites/gov_glance-2011-en/05/01/index.html?contentType=&itemId=/content/chapter/gov_glance-2011-27-en&containerItemId=/content/serial/22214399&accessItemIds=/content/book/gov_glance-2011-en&mimeType=text/html
32. Data from 2008; OECD, Employment in General Government and Public Corporations as a Percentage of the Labor Force, 2000 and 2008. Available at: http://www.oecd-ilibrary.org/sites/gov_glance-2011-en/05/01/index.html?contentType=&itemId=/content/chapter/gov_glance-2011-27-en&containerItemId=/content/serial/22214399&accessItemIds=/content/book/gov_glance-2011-en&mimeType=text/html

33. Blavoukos and Pagoulatos 2008.
34. Corriere della sera 1996.
35. Alessandro Santoro 2010.
36. La Repubblica 2008.
37. Corriere della sera 2008.
38. See data from Eurostat 2013. Also, Yglesias 2012.
39. Trigilia 1986.
40. Caruana, Larrinaga, and Matés 2011.
41. Il Venerdi' della Repubblica 2011.
42. Andrews 2010.
43. See Fernández-Villaverde 2013, pp. 15–16.
44. For the Spanish case, see Jordana 2013.
45. Data from Eurostat 2012. Available at: http://epp.eurostat.ec.europa.eu/statistics_explained/index.php/Electricity_and_natural_gas_price_statistics
46. Ragazzi 2006.
47. Data from Eurostat 2014. At-risk-of-poverty rate anchored at a fixed moment in time (2005) (percentage of the population whose equivalent disposable income is below the "at-risk-of-poverty threshold" calculated in the standard way for the base year, currently 2005, and then adjusted for inflation). Available at: http://epp.eurostat.ec.europa.eu/portal/page/portal/income_social_inclusion_living_conditions/data/main_tables
48. Data from Eurostat 2014, Unemployment rate—LFS adjusted series. Available at: http://epp.eurostat.ec.europa.eu/portal/page/portal/employment_unemployment_lfs/ data/main_tables
49. Busch et al. 2013.
50. Lynch 2006.
51. Pensions were the main income in 26 percent of Spanish households in 2012. AnsaMed 2013.
52. See Busch et al. 2013, pp. 10–13.
53. Carinci 2012.
54. Dubin 2013.
55. The Euro Plus Pact was quite open about its preferences in this regard; see European Council 2011a.
56. Eichengreen 1996; see also Eichengreen 2012, and Matthijs 2014b.
57. Blyth and Katz 2005.
58. Grillo 2013.
59. Dericquebourg 2013.
60. Toharia 2012.
61. See the data on declining public confidence in democratic institutions in Alonso 2013.
62. PEW Research 2013.
63. Hirschman 1970.

CHAPTER 9

1. I thank the Department of Political Science at Brigham Young University, the Austrian Marshall Fund, and the SAIS Center for Transatlantic Relations for research support. Mark Blyth, Anke Hassel, Matthias Matthijs, Waltraud Schelkle, and Tobias Schulze-Cleven provided very useful feedback on earlier versions. The usual disclaimers apply.

2. See Jones 2010. Also, Adam Posen's comment that "Merkel does not get basic economics" was widely reported. See Spiegel Online 2009.

3. See Shaw 2013.

4. Silvia 2011; Dullien and Guerot 2012. For the author's more skeptical analysis of the ordoliberal angle, see Jacoby 2014b.

5. Zimmermann 2012.

6. After some false starts in the 1990s (e.g., Schedler and Santiso 1998) that sparked little follow-up, Pierson 2004; Goetz and Meyer-Sahling 2009; Dyson 2009; and Meyer-Sahling, and Goetz 2009 all pushed forward the agenda on time and timing.

7. See Abraham Newman's Chapter 6 in this volume.

8. If the post-outright monetary transactions period (e.g., after June 2012) turns into a permanent normalization of the euro, the main argument of this chapter—that much trouble still lies ahead—will be disconfirmed.

9. Bibow 2013; Scharpf 2011; Jacoby 2011; Dullien and Fritsche 2009.

10. See Erik Jones's Chapter 3 in this volume.

11. C.f., Eichengreen 2010.

12. To be sure, while it brought no electoral earthquake, the May 2014 European elections did show some differences from the general election results of six months earlier. The SPD finished only 8 percent behind the CDU/CSU (compared to its 16 percent deficit vis-à-vis the CDU in both the 2013 German election and the 2009 European Parliament elections). More important, perhaps, the Alternative für Deutschland (AfD) increased its general election vote totals from 4.8 percent to just over 7 percent. AfD's only meaningful electoral proposition is to end German support for Eurozone bailouts and to persuade weaker Eurozone states to voluntarily withdraw from a monetary union that offers them nothing but austerity and structural reform. The core of the ordoliberal perspective on the Eurozone resides in the AfD and, to some extent, in the Free Democratic Party, which has done very poorly in both the German and European Parliament elections. See Jacoby 2014b.

13. Bibow 2013.

14. Whitlock 2009.

15. The Economist 2011c.

16. Spiegel Online 2012.

17. Bloomberg News 2012a.

18. Wall Street Journal 2013.

19. Euractiv 2014a.
20. A loose translation: "when I dream of Germany in the night, instead of sleep my mind feels fright." See Fischer 2010.
21. Schmidt 2011.
22. E.g., Schwarzer and Lang 2012.
23. See, for example, Schelkle 2012; Zohlnhoefer 2011; and Bergsten and Kirkegaard 2012.
24. Schwarzer 2013; Vail, Chapter 7 in this volume.
25. Mabbett and Schelkle 2013.
26. The Court said Bundestag approval would be required for any increase above the €190 billion (of the ESM total of €500 billion) already committed by Germany.
27. Sinn 2012.
28. CESIfo Institue 2012.
29. Bloomberg Business Week 2012. Here, too, there are measurement controversies. While Germany is responsible for 6 percent of IMF assistance and 26 percent of ECB measures, Sinn notes that in certain default scenarios, the remaining Eurozone states would have to absorb burdens from the defaulting states. He puts the worst-case scenario for Germany at 41 percent of ECB exposure. See CESIfo Institute 2012.
30. Strupczewski 2013.
31. Blyth 2013a.
32. See Abraham Newman's Chapter 6 in this volume for a more detailed analysis of German politicians' choice to play up the "moral hazard frame" and play down the "contagion" and "trading" frames. The latter problem is the focus of this section. Erik Jones's Chapter 3 and Jonathan Hopkin's Chapter 8 report these same events from the perspective of southern Europe.
33. And despite increased critical attention—including from the US government— the surplus hasn't really shrunk. According to the Ifo Institute, an economics think tank based in Munich, the surplus for 2013 was 7.3 percent of GDP; it is estimated to be 7.4 percent in 2014. See Sinn 2014.
34. Blyth 2013.
35. Scharpf 2012a; Jacoby 2014a.
36. Bibow 2013; Jones, Chapter 3 in this volume.
37. Bastasin 2013.
38. By contrast, Germany's service sector is not terribly competitive. Its last surplus was in 1961.
39. For a characterization of Germany as Europe's "Company Store," see Jacoby 2011.
40. For a representative effort to deflect these criticisms, see then-Foreign Minister Guido Westerwelle's Paris speech. Westerwelle 2013.
41. Goetz and Meyer-Sahling 2009, pp. 180–183.
42. To be sure, this is less true of the junior partner (SPD) than of the senior partner (CDU-CSU). Still, their coalition agreement contains an explicit disavowal

of any form of debt mutualization and several reiterations of the CDU-CSU's basic policy line across the crisis. It is not clear the SPD sought in the agreement any important changes in policy toward the Eurozone. In any event, they achieved none.

43. Most references to Spain are from the Left Party, which has not made electoral headway with the argument that the suffering in the Eurozone periphery is linked to Germany's export dominance. Those ordoliberals who now hope to see Germany use a different currency from Spain, Greece, and Portugal also stress the enormous suffering in the South that is a predictable consequence of clinging to a common currency and forcing all adjustment through domestic wages, prices, and employment (Sinn 2012, 2013; Kerber 2013). In that sense, the German left and right have made very similar arguments, while the rest of the nation "plugs and shrugs."

44. Bastasin 2013.

45. GMFUS 2012, chart 10.

46. Kaiser 2011.

47. Almunia et al. 2010.

48. See Vail 2010; Farrell 2010; Blyth 2013a.

49. Steinbrück and Steinmeier 2010.

50. Bundestag Drucksache 17/214: 26201.

51. Beck 2012.

52. See Chapter 6 in this volume.

53. A related metaphor with an even more pessimistic twist was Finance Minister's Schäuble's February 2012 reference to Greece as potentially a "bottomless pit."

54. For some (e.g., Beck 2012), German delay has, itself, been a tool for exercising power. While this chapter does not deny that German delays can increase the desperation of their European partners to find a deal and thus lead to terms more comfortable for Germany, the stress here is on Germany's own dilemmas of disorientation.

55. Mabbett and Schelkle 2013.

56. See Erik Jones's Chapter 3 in this volume.

57. Gros 2013; Fuertes, Kalotychou, and Saka 2014.

58. Admati and Hellwig 2013.

59. Expertenrat 2011.

60. This was a dated and bizarre metaphor. The bazooka is no longer a particularly fearsome weapon. It was also highly visible and often got the user quickly killed for his efforts.

61. Sinn 2013.

62. Admati and Helwig 2013.

63. German voters thus generally do not understand that the persistent current account surpluses are linked to Germany's low—relative to other OECD countries—private consumption levels and low domestic investment levels.

Neither do they see the contribution of the savings represented by such surpluses to broader deflationary pressures in the Eurozone. While such phenomena are obviously complex in their own right, it is not helpful that the modal German response to the imbalances worries seems to be, "What do they want us to do? Make inferior products?"

64. And does nothing to address a near-decade of accumulated debts.

65. An important caveat here is that the Constitutional Court may still prohibit German and Bundesbank participation in OMT, contingent upon a review by the European Court of Justice.

66. It also points to the fact that ordoliberal ideology makes a weak explanatory cause of crisis behavior simply because ordoliberals are on all sides of every important question. Ideology underdetermines behavior in this case (Jacoby 2014b).

67. Beck 2012.

68. Germany's own earlier and more aggressive labor market reforms came precisely during a period in which state spending was expanding rather than contracting. This fact seems to have escaped the German popular imagination, which often implies some version of "we made the tough choices to promote competitiveness and now so must others" (Privitera 2013; Bastasin 2013).

69. The most recent agreement on bank resolution at the EU level calls for a minimum of 8 percent participation from private sources—creditors and owners—before public money can be used.

70. Still, Gros 2013 shows that German banks are still the most exposed to sovereign debt (their own state's and others') of any banks in Europe.

71. Paterson and Bulmer 2010.

72. Zimmermann 2012.

73. Privitera 2013; Bibow 2013. This triumphalist narrative also tends to obscure that Germany has also been hit by the crisis. Most important, there have been spectacular bailouts of a few financial institutions (with perhaps more trouble for the *Landesbanken* after the Asset Quality Reviews) and also much more quiet use by German banks of swaps with the US Federal Reserve and ECB LTRO provisions, as German banks are particularly reliant on wholesale funding.

74. These figures should be treated with caution. Cost considerations meant that Pew could sample in only eight EU members (Germany, Britain, France, Italy, Spain, Greece, Poland, and the Czech Republic).

75. Strupczenwski 2013.

76. Fratzscher 2013.

77. Eichengreen 2010.

78. Véron 2013a, p. 4.

79. Schäuble 2013a.

80. Véron 2013a, pp. 5–6.

81. The Sparkassen continue to push for upward revision of this figure to €45 or even €70 billion.

82. The number of banks could go as high as 200.
83. Véron 2013a, p. 8.
84. Véron 2013a, p. 9.
85. The December 2013 coalition agreement between CDU/CSU and SPD foresees some possibility of ESM use for bank recapitalization up to 60 billion euro after several conditions have been met (Bartsch 2013).
86. Véron 2013a, p. 13.
87. Münchau 2013.
88. Kapila 2013.
89. Jones's Chapter 3 in this volume.
90. Gros 2013.
91. Arnold and Fleming 2014.
92. For an excellent survey, see Oliver Wyman 2013.
93. Horrobin and Steinhauser 2013.
94. O'Donnel and Breidthardt 2013.
95. Grant 2013.
96. Asmussen 2013a.
97. See, for example, Schoenmaker and Gros 2012, among many others.
98. Schoenmaker and Gros 2012, p. 6.
99. Goetz and Mayer-Sahling 2009.
100. Sommer 2013.
101. Spiegel Online 2013.
102. Bartsch 2013.
103. Data from the Bundesbank.
104. Thus, even authors very sympathetic to Germany on the imbalances question are likely to be disappointed in its response to their calls for sharp write-downs of German claims in peripheral Europe. See Rogoff 2014.
105. The notion that the imbalances can be corrected is actually the position of the Commission, with its excessive imbalance procedure.
106. Katzenstein 1987.
107. Watt 2014.

CHAPTER 10

1. Praet 2012.
2. Recent scholarly examples: Gross 2011; McCormick 2012; Schmitter 2012; Lefkofridi and Schmitter 2014. Examples of policymakers: Merkel 2010a; Van Rompuy 2011; Fischer 2012; Schäuble 2012a; Hollande 2013a.
3. Monnet 1978, p. 417.
4. Reinhart and Rogoff 2009.
5. We want to emphasize that we are mainly focused in this chapter on the "big" steps in European integration. It goes without saying that plenty of smaller

specific crises, in particular policy domains, have in fact directly sparked institutional innovation (e.g., in consumer rights policy or environmental policy).

6. Haas 1958.
7. Haas 1958; see also Lindberg 1963 and Schmitter 1970.
8. Monnet 1978, p. 109. Politicians and policymakers often quote this passage of Monnet's memoirs. For example, the Deputy Managing Director of the IMF Nemat Shafik 2012.
9. Matthijs 2013, 2014c.
10. Delors 2001.
11. Haas 1975. See also latter-day "neofunctionalists," including Burley and Mattli 1993; and Schmitter 2004.
12. Moravcsik 1993.
13. See Moravcsik 1998.
14. The most direct connection between neofunctionalism and crisis came from Schmitter 1970, who revised Haas's basic neofunctionalist paradigm to take into account the role of crises in the process of integration. Lefkofridi and Schmitter 2014, in revisiting Schmitter's 1970 framework, argued that "[c]rises have been an integral part of the process of European integration and, by and large, they have had positive effects."
15. We leave out the Constitutional Treaty that became the Lisbon Treaty, since it is obvious that no pressing crisis drove this initiative (which had no *a priori* policy focus at all).
16. For one of the closest and best-researched accounts, see Duchêne 1994.
17. Willis 1968, p. 100.
18. Gillingham 1991, p. 269.
19. Fursdon 1980, p. 55.
20. See, among others, D'Abzac-Epezy and Vial 1995; Guillen 1983; Sauvage 1993.
21. Milward 1992.
22. For example, see Raymond Aron's column in *Le Figaro*, June 3, 1955.
23. Deniau 1994, p. 54.
24. See Lynch 1997.
25. Milward 1992, pp. 167–171.
26. Milward 1992, p. 283.
27. Marjolin 1986, p. 292.
28. For a full account, see Parsons 2003.
29. See Parsons 2003, pp. 160–170.
30. Sandholtz and Zysman 1989.
31. Attribution of the Thatcher cite is difficult, but it is widely quoted, as in Parker 2008.
32. See Parsons 2010.
33. Delwit 1995, p. 104; Haywood 1989, 1993.
34. Saint-Ouen 1988; Parsons 2003, pp. 195–200.

35. Védrine 1996, p. 416; Dyson 1994, p. 125.
36. See Aeschimann and Riché 1997.
37. Criddle 1993.
38. Pop 2013.
39. See, for example, Martin Feldstein 1997.
40. For a nuanced discussion of the motivations to eastern enlargement, see Schimmelfennig 2003.
41. Parsons 2003.
42. Kahler and Lake 2013, p. 1.
43. On this point, see Chapter 9, by Wade Jacoby on "the timing of politics and the politics of timing," in this volume.
44. Matthijs 2014a, p. 215.
45. For "crises" defined as situations needing a decisive intervention, see Hay 1999 and Matthijs 2011.
46. Lasswell 1936.
47. Matthijs 2014b.
48. You could argue that the Great Recession re-politicized monetary policy world-wide, not least in the United States and Japan.
49. For example, see North 1993.
50. Giavazzi and Pagnano 1988; McNamara 1998.
51. Barro and Gordon 1983.
52. Berman and McNamara 1999.
53. See Wade Jacoby's Chapter 9 on the "timing of politics and the politics of timing" in this book.
54. Matthijs 2014b.
55. Lucas Papademos in Greece, and Mario Monti in Italy, who both took office in November 2011.
56. Matthijs 2014b.
57. See Erik Jones's Chapter 3, "Forgotten Financial Union," in this volume.
58. Norman 2013.
59. Reuters.com 2013b.
60. As German Finance Minister Wolfgang Schäuble said on October 11, 2013. Reuters.com 2013a.
61. According to Finance Watch, www.finance-watch.org.
62. Herring 2013.
63. Except the "Constitutional Treaty," which became the Lisbon Treaty. One reason that it was such a failure was that it was the only major attempt to renegotiate the EU treaties for which no one even claimed a connection to a particular policy problem.
64. See Parsons and Fontana 2014; and on the possibility of the UK leaving the EU, see Matthijs 2013 and 2014c.
65. Matthijs 2012a, p. 50.

CHAPTER 11

1. Some portions of this chapter draw on material in Helleiner 2014.
2. For a historical critique of OCA theory's inability to explain the emergence of national "territorial currencies," see Helleiner 2003.
3. Helleiner 2013, chap. 8.
4. Broz 2007.
5. See especially Henning 1998.
6. European Commission 1990, pp. 191, 194, 195.
7. European Commission 1990, p. 182.
8. Quoted in Helleiner 1994, p. 161.
9. Global Research 2008.
10. Bertuch-Samuels and Ramlogan 2007.
11. Kester 2007.
12. Quote from The Economist 2006, p. 28.
13. Wolf 2008.
14. See, for example, Kirshner 2008, p. 428; Dieter 2007; Helleiner 2009; James 2009, pp. 224, 227.
15. Wade 2009; Chin and Helleiner 2008.
16. Quote from Kirshner 2008; see also Dieter 2007; Murphy 2006, p. 62.
17. The Economist 2007, p. 15.
18. Soros 2009.
19. Paulson 2009; Sorkin 2009, p. 222.
20. Münchau 2008.
21. Benoit 2008.
22. McCauley and McGuire 2009, p. 85.
23. McCauley and McGuire 2009; Kohler 2010.
24. For the link between key currency status and the power of the issuing state, see, for example, James 2009; Chey 2012.
25. Cooper 2009, pp. 1–2.
26. Cohen 2010.
27. See, for example, Oakley and Tett 2008.
28. McCauley and McGuire 2009.
29. McDowell 2012; Allen and Moessner 2010; McGuire and von Peter 2009; Schwartz 2009.
30. Considerable portions of the enormous AIG bailout, for example, ended up in the hands of Eurozone banks that had been AIG counterparties, such as Société Génerale and Deutsche Bank (Barofsky 2012, chap. 10).
31. Broz 2012.
32. McDowell 2012; Allen and Moessner 2010; McGuire and von Peter 2009.
33. Wessel 2009, p. 141.
34. The Fed also extended swaps to other European authorities such as the Swiss National Bank, the Bank of England, and the central banks of Sweden, Norway, and Denmark.

35. For a broader argument about this subordination before the crisis, see Cafruny and Ryner 2007.

36. Allen and Moessner 2010, 2011.

37. Board of Governors 2012.

38. Paulson 2009, p. 242.

39. Strange 2011. The share of China's reserves held in dollars is not public information, but a leak in September 2010 revealed that 65 percent (or almost $1.6 trillion) of its $2.45 trillion reserves at the time were in dollars (Zhou and Rabinovitch 2010). Since its total reserves were not quite that size at the time the crisis broke out, it is quite certain that China's holdings of dollars rose during the crisis (even if the share of reserves in dollars may have declined).

40. Otero-Iglesias and Steinberg 2012, p. 323.

41. Obstfeld et al. 2009.

42. Gallagher and Shrestha 2012.

43. Quoted in Sender 2009. See also Otero-Iglesias and Steinberg 2013, p. 194–195.

44. Quotes from Otero-Iglesias and Steinberg 2013, p. 193.

45. Kester 2007; ECB 2013, p. 20. For growing official scepticism in emerging market countries, see Otero-Iglesias and Steinberg 2012, 2013.

46. Momani 2008; Murphy 2006; Otero-Iglesias and Steinberg 2012; Posen 2008.

47. Otero-Iglesias and Steinberg 2012, p. 318.

48. Dooley et al. 2003.

49. Otero-Iglesias and Steinberg 2012, p. 321–324.

50. Blustein 2012.

51. Paulson 2009, pp. 161, 242, 318; Sorkin 2009, pp. 269–274, 444–453, 469–470, 482, 509, 518.

52. See, for example, Drezner 2009; Tett 2009, p. 211; Paulson 2009, pp. 233, 318; Sorkin 2009.

53. Kirshner 1995, p. 118. See also Drezner 2009. Statistic from Cohen 2008, p. 462.

54. Quoted in Bradsher 2009.

55. Strange 1988.

56. See, for example, Bowker 2013.

57. European Central Bank 2013, p. 8.

58. Quote from McNamara 2008. p. 450.

59. Jörg Asmussen quoted in Otero-Iglesias and Zhang 2012, p. 23.

60. Sarkozy 2010a. He had made the same point in July 2009: "We cannot stick with one single currency . . . we've still got the Bretton Woods system of 1945 . . . 60 years afterwards, we've got to ask: shouldn't a politically multipolar world correspond to an economically multi-currency world?" Quoted in Otero-Iglesias and Steinberg 2012, p. 320.

61. Sarkozy 2010b.

62. This argument had been given particular attention by a high-profile UN Commission of Experts (2009) chaired by Nobel Prize–winning economist Joseph Stiglitz.

63. Quoted in Chin 2014.
64. Zhou 2009.
65. Quoted in Otero-Iglesias and Steinberg 2012, p. 320.
66. Chin 2014.
67. Otero-Iglesias and Zhang 2012.
68. Chin 2014; Kirshner 2014.
69. The strengthening of the SDR was supported not just by Sarkozy but also by a group of prominent experts convened under a "Palais Royal" initiative by three prominent former Europeans officials in early 2011: Michel Camdessus, Alexander Lamfalussy, and Tommaso Padoa-Schioppa (2011).
70. Otero-Iglesias and Zhang 2012, p. 15; Chin 2014.
71. Helleiner 2014.
72. Quoted in Otero-Iglesias 2013, p. 5.
73. Otero-Iglesias 2013; Otero-Iglesias and Steinberg 2013; James 2011, pp. 531–532.
74. Sender 2011.
75. Jiang 2014.
76. IMS = International Monetary System. See Otero-Iglesias and Steinberg 2013, p. 326.
77. Otero-Iglesias 2013; Otero-Iglesias and Steinberg 2013, p. 325; Chin 2014.
78. Jiang 2014.
79. Otero-Iglesias 2013.

CHAPTER 12

1. Quoted in Rachman 2008.
2. See, for example, Bergsten and Kirkegaard 2012; *The Independent* 2013; Talbott 2014; Chambers 2014; and also Jones 2014.
3. See European Commission 2013b.
4. See Taylor and Emmott 2014.
5. See Chapter 2 in this volume.
6. Henning and Kessler 2012, p. 7.
7. Henning and Kessler 2012, p. 9.
8. Henning and Kessler 2012, pp. 10–14.
9. The single resolution mechanism, designed to resolve those banks if they get into (more) trouble, still has years to go before it can be fully operational and effective.
10. International Monetary Fund 2014. *World Economic Outlook Database*. Washington, DC. Authors' calculations.
11. On the decline of the western world and the rise of the rest, see Matthijs 2012a.
12. See Chapter 10 in this volume.
13. See Helleiner and Kirshner 2014.
14. Interview with Romano Prodi at Brown University (Providence, RI), spring 2011.
15. As Dustmann et al. point out, however, this is a case of confusing causation and correlation. See Dustmann et al. 2014.

16. Interview with Romano Prodi at Brown University (Providence, RI), spring 2011.

17. International Monetary Fund. 2013. *World Economic Outlook Database.* Washington, DC. Available at: http://www.imf.org/external/pubs/ft/weo/2013/02/weodata/index.aspx. Authors' calculations.

18. Matthijs 2014b.

19. Merkel 2010b.

20. Van Rompuy 2012; Van Rompuy et al. 2012.

21. European Commission 2012b.

22. It remains unclear why the Commission felt the need to have its own report on the future of the Eurozone, which resembles the "Four Presidents' Report" so closely. The most likely reason is for the Commission to try to win back the legislative initiative after most of the institutional innovations during the euro crisis came from the Council, which includes only Europe's heads of state and government.

23. Enderlein et al. 2012.

24. Glienicker Group 2013; Eiffel Group 2014; and Legrain 2014.

25. Glienicker Group 2013.

26. Glienicker Group 2013.

27. Eiffel Group 2014.

28. Eiffel Group 2014.

29. Legrain 2014.

30. Legrain 2014, p. 10.

31. Legrain 2014, p. 39.

32. Taleb 2007.

33. This part of the chapter borrows from, extends, and builds on Blyth 2009 and Matthijs 2012b.

34. Black swan examples are the terrorist attacks of 9/11, the popular uprisings of the Arab Spring, or the London riots of August 2011. Also, note that all three types of "swans" can be positive as well as negative. However, given that it is frequency times impact that matters, negative swans tend to matter much more than positive ones for future outcomes.

35. A fuller version of this argument is developed in Blyth 2014b.

36. See Lawton 2013.

37. Blyth 2013b.

38. The EU Treaty on Stability, Coordination and Governance is available online at: http://www.european-council.europa.eu/media/639235/stootscg26_en12.pdf

39. Treaty on Stability, Coordination and Governance, Article 3.1(a).

40. Treaty on Stability, Coordination and Governance, page 5.

41. Treaty on Stability, Coordination and Governance, Article 3.1(e).

42. For more information on the 'Six-Pack,' see European Commission 2012a.

43. Hall 2014; and Hall and Soskice, eds., 2001.

Bibliography

Abdelal, Rawi. 1998. "The Politics of Monetary Leadership and Followership: Stability in the European Monetary System since the Currency Crisis of 1992." *Political Studies* 46(2): 236–259.

Abdelal, Rawi, Mark Blyth, and Craig Parsons. 2010. *Constructing the International Economy*. Ithaca, NY: Cornell University Press.

Admati, Anat, and Hellwig, Martin. 2013. *The Bankers' New Clothes*. Princeton, NJ: Princeton University Press.

Aeschimann, Eric, and Patrick Riché. 1996. *La guerre de sept ans*. Paris: Calmann-Lévy.

Agence France Presse Online. 2008a. "Crise économique: Sarkozy content d'avoir fait les 'bons choix'" (January 23).

Agence France Presse Online. 2008b. "L'Eurogroupe a adopté un plan d'action pour rétablir la confiance des marchés" (October 12).

Agence France Presse Wire Service. 1997 (October 14).

Alesina, Alberto, Silvia Ardagna, and Vincenzo Galasso. 2008. "The Euro and Structural Reforms." *NBER Working Paper 14479*. Available at: http://www.nber.org/papers/w14479.

Allen, William, and Richhild Moessner. 2010. "Central Bank Co-operation and International Liquidity in the Financial Crisis of 2008–9." *BIS Working Papers* No. 310 (May).

Allen, William, and Richhild Moessner. 2011. "The International Liquidity Crisis of 2008–2009." *World Economics* 12(2): 183–198.

Almunia, Miguel, Agustin Benetrix, Barry Eichengreen, Kevin O'Rourke, and Gisela Rua. 2010. "From Great Depression to Great Credit Crisis: Similarities, Differences and Lessons." *Economic Policy* 25(62): 219–265.

Alonso, Sonia. 2013. "The Growing Ideological and Economic Breach Between Northern and Southern EU Countries Is Pushing Europe Towards a Perfect Storm." *LSE EUROPP Blog* (July 22). Available at: http://blogs.lse.ac.uk/europpblog/2013/07/22/the-growing-economic-and-ideological-breach-between-northern-and-southern-eu-countries-is-pushing-europe-towards-a-perfect-storm/.

Anderson, Benedict. 1983. *Imagined Communities*. New York: Verso.

Andersson, Malin, Arne Gieseck, Beatrice Pierluigi, and Nick Vidalis. 2008. "Wage Growth Dispersion across the Euro Area Countries: Some Stylized Facts." *ECB Occasional Paper Series* No. 90 (July).

Andrews, Dan. 2010. "Real House Prices in OECD Countries." *OECD Economics Department Working Papers* No. 831. Paris: OECD.

AnsaMed. 2013. "Crisis, Spain: Families Supported by Pensioners Tripled." *Ansa.Med* (May 20). Available at: http://www.ansamed.info/ansamed/en/news/nations/spain/2013/05/20/Crisis-Spain-families-supported-pensioners-tripled_8735227.html.

Armingeon, Klaus, and Lucio Baccaro. 2013. "The Sorrows of the Young Euro: Policy Responses to the Sovereign Debt Crisis." In Nancy Bermeo and Jonas Pontusson, eds. *Coping with Crisis*. New York: Russell Sage Foundation.

Arnold, Martin, and Sam Fleming. 2014. "European Banks Raise Capital Ahead of Stress Tests." *Financial Times* (July 3). Available at: http://www.ft.com/cms/s/0/e4d05a72-0141-11e4-9750-00144feab7de.html#axzz371RsYDDz.

Aron, Raymond. 1955. Column in *Le Figaro* (June 3).

Arslanalp, Serkan, and Takahiro Tsuda. 2012. "Tracking Global Demand for Advanced Economy Sovereign Debt." *IMF Working Paper* WP/12/284. Washington, DC: IMF (December).

Asmussen, Jörg. 2013a. *Building Banking Union*. Speech given at the Atlantic Council, London (July 9).

Asmussen, Jörg. 2013b. "Fünf Jahre Krise—Wo Steht Europa Heute?" Frankfurt: ECB (November 27).

Baccaro, Lucio, and Valeria Pulignano. 2011. "Employment Relations in Italy." In Greg Bamber, Russell Lanbury, and Nick Wailes, eds. *International and Comparative Industrial Relations*. London: Sage.

Banchoff, Thomas. 1999. "German Identity and European Integration." *European Journal of International Relations* 5(3): 259–289.

Bank for International Settlements. 2010. *BIS Quarterly Review*. Basel: BIS (December).

Barbier, Cécile. 2012. "La prise d'autorité de la Banque centrale européenne et les dangers démocratiques de la nouvelle gouvernance économique dans l'Union européenne." Research Paper for *Observatoire Social Européen*, no. 9 (November).

Barbier, Jean-Claude. 2008. *La longue marche vers l'Europe Sociale*. Paris: PUF.

Barofsky, Neil. 2012. *Bailout*. New York: Free Press.

Barro, Robert J., and David B. Gordon. 1983. "A Positive Theory of Monetary Policy in a Natural Rate Model." *Journal of Political Economy* 91(4): 589–610.

Bastasin, Carlo. 2012. *Saving Europe: How National Politics Nearly Destroyed the Euro*. Washington, DC: The Brookings Institution.

Bastasin, Carlo. 2013. "Germany: A Global Miracle and a European Challenge." *Brookings Global Economy and Development Working* Paper No. 58.

Bayoumi, Tamim, and Barry Eichengreen. 1993. "Ever Closer to Heaven? An Optimum-Currency-Area Index for European Countries." *European Economic Review* 41: 761–770.

BBC. 2010. "Greece Crisis: Fears Grow That It Could Spread." *BBC News* (April 28).

Beck, Ulrich. 2012. *German Europe*. Cambridge: Polity.

Benoit, Bertrand. 2008. "US 'Will Lose Financial Superpower Status.'" *Financial Times* (September 25).

Benoit, Bertrand, and Tony Barber. 2009. "Germany Ready to Help Eurozone Members." *Financial Times* (February 18).

Bensel, Richard. 1991. *Yankee Leviathan: The Origins of Central State Authority in America 1859–1877*. New York: Cambridge University Press.

Benz, Arthur, and Yannis Papadopoulos. 2006. *Governance and Democracy*. London: Routledge.

Berentsen, William H. 2006. "Changing Regional Inequalities in United Germany." *Eurasian Geography and Economics* 47(4): 462–477.

Berghahn, Volker, and Brigitte Young. 2013. "Reflections on Werner Bonefeld's 'Freedom and the Strong State: On German Ordoliberalism' and the Continuing Importance of the Ideas of Ordoliberalism to Understand Germany's (Contested) Role in Resolving the Eurozone Crisis." *New Political Economy* 18(5): 1–11.

Bergman, Michael. 1999. "Do Monetary Unions Make Economic Sense? Evidence from the Scandinavian Currency Union, 1873–1913." *Scandinavian Journal of Economics* 101(3): 363–377.

Bergman, Michael, Stefan Gerlach, and Lars Jonung. 1993. "The Rise and Fall of the Scandinavian Currency Union, 1873–1920." *European Economic Review* 37(2–3): 507–517.

Bergsten, C. Fred, and Jacob Funk Kirkegaard. 2012. "The Coming Resolution of the European Crisis." Peterson Institute for International Economics, Policy Brief 12-1.

Berman, Sheri. 2006. *The Primacy of Politics: Social Democracy and the Making of Europe's Twentieth Century*. New York: Cambridge University Press.

Berman, Sheri, and Kathleen R. McNamara. 1996. "Bank on Democracy: Why Central Banks Need Public Oversight." *Foreign Affairs* 78(2): 2–8.

Bibow, Jörg. 2012. "The Euroland Crisis and Germany's Euro Trilemma." *International Review of Applied Economics* 27(3): 360–385.

Binder, Sarah, and Mark Spindel. 2013. "Monetary Politics: The Origins of the Federal Reserve." *Studies in American Political Development* 27(1): 1–13.

Black, Jeff, and Christian Vits. 2010. "Business Confidence in Germany Unexpectedly Surges to Record in November." *Bloomberg* (November 24).

Blanchard, Olivier, and Daniel Leigh. 2013. "Growth Forecast Errors and Fiscal Multipliers." IMF Working Paper WP/13/1. Washington, DC: International Monetary Fund.

Blavoukos, Spyros, and George Pagoulatos. 2008. "Fiscal Adjustment in Southern Europe: The Limits of EMU Conditionality." *GreeSE* Paper No. 12, Hellenic Observatory Papers on Greece and Southeast Europe, London School of Economics (March). Available at: http://www.lse.ac.uk/europeanInstitute/research/hellenicObservatory/pdf/GreeSE/GreeSE12.pdf.

Bloomberg Business Week. 2012. "Bloomberg View: Germany's Banks Must Assist in Europe's Cleanup." *Businessweek* (May 24). Available at: http://www.businessweek.com/articles/2012-05-24/bloomberg-view-germanys-banks-must-assist-in-europes-cleanup.

Bloomberg News. 2009. "Merkel's Coalition Forges Extra $66 Billion Stimulus." *Bloomberg* (January 13).

Bloomberg News. 2007. "Supermodel Bündchen Joins Hedge Funds Dumping Dollars." *Bloomberg* (November 5). Available at: http://www.bloomberg.com/apps/news?pid=newsarchive&sid=aCs.keWwNdiY.

Bloomberg News. 2008. "G-20 Pits Bush Versus Sarkozy-Merkel Regulation Push." *Bloomberg* (November 10).

Bloomberg News. 2012a. "Merkel's Isolation Deepens as Draghi Critizes Strategy." *Bloomberg* (June 1). Available at: http://www.bloomberg.com/news/2012-05-31/merkel-s-isolation-deepens-as-draghi-criticzes-strategy.html.

Bloomberg News. 2012b. "Merkel's Frugal Stance on Greece Aid No. 1 Vote-Winner, CDU Says." *Bloomberg* (September 4).

Blustein, Paul. 2012. "A Flop and a Debacle: Inside the IMF's Global Rebalancing Efforts." *CIGI Papers* No. 4. Waterloo: Center for International Governance Innovation.

Blyth, Mark. 2002. *Great Transformations: Economic Ideas and Institutional Change in the Twentieth Century*. New York: Cambridge University Press.

Blyth, Mark. 2009. "Coping with the Black Swan: The Unsettling World of Nassim Taleb." *Critical Review* 21(4): 447–465.

Blyth, Mark. 2013a. *Austerity: The History of a Dangerous Idea*. New York: Oxford University Press.

Blyth, Mark. 2013b. "Deutschland schafft das nicht." *Der Spiegel* 42 (October 14). Available at: http://www.spiegel.de/spiegel/print/d-116119661.html.

Blyth, Mark. 2014a. "The Sovereign Debt Crisis That Isn't: Or, How to Turn a Lending Crisis into a Spending Crisis and Pocket the Spread." Paper presented at annual International Conference of Europeanists (Council of European Studies) in Washington, DC (March 15).

Blyth, Mark. 2014b. "Europe's Goldilocks Dilemma." *Foreign Policy* (July 14). Available at: http://www.foreignpolicy.com/articles/2014/07/14/europe_goldilocks_dilemma_austerity_growth.

Blyth, Mark, and Richard Katz. 2005. "From Catch-All Politics to Cartelization: The Political Economy of the Cartel Party." *West European Politics* 28(1): 33–60.

Board of Governors of the Federal Reserve System. 2012. *Central Bank Liquidity Swap Lines* (last updated December 13, 2012; accessed January 18, 2013). Available at: http://www.federalreserve.gov/newsevents/reform_swaplines.htm.

Boell, Sven, and Christian Reiermann. 2013. "German Government to Gamble on Stimulus." *Der Spiegel* (May 27).

Bordo, Michael. 2004. "The United States as a Monetary Union and the Euro: A Historical Perspective." *Cato Journal* 24(1–2): 163–170.

Bosco, Anna, and Susannah Verney. 2012. "Electoral Epidemic: The Political Cost of Economic Crisis in Southern Europe, 2010–11." *South European Society and Politics* 17(2): 129–154.

Boutté, Gilbert. 2010. *Nicolas Sarkozy face à la crise*. Paris: L'Harmattan.

Bowker, Tom. 2013. "Euro's International Role Hampered by Continued Fragmentation." *Central Banking* (July 5).

Boyer, Robert, and Mario Dehove. 2001. "Du gouvernement économique au gouvernement tout court." *Critique Internationale* No. 11.

Bradsher, Keith. 2009. "China Slows Purchases of US and Other Bonds." *New York Times* (April 12). Available at: http://www.nytimes.com/2009/04/13/business/global/13yuan.html?_r=0.

Braun, Benjamin. 2013. "Preparedness, Crisis Management and Policy Change: The Euro Area at the Critical Juncture of 2008–2013." *British Journal of Political and International Relations*. Available at doi: 10.1111/1467-856X.12026.

Brennan, Michael. 2013. "We Never Saw Crash Coming—We Had No Plan B, Cowen Admits." *The Independent* (August 28).

Broyer, Claudia, Ann-Katrin Petersen, and Rolf Schneider. 2012. "Impact of the Euro Crisis on the German Economy." *Allianz Working Paper* 154 (September 25).

Broz, J. Lawrence. 1997. *The International Origins of the Federal Reserve System*. Ithaca, NY: Cornell University Press.

Broz, J. Lawrence. 2012. *The Federal Reserve as Global Lender of Last Resort, 2007–2010* (November 14 draft). Mimeo.

Bulmer, Simon, and William Paterson. 1996. "Germany in the European Union: Gentle Giant or Emergent Leader?" *International Affairs* 72(1): 9–32.

Burley, Anne-Marie, and Walter Mattli. 1993. "Europe before the Court: A Political Theory of Legal Integration." *International Organization* 47(1): 41–76.

Burnham, Walter Dean. 1970. *Critical Elections and the Mainsprings of American Politics*. New York: W. W. Norton.

Busch, Klaus, Christophe Hermann, Karl Hinrichs, and Thorsten Schulten. 2013. "Euro Crisis, Austerity Policy and the European Social Model." *International Policy Analysis*, Friedrich Ebert Stiftung (February). Available at: http://library.fes.de/pdf-files/id/ipa/09656.pdf.

Cafruny, Alan, and Magnus Ryner. 2007. "Monetary Union and the Transatlantic and Social Dimensions of Europe's Crisis." *New Political Economy* 12(2): 141–165.

Bibliography

Calleo, David P. 2003. *Rethinking Europe's Future*. Princeton, NJ: Princeton University Press.

Calleo, David P. 2011. "Monetary Crisis in a Less Than Perfect Union." In Robert M. Solow and Daniel S. Hamilton, eds. *Europe's Economic Crisis: Transatlantic Perspectives*, 45–62. Washington, DC: Center for Transatlantic Relations.

Camdessus, Michel, Alexander Lamfalussy, and Tommaso Padoa-Schioppa. 2011. *Reform of the International Monetary System* (February 8). Paris: Palais-Royale Initiative.

Caporaso, James, and Sidney Tarrow. 2008. "Polanyi in Brussels: European Institutions and the Embedding of Markets in Society." RECON Online Working Paper 2008/01. Available at: www.reconproject.eu/projectweb/portalproject/RECONWorkingPapers.html.

Carinci, Maria Teresa. 2012. "The Italian Labour Market Reform under the Monti Government (Law No. 92/2012)." *European Law Journal* 3(4): 305–316.

Carnegy, Hugh. 2013a. "Hollande Wrestles with Austerity Demands." *Financial Times* online (February 18). Available at: http://www.ft.com/intl/cms/s/0/obdd9f80-79d0-11e2-9015-00144feabdco.html?siteedition=intl#axzz3FBZ5N9mN.

Carnegy, Hugh. 2013b. "France Misses 2012 Deficit Target." *Financial Times* online (March 29). Available at: http://www.ft.com/intl/cms/s/0/7d3aeof8-984c-11e2-a853-00144feabdco.html#axzz3FBZ5N9mN.

Carnegy, Hugh. 2013c. "French Socialists Attack 'Selfish' Merkel." *Financial Times* online (April 26). Available at: http://www.ft.com/intl/cms/s/0/b933ccc8-ae72-11e2-8316-00144feabdco.html#axzz3FBZ5N9mN.

Caruana, Leonardo, Carlos Larrinaga, and Juan Manuel Matés. 2011. "La pequeña y mediana empresa en la edad de oro de la economía española: Estado de la cuestión." *Investigaciones de Historia Económica* 7(2): 322–333.

CESIfo Institute. 2012. "The Exposure Level—Bailout Measures for the Eurozone Countries and Germany's Exposure." (July 10). Available at http://www.cesifo-group.de/ifoHome/policy/Haftungspegel.html.

Chambers, Clem. 2014. "Europe and the End of the Euro Crisis." *Forbes* (May 27). Available at: http://www.forbes.com/sites/investor/2014/05/27/europe-and-the-end-of-the-euro-crisis/.

Chey, Hyoung-Kyu. 2012. "Theories of International Currency and the Future of the World Monetary Order." *International Studies Review* 14(1): 51–77.

Chin, Gregory. 2014. "China's Rising Monetary Power." In Eric Helleiner and Jonathan Kirshner, eds. *The Great Wall of Money: Power and Politics in China's International Monetary Relations*. Ithaca, NY: Cornell University Press.

Chin, Gregory, and Eric Helleiner. 2008. "China as a Creditor: A Rising Financial Power?" *Journal of International Affairs* 61(2): 87–102.

Cœuré, Benoît. 2013. "The Future of Europe: Building on Our Strengths." Frankfurt: ECB (December 6).

Cohen, Benjamin. 2008. "The International Monetary System." *International Affairs* 84(3): 455–470.

Cohen, Benjamin. 2010. *The Future of Global Currency*. London: Routledge.

Cohen, Elie. 1989. *L'Etat brancardier: Politiques du déclin industriel (1974–1984)*. Paris: Calmann-Lévy.

Congressional Oversight Panel. 2010. *The Global Context and International Effects of the TARP* (August 12).

Cooper, Richard. 2009. "The Future of the Dollar." Peterson Institute of International Economics, *Policy Brief* 9-21 (September).

Cornudet, Cécile. 2008. "Nicolas Sarkozy répond à la crise économique par un effort public massif." *Les Echos* (December 5).

Cornudet, Cécile. 2009. "Sarkozy veut prendre le temps d'expliquer sa politique anti-crise." *Les Echos* (February 2).

Corriere della sera. 1996. "Eurotassa con il bonus." *Corriere della sera* (October 31). Available at: http://archiviostorico.corriere.it/1996/ottobre/31/Eurotassa_con_bonus_co_0_9610316799.shtml.

Corriere della sera. 2008. "Il reddito degli italiani su internet poi arriva lo stop del garante." *Corriere della sera* (May 1).

Council of Europe. 2013. "Safeguarding Human Rights in Times of Economic Crisis." Issue Paper, November.

Council of the European Union. 2010. "Press Release: Economic and Financial Affairs." Brussels (May 9/10).

Cour des Comptes. 2012. *L'Etat et le financement de l'économie*. Rapport public thématique (July).

Cowell, Alan, and Nicholas Kulish. 2012. "Austerity Faces Sharper Debate after European Elections." *New York Times* online (May 7). Available at: http://www.nytimes.com/2012/05/08/world/europe/francois-hollandes-victory-sharpens-european-austerity-debate.html?pagewanted=all&_r=0.

Crespy, Amandine, and Vivien A. Schmidt. 2012. "The Clash of Titans / The White Knight and the Iron Lady: France, Germany and the Discursive Double Game of EMU Reform." Paper prepared for presentation to the ECSA-Canada Biennial Conference (April 27–28).

Creuset, Patrick. 2014. "Political Contagion in the Eurozone." *St. Anthony's International Review* 9(2): 93–113.

Criddle, Byron. 1993. "The French Referendum on the Maastricht Treaty." *Parliamentary Affairs* 46(2): 228–239.

Czuczka, Tony. 2012. "Merkel Hardens Resistance to Euro-Area Debt Sharing." *Bloomberg* (June 25).

Czuczka, Tony, and Brian Parkin. 2011. "Merkel Rejects Euro Bonds Again after Auction." *Bloomberg* (November 24, 2011).

D'Abzac-Epezy, Claude, and Phillipe Vial. 1995. "French Military Elites and the Idea of Europe, 1947–1954." In Anne Deighton, ed. *Building Postwar Europe*. New York: St. Martin's.

Dalton, Matthew. 2013. "EU Balks at Rule Change That Could Ease Austerity." *Wall Street Journal* (September 24). Available at: http://online.wsj.com/news/articles/SB10001424052702304213904579095481787193644.

Darvas, Zsolt, Jean Pisani-Ferry, and Guntram Wolff. 2013. "Europe's Growth Problem (and What to Do About It)." *Bruegel Policy Brief* 2013/03 (April).

Daripa, Arup, Sandeep Kapur, and Stephen Wright. 2013. "Labour's Record on Financial Regulation." *Oxford Review of Economic Policy* 29(1): 71–94.

Das, Satyajit. 2012. "The Euro-Zone Debt Crisis—It's Now ABOUT Germany, NOT UP TO Germany!" Naked Capitalism. Available at: http://www.naked-capitalism.com/2012/06/satyajit-das-the-euro-zone-debt-crisis-its-now-about-ger-many-not-up-to-germany.html (accessed August 6, 2013).

De Cecco, Marcello. 1998. "The Euro and the Italian Economy." *The International Spectator* 33(2): 33–42.

De Grauwe, Paul. 2011. "The Governance of a Fragile Eurozone." *CEPS Working Documents* 346 (May).

De Grauwe, Paul, and Yumei Ji. 2012. "Mispricing of Sovereign Risk and Multiple Equilibria in the Eurozone." *CEPS Working Documents* 361 (January).

De Grauwe, Paul, and Yumei Ji. 2013. "Panic-Driven Austerity in the Eurozone and Its Implications." *Vox EU* (February 21).

De Larosière, Jacques. 2009. *The High Level Group of Financial Supervision in the EU: Report*. Brussels: European Commission (February 25).

Dehousse, Renaud. 2011. "Référendum grec: une irresponsabilité choquante Telos." (November 2). Available at: http://www.telos-eu.com/fr/article/referendum-g rec-une-irresponsabilite-choquante.

Delacroix, Guillaume. 2008. "10 milliards d'investissements publics accélérés et un Code de marchés publics allégé." *Les Echos* (December 5).

Delors, Jacques. 2001. "Where Is the European Union Heading." *Series of Conferences in the United States*. Available at http://www.notre-europe.eu/media/ discoursivo1-en.pdf?pdf=ok.

Delpla, Jacques, and Jakob von Weizsäcker. 2010. "The Blue Bond Proposal." *Bruegel Policy Brief*. Brussels (May).

Delwit, Pascal. 1995. *Les partis socialistes et l'intégration européenne: France, Grande Bretagne, Belgique*. Brussels: Université de Bruxelles.

Deniau, Jean-Francois. 1994. *La découverte de l'Europe*. Paris: Seuil.

Dericquebourg, Baptiste. 2013. "Where Syriza Stands." *Le Monde Diplomatique* (July 7). Available at: http://mondediplo.com/2013/07/07syriza.

Dieter, Heribert. 2007. "The US Economy and the Sustainability of Bretton Woods II." *Journal of Australian Political Economy* 55: 48–76.

Direction de l'Animation de la Recherche, des Etudes, et des Statistiques (DARES). 2002. "Le passage à 35 heures vu par les employeurs." *Premières Synthèses* (April).

Donahue, Patrick, and Tony Czucka. 2012. "Merkel Rejects Stimulus in Challenge to Hollande's Growth Plans." *Bloomberg* (May 2).

Dooley Michael, Folkerts-Landau David, Garber Peter. 2003. "An Essay on the Revived Bretton Woods System." *NBER Working Paper 9971*. Cambridge, MA: National Bureau of Economic Research.

Dornbusch, Rudiger. 1993. "The End of the German Miracle." *Journal of Economic Literature* 31(2): 881–885.

Draghi, Mario. 2011a. "Introductory Statement to the Press Conference (with Q&A)." Frankfurt: ECB (November 3).

Draghi, Mario. 2011b. "Introductory Statement to the Press Conference (with Q&A)." Frankfurt: ECB (December 8).

Draghi, Mario. 2012a. "Speech at the Global Investment Conference in London." Frankfurt: ECB (July 26).

Draghi, Mario. 2012b. "Introductory Statement to the Press Conference (with Q&A)." Frankfurt: ECB (August 2).

Draghi, Mario. 2012c. "Introductory Statement to the Press Conference (with Q&A)." Frankfurt: ECB (September 6).

Draghi, Mario. 2013. "Introductory Statement to the Press Conference (with Q&A)." Frankfurt: ECB (April 4).

Draghi, Mario. 2014. "Introductory Statement to the Press Conference (with Q&A)." Frankfurt: ECB (January 9).

Drezner, Dan. 2009. "Bad Debts: Assessing China's Financial Influence in Great Power Politics." *International Security* 34(2): 7–45.

Driffill, John, and Marcus Miller. 2003. "No Credit for Transition: European Institutions and German Unemployment." *Scottish Journal of Political Economy* 50(1): 41–60.

Dubin, Ken. 2013. "Redefining Insiders: Labour Market and Pension Reform in Spain." Paper presented at 20th Conference of Europeanists, Amsterdam (June 25–27).

Duchêne, Francois. 1994. *Jean Monnet: First Statesman of Interdependence.* New York: W. W. Norton.

Duchesne, Sophie, Elizabeth Frazer, Florence Haegel, and Virginie Van Ingelgom. 2013. *Citizens' Reactions to Europe Compared: Overlooking Europe.* Basingstoke, UK: Palgrave.

Duffy, David. 2012. "Irish Housing: A Role for Loan-to-Value Limits?" *Renewal Paper Series 7.* Dublin: Economic and Social Research Institute (February).

Dullien, Sebastian, and Ulrich Fritsche. 2009. "How Bad Is Divergence in the Euro-Zone? Lessons from the United States of America and Germany." *Journal of Post-Keynesian Economics* 31(3): 431–457.

Dullien, Sebastian, and Ulrike Guerot. 2012. "The Long Shadow of Ordoliberalism: Germany's Approach to the Euro Crisis." *European Council on Foreign Relations*, Policy Brief 49.

Dustmann, Christian, Bernd Fitzenberger, Uta Schonberg, and Alexandra Spitz-Oener. 2014. "From Sick Man of Europe to Economic Superstar: Germany's Resurgent Economy." *Journal of Economic Perspectives* 28(1): 167–188.

Dyson, Kenneth. 2009. "The Evolving Timescapes of European Economic Governance: Contesting and Using Time." *Journal of European Public Policy* 16(2): 286–306.

Dyson, Kenneth, and Kevin Featherstone. 1999. *The Road to Maastricht: Negotiating Economic and Monetary Union*. Oxford: Oxford University Press.

Easton, David. 1965. *A Systems Analysis of Political Life*. New York: Wiley.

The Economist. 2006. "A Topsy-Turvy World." *The Economist* (September 16): 28

The Economist. 2007. "The Panic about the Dollar." *The Economist* (December 1): 15.

The Economist. 2009. "Vive la Différence." *The Economist*. (May 9). Available at: http://www.economist.com/node/13610197.

The Economist. 2011a. "Profligacy Is Not the Problem." *The Economist* (September 17). Available at: http://www.economist.com/node/21529087.

The Economist. 2011b. "Charlemagne: The Driver and the Passenger." *The Economist* (October 15). Available at: http://www.economist.com/node/21532283.

The Economist. 2011c. "Sikorski: German Inaction Scarier Than Germans in Action." *The Economist* (November 29). Available at: http://www.economist.com/blogs/easternapproaches/2011/11/polands-appeal-germany.

The Economist. 2012. "President Hollande." *The Economist* (May 12–18). Available at: http://www.economist.com/node/21554548.

The Economist. 2013. "Not Everyone Can Be Germany." *The Economist* (January 15). Available at: http://www.economist.com/blogs/freeexchange/2013/01/euro-crisis-0.

Economist Intelligence Unit. 2011. *Country Report: France*. London: EIU (March).

Eichengreen, Barry. 1991. "Is Europe an Optimum Currency Area?" *NBER Working Paper 3579* (January).

Eichengreen, Barry. 1996. *Golden Fetters: The Gold Standard and the Great Depression 1919–39*. New York: Oxford University Press.

Eichengreen, Barry. 2005. "Sterling's Past, Dollar's Future: Historical Perspectives on Reserve Currency Competition." *NBER Working Paper 11336*. Available at: http://www.nber.org/papers/w11336.

Eichengreen, Barry. 2008. "Sui Generis EMU." *European Economy* Economic Papers 303 (February).

Eichengreen, Barry. 2010. *Exorbitant Privilege: The Rise and Fall of the Dollar and the Future of the International Monetary System*. New York: Oxford University Press.

Eichengreen, Barry. 2012. "Is Europe on a Cross of Gold?" *Project Syndicate* (May 11). Available at: http://www.project-syndicate.org/commentary/is-europe-on-a-cross-of-gold-.

Eichengreen, Barry. 2013. "The ECB: A Bridge Too Far." *Social Europe Journal* (December). Available at: http://www.social-europe.eu/2013/12/ecbs-bridge-far/.

Eiffel Group. 2014. "For a Euro Community." Available at: http://www.groupe-eiffel.eu/our-manifesto/.

Einaudi, Luca. 2001. *Money and Politics: European Monetary Unification and the International Gold Standard, 1865–1873*. Oxford: Oxford University Press.

Elster, Jon, ed. 1986. "Introduction." In *Rational Choice*. New York: New York University Press.

Enderlein, Henrik, et al. 2012. "Completing the Euro—A Road Map Towards Fiscal Union in Europe." Report of the Tommaso Padoa-Schioppa. *Notre*

Europe Study no. 92. Available at: http://www.notre-europe.eu/media/completingtheeuroreportpadoa-schioppagroupnejune2012.pdf?pdf=ok.

Euractiv. 2014a. "Brussels Renews Criticism of German Trade Surplus." *Euractiv.com* (March 7). Available at: http://www.euractiv.com/sections/euro-finance/brussels-renews-criticism-german-trade-surplus-300733.

Euractiv. 2014b. "Germany's Bundesbank Opens Up to Quantitative Easing." *Euroactiv.com* (March 26). Available at: http://www.euractiv.com/sections/euro-finance/germanys-bundesbank-opens-quantitative-easing-301143.

Euro Area. 2012. "Euro Area Summit Statement." Brussels: Council of the European Union (June 29).

Euronews. 2013. "Poll Boost for Germany's Merkel as She Gears Up for Third Term Bid." *Euronews* (April 5).

European Central Bank. 1999. *Possible Effects of EMU on the EU Banking System in the Medium to Long Term.* Frankfurt: ECB (February).

European Central Bank. 2011a. "Press Release: Statement by the President of the ECB." Frankfurt (August 7).

European Central Bank. 2011b. "Press Release: ECB Announces Measures to Support Bank Lending and Money Market Activity." Frankfurt (December 8).

European Central Bank. 2012a. "The Euro Area Bank Lending Survey." Frankfurt: ECB (January).

European Central Bank. 2012b. "Verbatim of the Remarks Made by Mario Draghi." London (July 26).

European Central Bank. 2012c. "Press Release: Technical Features of Outright Monetary Transactions." Frankfurt: ECB (September 6).

European Central Bank. 2013. *The International Role of the Euro* (July). Frankfurt: ECB.

European Commission. 1990. "One Market, One Money." *European Economy* 44.

European Commission. 2005. "Country Study: Spain in EMU: A Virtuous Long-Lasting Cycle?" *Occasional Papers* No. 14. Brussels: European Commission Directorate Generale of Economic and Financial Affairs.

European Commission. 2012a. "Six-Pack? Two-Pack? Fiscal Compact? A Short Guide to the New EU Fiscal Governance." *Press Release* (March 14). Available at: http://ec.europa.eu/economy_finance/articles/governance/2012-03-14_six_pack_en.htm.

European Commission. 2012b. "A Blueprint for a Deep and Genuine Economic and Monetary Union: Launching a European Debate." Brussels: Communication from the Commission (November 30). Available at: http://ec.europa.eu/commission_2010-2014/president/news/archives/2012/11/pdf/blueprint_en.pdf.

European Commission. 2013a. "Public Opinion in the European Union." *Eurobarometer 79* (May 2013). Available at: http://ec.europa.eu/public_opinion/archives/eb/eb79/eb79_en.htm.

European Commission. 2013b. "Public Opinion in the European Union." *Standard Eurobarometer* 80 (Autumn): Available at: http://ec.europa.eu/public_opinion/archives/eb/eb80/eb80_first_en.pdf.

European Council. 2005. "Presidency Conclusions." Brussels (March 22–23).

European Council. 2010. "Strengthening Economic Governance in the EU: Report of the Task Force to the European Council." Brussels (October 21).

European Council. 2011a. "The Euro Plus Pact: Stronger Economic Policy Coordination for Competitiveness and Convergence." *Conclusions of the European Council of 24–5 March 2011*. Annex 1, EUCO 10/1/11 REV1. Brussels: European Council.

European Council. 2011b. "Statement by the Euro Area Heads of State or Government." Brussels (December 9).

European Council. 2012a. "Treaty on Stability, Coordination and Governance Signed" (February 3). Available at: http://www.european-council.europa.eu/home-page/highlights/treaty-on-stability,-coordination-and-governance-signed?lang=en.

European Council. 2012b. "Conclusions." Brussels (June 29).

European Council. 2012c. "Euro Area Summit Statement." Brussels (June 29).

European Council. 2012d. "European Council 18/19 October 2012, Conclusions." Brussels: European Council, EUCO 156/12 (October 19).

European Council. 2012e. "European Council 13/14 December 2012, Conclusions." Brussels: European Council, EUCO 205/12 (December 14).

European Parliament. 2008. "Resolution on the EMU@10: The First Ten Years of Economic and Monetary Union and Future Challenges." Brussels (November 18).

European Union. 1992. "Treaty on European Union, Treaty of Maastricht." *Official Journal of the European Communities* C 325/5.

European Union. 2007. "Treaty of Lisbon Amending the Treaty on European Union and the Treaty Establishing the European Community." *Official Journal of the European Communities* C 306/01.

Eurostat. 2008. *Report on the EDP Follow-Up Methodological Visit to Greece, 15–19 September 2008*. Brussels: European Commission.

Eurostat. 2013. "Nearly 40% of Persons Employed by Non-Financial Enterprises in the EU28 Worked for SMEs in 2011." *Eurosta News Release 175/2013* (November 2013). Available at: http://epp.eurostat.ec.europa.eu/cache/ITY_PUBLIC/4-25112013-AP/EN/4-25112013-AP-EN.PDF.

Evans, Peter B., Dietrich Rueschemeyer, and Theda Skocpol. 1985. *Bringing the State Back In*. Cambridge: Cambridge University Press.

Everson, Michelle, and Christian Joerges. 2012. "Reconfiguring the Politics–Law Relationship in the Integration Project Through Conflicts–Law Constitutionalism." *European Law Journal* 18(5): 644–666.

Ewing, Jack. 2010. "Debt Burden Falls Heavily on Germany and France," *New York Times* (June 13).

Expertenrat (2011). "Strategien für den Ausstieg des Bundes aus krisenbedingten Beteiligungen an Banken: Gutachten des von der Bundesregierung eingesezten Expertenrats." Available at: http://www.bundesfinanzministerium.de/Content/DE/Standardartikel/Themen/Internationales_Finanzmarkt/

Finanzmarktpolitik/2011-02-15-gutachten-bankenbeteiligung-anlage.pdf?__ blob=publicationFile&v=3 (accessed July 25, 2013).

Fabbrini, Sergio. 2013. "Intergovernmentalism and Its Limits: Assessing the European Union's Answer to the Euro Crisis." *Comparative Political Studies* 46(9): 1003–1029.

Feldstein, Martin. 1997. "EMU and International Conflict." *Foreign Affairs* 76(6): 60–73.

Fernández-Villaverde, Jesús, Luis Garicano, and Tano Santos. 2013. "Political Credit Cycles: The Case of the Euro Zone." *NBER Working Paper* No. 18899 (March).

Ferrera, Maurizio, and Elisabetta Gualmini. 2004. *Rescued by Europe?* Amsterdam: Amsterdam University Press.

Fischer, Joschka. 2010. "Europas Rolle in der Welt." Heinrich-Heine Universität, Düsseldorf (April 28). Available at: http://www.youtube.com/watch?v=1g7AP2Qrrn4.

Fischer, Joschka. 2012. "Krise als Reformbeschleuniger." *Süddeutsche Zeitung* (October 4). Available at: http://www.sueddeutsche.de/politik/neue-politik-in-der-eu-krise-als-reformbeschleuniger-1.1486319.

Flandreau, Marc. 2000. "The Economics and Politics of Monetary Unions: A Reassessment of the Latin Monetary Union, 1865–71." *Financial History Review* 7(1): 25–44.

Flandreau, Marc. 2003. "The Bank, the States, and the Market: an Austro-Hungarian Tale for Euroland, 1867–1914." In Forrest Caipe and Geoffrey E. Wood, eds. *Monetary Unions: Theory, History, Public Choice.* London: Routledge.

Flandreau, Marc. 2005. "The Logic of Compromise: Monetary Bargaining in Austria-Hungary, 1867–1913." Sciences-Po: Unpublished manuscript.

Flandreau, Marc, Jacques le Cacheaux, and Frederic Zumer. 1998. "Stability Without a Pact? Lessons from the European Gold Standard 1880–1914." *Economic Policy* 13(26): 115–162.

Focus Magazin. 2004. "Interview with Horst Köhler in 'Einmischen statt abwenden.'" *Focus Magazin* 38 (September 13).

Follesdal, Andreas. 2006. "The Legitimacy Deficits of the European Union." *Journal of Political Philosophy* 14(4): 441–468.

Foreman-Peck, James. 2006. "Lessons from Italian Monetary Unification." *Working Paper* 1013. Vienna: Österreichische Nationalbank.

Frankel, Jeffrey A., and Andrew K. Rose. 1997. "Is EMU More Justifiable ex post Than ex ante." *European Economic Review* 41: 753–760.

Frankel, Jeffrey A., and Andrew K. Rose. 1998. "The Endogeneity of the Optimum Currency Area Criteria." *Economic Journal* 108: 1009–1025.

Franklin, Mark, and Cees van der Eijk. 2007. "The Sleeping Giant." In Wouter Van der Brug, and Cees Van der Eijk, eds. *European Elections and Domestic Politics.* Notre Dame, IN: University of Notre Dame Press.

Friedberg, Aaron. 2012. "Beyond the Euro Crisis: Implications for U.S. Strategy." *The Euro Future Project Paper Series.* The German Marshall Fund (October).

Friedman, Milton. 1953. *Essays in Positive Economics*. Chicago: University of Chicago Press.

Fuertes, Ana-Maria, Elena Kalotychou, and Orkun Saka. 2014. "ECB Policy and Eurozone Fragility: Was DeGrauwe Right?" Economic Policy: CEPS Working Documents (June 20).

Fursdon, Edward. 1980. *The European Defense Community: A History*. New York: St. Martin's Press.

Gallagher, Kevin, and Elen Shrestha. 2012. "The Social Cost of Self-Insurance: Financial Crisis, Reserve Accumulation, and Developing Countries." *Global Policy* 3(4): 501–509.

Gallup. 2013. "Debating Europe: Austerity Policies" (September).

Gangahar, Anuj, and Adam Jones. 2007. "BNP Paribas Investment Funds Hit by Volatility." *Financial Times* (August 9).

Garber, Peter, and Michael Spencer. 1994. "The Dissolution of the Austro-Hungarian Empire: Lessons for Currency Reform." *Essays in International Finance* no. 191. International Finance Section, Department of Economics, Princeton University (February).

German Institute for Economic Research. 2009. "Real Wages in Germany: Numerous Years of Decline." *German Institute for Economic Research Weekly Report*. 5(28).

German Marshall Fund of the United States. 2012. *Transatlantic Trends: Key Findings 2012*. Washington, DC. Available at: http://trends.gmfus.org/files/2012/09/TT-2012-Key-Findings-Report.pdf.

Giavazzi, Francesco, and Marco Pagnano. 1988. "The Advantages of Tying One's Hands: EMS Discipline and Central Bank Credibility." *European Economic Review* 32(5): 1055–1075.

Giersch, Herbert, and Hans-Werner Sinn. 2000. "Wirtschaftliche Einheit mit Mühen," *Frankfurter Allgemeine Zeitung* (September 29).

Gilbert, Mark. 2012. *European Integration: A Concise History*. Lanham: Rowman & Littlefield.

Gillingham, John. 1991. *Coal, Steel, and the Rebirth of Europe, 1945–1955*. Cambridge: Cambridge University Press.

Glienicker Group. 2013. "Towards a Euro Union." (The original version was published in German by Die Zeit on October 17). Available at: http://www.glienickergruppe.eu/english.html.

Global Research. 2008. "Sarkozy-US Dollar No Longer Only Currency in World." (November 13). Available at: www.globalresearch.ca/sarkozy-us-dollar-no-longer-only-currency-in-world/10942.

Goetz, Klaus, and Jan-Hinrik Meyer-Sahling. 2009. "Political Time in the EU: Dimensions, Perspectives, Theories." *Journal of European Public Policy* 16(2): 180–201.

Gomez, Juan. "Germany Rejects Rajoy Request for Stimulus Measures." *El País* (January 16).

Gore, Gareth, and Roy, Sudip. 2012. "German Banks Win Big from Spain Bailout." *Reuters* (June 29).

Grant, Charles. 2013. "Germany's Plans for Treaty Change—and What They Mean for Britain." (March 28). Available at: http://www.cer.org.uk/insights/germany%E2%80%99s-plans-treaty-change-%E2%80%93-and-what-they-mean-britain.

Grieco, Joseph M. 1996. "State Interests and Institutional Rule Trajectories: A Neorealist Interpretation of the Maastricht Treaty and European Economic and Monetary Union." *Security Studies* 5(3): 261–306.

Grillo, Beppe. 2013. *Lettera agli italiani* (February 6). Available at: http://www.beppe-grillo.it/2013/02/lettera_agli_italiani.html.

Gros, Daniel, and Thomas Mayer. 2004. "The Dog That Lost Its Bark: The Commission and the Stability Pact." *CEPS Policy Brief* 58 (November).

Gros, Daniel. 2013. "EZ Banking Union with a Sovereign Virus." *VOX* (June 14). Available at: http://www.voxeu.org/article/ez-banking-union-sovereign-virus (accessed July 6, 2013).

Gross, Stephen. 2011. "History's Lessons for the European Debt Crisis." Berkeley Blog. Available at: http://blogs.berkeley.edu/2011/07/26/historys-lessons-for-the-european-debt-crisis/.

Guillen, Pierre. 1983. "Les chefs militaires français, le réarmement de l'Allemagne et la CED (1950-1954)." *Revue d'histoire de la deuxième guerre mondiale et des conflits contemporains* 129: 3–33.

Haas, Ernst B. 1958. *The Uniting of Europe: Political, Economic, and Social Forces, 1950–1957*. London: Stevens.

Haas, Ernst B. 1968. *Beyond the Nation State: Functionalism and International Organization*. Palo Alto, CA: Stanford University Press.

Haas, Ernst B. 1975. *The Obsolescence of Regional Integration Theory*. Research Series: Institute of International Studies, University of California, Berkeley No. 25.

Habermas, Jürgen. 2011: *Zur Verfassung Europas. Ein Essay*. Berlin: Suhrkamp.

Hall, Ben. "Six Ways Cyprus Has Hurt the Eurozone." *Financial Times* (March 25).

Hall, Peter. 1986. *Governing the Economy: The Politics of State Intervention in Britain and France*. New York: Oxford University Press.

Hall, Peter. 2012. "The Economics and Politics of the Euro Crisis." *German Politics* 21(4): 355–371.

Hall, Peter. 2014. "Varieties of Capitalism and the Euro Crisis." *West European Politics* 37(6): 1223–1243.

Hall, Peter, and David Soskice. 2001. *Varieties of Capitalism: The Institutional Foundations of Comparative Advantage*. Oxford: Oxford University Press.

Hamilton, Alexander, James Madison, and John Jay. 1987 [1788]. *The Federalist Papers*. London: Penguin Books.

Hancké, Bob. 2012. "Worlds Apart? Labour Unions, Wages and Monetary Integration in Continental Europe." Working Paper 128. Vienna: Institute for Advanced Studies.

Harding, Rebecca, and William Edgar Paterson. 2000. *The Future of the German Economy: An End to the Miracle?* Manchester: Manchester University Press.

Hawley, Charles. 2011. "The Return of 'Madame Non.'" *Der Spiegel Online* (November 24).

Hay, Colin. 1999. "Crisis and the Structural Transformation of the State: Interrogating the Process of Change." *British Journal of Politics and International Relations* 1(3): 317–344.

Haywood, Elizabeth E. 1989. "The French Socialists and European Institutional Reform." *Journal of European Integration* 12(2–3): 121–149.

Haywood, Elizabeth E. 1993. "The European Policy of François Mitterrand." *Journal of Common Market Studies* 31(2): 269–282.

Heipertz, Martin, and Amy Verdun. 2010. *Ruling Europe: The Politics of the Stability and Growth Pact.* Cambridge: Cambridge University Press.

Helleiner, Eric. 1994. *States and the Reemergence of Global Finance.* Ithaca, NY: Cornell University Press.

Helleiner, Eric. 2003. *The Making of National Money: Territorial Currencies in Historical Perspective.* Ithaca, NY: Cornell University Press.

Helleiner, Eric. 2008. "Political Determinants of International Currencies: What Future for the Dollar?" *Review of International Political Economy* 15(3): 354–378.

Helleiner, Eric. 2009. "Enduring Top Currency, Fragile Negotiated Currency: Politics and the Dollar's International Role." In Eric Helleiner and Jonathan Kirshner, eds. *The Future of the Dollar.* Ithaca, NY: Cornell University Press.

Helleiner, Eric. 2014. *The Status Quo Crisis: Global Financial Governance after the 2008 Meltdown.* Oxford: Oxford University Press.

Helleiner, Eric, and Jonathan Kirshner, eds. 2014. *The Great Wall of Money: Power and Politics in China's International Monetary Relations.* Ithaca, NY: Cornell University Press.

Hendriksen, Ingrid, and Niels Kaergard. 1995. "The Scandinavian Currency Union 1875–1914." In Jaime Reis, ed. *International Monetary Standards in Historical Perspective.* London: Palgrave Macmillan.

Henning, C. Randall. 1998. "Systemic Conflict and Regional Monetary Integration: The Case of Europe." *International Organization* 52: 537–574.

Henning, C. Randall, and Martin Kessler. 2012. "Fiscal Federalism: US History for Architects of Europe's Fiscal Union." *Bruegel Essay and Lecture Series.* Available at: http://www.bruegel.org/download/parent/669-fiscal-federalism-us-history-for-architects-of-europes-fiscal-union/file/1537-fiscal-federalism-us-history-for-architects-of-europes-fiscal-union/.

Héritier, Adrienne, and Dirk Lehmkuhl. 2011. "New Modes of Governance and Democratic Accountability." *Government and Opposition* 46(1): 126–144.

Hirschman, Albert. 1970. *Exit, Voice and Loyalty: Responses to Decline in Firms, Organizations and States.* Cambridge, MA: Harvard University Press.

Hix, Simon. 2008. *What's Wrong with the European Union and How to Fix It.* Cambridge: Polity Press.

Hollande, François. 2012. "Declaration to the French People." December 31. Available at: http://www.elysee.fr/photos/v-ux-aux-francais-2/.

Hollande, François. 2013a. "Speech to the Nikkei Economic Conference." Quoted in *CBS News* (June 6). Available at: http://www.cbsnews.com/8301-505123_162-57588410/french-president-francois-hollande-claims-eurozone-crisis-is-over/.

Hollande, François. 2013b. "Entretien télévisé en direct sur TF1 et France 2." Paris (July 14). Available at: http://www.elysee.fr/chronologie/#e3957,2013-07-14,entre tien-televise-en-direct-sur-tf1-et-france.

Hollande, François, and Angela Merkel. 2013. "Joint Press Conference." Berlin (January 21).

Holtfrerich, Carl-Ludwig. 1989. "The Monetary Unification Process in 19th Century Germany: Relevance and Lessons for Europe Today." In Marcello de Cecco and Alberto Giovannini, eds. *A European Central Bank?* Cambridge: Cambridge University Press.

Holtfrerich, Carl-Ludwig. 1993. "Did Monetary Unification Precede or Follow Political Unification of Germany in the 19th Century?" *European Economic Review* 37(2–3): 518–524.

Hooghe, Liesbeth, and Gary Marks. 2009. "A Postfunctionalist Theory of European Integration: From Permissive Consensus to Constraining Dissensus." *British Journal of Political Science* 39(1): 1–23.

Hopkin, Jonathan, and Mark Blyth. 2012. "What Can Okun Teach Polanyi? Efficiency, Regulation and Equality in the OECD." *Review of International Political Economy* 19(1): 1–33.

Hopkin, Jonathan. 2012a. "A Slow Fuse: Italy and the EU Debt Crisis." *The International Spectator* 47(4): 35–48.

Hopkin, Jonathan. 2012b. "Clientelism, Corruption and Political Cartels: Informal Governance in Southern Europe." In Thomas Christiansen and Christine Neuhold, eds. *International Handbook on Informal Governance*. Cheltenham, UK: Edward Elgar.

Höpner, Martin, and Armin Schäfer. 2007. "A New Phase of European Integration: Organized Capitalisms in Post-Ricardian Europe." *MOIFG Discussion* Paper No. 2007/4. Available at: http://ssrn.com/abstract=976162.

Horrobin, William, and Gabriele Steinhauser. 2013. "Germany, France Unite on Banks." *Wall Street Journal* (May 30). Available at: http://online.wsj.com/news/articles/SB10001424127887323728204578515501321397738.

Horton, Mark A. 2011. "Comparing Transatlantic Responses to the Financial Crisis: The Fiscal Policy Response." In Jean Pisani-Ferry, Adam Posen, and Fabrizio Saccomanni, eds. *An Ocean Apart? Comparing Transatlantic Responses to the Financial Crisis*. Paris: Breugel, 2011.

Howarth, David, and Lucia Quaglia. 2013. "Banking Union as Holy Grail: Rebuilding the Single Market in Financial Services, Stabilizing Europe's Banks and 'Completing' Economic and Monetary Union." *The JCMS Annual Review of the European Union in 2012* 51: 103–123.

Huffington Post. 2012. "Germany Continues Push for Austerity Ahead of Meeting Between Merkel, Sarkozy." *Huffington Post* online (January 9). Available at: http://www.huffingtonpost.com/2012/01/09/european-debt-crisis-germany-continues-push-austerity-merkel-sarkozy_n_1193564.html.

Il Venerdi' della Repubblica. 2011. "Intervista a Marcello di Cecco." *Il Venerdi' della Repubblica* (August 25).

ILO. 2010. *World Social Security Report: Providing Coverage in Times of Crisis and Beyond, 2010–2011.* Geneva: ILO.

The Independent. 2013. "Jose Manuel Barroso: End Is in Sight for Eurozone Crisis, But Recovery Threatened by 'Political Instability.'" *The Independent* (September 11). Available at: http://www.independent.co.uk/news/world/europe/jose-manuel-barroso-end-is-in-sight-for-eurozone-crisis-but-recovery-threatened-by-political-instability-8809201.html.

International Monetary Fund. 2007. *Financial Integration in the Nordic-Baltic Region: Challenges for Financial Policies.* Washington, DC: IMF.

International Monetary Fund. 2011. *Spain: Selected Issues.* Washington, DC: IMF (July 8).

International Monetary Fund. 2012. "World Economic Outlook: Coping with High Debt and Sluggish Growth." *IMF World Economic and Financial Surveys.*

International Monetary Fund. 2013. *Greece: Ex Post Evaluation of Exceptional Access under the 2010 Stand-By-Arrangement.* IMF Country Report No. 13/156 (June).

International Monetary Fund. 2014. *World Economic Outlook Database.* Washington, DC.

Irwin, Neil. 2013. *The Alchemists: Three Central Bankers and a World on Fire.* New York: Penguin Press.

Italian Treasury. 2011. *Quarterly Bulletin No. 51.* Rome: Ministero dell'Economia e della Finanza (October).

Jabko, Nicolas. 2006. *Playing the Market: A Political Strategy for Integrating Europe, 1985–2005.* Ithaca, NY: Cornell University Press.

Jabko, Nicolas, and Massoc, Elsa. 2012. "French Capitalism under Stress: How Nicolas Sarkozy Rescued the Banks." *Review of International Political Economy* 19(4): 562–585.

Jacoby, Wade. 2011. "Germany: Europe's Company Store." *Crooked Timber* (January 19). Available at: http://crookedtimber.org/2011/01/19/germany-europes-company-store/ (accessed May 6, 2013).

Jacoby, Wade. 2014a. "The EU Factor in Fat Times and in Lean: Did the EU Amplify the Boom and Soften the Bust?" *Journal of Common Market Studies* 52(1): 55–70.

Jacoby, Wade. 2014b. "The Politics of the Eurozone Crisis: Two Puzzles Behind the German Consensus." *German Politics and Society* 32(2): 70–85.

James, Harold. 2009. *The Creation and Destruction of Value.* Cambridge, MA: Harvard University Press.

James, Harold. 2011. "International Order after the Financial Crisis." *International Affairs* 87(3): 525–537.

Jenkins, Patrick. 2012. "Spain's Balancing Act to Avert Doom Loop." *Financial Times* (June 11).

Jiang, Yang. 2014. "The Limits of China's Monetary Diplomacy." In Eric Helleiner and Jonathan Kirshner, eds. *The Great Wall of Money: Power and Politics in China's International Monetary Relations.* Ithaca, NY: Cornell University Press.

Johnson, Corey. 2011. "Mezzogiorno Without the Mafia: Modern-Day Meridionalisti and the Making of a 'Space of Backwardness' in Eastern Germany." *National Identities* 13(2): 157–176.

Join-Lambert, Marie-Thérèse et al., eds. 1997. *Politiques sociales*, 2nd ed. Paris: Presses de Sciences Po et Dalloz.

Jones, Erik. 2010. "Merkel's Folly." *Survival* 52(3): 21–38.

Jones, Erik. 2013a. "The Collapse of the Brussels-Frankfurt Consensus and the Future of the Euro." In Vivien A. Schmidt and Mark Thatcher, eds. *Resilient Liberalism: European Political Economy Through Boom and Bust.* Cambridge: Cambridge University Press.

Jones, Erik. 2013b. "The Euro Crisis: No Plan B." *Survival* 55(3): 81–94.

Jones, Erik. 2014. *The Year the European Crisis Ended.* Basingstoke, UK: Palgrave Macmillan.

Jonung, Lars. 2007. "The Scandinavian Monetary Union, 1873–1924." In Philip Cottrell, Gerrasimos Notaras, and Gabriel Tortella, eds. *From the Athenian Tetradrachm to the Euro.* London: Ashgate.

Jordana, Jacint. 2013. "Multiple Crises or Multiple Adjustments? Dismantling Public Policies in Spain." Paper presented at the Conference of Europeanists, Amsterdam (June 25–27).

Judt, Tony. 2006 [2005]. *Postwar: A History of Europe since 1945.* New York: Penguin.

Juncker, Jean-Claude, and Giulio Tremonti. 2010. "E Bonds Would End the Crisis." *Financial Times* (December 5).

Kahler, Miles, and David A. Lake, eds. 2013. *Politics in the New Hard Times.* Ithaca, NY: Cornell University Press.

Kaiser, Stefan. 2011. "Myth of German Economic Discipline." *VOXEurop* (November 21). Available at: http://www.presseurop.eu/en/content/ article/1194641-myth-german-economic-discipline.

Kambas, Michele, Stephen Grey, and Stelios Orphanides. 2013. "Why Did Cypriot Banks Keep Buying Greek Bonds?" *Reuters* (April 30).

Kapila, Jennifer. 2013. "Jennifer Kapila on Europe 'Ignoring the Scale of Bank Losses.'" *Roubini Global Economics* (June 26).

Katzenstein, Peter. 1987. *Policy and Politics in West Germany: The Growth of a Semisovereign State.* Philadelphia: Temple University Press.

Katzenstein, Peter. 1997. *Tamed Power: Germany in Europe.* Ithaca, NY: Cornell University Press.

Kenen, Peter B. 1969. "The Theory of Optimal Currency Areas: An Eclectic View." In Robert Mundell and Alexander Swoboda, eds. *Monetary Problems of the International Economy.* Chicago, IL: University of Chicago Press.

Kester, Anne. 2007. "Reserve Dominance of the U.S. Dollar Declining." *IMF Survey.* (September 12).

Kindleberger, Charles. 2013. *The World in Depression, 1929–1939.* Berkeley, CA: University of California Press.

Kingsley, Patrick. 2012. "Financial Crisis: Timeline." *The Guardian* (August 6).

Kirshner, Jonathan. 1995. *Currency and Coercion: The Political Economy of International Monetary Power.* Princeton, NJ: Princeton University Press.

Kirshner, Jonathan, ed. 2003. "The Inescapable Politics of Money." In *Monetary Orders: Ambiguous Economics, Ubiquitous Politics.* Ithaca, NY: Cornell University Press.

Kirshner, Jonathan. 2008. "Dollar Primacy and American Power." *Review of International Political Economy* 15(3): 418–438.

Kirshner, Jonathan. 2014. *American Power after the Financial Crisis.* Ithaca, NY: Cornell University Press.

Kitschelt, Herbert, and Wolfgang Streeck. 2003. "From Stability of Stagnation: Germany at the Beginning of the Twenty-First Century." *West European Politics* 26(4): 1–34.

Kohler, Marion. 2010. "Exchange Rates during Financial Crises." *BIS Quarterly Review* (March): 39–50.

Kriesi, Hanspeter, et al. 2008. *West European Politics in the Age of Globalization.* Cambridge: Cambridge University Press.

Krugman, Paul. 2012a. "Europe's Austerity Madness." *Conscience of a Liberal* blog, *New York Times* (September 27). Available at: http://www.nytimes.com/2012/09/28/opinion/krugman-europes-austerity-madness.html?_r=0.

Krugman, Paul. 2012b. "European Crisis Realities." *Conscience of a Liberal* blog, *New York Times* (February 25). Available at: http://krugman.blogs.nytimes.com/2012/02/25/european-crisis-realities/.

Kulish, Nicholas. 2008. "Crisis Comes to Hungary in Foreign Currency Loans." *New York Times* (October 19). Available at: http://www.nytimes.com/2008/10/19/world/europe/19hungary.html?pagewanted=print.

La Republica. 2008. "Chiuso il caso Visco-Speciale. Archiviazione per il viceministro." La Repubblica. (March 11). Available at: http://www.repubblica.it/2007/12/sezioni/politica/speciale-caso2/visco-archivia/visco-archivia.html.

Laffan, Brigid. 2014. "Testing Times: The Growing Primacy of Responsibility in the Euro Area." *West European Politics* 37(2): 270–287.

Lasswell, Harold D. 1958. *Politics: Who Gets What, When, and How.* New York: Meridian Books.

Lawton, Christopher. 2013. "Euro-Zone Banking Assets Reach $39.86 Trillion: Asset Total Is Three Times the Size of Euro-Zone GDP." *Wall Street* Journal (November 4). Available at: http://online.wsj.com/news/articles/SB10001424052702303936904579177412896271796.

Lefkofridi, Zoe, and Phillipe C. Schmitter. 2014. "Transcending or Descending? European Integration in Times of Crisis." *European Political Science Review.* Available on CJO2014. doi:10.1017/S1755773914000046.

Legrain, Philippe. 2014. "How to Finish the Euro House." *Centre for European Reform* (June). Available at: http://www.cer.org.uk/sites/default/files/publications/attachments/pdf/2014/report_legrain_euro_house_june14-9111.pdf.

Lerner, Abba P. 1972. "The Economics and Politics of Consumer Sovereignty." *American Economic Review* 62(1–2): 258–266.

Levy, Jonah D. 1999. *Tocqueville's Revenge: State, Society, and Economy in Contemporary France.* Cambridge, MA: Harvard University Press.

Levy, Jonah D., Mari Miura, and Gene Park. 2006. "Exiting Etatisme? New Directions in State Policy in France and Japan." In Jonah D. Levy, ed. *The State after Statism: New State Activities in the Age of Liberalization.* Cambridge, MA: Harvard University Press.

Lindberg, Leon N. 1963. *The Political Dynamics of European Economic Integration.* Stanford, CA: Stanford University Press.

Loriaux, Michael. 1991. *France after Hegemony: International Change and Financial Reform.* Ithaca, NY: Cornell University Press.

Lynch, Frances M. B. 1997. *France and the International Economy: From Vichy to the Treaties of Rome.* New York: Routledge.

Lynch, Julia. 2006. *Age in the Welfare State.* New York: Cambridge University Press.

Mabbett, Deborah, and Waltraud Schelkle. 2013. "Searching under the Lamp-Post: The Evolution of Fiscal Surveillance." Paper presented at the Conference of the Council for European Studies, Amsterdam (June 25–27).

Mair, Peter. 2006. "Political Parties and Party Systems." In Paolo Graziano and Maarten Vink, eds. *Europeanization.* Basingstoke, UK: Palgrave Macmillan.

Mair, Peter. 2013. "Smaghi vs. the Parties: Representative Government and Institutional Constraints." In Armin Schäfer and Wolfgang Streeck, eds. *Politics in the Age of Austerity.* Cambridge: Polity.

Mair, Peter, and Jacques Thomassen. 2010. "Political Representation and Government in the European Union." *European Journal of Public Policy* 17: 2035.

Majone, Giandomenico.1998. "Europe's Democratic Deficit." *European Law Journal* 4(1): 5–28.

Mallaby, Sebastian. 2012. "Europe's Optional Catastrophe." *Foreign Affairs* (July 1).

Mallet, Victor, and Peter Spiegel. 2012. "Rajoy Presents Spain Bailout as 'Victory.'" *Financial Times* (June 11).

March, James G. 1994. *A Primer on Decision Making: How Decisions Happen.* New York: The Free Press.

Marjolin, Robert. 1986. *Le travail d'une vie: mémoires, 1911–1986.* Paris: R. Laffont.

Markovits, Andrei. 2013. "The Virtual Absence of Germany's Concrete Effects on Europe in the Current Campaign for the Bundestag." *Huffington Post* (September 17).

Markus Kerber. 2013. "Der Europaische Stabilitatsmechanismus ist eine Hydra." *Wirtschaftsdienst* (July 7).

Marsh, David. 2011. *The Euro: The Battle for the New Global Currency.* 2nd ed. New Haven, CT: Yale University Press.

Martinuzzi, Elisa, Zijing Wu, and Charles Plenty. 2012. "Bankia IPO Causes Shareholders $2 Billion Loss Post Bailout." *Bloomberg* (May 16).

Matthijs, Matthias. 2011. *Ideas and Economic Crises in Britain from Attlee to Blair (1945–2005)*. New York: Routledge.

Matthijs, Matthias. 2012a. "Crying Wolf Again? The Decline of Western Economic Influence after the Great Recession." *The International Spectator* 47(3): 37–52.

Matthijs, Matthias. 2012b. "White, Grey, and Black (Euro) Swans: Dealing with Transatlantic Financial Risk in 2012." *AICGS—Transatlantic Perspectives* (April 3). Available at: http://www.aicgs.org/publication/white-grey-and-black-euro-sw ans-dealing-with-transatlantic-financial-risk-in-2012/.

Matthijs, Matthias. 2013. "David Cameron's Dangerous Game." *Foreign Affairs* 92(5): 10–16.

Matthijs, Matthias. 2014a. "The Eurozone Crisis: Growing Pains or Doomed from the Start?" In Manuela Moschella, and Catherine Weaver, eds. *Routledge Handbook of Global Economic Governance*. London: Routledge.

Matthijs, Matthias. 2014b. "Mediterranean Blues: The Crisis in Southern Europe." *Journal of Democracy* 25(1): 101–115.

Matthijs, Matthias. 2014c. "Britain and Europe: The End of the Affair?" *Current History* 113(761): 91–97.

Matthijs, Matthias, and Mark Blyth. 2011. "Why Only Germany Can Fix the Euro: Reading Kindleberger in Berlin." *Foreign Affairs* (November 17). Available at: http://www.foreignaffairs.com/print/133968.

Mattli, Walter. 1999. *The Logic of Regional Integration: Europe and Beyond*. New York: Cambridge University Press.

McCauley, Robert N., and Patrick McGuire. 2009. "Dollar Appreciation in 2008: Safe Haven, Carry Trades, Dollar Shortage and Overhedging." *BIS Quarterly Review* (December): 85–93.

McCormick, John. 2012. "Crisis and the Future of Europe." *Cicero Foundation Great Debate* Paper No. 12/06. Available at: http://www.cicerofoundation.org/lectures/JohnMcCormick_Crisis_Europe.pdf

McDowell, Daniel. 2012. "The US as Sovereign International Last-Resort Lender: The Fed's Currency Swap Program during the Great Panic of 2007–09." *New Political Economy* 17(2).

McGuire, Patrick, and Goetz von Peter. 2009. "The US Dollar Shortage in Global Banking." *BIS Quarterly Review* (March): 47–63.

McNamara, Kathleen R. 1998. *The Currency of Ideas: Monetary Politics in the European Union*. Ithaca, NY: Cornell University Press.

McNamara, Kathleen. 2002. "Statebuilding and the Territorialization of Money: Creating the American Greenback." In David M. Andrews, C. Randall Henning, and Louis W. Pauly, eds. *Governing the World's Money*. Ithaca, NY: Cornell University Press.

McNamara, Kathleen. 2003. "Towards a Federal Europe? The Euro and Institutional Change in Historical Perspective." In Tanja A. Börzel and Rachel A. Cichowski, eds. *State of the European Union*, Vol. 6: *Law, Politics, and Society*. Oxford: Oxford University Press.

McNamara, Kathleen. 2008. "A Rivalry in the Making? The Euro and International Monetary Power." *Review of International Political Economy* 15(3): 439–459.

McNamara, Kathleen. 2011. "Historicizing the Unique: Why EMU Has No Fiscal Authority and Why It Matters." Mortara Center Working Paper (November).

Merkel, Angela. 2010a. "Speech at the Awarding of the Charlemagne Prize" (May 13). Available at: http://www.bundesregierung.de/Content/DE/Bulletin/2010/05/52-3-bk-karlspreis.html.

Merkel, Angela. 2010b. "Speech by Federal Chancellor Angela Merkel at the Opening Ceremony of the 61st Academic Year of the College of Europe in Bruges on 2 November 2010." Available at: http://www.bruessel.diplo.de/contentblob/2959854/Daten/.

Merler, Silvia, and Jean Pisani-Ferry. 2012. "Sudden Stops in the Euro Area." *Bruegel Policy Contribution* 2012/06 (March).

Mersch, Yves. 2014. "Europe after the Warm Reboot." Frankfurt: ECB (January 13).

Meyer-Sahling, Jan-Hinrik, and Klaus H. Goetz. 2009. "The EU Timescape: From Notion to Research Agenda." *Journal of European Public Policy* 16(2): 325–336.

Milner, Susan. 2011. "France: Steering Out of Crisis?" In Pompeo Della Posta and Leila Simona Talani, ed. *Europe and the Financial Crisis*. Houndmills, UK: Palgrave Macmillan, 2011.

Milward, Alan S. 1992. *The European Rescue of the Nation-State*. Berkeley, CA: University of California Press.

Milward, Alan S. 2000. *The European Rescue of the Nation State*. 2nd ed. London: Routledge.

MNI. 2011. "Germany Rejects Calls for Additional Stimulus" (September 23).

Moïsi, Dominique. 2013. "Hollande Must Heed Lessons of Louis XVI." *Financial Times* online (April 9). Available at: http://www.ft.com/intl/cms/s/0/c452f694-a038-11e2-a6e1-00144feabdco.html#axzz3FBZ5N9mN.

Momani, Bessma. 2008. "Gulf Cooperation Council Oil Exporters and the Future of the Dollar." *New Political Economy* 13(3): 293–314.

Mongelli, Francesco Paolo. 2002. "'New' Views on the Optimum Currency Area Theory: What Is EMU Telling Us?" *ECB Working* Paper No. 138.

Monnet, Jean. 1978. *Memoirs*. Garden City, NY: Doubleday.

Moravcsik, Andrew. 1993. "Preferences and Power in the European Community: A Liberal Intergovernmentalist Approach." *Journal of Common Market Studies* 31(4): 473–524.

Moravcsik, Andrew. 1998. *The Choice for Europe: Social Purpose and State Power from Messina to Maastricht*. Ithaca, NY: Cornell University Press.

Moravcsik, Andrew. 2002. "Reassessing Legitimacy in the European Union." *Journal of Common Market Studies* 40(4): 603–624.

Moravcsik, Andrew. 2012. "Europe after the Crisis." *Foreign Affairs* (May 1).

Müller, Uwe. 2006. *Supergau deutsche Einheit*. Reinbek: Rowohlt Taschenbuch Verlag.

Münchau, Wolfgang. 2008. "The Crisis Could Bring Euro Centre-Stage." *Financial Times* (March 24). Available at: http://www.ft.com/intl/cms/s/0/5fe5773a-f8eb-11dc-bcf3-000077b07658.html.

Münchau, Wolfgang. 2010. "Germany's Rebound Is No Cause for Cheer." *Financial Times* (August 29). Available at: http://www.ft.com/intl/cms/s/0/2becafc4-b398-11df-81aa-00144feabdco.html.

Münchau, Wolfgang. 2013. "Europe Is Ignoring the Scale of Bank Losses." *Financial Times* (June 23). Available at: http://www.ft.com/intl/cms/s/0/f4577204-d9ca-1 1e2-98fa-00144feab7de.html#axzz3FUASPVGk.

Mundell, Robert. 1961. "A Theory of Optimal Currency Areas." *The American Economic Review* 51(4): 657–665.

Murphy, R. Taggart. 2006. "East Asia's Dollars." *New Left Review* 40: 39–64.

Newman, Abraham L. 2010. "Flight from Risk: Unified Germany and the Role of Beliefs in the European Response to the Financial Crisis." *German Politics & Society* 28(2): 151–164.

North, Douglas. 1993. "Institutions and Credible Commitment." *Journal of Institutional and Theoretical Economics* 149(1): 11–23.

Novak, Stephanie. 2010. "Decision Rules, Social Norms and the Expression of Disagreement: The Case of Qualified-Majority Voting in the Council of the European Union." *Social Science Information* 49(1): 83–97.

O'Donnel, John, and Annika Breidthardt. 2013. "EU's Scaled-Down Agency to Shut Banks Fails to Please Germany." *Reuters* (July 10). Available at: http://uk.reuters.com/article/2013/07/10/uk-eu-bankingunion-idUKBRE96908H20130710.

O'Rourke, Kevin H., and Alan M. Taylor. 2013. "Cross of Euros." *Journal of Economic Perspectives* 27(3): 167–192.

Oakley, David, and Gillian Tett. 2008. "Credit Markets Point to Strains in Rich Economies." *Financial Times* (October 8). Available at: http://www.ft.com/intl/cms/s/0/093b1f64-94ab-11dd-953e-000077b07658.html.

Obstfeld, Maurice. 2013. "Finance at Center State: Some Lessons of the Euro Crisis." *European Economy: Economic Papers* 493. Brussels: European Commission (April).

Obstfeld, Maurice, Jay C. Shambaugh, and Alan M. Taylor. 2009. "Financial Instability, Reserves, and Central Bank Swap Lines in the Panic of 2008." *American Economic Review: Papers and Proceedings* 99(2): 480–486.

Ockrent, Christine. 2011. "Can 'Merkozy' Save the Day?" *New York Times* (December 8). Available at: http://www.nytimes.com/2011/12/09/opinion/can-merkozy-save-the-day.html?_r=0.

OECD. 2009. *OECD Economic Outlook, Interim Report*. Paris: OECD.

OECD. 2011. *Main Economic Indicators*. Volume 2011/5. Paris: OECD.

OECD. 2012. "OECD Country Statistical Profile: France 2011–2012." Available at: http://www.oecd-ilibrary.org.

OECD. 2013. "Government Deficit / Surplus as a Percentage of GDP." *Economics: Key Tables from OECD* (November 20).

Oliver, Wyman. 2014. "The Shape of Things to Come: What Recent History Tells Us about the Future of European Banking." Marsh & McLennan. Available at: http://www.oliverwyman.com/content/dam/oliver-wyman/global/en/files/archive/2013/Oliver_Wyman_The_Shape_of_Things_to_Come.pdf.

Osborne, Alistair. 2013. " 'Stick Two Fingers Up at Britain and Germany' joked Anglo Irish Bank boss." *The Telegraph* (June 25).

Otero-Iglesias, Miguel. 2013. *The Euro for China: Too Big to Fail*. Mimeo.

Otero-Iglesias, Miguel, and Federico Steinberg. 2012. "Is the Dollar Becoming a Negotiated Currency? Evidence from the Emerging Markets." *New Political Economy* 18(3): 309–336.

Otero-Iglesias, Miguel, and Federico Steinberg. 2013. "Reframing the Euro versus Dollar Debt." *Review of International Political Economy* 20(1): 180–214.

Otero-Iglesias, Miguel, and Ming Zhang. 2012. "EU-China Collaboration in the Reform of the International Monetary System: Much Ado about Nothing?" Research Center for International Finance, Working Paper No. 21012W07.

Parsons, Craig. 2003. *A Certain Idea of Europe*. Ithaca, NY: Cornell University Press.

Parsons, Craig, and Cary Fontana. 2014. " 'One Woman's Prejudice'? How Margaret Thatcher Caused British Anti-Europeanism." Draft.

Paterson, William E., and Simon Bulmer. 2010. "Germany and the European Union: From 'Tamed Power' to 'Normalized Power'?" *International Affairs* 86(5): 1051–1073.

Paulson Hank. 2009. *On the Brink*. New York: Business Press.

Peel, Quentin, and Hugh Carnegy. 2013. "Europe: An Uneven Entente." *Financial Times* online (January 20). Available at: http://www.ft.com/intl/cms/s/0/37c2ae62-6182-11e2-9545-00144feab49a.html#axzz3FBZ5N9mN.

Pelkmans, Jacques. 1987. "The New Approach to Technical Harmonization and Standardization." *Journal of Common Market Studies* 25(3): 249–269.

Pérez, Claudi. 2013. "Quién manda en España." *El Pais.com* (December 1). Available at: http://economia.elpais.com/economia/2013/12/01/actualidad/1385930804_761372.html.

PEW Research. 2013. "The New Sick Man of Europe." *Global Attitudes Project* (May 13).

Pierson, Paul. 1996. "The Path to European Integration: A Historical Institutionalist Analysis." *Comparative Political Studies* 29(2): 123–163.

Pierson, Paul. 2004. *Politics in Time: History, Institutions, and Social Analysis*. Princeton, NJ: Princeton University Press.

Pisani-Ferry, Jean. 2006. "Only One Bed for Two Dreams: A Critical Retrospective on the Debate over the Economic Governance of the Euro Area." *Journal of Common Market Studies* 44(4): 823–844.

Poggi, Gianfranco. 1978. *The Development of the Modern State*. Stanford, CA: Stanford University Press.

Polanyi, Karl. 1944. *The Great Transformation: The Political and Economic Origins of Our Time*. Boston: Beacon Press.

Polanyi, Karl. 1957. *The Great Transformation*. New York: Beacon Press, 1957.

Posen, Adam. 2008. "Why the Euro Will Not Rival the Dollar." *International Finance* 11(1): 75–100.

Praet, Peter. 2012. "European Financial Integration in Times of Crisis." *ICMA Annual General Meeting and Conference* (May 25). Available at: http://www.ecb.europa. eu/press/key/date/2012/html/sp120525.en.html.

Prasad, Eswar, and Isaac Sorkin. 2009. "Assessing the G-20 Stimulus Plans: A Deeper Look." *Brookings Institution Working Paper* (December 14).

Privitera, Alexander. 2013. "Not All European Countries Can Be Germany." *Financial Times* (April 29). Available at: http://www.ft.com/intl/cms/s/0/db0ea83e-b0cc-1 1e2-9f24-00144feabdco.html#axzz3FBZ5N9mN.

Puetter, Uwe. 2012. "Europe's Deliberative Intergovernmentalism: The Role of the Council and European Council in EU Economic Governance." *Journal of European Public Policy* 19(2): 161–178.

Rachman, Gideon. 2008. "Super-Sarko's Plans for the World." *Financial Times* (October 20). Available at: http://www.ft.com/intl/cms/s/0/c30faa84-9ebc-1 1dd-98bd-000077b07658.html#axzz36cVoowIW.

Ragazzi, Giorgio. 2006. "Un limite ai profitti in autostrada." *Lavoce.info* (July 19). Available at: http://archivio.lavoce.info/articoli/-infrastruttre_trasporti/pagina2287.html.

Rehn, Olli. 2013. "Recovery Is Within Reach." Available at: http://blogs.ec.europa.eu/ rehn/recovery-is-within-reach/.

Reinhart, Carmen, and Kenneth Rogoff. 2009. *This Time Is Different: Eight Centuries of Financial Folly*. Princeton, NJ: Princeton University Press.

Reisenbichler, Alexander, and Kimberly J. Morgan. 2012. "From 'Sick Man' to 'Miracle': Explaining the Robustness of the German Labor Market during and after the Financial Crisis 2008–09." *Politics & Society* 40(4): 549–579.

Reuters.com. 2013a. "Berlin Committed to European Banking Union Solution: German Finance Minister." *Reuters.com* (October 11). Available at: http://www.reuters.com/ article/2013/10/12/us-imf-eurozone-bankingunion-germany-idUSBRE99B0IU20131012.

Reuters.com. 2013b. "Euro Zone Crisis Over for Now: ZEW Economist." *Reuters. com* (October 15). Available at: http://uk.reuters.com/article/2013/10/15/ uk-germany-economy-zew-economist-idUKBRE99E07V20131015.

Rhodes, Martin. 2001. "The Political Economy of Social Pacts." In Paul Pierson, ed. *The New Politics of the Welfare State*. New York: Oxford University Press.

Risse, Thomas. 2003. "The Euro Between National and European Identity." *Journal of European Public Policy* 10(4): 487–505.

Rockoff, Hugh. 2003. "How Long Did It Take the United States to Become an Optimal Currency Area?" In Forrest Capie, ed. *Monetary Unions: Theory, History, Public Choice*. London: Routledge.

Rogoff, Kenneth. 2014. "The German Locomotive Is Moving Fast Enough." *Frankfurter Allgemeine Zeitung* blog (June 24). Available at: http://blogs.faz.net/fazit/2014/06/24/german-locomotive-moving-fast-enough-4185/.

Ronald I. McKinnon. 1963. "Optimum Currency Areas." *The American Economic Review* 53(4): 717–725.

Rose, Andrew. 2008. "Is EMU Becoming an Optimum Currency Area? The Evidence on Trade and Business Cycle Synchronization." Available at: http://faculty.haas.berkeley.edu/arose/EMUMetaECB.pdf (accessed June 12, 2013).

Rosenthal, John. 2012. "Germany and the Euro Crisis: Is the Powerhouse Really So Pure?" *World Affairs Journal* (May/June). Available at: http://www.worldaffairsjournal.org/article/germany-and-euro-crisis-powerhouse-really-so-pure.

Royo, Sebastián. 2001. " 'Still the Century of Corporatism'? Corporatism in Southern Europe: Spain and Portugal in Comparative Perspective." *Centre for European Studies Working Paper Series* 75. Cambridge, MA: Harvard University.

Royo, Sebastián. 2013. *Lessons from the Economic Crisis in Spain*. Basingstoke, UK: Palgrave.

Saint-Ouen, François. 1988. "Le RPR est-il devenu européen?" *Revue politique et parlementaire* 90(933): 51–54.

Sandholtz, Wayne, and John Zysman. 1989. "1992: Recasting the European Bargain." *World Politics* 41(1): 42–95.

Santoro, Alessandro. 2010. "Sull'evasione parlano i dati." *LaVoce* (May 25). Available at: http://archivio.lavoce.info/articoli/pagina1001732.html.

Sarkozy, Nicolas. 2008. "Speech by President Sarkozy before the European Parliament." Strasbourg (October 21).

Sarkozy, Nicolas. 2010a. "Speech by the President of the Republic." 18th Ambassadors' Conference, Elysée Palace (August 25). Available at: http://www.diplomatie.gouv.fr/en/ministry_158/events_5815/speech-by-the-president-of-the-republic_14177.html.

Sarkozy, Nicolas. 2010b. "50th Anniversary of the Signature of the Convention of the Organization for Economic Cooperation and Development—Speech by Nicolas Sarkozy, President of the Republic" (December 13). Available at: http://ambafrance-us.org/spip.php?article2050.

Sauvage, Jean-Christophe. 1993. "La vision de l'Allemagne à l'IHEDN sous la IVe République." *Revue d'histoire diplomatique* 107(2): 97–118.

Scharpf, Fritz W. 1999. *Governing in Europe*. Oxford: Oxford University Press.

Scharpf, Fritz. 2012a. "Monetary Union, Fiscal Crisis, and the Preemption of Democracy." *MPIfG*, Discussion Paper 11/11.

Scharpf, Fritz W. 2012b. "Monetary Union, Fiscal Crisis and the Pre-emption of Democracy." In Joachim Jens Hesse, ed. *Zeitschrift für Staats- und Europawissenschaften* 9(2): 163–198.

Scharpf, Fritz W. 2013. "Monetary Union, Fiscal Crisis and the Disabling of Democratic Accountability." In Armin Schäfer and Wolfgang Streeck, eds. *Politics in the Age of Austerity* Cambridge: Polity.

Scharpf, Fritz W. 2014. "Political Legitimacy in a Non-optimal Currency Area." In Olaf Cramme and Sara B. Hobolt, eds. *Democratic Politics in a European Union under Stress*. Oxford: Oxford University Press.

Schäuble, Wolfgang. 2010. "Rede des Bundesministers der Finanzen Dr. Wolfgang Schäuble an der Université Paris-Sorbonne" (November 2).

Schäuble, Wolfgang. 2011. "Why Austerity Is Only Cure for the Eurozone." *Financial Times* (September 5). Available at: http://www.ft.com/intl/cms/s/0/97 b826e2-d7ab-11e0-a06b-00144feabdc0.html#axzz379EKqpLj.

Schäuble, Wolfgang. 2012a. "Interview with Der Spiegel" (June 25). Available at: http://www.spiegel.de/spiegel/finanzminister-schaeuble-ueber-die-geburtsfehler-des-euro-a-840867.html.

Schäuble, Wolfang. 2012b. "Building a Sturdier Euro." *Wall Street Journal* (December 12). Available at: http://online.wsj.com/news/articles/SB10001424127887323981504578174812451337722.

Schäuble, Wolfgang. 2013a. "Banking Union Must Be Built on Firm Foundations." *Financial Times* (May 12).

Schäuble, Wolfgang. 2013b. "We Germans Don't Want a German Europe." *The Guardian* (July 19).

Schäuble, Wolfgang. 2013c. "Ignore the Doomsayers: Europe Is Being Fixed." *Financial Times* (September 16).

Schedler, Andreas, and Javier Santiso. 1998. "Democracy and Time: An Invitation." *International Political Science Review* 19(1): 5–18.

Schelkle, Waltraud. 2012. "Policymaking in Hard Times: French and German Responses to the Eurozone Crisis." In Jonas Pontusson and Nancy Bermeo, eds. *Coping with Crisis: Government Reactions to the Great Recession*. Ithaca, NY: Cornell University Press.

Schelkle, Waltraud. 2014. "The Insurance Potential of a Non-Optimum Currency Area." In Olaf Cramme and Sara B. Hobolt, eds. *Democratic Politics in a European Union under Stress*. Oxford: Oxford University Press.

Schimmelfennig, Frank. 2003. *The EU, NATO, and the Integration of Europe: Rules and Rhetoric*. Cambridge: Cambridge University Press.

Schmidt, Helmut. 2011. "Vortrag zur künftigen Rolle Deutschlands in Europa." Rede auf dem SPD Parteitag (December 3). Available at: http://www.youtube.com/watch?v=CHhu3zsGdWw.

Schmidt, Vivien A. 2006. *Democracy in Europe*. Oxford: Oxford University Press.

Schmidt, Vivien A. 2013a. "Democracy and Legitimacy in the European Union Revisited: Input, Output and 'Throughput.'" *Political Studies* 61(1): 2–22.

Schmidt, Vivien A. 2013b. "Speaking to the Markets or to the People? A Discursive Institutionalist Analysis of EU Leaders' Discourse during the Eurozone Crisis," *British Journal of Politics and International Relations* 16(1): 188–209.

Schmidt, Vivien A. 2013c. "In the Light and the Shadow of the Single Currency: European Identity and Citizenship." In Giovanni Moro, ed. *The*

Single Currency and European Citizenship: Unveiling the Other Side of the Coin. New York: Bloomsbury.

Schmidt, Vivien A., and Mark Thatcher. 2013. "Introduction: The Resilience of Neo-Liberal Ideas." In Vivien A. Schmidt and Mark Thatcher, eds. *Resilient Liberalism: European Political Economy Through Boom and Bust.* Cambridge: Cambridge University Press.

Schmitter, Phillipe C. 1970. "A Revised Theory of Regional Integration." *International Organization* 24(4): 836–868.

Schmitter, Phillipe. 2004. "Neo-Neofunctionalism." In Antje Wiener and Thomas Diez, eds. *European Integration Theory.* Oxford: Oxford University Press.

Schmitter, Phillipe. 2012. "A Way Forward?" *Journal of Democracy* 23(4): 39–46.

Schoenmaker, Dirk, and Daniel Gros. 2012. "A European Deposit Insurance and Resolution Fund: An Update." *DSF Policy Paper* 26.

Schreiber, Kristin. 1991. "The New Approach to Technical Harmonization and Standards." In Leon Hurwitz and Christian Lequesne, eds. *The State of the European Community: Policies, Institutions, and Debates in the Transition Years.* Boulder, CO: Lynne Rienner Publishers.

Schwartz, Herman. 2009. *Subprime Nation.* Ithaca, NY: Cornell University Press.

Schwartz, Nelson D. 2009. "France, Unlike U.S., Is Deep into Stimulus Projects." *New York Times* (July 7).

Schwarzer, Daniela. 2013. "Crisis and Reform in the Euro Area." *Current History* 112(752): 83–87.

Schwarzer, Daniela, and Kai-Olaf Lang. 2012. "The Myth of German Hegemony: Why Berlin Can't Save Europe Alone." *Foreign Affairs* 91(5).

Sender, Henny. 2009. "China to Stick with US bonds." *Financial Times* (February 12).

Sender, Henny. 2011. "China Has Much to Gain from Shoring Up the Euro." *Financial Times* (February 4).

Sfakianasis, John. 2012. "The Cost of Protecting Greece's Public Sector." *New York Times* (October 12).

Shafik, Nemat. 2012. "Reviving Growth in Europe." *Brussels Economic* Forum, Brussels (May 31). Available at: http://www.imf.org/external/np/speeches/2012/053112.htm.

Shaw, Mark. 2013. "Still Mentioning the War? Perceptions of Germany in Britain during the Eurozone Crisis." IASGP Annual Conference, London (May 12).

Shin, Hyon Song. 2012. "Global Banking Glut and Loan Risk Premium." Paper presented at the Mundell-Fleming Lecture, 2011 IMF Annual Research Conference, November 10–11, 2011. Available at: http://www.princeton.edu/~hsshin/www/mundell_fleming_lecture.pdf.

Sikorski, Radoslaw. 2011. "I Fear Germany's Power Less Than Her Inactivity." *Financial Times* (November 28).

Silvia, Stephen. 2011. "Why do German and US Reactions to the Financial Crisis Differ?" *German Politics and Society* 29(4): 68–77.

Simoni, Marco. 2012. *Senz'alibi. Perche' il capitalismo italiano non cresce piu.* Venice: Marsilio.

Sinn, Hans-Werner. 2012. "TARGET Losses in Case of a Euro Breakup," *VOX* (October 22). Available at: http://www.voxeu.org/article/target-losses-case-e uro-breakup (accessed August 6, 2013).

Sinn, Hans-Werner. 2013. *Verspielt nicht eure Zukunft!* Munich: Redline Verlag.

Sinn, Hans-Werner. 2014. "Weltmeister beim Kapitalexport." *Wirtschaftswoche* 4: 40 (January 1). Available at: http://www.cesifo-group.de/de/ifoHome/policy/ Staff-Comments-in-the-Media/Press-articles-by-staff/Archive/Eigene-Artikel-2014/ medienecho_ifostimme-wirtschaftswoche-20-01-2014.html.

Skidelsky, Robert. 2009. *Keynes: The Return of the Master.* New York: Public Affairs.

Skidelsky, Robert. 2013. "Austere Illusions." *Social Europe* (May 22). Available online at http://www.social-europe.eu/2013/05/austere-illusions/

Skowronek, Stephen. 1982. *Building a New American State: the Expansion of National Administrative Capacities, 1977–1920.* Cambridge: Cambridge University Press.

Smismans, Stijn. 2003. "European Civil Society. Shaped by Discourses and Institutional Interests." *European Law Journal* 9(4): 473–495.

Sommer, Sarah. 2013. "Adiós Alemania: Many Immigrants Leave Germany within a Year." *Der Spiegel Online International* (June 13). Available at: http://www.spiegel. de/international/germany/oecd-study-finds-large-numbers-of-immigrants-leave-g ermany-a-905583.html.

Sorkin, Andrew. 2009. *Too Big To Fail.* New York: Viking.

Soros, George. 2009. *The New Paradigm for Financial Markets.* New York: Public Affairs.

Der Spiegel. 2013. "Crisis Has Saved Germany 40 Billion Euros." *Der Spiegel* (August 19).

Spiegel Online. 2009. "US Economist Adam Posen: Merkel Does Not Get Basic Economics." *Der Spiegel Online International* (March 31). Available at: http:// www.spiegel.de/international/world/us-economist-adam-posen-merkel-d oes-not-get-basic-economics-a-616561.html.

Spiegel Online. 2012. "US Deficit 'Higher Than Euro Zone's': Germany Rejects Obama's Criticism in Euro Crisis." *Der Spiegel Online International* (June 25). Available at: http://www.spiegel.de/international/europe/german-finance- minister-rejects-obama-criticism-of-crisis-management-a-840749.html.

Spiegel Online. 2013. "'Germany Is Critical': IMF Calls on Berlin to Loosen Pocketbook." *Der Spiegel Online International* (August 7). Available at: http:// www.spiegel.de/international/business/imf-tells-germany-to-loosen-its-fiscal-s tance-a-915268.html.

Spiegel, Peter. 2013. "Cyprus Rescue Signals New Line on Bailouts." *Financial Times* (March 25). Available at: http://www.ft.com/intl/cms/s/0/68c9c18e-955e-11e2- a151-00144feabdco.html#axzz3FUASPVGk.

Spiegel, Peter, and Joshua Chaffin. 2012. "Europe Agrees Crisis-Fighting Measures." *Financial Times* (June 29). Available at: http://www.ft.com/intl/cms/s/0/55 13d3d4-c19f-11e1-8eca-00144feabdco.html?siteedition=intl#axzz3FUASPVGk.

Spiegel, Peter, and Peter Ehrlich. 2013. "Eurozone Anti-austerity Camp on the Rise." *Financial Times* (April 21). Available at: http://www.ft.com/intl/cms/s/0/ac3da0e4-a845-11e2-b031-00144feabdco.html#axzz3FUASPVGk.

Spruyt, Hendrik. 1996. *The Sovereign State and Its Competitors*. Princeton, NJ: Princeton University Press.

Steinhauser, Gabriele, Matina Stevis, and Marcus Walker. 2013. "Cyprus Rescue Risks Backlash." *Wall Street Journal* (March 17).

Steinmeier, Frank-Walter, and Peer Steinbrück. 2010. "Germany Must Lead Fightback." *Financial Times* (December 14).

Strange, Gerard. 2011. "China's Post-Listian Rise: Beyond Radical Globalisation Theory and the Political Economy of Neoliberal Hegemony." *New Political Economy* 16(5): 539–559.

Strange, Susan. 1988. *States and Markets*. New York: Basil Blackwell.

Streeck, Wolfgang, and Anke Hassel. 2003. "The Crumbling Pillars of Social Partnership." *West European Politics* 26(4): 101–124.

Streeck, Wolfgang, and Christine Trampusch. 2005. "Economic Reform and the Political Economy of the German Welfare State." *German Politics* 14(2): 174–195.

Strupczewski, Jan. 2013. "What Taxpayer Bailouts? Euro Crisis Saves Germany Money." *Reuters.com* (May 2013). Available at: http://uk.reuters.com/article/2013/05/02/uk-eurozone-bailouts-idUKBRE9410C920130502.

Taggart, Paul, and Aleks Szczerbiak. 2013. "Coming in from the Cold? Euroscepticism, Government Participation and Party Positions on Europe." *Journal of Common Market Studies* 51(1): 17–37.

Talbott, Strobe. 2014. "Monnet's Brandy and Europe's Fate." *Brookings Essays* (February 11). Available at: http://www.brookings.edu/research/essays/2014/monnets-brandy-and-europes-fate

Taleb, Nassim Nicholas. 2007. *The Black Swan: The Impact of the Highly Improbable*. New York: Random House.

Taleb, Nassim Nicholas. 2010. *The Black Swan: The Impact of the Highly Improbable*. 2nd ed. New York: Random House.

Taylor, Paul, and Robin Emmott. 2014. "Euroskeptic Election Surge Gives EU Headache." *Reuters* (May 26). Available at: http://www.reuters.com/article/2014/05/26/us-eu-election-idUSBREA4N0DK20140526

Thorhallsson, Baldur. 2013. "The Icelandic Economic Collapse: How to Overcome Constraints Associated With Smallness?" *European Political Science* 12(3): 320–332.

Tilford, Simon, and Philip Whyte. 2011. *The Libson Scorecard X: The Road to 2020*. London: Centre for European Reform. Available at: http://www.cer.org.uk/sites/default/files/publications/attachments/pdf/2011/rp_967-251.pdf.

Tilly, Charles, ed. 1975. *The Formation of National States in Western Europe*. Princeton, NJ: Princeton University Press.

Tilly, Charles. 1985. "War Making and State Making as Organized Crime." In Peter B. Evans, Dietrich Rueschemeyer, and Theda Skocpol, eds. *Bringing the State Back In*. Cambridge: Cambridge University Press.

Toharia, José Juan. 2012. "Hipotético referendum sobre la independencia de Cataluña." *El País Metroscopia Blog* (November 21). Available at: http://blogs.elpais.com/metroscopia/2012/11/hipotetico-referendum-sobre-la-independencia-de-catalunya.html.

Toniolo, Gianni, Leandro Conte, and Giovanni Vecchi. 2003. "Monetary Union, Institutions and Financial Market Integration: Italy 1862–1905." CEPR Discussion Paper no. 3684 (January).

Traut-Mattausch, Eva, Stefan Schulz-Hardt, Tobias Greitemeyer, and Dieter Frey (2004). "Expectancy Confirmation in Spite of Disconfirming Evidence: The Case of Price Increases Due to the Introduction of the Euro." *European Journal of Social Psychology* 34(6): 739–760.

"Treaty on Stability, Coordination and Governance in the Economic and Monetary Union." 2012. Brussels (March 2).

Trichet, Jean-Claude. 2005. "Governance and Structure of European Finance after EU Enlargement." SUERF/UNICREDIT Conference, Frankfurt (March 9). Available at: http://www.ecb.int/press/key/date/2005/html/sp050309.en.html.

Trichet, Jean-Claude. 2009. "Introductory Comments with Q and A." *European Central Bank*. Press Conference, May 7. Available at: http://www.ecb.europa.eu/press/pressconf/2009/html/is090507.en.html.

Trigilia, Carlo. 1986. *Grandi partiti e piccole imprese*. Bologna: Il Mulino.

United Nations, Commission of Experts of the President of the United Nations General Assembly on Reforms of the International Monetary and Financial System. 2009. *Report of the Commission of Experts of the President of the United Nations General Assembly on Reforms of the International Monetary and Financial System* (September 21). New York: United Nations.

US Treasury Department. 2013. *Report to Congress on International Economic and Exchange Rate Policies* (October 30).

Usherwood, Simon, and Nick Startin. 2013. "Euroscepticism as a Persistent Phenomenon." *Journal of Common Market Studies* 51(1): 1–16.

Vail, Mark I. 2009. "Left of Eden: The Changing Politics of Economic Inequality in Contemporary Germany." *German Politics* 18(4): 559–576.

Vail, Mark I. 2010. *Recasting Welfare Capitalism: Economic Adjustment in Contemporary France and Germany*. Philadelphia: Temple University Press.

Vail, Mark I. 2014. "Varieties of Liberalism: Keynesian Responses to the Great Recession in France and Germany." *Governance* 27(1): 63–85.

Van Rompuy, Herman. 2011. "Speech by President of the European Council at the annual 'State of Europe' event" (October 11). Available at: http://www.consilium.europa.eu/uedocs/cms_data/docs/pressdata/en/ec/132796.pdf.

Van Rompuy, Herman. 2012. "Towards a Genuine Economic and Monetary Union," *European Council* (June 26). Available at: http://ec.europa.eu/economy_finance/crisis/documents/131201_en.pdf.

Van Rompuy, Herman. 2013. "Remarks by President Van Rompuy Following the First Session of the European Council." Brussels (December 20).

Van Rompuy, Herman et al. 2012. "Towards a Genuine Economic and Monetary Union." European Council. (December 5). Available at: http://www.consilium. europa.eu/uedocs/cms_Data/docs/pressdata/en/ec/134069.pdf.

Vandevyvere, Windy, and Andreas Zenthoefer. 2012. "The Housing Market in the Netherlands." *European Economy: Economic Papers* 457. Brussels: European Commission (June).

Véron, Nicolas. 2013a. "A Realistic Bridge Towards European Banking Union." *Peterson Institute for International Economics, Policy Brief* 13–17.

Véron, Nicolas. 2013b. "The European Crisis and Banking Nationalism" (October). Available at: http://veron.typepad.com/main/2013/10/the-european-crisis-and-banking-nationalism.html.

Vipond, Peter. 1991. "Financial Services and the Internal Market." In Leon Hurwitz and Christian Lequesne, eds. *The State of the European Community: Policies, Institutions, and Debates in the Transition Years*. Boulder, CO: Lynne Rienner Publishers.

Vitzthum, Thomas. 2011. "Kanzlerin Merkel will neue Regeln für Europas Sünder." *Hamburger Abendblatt* (December 3).

Wade, Robert. 2009. "From Global Imbalances to Global Reorganisations." *Cambridge Journal of Economics* 33(4): 539–562.

Wall Street Journal. 2013. "Barnier Criticzes German Proposal for Winding Down Euro-Zone Banks." *Wall Street Journal* (July 12). Available at: http://online.wsj. com/article/SB10001424127887324879504578601780260101590.html.

Watt, Andrew. 2014. "Karlsruhe's Underappreciated Threat to the Euro." *Social Europe Journal* (February 11). Available at: http://www.social-europe.eu/2014/02/karlsruhes-underappreciated-threat-euro/.

Weber, Eugen. 1976. *Peasants into Frenchmen*. Stanford, CA: Stanford University Press.

Wessell, David. 2009. *In Fed We Trust*. New York: Crown Business.

Westerwelle, Guido. 2013. " 'Frankreich, Deutschland und die Zukunft Europas'— Rede von Außenminister Westerwelle beim Le-Monde-Diskussionsforum in Paris" (May 24). Available at: http://www.auswaertiges-amt.de/DE/Infoservice/Presse/Reden/2013/130524-BM_Le_Monde.html.

White, Sharon. 2012. *Review of HM Treasury's Management Response to the Financial Crisis*. London: HM Treasury (March).

Whitlock, Craig. 2009. "EU Denies Hungary's Bailout Request for Eastern Europe." *Washington Post* (March 2). Available at: http://www.washingtonpost.com/wp-dyn/content/article/2009/03/01/AR2009030100389.html.

Willis, F. Roy. 1968. *France, Germany, and the New Europe, 1945–1967.* Stanford, CA: Stanford University Press.

Wittrock, Philipp. 2012. "Savings vs. Stimulus: Can Merkel Teach Hollande Austerity?" *Der Spiegel* online (May 7). Available at: http://www.spiegel.de/international/europe/chancellor-merkel-wants-to-teach-president-hollande-merits-of-austerity-a-831845.html.

Wolf, Martin. 2008. *Fixing Global Finance.* Baltimore, MD: Johns Hopkins University Press.

Wolf, Martin. 2013. "Germany's Strange Parallel Universe." *Financial Times* (September 24). Available at: http://www.ft.com/intl/cms/s/0/b3faf9b0-2489-11e3-8905-00144feab7de.html#axzz3FUASPVGk.

Wolff, Guntram B. 2012. "A Budget for Europe's Monetary Union." *Bruegel Policy Contribution*, Issue 2012/22 (December).

Woodruff, David. 1999. *Money Unmade: Barter and the Fate of Russian Capitalism.* Ithaca, NY: Cornell University Press.

Yglesias, Matt. 2012. "Southern Europe's Small Business Problem." *Slate* (July 6). Available at: http://www.slate.com/articles/business/small_business/2012/07/the_small_business_problem_why_greece_italy_and_spain_have_too_many_small_firms_.html.

Zhou Xiaochuan. 2009. "Reform the International Monetary System." *BIS Review* 41: 1–3. Online available at http://www.bis.org/review/r090402c.pdf?frames=0

Zhou Xin, and Simon Rabinovitch. 2010. "Heavy in Dollars, China Warns of Depreciation." *Reuters.* September 3. Available at: http://www.reuters.com/article/2010/09/03/us-china-economy-reserves-idUSTRE6820G520100903.

Zimmermann, Hubert. 2012. "No Country for the Market: The Regulation of Finance in Germany after the Crisis." *German Politics* 21(4): 484–501.

Zohlnhöfer, Reimut. 2011. "Between a Rock and a Hard Place: The Grand Coalition's Response to the Economic Crisis." *German Politics* 20(2): 227–242.

Zürn, Michael. 2000. "Democratic Governance Beyond the Nation-State." *European Journal of International Relations* 6(2): 183–221.

Index